T0374760

Until I Find You

Until I Find You

Disappeared Children and Coercive Adoptions in Guatemala

Rachel Nolan

Harvard University Press

CAMBRIDGE, MASSACHUSETTS   LONDON, ENGLAND   2024

First printing

LIBRARY OF CONGRESS CATALOGING-IN-PUBLICATION DATA

Names: Nolan, Rachel, author.
Title: Until I find you : disappeared children and coercive adoptions in Guatemala /
    Rachel Nolan.
Description: Cambridge, Massachusetts ; London, England : Harvard University
    Press, 2024. | Includes bibliographical references and index. Identifiers:
    LCCN 2023017400 | ISBN 9780674270350 (cloth)
Subjects: LCSH: Adoption—Corrupt practices—Guatemala. | Intercountry
    adoption—Guatemala. | Interracial adoption—Guatemala. | Wrongful
    adoption—Guatemala. | Adoption agencies—Guatemala. | Disappeared persons—
    Guatemala. | Indian children—Guatemala. | Guatemala—History—Civil War,
    1960–1996.
Classification: LCC HV875.5 .N65 2024 | DDC 362.734097281—dc23/eng/20230601
LC record available at https://lccn.loc.gov/2023017400

*For my parents, Susan Baronoff and Peter Nolan,
with love and appreciation*

Contents

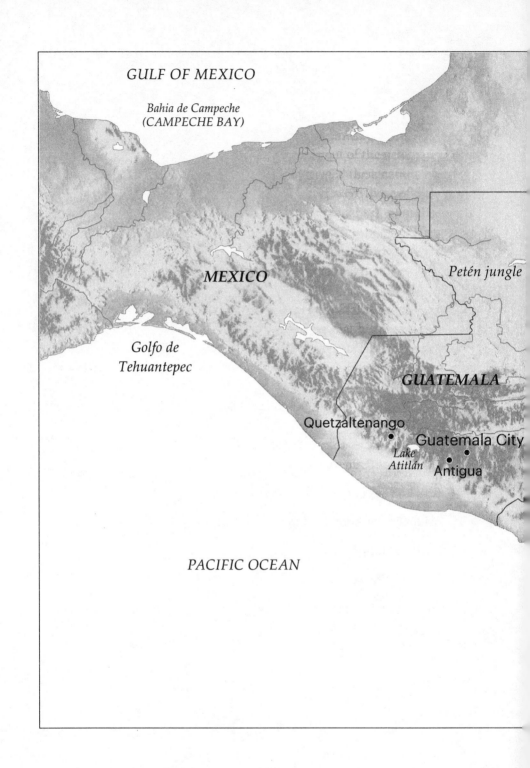

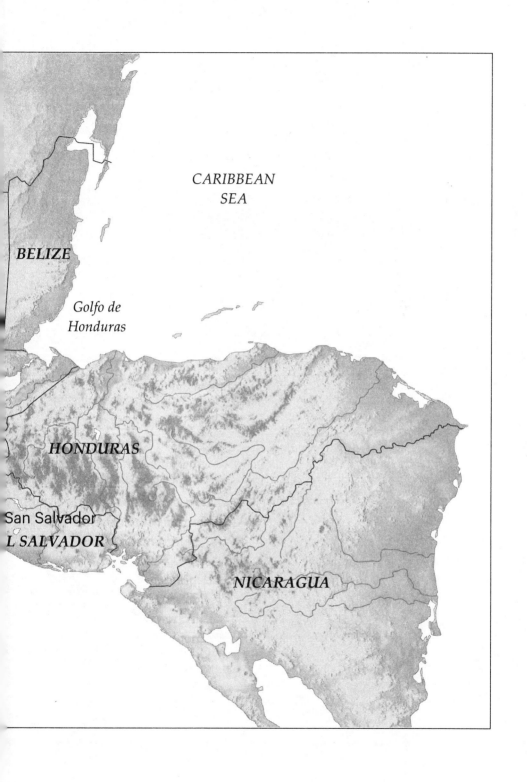

CARIBBEAN
SEA

BELIZE

Golfo de
Honduras

HONDURAS

San Salvador
L SALVADOR

NICARAGUA

Learning the truth is painful, but it is without question a highly beneficial and liberating act.

—Bishop Juan José Gerardi, 1998

Introduction

In 2009, Dolores Preat went looking for her birth mother. She had been adopted as a five-year-old from Guatemala by a Belgian family in 1984. Preat's adoptive parents had shown her paperwork given to them by their adoption lawyer saying that her birth mother was originally from an area brutalized during one of the longest-running and bloodiest armed conflicts in Latin American history.[1] An estimated 200,000 people died during the war that ravaged the country from 1960 to 1996. Preat consulted the paperwork to see what she could learn. The file listed Preat's birth mother as Rosario Colop Chim, and included her address in Colonia Limón, a slum in Guatemala City. Preat, like many adults adopted as children, wanted to meet her birth family. At age thirty-two she booked a plane ticket to Guatemala to visit her birth mother, unannounced.

Preat managed to trace Colop Chim to her home in a town called Zunil, located just outside Quetzaltenango, the country's second largest city and the commercial hub for Guatemala's Indigenous middle class.[2] Zunil is a small town sitting in a green valley at the base of a volcano. Its name means "reed whistle" in the Indigenous Maya language K'iche'. Preat speaks neither K'iche', one of Guatemala's twenty-two Indigenous languages, nor much Spanish. In Guatemala, Indigenous people make up about half the population, identified and differentiated by language, by town of origin, and—especially among women—by wearing brightly colored handwoven clothing.[3] Racism against Indigenous people poisoned and continues to poison life there, and the Guatemalan elite thinks of itself not as mixed-race *(mestizo)*, but as white.[4] According to the adoption file, like many Indigenous girls, Colop Chim had moved to the capital to work when she was young, then returned to her hometown.

Zunil is a series of concrete block and adobe houses laid out along cobblestone and dirt roads surrounding a soccer field and church. Preat had no trouble finding the right house. When she showed up, Colop Chim wasn't there, but her sister was. The sister was confused. Colop Chim had never given up a child for adoption, she said. But someone had kidnapped a girl from across the street in 1984, and her family had been looking for the girl ever since. Preat crossed the street and met a woman nearly her age with a very familiar face—just like her own face. The woman's mother tearfully recounted the kidnapping. Testimony given for a later criminal case captured the emotion of the moment: "The family gathered, Dolores told them about the adoption, and all was confusion. Her aunts and uncles arrived and one of them said that on seeing Dolores he felt the call of blood."[5] DNA tests confirmed what Preat also felt right away. The woman with the familiar face was her sister, and her mother Preat's own birth mother. Rosario Colop Chim was not Preat's mother at all, but her kidnapper. After stealing her neighbor's child, she posed as her birth mother to sign legal consent forms for the adoption. Colop Chim worked as a *jaladora*—a "puller," or baby broker—for a lawyer in Guatemala City who arranged private adoptions.

Preat brought a criminal case against Colop Chim. Her lawyers sidestepped the statute of limitations by arguing that this was more than a simple kidnapping. Preat had been "disappeared," that most Latin American of crimes. Forced disappearance constituted an ongoing crime, the prosecution argued, because of the anguish and uncertainty that Preat's family experienced every day since the kidnapping and because of her own long-term mistaken understanding of her identity. Her lawyer explained to me that this was a legal strategy pioneered in Argentina, one of the few ways to convict war criminals who were otherwise let off the hook by statutes of limitation or amnesty laws. Jorge Rafael Videla, who had been in and out of prison for various crimes committed during his 1976–1981 dictatorship, was finally sentenced in 2012 to fifty years of prison for ordering the forced disappearance and illegal adoptions of children—crimes not covered by amnesty. He died in prison. Preat's criminal complaint said that "in the eyes of her biological family she was a disappeared child and in her own eyes she was a rejected child." She sought criminal charges against her kidnapper and baby broker, "to demand justice and penal responsibility for the people who snatched her away from her family, identity, and culture." In 2015, Colop Chim was convicted and sentenced to fifteen years in prison. While the crime was not unique, the series of events leading to its punishment were. Only because the kidnapper lived across the street from her birth family did Preat learn the truth.[6]

The history of adoption from Guatemala has many threads, most of them disquieting in one way or another. In addition to kidnappings, children were forcibly disappeared during the armed conflict, Indigenous children were separated from their families and communities in large numbers, and women—often single mothers facing extreme poverty—decided to relinquish or were coerced into relinquishing children for what became a commercialized global market. These stories first drew my attention when I read a statistic so startling that I thought it must be wrong: at the height of the adoption boom in the 2000s, one in 100 children born in Guatemala was placed for adoption with a family abroad.[7] Guatemala overtook other "sender" countries, including South Korea and Russia, until it was second only to China for the number of children adopted abroad—in absolute numbers, not adjusted for population.[8] Guatemala's population in 2006 was only 14 million people, yet it provided the second-highest number of children to what had become a world adoption market. How was this possible? And who were these children?

While most accounts of international adoption focus on the racial, social, and economic differences between countries of origin and countries of adoption, I found that the internal dynamics of a "sender" country can be equally if not more important. Conditions of social inequality and racial difference within Guatemala were crucial to producing adoptable children.[9] Guatemala has one of the most unequal distributions of wealth in the world and is still reeling in the aftermath of what is often called a civil war, but which might more properly be called state terror because the majority of the violence was perpetrated by the government against civilians, especially Indigenous people.[10] It is also the only country in the world to have fully privatized adoptions, for a period lasting from 1977 to 2007. This highly unusual set of laws provided very speedy adoptions of newborns, who were preferred by most adoptive parents, and a moneymaking opportunity for criminal adoption rings. According to the U.S. Department of State, a total of 29,807 Guatemalan children were adopted in the United States, 52.8 percent girls and 47.2 percent boys. Seventy percent of the total adoptees were under the age of one. Sweden and Canada were also popular early destinations for Guatemalan adoptees, joined later by France, the United Kingdom, Belgium, the Netherlands, Italy,

Germany, and other countries. Between the United States, Canada, and Europe, there are likely now about 40,000 Guatemalan adoptees living abroad around the world.[11]

The early years of Guatemala's adoption boom coincided with the bloodiest episode of Latin America's Cold War, an armed conflict that escalated into genocide perpetrated by the Guatemalan army against Indigenous Maya peoples especially between the years 1981 and 1983.[12] Many children were murdered, while others were forcibly disappeared by army officials and ended up as unpaid domestic servants or adopted by both Guatemalan and foreign families. A report by a truth commission sponsored by the United Nations found that 5,000 children were forcibly disappeared during the war. A later report focusing on crimes committed against children estimated that at least 500 of the disappeared were put up for adoption, though human rights groups caution that the number is likely higher.[13]

As in other "sender" countries, large-scale international adoption began only in the second half of the twentieth century. Social workers at the largest Guatemalan public orphanage organized their first case through a state-run adoption program created in 1968. A massive earthquake in 1976 orphaned thousands of children, and lawyers took the opportunity to push for a separate track for privatized adoptions. They were successful, and Guatemala became the only country in the world to allow lawyers to match children to families and complete adoptions without judicial oversight. This created an unregulated market for children based on foreign demand, and a strong and growing profit motive in Guatemala. Guatemalan public opinion turned against international adoptions in the 1990s, when numbers of adoptees leaving the country ballooned, unfounded rumors of organ trafficking circulated, and several foreign tourists and Guatemalans wrongfully suspected of child theft were attacked, beaten, and in some cases killed. Guatemalan newspapers published a barrage of articles about what they called "children for export."

This book is based on a vast set of adoption files, police records, court cases, and other archival sources, along with interviews, that show how Guatemalan children came to be adopted in such large numbers. There were roughly five sets of circumstances. Hundreds of children were forcibly disappeared as part of the political violence, mostly from Indigenous communities. The genocide-era adoptions of disappeared children run like a toxic stream through the larger history of adoptions from Guatemala. Then there were children who were kidnapped in unknown numbers, because falsified adoption paperwork makes it

impossible to say for sure. There were true orphans, through death or abandonment, in smaller proportions than one might expect. (Adoption files indicated
these to be well under 10 percent of cases.) The last two groups were the largest.
There were children who were coerced away from their families, often desperately poor single mothers. The mothers were coerced into relinquishing their
children either directly, by baby brokers, lawyers, or family members, or indirectly, through the constraints of misogyny, poverty, and social exclusion. It is
impossible to know whether, under other circumstances, these women would
have wished to keep them. Finally, there were children who were relinquished
by birth mothers who wished to place them in adoption. Written sources can
make it difficult to ascertain the true circumstances of any given adoption,
never mind the level of informed consent. Birth mothers, social workers,
lawyers, and adoptive parents had clashing views of who made a good parent,
what counted as a broken family (*familia desintegrada,* literally "disintegrated
family" in Spanish), and what circumstances made a child adoptable. I found
ample support for historian Laura Briggs's caution against rushing to label international adoption as either rescue or kidnapping.[14]

Foreign families adopted from Guatemala for forty years, often without full
information about the origins of the babies and children they welcomed into
their homes. Moving a child from one country to another, one family to another, demanded constant negotiations across geographical distance and
across inequalities of power and resources. First came local determinations
about which children were adoptable, who counted as abandoned or orphaned, and how to secure consent from birth mothers. Second came diplo-
macy and correspondence between adoption agency workers and social
workers in Guatemala, various European countries, the United States, and
Canada, setting the parameters for adoptions. Last came the actual transfer
of children. Much information was lost or suppressed along the way. While
often initiated with the best of intentions in wealthier countries, international
adoptions were the result of immiseration in sender countries, where they
were bound up in violent conflicts over politics, local racial divisions, and
enforcing often misogynistic ideas about the role and place of women.

In 2008, Guatemala closed all international adoptions. It is still widely cited
as the worst-case scenario for international adoption, a case study in all that
can go wrong when families in rich countries participate, often unwittingly, in
a commercial market for children from poor countries. In Guatemala, I often
heard that adoption was "just a business." "Some countries export bananas,"

one lawyer who arranged private adoptions told *The Economist* in 2016. "We exported babies."[15] In contrast, many people in wealthy countries had long seen international adoptions as selfless acts of charity, though this began to change after scandals in Guatemala and elsewhere.[16] Dawning awareness of ethical concerns is one reason international adoption is declining around the world. The United States remains the largest receiving country, but the high-water mark was 22,884 children adopted from all over the world in 2004. Since then, numbers of international adoptions are falling fast, even as international surrogacy, which raises parallel ethical issues, is on the rise.[17]

Even supporters of international adoption, like conservative author Arthur Brooks, acknowledge that national pride and "worries about corruption and human trafficking" cause some sender countries to close adoptions. He writes, though, that the children left unadopted are "too high a price to pay for bureaucratic screw-tightening."[18] Legal scholar Elizabeth Bartholet, the most prominent defender of adoptions from Guatemala, criticized the "righteous condemnation" by international organizations, including UNICEF, for "alleged adoption abuses" there. For Bartholet, critics of international adoptions "have made no effort to weigh the costs and benefits" of suspending them.[19] In an interview, she acknowledged fraud but told me that she believes the response should be to address the illegality, not, as she put it, to "shut the whole thing down." "There is a huge cost to be paid by the children who are denied adoptive homes and typically end up in institutions," she added.[20] The problem with this view is that most of the children adopted from Guatemala were not orphans but were sourced on demand by adoption lawyers.

During the years that privatized adoptions were legal in Guatemala, a small group of well-connected lawyers and other elites ran and profited from the adoption process. The sister-in-law of a former dictator, Ofelia Rosal de Gamas, worked with the agency that oversaw Dolores Preat's adoption. Preat's adoptive parents were, naturally, horrified by the discovery that they had adopted a kidnapped child. The agency led them to "believe that her family didn't want her and that's why they found her another family and sent her to Belgium for adoption."[21] Preat's story is unusual in that it involves an outright kidnapping, and in that Preat was not a baby when she was adopted. But in other ways it is representative. Like many other adoptions, Preat's case involved a baby broker tasked with searching for children.[22] It involved falsified paperwork, and lies told to the adoptive family. It involved a child who had living family members in Guatemala.

Perhaps the most unusual feature of Preat's story is that in the end she managed to learn the truth of where she came from and the circumstances of her adoption. Because falsified documents were common, even in cases that did not involve kidnappings, many other adoptees with questions about their pasts have had less success. Adoptees—now grown up—and birth families continue to search for one another. As they do so, the adoptees try to learn which part of the story they belong to. Were they the disappeared or stolen children of the war? Were they really orphans? Did a baby broker approach their pregnant mother at a bus stop or market to let her know she had options? Perhaps most painful—did their mother not want them? Or was she the victim of a crime or war crime? Did she simply lack the money to buy them milk?

These stories echo a much longer, often violent history of governments that stole children and assigned them new families in places as far flung as the United States, Argentina, Spain, Australia, Chile, and Canada. Two older logics surface in these histories: who can afford to raise a child and be considered a good mother, and whether children deemed undesirable or dangerous by the powerful—because they are too Indigenous or too poor—are to be taken and reassigned, given a new identity and a new family, supposedly in their own best interests or for the good of society. The category of child is itself distorted in Guatemala, as in other countries with Indigenous and poor populations.[23] Historian Deborah Levenson-Estrada wrote, "Street children are called children, no matter their age; gang members are youth criminals, not children; and the elite have applied the term *niños* to Mayas of all ages since the 1500s."[24] In the eyes of paternalistic, racist empires, the "darker nations" have long seemed like children themselves, in need of saving.[25] One way to civilize supposedly childish nations is to reform adults. Another is to transplant their children to be raised by others, in allegedly civilized families. When children are removed by force, whether by a fascist state, religious groups, or a colonial regime, the devastating act negates their families' most intimate right, to have and raise desired children. This book is about Guatemala, but in its broadest strokes the story resembles that of many countries where Indigenous children have been separated from their families, where people have preyed on birth mothers to profit from commercial adoptions, or where families have struggled to keep and raise their children in the face of mass violence, untenable economic pressures, and unfreedom for women.

Adoptions as Political Violence

Telling the history of adoptions from Guatemala involves retelling the story of the Guatemalan armed conflict from a different perspective. Widening the view from the guerrillas, from the army, and from tallying the horrifying death toll, adoptions come into focus as a tool of political violence. To call what happened in Guatemala between 1960 and 1996 a war at all is somewhat misleading. A small leftist insurgency was brutally crushed by the army, police, and armed "civil defense patrols" made up of forcibly recruited civilians. The government engaged in mass murder of its own people on a scale closer to Pol Pot's Cambodia or Stalinist Russia than other Cold War conflicts in Latin America. Those who were attempting to overthrow Guatemala's right-wing regimes were killed alongside those who simply wished to be left to raise their crops. By the end of the thirty-six-year armed conflict, an estimated 200,000 Guatemalans had died. Exhumations are ongoing.

There were two truth commissions in Guatemala, whose similar findings were unwelcome, to put it mildly, among the army. The first was led by the Catholic Church and directed by Bishop Juan José Gerardi of Guatemala City. It gathered extensive testimonies and evidence for a four-volume report called *Guatemala: Nunca Más!* ("Never Again!"). The report asserted that government forces were responsible for 90 percent of documented human rights violations during the war. In 1998, two days after its publication, Bishop Gerardi was beaten to death inside the garage of his parish house in the capital. Three army officers went to jail for his assassination, though evidence pointed even higher up the chain of command.[26] A year later, a second truth commission report, sponsored by the United Nations and also based on exhaustive documentation and interviews, was published. This truth commission found that the Guatemalan government was responsible for 93 percent of human rights violations, and that fully 83 percent of those killed in the war were Indigenous.[27] The state's counterinsurgent strategy, under the directive to "drain the sea to kill the fish," escalated into what the UN-backed truth commission called "genocidal acts."[28]

Through ongoing investigations and human rights trials, even more evidence has come to support the findings of these commissions in the decades since their publication. Former and current military personnel and their supporters have tried to deny their crimes, but the patient work of forensic anthropologists, Guatemalans trained by Argentine colleagues who helped provide proof of war crimes in their own country, have dug up mass grave after mass

Vigil for Bishop Juan José Gerardi on the fifteenth anniversary of his murder in Guatemala City in 1998. The banner reads "Witnesses of Truth." *Reuters / Alamy Stock Photo.*

grave. Forensic anthropologists proved definitively that the truth commissions had not exaggerated the scale of the government's crimes. The bones told the truth of what had happened.[29] Many of the bodies found in mass graves were people who had been forcibly disappeared by the army. One of the truth commissions was able to document 6,159 people forcibly disappeared during the conflict, but now the number is thought to be more like 45,000 people, the highest per capita number of people "disappeared" by the government anywhere in Latin America. Indeed, the verb was first perverted into the transitive form during this conflict. The term was coined and the practice deployed as a tool of state repression for the first time in Guatemala beginning in 1966.[30] Anthropologist Diane Nelson cautioned that calculating figures and a fixation on the round number of 200,000 deaths obscures other crimes that were less immediately obvious in the aftermath of the war.[31] Sexual violence is one example. Forcible adoptions, including of disappeared children, are another.

It is hard to avoid the sense that this conflict would be better known in the United States and around the world if most of the victims were seen as white, like many of the disappeared in Chile and Argentina during those countries' periods of state terror, or had they been students and intellectuals or lived in cities. Instead, the majority of victims were Indigenous families working the land in remote towns. Ricardo Falla, a priest and anthropologist who joined a community fleeing the army into the jungle, later wrote that the war, often called the "armed internal conflict" in Guatemala, was not made up of battles but rather "collective torture."[32] Army officials spoke openly, even bragged, of wiping more than 400 villages off the map. They invaded, raped, and murdered inhabitants, and burned to the ground the cornfields that sustain Indigenous communities and are considered sacred. Generals bragged of "saving" children.

The Guatemalan war was so long and so bloody, wrote Greg Grandin, that it "is composed of many stories, as many as there are individuals, families, and communities that lived through it, and each story has a different turning point and climax."[33] Seen for a moment in the bird's-eye view, the war had roughly three phases. It began with a guerrilla group that formed after the 1954 coup, backed by the U.S. Central Intelligence Agency, against a democratically elected president, Jacobo Árbenz. The puppet dictator installed by the CIA rolled back Árbenz's moderate attempts at land reform, and former members of the military—bitter that a series of dictators had sold out the country to North Americans—built up a guerrilla insurgency in the eastern part of the country. From about 1963 to 1978, the government, along with its death squads, targeted student activists, trade unionists, and guerrilla leaders.[34] The second phase of the war involved mass repression and murder of Indigenous peoples. Since the Spanish colonial invasion of the Americas, those in control of Guatemala had feared a *motín de indios* (Indian rebellion), in which Indigenous people would take stock of their larger numbers and riot to take back what was, or used to be, theirs. In May 1978, a group of K'ekchi' Maya women and men gathered in Panzós, a town in the mountainous highlands, to protest threats to their land titles, which were consistently ignored as *ladinos* encroached on Indigenous territory. (*Ladino* is a word used only in Guatemala to mean non-Indigenous people.) Army soldiers fired on the unarmed crowd, violently overreacting and, as Grandin wrote, "conjuring the riot they have long feared."[35] The Panzós Massacre was the opening shot in a scorched-earth campaign in majority Maya areas that escalated in 1981. The military alleged, without evidence, that Indigenous people were especially susceptible to communist ideology and were harboring guerrillas on a wide scale. The most violent phase of the war, including the genocide, occurred in the early to mid-1980s. In the third phase of the war, a transition to democracy in 1985 decreased violence for a few years. But the military still held

Child victim of aerial bombardment in an army detention center in Nebaj, an Ixil Maya town, in 1983. In this case, she was accompanied by her family. *Courtesy of Jean-Marie Simon.*

behind-the-scenes political power and used death squads to assassinate political leaders, Catholic lay leaders called catechists, and trade unionists until peace accords were signed in 1996.

At least 250,000 Guatemalan children lost one or both parents during the armed conflict. Child survivors of massacres, disappeared by the army during the second phase of the war, along with children forcibly separated from their parents, were placed for adoption in Guatemala and abroad.[36] Official support for searches quickly dried up, and those searching for disappeared children in Guatemala rely on a nonprofit organization called La Liga Guatemalteca de Higiene Mental (Guatemalan League for Mental Hygiene), or La Liga. The group is run by Marco Antonio Garavito, a compact, warm man with a mustache, who was trained as a social psychologist. He is known to everyone as Maco, and works with a small staff out of an unmarked office in downtown Guatemala City. Garavito estimates that the number of disappeared children who were later disappeared may be closer to 800. The organization is approached by more survivors each year, and must continually revise estimates upward.[37] The coordinator of one of several evanescent commissions tasked with searching for missing children after the war said in an interview that many victims of state terror reported disappeared adult family members to truth commissions but not children. Disappeared children were under-reported because of stigma around being a bad parent, "for fear that it would be thought that they had abandoned them."[38] The Catholic Church followed up its truth commission with a report focusing only on disappeared children, published in 2000. Parents whose children had been forcibly disappeared during the war told human rights workers that they had seen them taken away in helicopters, and still suffered from the memory that "we didn't have the means to go around looking for them." One mother who somehow put to-gether the money and courage to inquire at an army base was told her child had been given directly to an orphanage "and now he doesn't have the same name and they gave him in adoption." Military officials told her the child was in the United States, but she said, "we don't know if that is true, since we don't have any confidence in what they tell us." The Catholic Church named this second report *Hasta Encontrarte,* "Until I Find You," after the testimony of a mother who said of her disappeared child, "I settle for now for a star to wish on and I will not give up until I find you."[39]

Separating parents from their children, disappearing children, and ar-ranging adoptions without the consent of surviving family members are acts of political violence. By the time disappearances and forcible adoptions were underway in Guatemala, this was a crime already considered part of geno-cide under international law. On 10 December 1948, the UN General Assembly adopted a resolution that legally defined genocide for the first time. The definition included five acts "committed with intent to destroy, in whole or in part, a national, ethnical, racial or religious group." The fifth act deemed con-stitutive of genocide: "Forcibly transferring children of the group to an-other group."[40]

Guatemala was the first country in the world to try a former dictator in national court and find him guilty of genocide. In 2013, Efraín Ríos Montt was tried for genocide and crimes against humanity committed during his rule from 1982 to 1983. Adoption files from the state orphanage were presented at the trial as evidence of genocide. At that time, the adoption files were housed at the Archivos de la Paz (the Peace Archives) in Guatemala City—a collec-tion mandated by the peace process but created only in 2008. Marco Tulio Álvarez, director of the archive, testified at Ríos Montt's trial that the army kidnapped children in "unknown numbers" for adoption.[41] Tulio Álvarez wrote in a report based on the archive's holdings that the army's treatment of children served many purposes during the war: "to terrorize the population in general," "to punish the parents through damage inflicted on the children," and "to obtain economic gains through the sale of children."[42]

To be clear, available adoption records do not show a concerted plan to use adoptions to cover up war crimes. What they do show is a consistent pattern of separating Maya children from their families and communities, assigning them non-Maya names, and giving them in adoption to non-Indigenous Guatemalan or foreign families. Genocide is age old, but the term was only widely recognized after World War II and the Nuremberg Trials. Barring the existence and discovery of notes like the Wannsee Conference minutes, in which Nazis spelled out their genocidal plans against the Jews, intent is very difficult to prove.[43] The strongest evidence for genocidal intent in Guatemala is to be found in a handful of army plans from the 1980s that became public after the war and speak of eradicating Indigenous families, and, in reference to their children, stamping out "bad seed."[44] Ríos Montt was convicted of genocide, but the sentence was later annulled on procedural grounds under political pressure.[45]

Many Guatemalans with right-wing views, including former military officials who maintain a political and economic stranglehold on the country, insist that no genocide occurred.[46] Historian Kirsten Weld calls this "an atmosphere of homegrown Holocaust denial."[47] Guatemala is surely the only country in the world where bumper stickers reading *"no hubo genocidio"* ("there was no genocide") were a common sight during a war crimes trial.[48] Graffiti reading *"Si hubo genocidio"* ("yes, there was a genocide") appeared on city walls during the trial and remains a common sight around Guatemala City, stenciled anew each year by members of HIJOS. The acronym stands for "Sons and Daughters for Identity and against Forgetting and Silence," a human rights group formed in 1999. HIJOS is now working with adoptees who suspect they may have been forcibly disappeared during the war and are searching for their birth parents.

Naturally, the first recovery efforts after the war involved counting and mourning the dead. Only several decades after the peace accords did Guatemalans come to terms more fully with crimes that left survivors: torture, rape, forcible adoptions. When I lived in Guatemala City, from 2015 to 2016, graffiti began to appear with one town's name: Sepur Zarco. Blocky letters announced: "There was and is gender violence in Guatemala." Fifteen women from that isolated K'ekchi' town testified in a 2016 trial that military officials had kidnapped them in 1982 and held them at a military base for more than a year, systematically raping them and forcing them to perform domestic tasks, including making tortillas and washing uniforms. The two surviving perpetrators were each sentenced to more than 100 years in jail. Asked why they came forward with their story so late, the survivors answered that human rights workers, historians, truth commission workers, and anthropologists had come to their village with other questions: How many were killed? Had their men cooperated with the guerrilla fighters before they died? No one asked about rape, and the women kept their counsel.[49] Garavito, the director of La Liga, describes a similar effect when it comes to the families of disappeared children: no one asked, so for a long time they didn't tell. One purpose of this book is to insist on asking about children, too, and to point out that stealing children, like sexual violence, is not a random, chaotic crime but a pattern, a known variant of political violence. Forcible adoptions were an important part of the history of repression in Guatemala and elsewhere.

The history of adoptions from Guatemala, like the rest of Guatemalan history, gives the lie to the all-too-common myth of Maya passivity. In the face of five centuries of racist violence and genocide, Maya communities have managed to resist often brutal pressures to culturally assimilate, while maintaining and continuously renewing their own community structures. An important limitation of this book is that all the written sources are in Spanish or English. I do not speak any of the twenty-two Mayan languages spoken in Guatemala, nor did the social workers who wrote adoption files nor the lawyers who arranged private adoptions. Even so, the archives clearly record Maya resistance to forced adoptions and Indigenous communities' desire and capacity to take in children orphaned by the war. Throughout the conflict, Maya families accused the government of disappearing their family members and perpetrating a genocide. In 1984, wives and mothers of the disappeared formed a human rights organization called GAM, the Grupo de Apoyo Mutuo (Group for Mutual Support), to advocate for the return of their loved ones. The majority of the members were Indigenous women. At a time when human rights activists were often targeted for assassination, together women marched holding posters with the faces of their disappeared husbands and children, demanding them back, or at the very least demanding to know what had happened to them. "At first we didn't blame the government because we thought that if we didn't blame them, the disappeared would appear," one member of GAM told the *Christian Science Monitor* in 1985. "But there comes a time when you have to tell the truth."[50]

As part of the slow process of recovery and reckoning after the war, more families began to search for missing children. Aside from a few short-lived committees that were thinly funded, if at all, this process has not been aided by the government. After the UN-backed truth commission report was published, an editorial in the *New York Times* observed: "Probably thousands of children disappeared in Guatemala's 36-year civil war, the vast majority taken by the security forces, typically after the army had attacked a Mayan Indian village and massacred many of its inhabitants. While most of the children were probably killed, there is reason to think that many of the younger children were adopted illegally by soldiers or taken to orphanages and later adopted by families in other countries, including the United States." The editorial noted efforts to find disappeared children in Argentina and El Salvador and continued, "With war increasingly fought in villages instead of battlefields, more nations need to find abducted children and connect them to their families." It concluded: "A priority for investigation should be the children who have disappeared. This is one instance where those presumed dead could indeed be brought back to life."[51]

After the signing of the peace accords in 1996, the search for missing children has emerged as an avenue for the recovery of historical memory, that collective narrative of the past that many countries find so difficult to cobble together and agree upon.[52] Guatemalans are still at odds over what the war was really about, and what it meant. Those who support the military see it as a heroic campaign that saved Guatemala from becoming "another Cuba."[53] Those who have read the truth commission reports and followed the human rights cases know that the government, police and army both, committed the vast majority of crimes—including genocide. Public discussion of what went wrong with adoptions is still dominated by stories of children trafficked by private lawyers, not of forcibly disappeared Indigenous children. Guatemalans tend to tell it as a story of corruption rather than mass terror, though the history of adoption in their country involved both.

Adoptions for Profit

In 2007, amid reports and rumors of adoption fraud and kidnappings, the Guatemalan government announced that it would close international adoptions the following year—for good. The shutdown followed a full-blown moral panic over adoptions in Guatemala, one way to deal with the past in an otherwise largely amnesiac state still unable to transition fully to peace. Disappeared children had been placed for adoption through state orphanages, but in even larger numbers through private adoptions. This was a legal process invented in Guatemala that was unique in the world. The private track, opened in 1977, caused the number of adoptions to surge by creating profit motives and an unregulated market for certain kinds of children. The market responded to demand, generally for children as young and as light-skinned as possible. The two ways of adopting from Guatemala, through private lawyers or from state orphanages, continued to coexist until the 1990s, when the relative ease and speed of private adoptions all but crowded out demand for state-run adoptions, which took much longer. U.S. families paid between US$20,000 and $40,000 per completed private adoption, of which at least $4,000 was a fee for the Guatemalan lawyer involved.[54] These were enormous sums in a poor country.

Women like Colop Chim, Dolores Preat's kidnapper, began working in the for-profit adoption market as *jaladoras,* baby brokers, sourcing adoptable children to lawyers for a fee. Adoption networks created to meet foreign demand represented a way out for some pregnant women constrained by extreme poverty, social stigma, or the inaccessibility of accessible or safe contraception or abortion—as well as to those who simply did not wish to raise children. Brokers also sought out children who could be parted from their birth mothers sometimes through outright theft but more usually through persuasion or coercion. Because of extreme disparities of wealth, social power, and education between lawyers and birth mothers—along with the enormous profits to be made—incentives for abuse by middlemen, or more often middlewomen, were strong. There are many documented cases in which either baby brokers or lawyers lied to, tricked, or intimidated birth mothers, or even threatened them with violence.

What was whispered and even shouted about abuses in the system in Guatemala took several decades to become more widely known outside the country. A study commissioned by UNICEF in 2000 argued that international adoptions created a commercial market for babies there that was driven more by financial considerations than by the well-being of the child. This had been common knowledge in Guatemala since the 1980s, but required the imprimatur of an international organization to trigger worldwide concern.[55]

While fully privatized adoptions are unique to Guatemala, coercion and kidnapping for adoption are not. Such abuses have been documented in countries as distant from one another as Ethiopia, India, Romania, Cambodia, Haiti, and Vietnam. Child trafficking for adoption is not limited to Latin America, Africa, or Asia, and has occurred, among many other places, across the U.S.-Canadian border.[56] Even when birth mothers are not paid outright, the system often involves a measure of commercialization or follows market logics. As sociologist Sarah Dorow writes, "Transnationally adopted children are not bought and sold, but neither are they given and received freely and altruistically; the people and institutions around them enter into social relationships of exchange, meaning, and value."[57] My aim in this book is not to expose abuses in international adoption, which are already widely known, but rather to show how closely legality may resemble illegality, how closely coercion may sit to consent.

Latin America as a region suffers extreme social inequality, and Guatemala is one of its most unequal countries. Over half of Guatemalans live below the poverty line, and over 16 percent live in extreme poverty.[58] By every measure of social well-being, from health to housing to access to education and opportunity, Indigenous people tend to be worse off and more marginalized than even poor members of the non-Indigenous population. Extreme inequality and imbalances of power within the country helped feed the adoption boom by creating an elite that enjoyed impunity even for adoption-related crimes and a ready supply of children whose parents did not earn enough to comfortably raise them. At their height, earnings from adoptions accounted for about one percent of Guatemala's GDP, and were lucrative for the tight circle of lawyers who processed them.[59] Lawyers, especially those based in Guatemala City with contacts abroad, were and remain an important section of the Guatemalan elite. They enjoyed such political influence that, despite widespread reporting on adoption fraud and abuses beginning in 1988, lawyers managed to block more than a dozen adoption reform bills in Congress.

Guatemala does not have to be a poor country. It is rich in natural resources, not to mention a strikingly hardworking population. The dire state of affairs there can be attributed to a small group who keep a stranglehold on power.[60] "G8" is the nickname for the eight families who are said to run the country, and it is not much of an exaggeration. These families are the most prominent among a small urban elite who also own *fincas,* sprawling plantations in the countryside. In a country where 60 percent of people farm to survive, only 2 percent of the population owns 70 percent of all productive farmland. Since the colonial period, the dominance of a few families has been built and consolidated through extreme exploitation, land theft, and systematic discrimination against the majority of the population, especially Maya families.[61] The terror of the war was joined to the structural violence of grinding poverty that predated and has outlived the armed conflict.

A designation repeatedly used in adoption files to justify placement with a new family is that the birth family is "broken." But a closer reading of case files shows that what most often broke apart families were pressures like economic exploitation, sexual violence, migration—first within Guatemala for seasonal agricultural work and then to the United States—and large-scale dislocation during the war. Guatemalan elites and the government created and maintained the conditions for families to unravel, then welfare bureaucrats and private lawyers used that brokenness to justify the need for adoptions.

Through their participation in the adoption system, poor and Indigenous Guatemalans who were exploited occasionally participated in exploitation of others like them. Indigenous women did participate in adoption rings as baby brokers or in other roles. I mention this to avoid the common oversimplification that poses *ladinos* (non-Indigenous Guatemalans) as villains and Indigenous Guatemalans as victims. Yet I am not suggesting that Indigenous people were the primary beneficiaries of a for-profit system, not by any means.[62] *Ladino* lawyers made by far the highest profits and exercised the most power over the system. An obvious way to track inequity even within adoption rings is to see who went to jail. Adoption lawyers trafficking in children enjoyed almost complete impunity, while those working the lower rungs of adoption rings did not. In Dolores Preat's case, only the baby broker went to jail. Justice has been faster in Guatemala than in Belgium, where there is an open criminal investigation into the agency that placed her.

Impunity was not and is not in itself remarkable in Guatemala. The wealthy and powerful enjoyed extraordinary silence about their crimes as well as the ability to remake law to their own economic benefit. Beginning in the 1980s, when for-profit adoptions became an object of first fascination then fear in Guatemala, women hired as baby brokers and nannies by adoption lawyers were regularly photographed, named, and shamed in the Guatemalan press. Lawyers, on the other hand, were rarely named and even more rarely investigated. Ofelia Rosal de Gamas was the sister-in-law of General Óscar Humberto Mejía Víctores, the dictator who ruled the country from 1983 to 1986. Police records show she was repeatedly investigated for adoption crimes, was named only a few times in the Guatemalan press, and never went to jail.[63] The only adoption lawyer sentenced to prison time was certainly involved in adoption fraud—including trafficking kidnapped children—but went to prison, by her own account, only after becoming something of an outcast from her own social class. Susana Luarca had been married to a Supreme Court justice and was investigated and imprisoned only after their divorce. Edmond Mulet, a Guatemalan lawyer who worked with Rosal de Gamas and was later investigated twice for adoption fraud in the 1980s, has gone on to have a prominent political career, running for president twice.

The country has seen some challenges to impunity, including for adoption crimes. Founded in 2006, the widely popular UN-backed International Commission against Impunity in Guatemala (Comisión Internacional Contra la Impunidad en Guatemala, or CICIG), made serious inroads into investigating the rich and politically powerful. CICIG supported a major national investigation into child trafficking for adoptions, helping to land Susana Luarca and others in prison. In a 2010 report, CICIG found that in 2007, the year before closure, Guatemalans made nearly $200 million from adoptions. In 2015, massive street protests against a corruption ring uncovered by CICIG and Guatemalan prosecutors helped bring down a president and vice-president, landing both in prison. Corrupt politicians and former military officials mounted a successful comeback, however, and conspired to have CICIG kicked out of the country in 2019.[64]

Existing research on adoptions from Guatemala tends to focus on the period from the 1990s to closure in 2008, when the boom was at its height. Most accounts of private adoption have been journalistic, focused on the most extreme cases of kidnapping and coercion, as in Erin Siegal McIntyre's meticulously researched account of the predations of one Florida-based adoption agency, Celebrate Children International, that did business in Guatemala.[65] The most extensive scholarship is by Laura Briggs and Karen Dubinsky, both of whom analyze Guatemalan adoptions together with those from other countries. Dubinsky notes that adoptions flow in one racial and economic direction, with whiter, richer families adopting browner, poorer children or babies.

Children from certain parts of the world suffering war, especially in areas where the United States has staged military interventions, were produced as adoptable for families in the U.S., Canada, and Europe. In Laura Briggs's account of adoptions from Guatemala, *Somebody's Children,* she noted that the story still "has to be written backwards" with "an account of the 1980s, when hundreds, probably thousands of children were kidnapped in Guatemala and adopted to Europe and the United States."[66] Access to adoption files and military records from the 1980s finally made it possible to write this history, which brings the story of earlier adoptions through state-run orphanages together with private adoptions in later decades.

The Disappearing Archive

The history of forcibly removing Indigenous children and the forcible disappearances of the children of those considered political opponents of the state is not unique to Guatemala. Illegal or gray adoptions have for a long time been associated with armed conflicts in Central America and the Southern Cone. The best-known cases occurred in Argentina, though families in Spain, Germany, and Chile all suffered forced adoptions overseen by totalitarian regimes.[67] Laura Briggs wrote, "Ironically, what most people in the international community know about the disappearance of children during the civil wars in Latin America is inversely related to the extent of what human rights activists believe happened in those countries. Where the problem was worst, we know the least."[68] Much has been written about Argentina; little has been written about El Salvador and Guatemala.[69] With a few highly publicized cases like that of Oscar Ramírez, the toddler disappeared after a massacre in Guatemala at Dos Erres, these stories are beginning to be told.[70]

The nearest parallel history is that of El Salvador, Guatemala's tiny neighbor, where existing adoption records remain closed to researchers for now. Human rights advocates estimate that during that country's armed conflict from 1979 to 1992, the government forcibly disappeared at least 3,000 children. The Association for the Search for Disappeared Children (Asociación Pro-Búsqueda de Niñas y Niños Desaparecidos), founded in 1994, has since documented 994 reports from the families of disappeared children, and more than 200 from children who were adopted abroad and are looking for their families in El Salvador. The director of Pro-Búsqueda, Eduardo García, who showed me around their offices in San Salvador, said families in the United States "rarely" take their calls about possible illegal adoptions.[71] Still, working with California-based doctors to develop a DNA database of family members with disappeared children, the organization has helped reunite 463 children with their families—about 100 of whom were adoptees.[72] In 2018, El Salvador's Ministry of Defense blocked the Supreme Court–ordered release of army documents that might have shed light on the whereabouts of some of these children. The ministry stated: "after having searched the institutional archives it has been established that no documents or registries of any kind related to the alleged operation have been found."[73]

What is unusual in Guatemala is both the sheer number of adoptions and the fact that the government body that oversaw those who passed through state orphanages kept meticulous files on each child that were, however briefly, opened to researchers. They are the most important source for this book. Only in rare instances have historians gained access to large sets of adoption files.[74] Researchers have never had access to wartime adoption records, if indeed they still exist, in Argentina or Chile. These files, which range from fifty to two hundred pages each, were compiled by social workers, who recorded extensive case histories of children's birth families, collected Guatemalan and foreign legal documents, and gathered letters and telegrams exchanged with agencies and adoptive families around the world.[75] Adoption files are generally closed to researchers to protect the privacy of children and families. But in Guatemala they were briefly opened as part of a special archive dedicated to investigating war crimes. After several years of research in these files, they became unavailable to me as well. When I traveled to Guatemala in 2014 to begin research for this book, the country's president, a former general who had served in an area where war crimes were committed, had recently closed the Archives of Peace.[76] An archivist at the Archivo General de Centroamérica, the country's national archive, suggested to me that the adoption files might have been returned to the Ministry of Social Welfare, a large white and blue tile-roofed complex in an out-of-the-way section of the capital. When I inquired at the gate, a security guard told me that there was no archive, but then asked if I wanted to talk to "the old man who keeps the papers."[77] That is how I met Mario Salguero, known to everyone as Don Marito, a courtly man in his seventies presiding over what turned out to be a minuscule but very active archive right next to the ministry's interior soccer field. Bureaucrats dropped off fresh paperwork every day, and Don Marito had the full set of 984 adoption files from the period 1968 to 1996, perfectly organized and stored.

Don Marito saw no problem with allowing me to consult the files, as long as I did not use the real names of children or families, but it was not up to him. He showed me how to file the Guatemalan equivalent of a Freedom of Information Act to gain official permission to read the adoption files.[78] Guatemala's Law of Access to Public Information, approved in 2008, is quite broad though unevenly applied and sometimes honored in the breach. The first time, my request was approved. In 2014 and 2015, I spent many hours at the tiny archive next to the soccer field, where Don Marito kindly brought me files and made me hot chocolate. He told me that the others who had found him and requested files were adoptees, now adults who wished to research their pasts. I sometimes found notes in adoption files that they had been photocopied for the adoptee in question.

Access to information is always political. In Guatemala, as elsewhere, it can be reversed at a moment's notice. When I tried to return to the archive in 2016, I submitted the same request under the Law of Access to Public Information to access the adoption files. This time, I was informed by an email written in vague bureaucratese that my request had been denied. I went to visit Don Marito, and he said he sincerely regretted he couldn't help me anymore. I later learned that around that time other researchers were denied permission to consult the same archive.

There are several possible reasons for being locked out. In 2015, two journalists, Sebastián Escalón and Pilar Crespo, published a series of articles in the investigative news outlet *Plaza Pública* based in part on archival material from the Ministry of Social Welfare. One widely read article was about Mulet, the repeat presidential candidate who had been arrested for trafficking children for adoption in the 1980s.[79] This cast an unflattering spotlight on the histories of adoptions, and some at the ministry may not have appreciated the attention. Another possibility is that the U.S. Embassy in Guatemala was not happy with my line of research. I received a Fulbright grant, funded by the U.S. Department of State, to research the history of adoptions. At an orientation session in Washington, D.C., program officers told me that before grants were awarded, embassy staff in the country in question were supposed to review applications. The embassy in Guatemala was late in its review but had flagged my application since it contained a "letter of affiliation" signed by Don Marito saying I had access to the adoption files. The Fulbright staff wanted to know: Would I be willing to avoid doing any research at all at the Ministry of Social Welfare? I politely declined.

Just before my return to Guatemala, I received an email from a program officer at the U.S. Department of State, asking if "postponing the archival portion of your research until you were off of Fulbright funding" was "something you would be open to?"[80] While I again considered how to say no, I received a follow-up email asking me to disregard the email and instead meet with a cultural attaché at the embassy on arrival. I did so, reporting to the bunker-like building in Zone 10 of the capital. Although the attaché emphasized the embassy's "respect for academic freedom," he said he also wanted me to see that these were "difficult" issues. I said that my research plans remained the same, left the embassy, and never heard from them again. When I returned to the Ministry of Social Welfare later that year, I was not granted access to the files.

As alluring as conspiratorial explanations may be, the most likely reason for later being denied access has nothing to do with critical journalism or the U.S. Embassy. The likeliest explanation is the prosaic fact that each new government brings in a new group of bureaucrats. The general-turned-president who had closed the Archives of Peace was himself forced out by CICIG's investigations and an extraordinary outpouring of street protests against corruption in 2015.[81] The Ministry of Social Welfare may simply have turned over to staff more concerned about the checkered past of adoptions or inclined to restrict access to archives. I had spent enough time with the adoption files for my purposes, but no other researcher I know of has been able to access this archive since 2016. I presume, and hope, that access is still granted to adoptees looking for more information about their own pasts.

Researching private adoptions presented a different challenge. I had not originally planned to conduct many interviews, but once I learned how frequently adoption files had been falsified, it seemed important to cross-check archival documents with interviews and vice versa whenever possible. To my surprise, lawyers who had arranged adoptions were willing, even eager, to talk. Most claimed that international adoptions had been closed prematurely and unfairly. Some clearly imagined a North American researcher might be a helpful ally in persuading the United States to reopen adoptions and to pressure Guatemala to do the same. Social workers were more reticent, though several women who held jobs with the Ministry of Social Welfare's adoption program did agree to talk. Those I interviewed tended to express the same view: that the reputation of adoptions in Guatemala was unfair, and that they had played only disinterested and humanitarian roles in the system.[82] During interviews with lawyers, I asked if it would be possible to read their adoption files. One adoption lawyer turned conservative congressman said yes. Fernando Linares Beltranena asked a secretary to haul out several massive blue plastic bins of adoption files and set me up in a conference room in his law office in a posh part of the capital to read them at my leisure. He asked only that I assign pseudonyms to children and families mentioned in the files.

During this research, many people asked if I planned to interview adoptees or birth mothers. Adoption files contained contact information, however dated, for both groups, but it seemed plainly unethical to get in touch that way. The files make it clear that some birth mothers gave up their children for adoption in secret. They may have since married, remarried, or found a new partner without mentioning this part of their pasts. As for adoptees, this book follows the story of how certain children came to be adopted, not their later experiences in the United States, Canada, and Europe, an important but distinct part of the history about which adoptees themselves have begun to research and write.[83] I did meet adult adoptees who are now searching for their birth parents in large numbers in Guatemala. In a repetition of some of the dynamics of baby brokering for private adoptions decades earlier, searching for birth mothers is now a private, for-profit business in Guatemala. Often "searchers" are middle-class Guatemalan women, and some are former baby brokers.

A final note on the ethics of researching and writing about adoptions: I am aware that the readers of this book will include adoptive parents, birth families, and adoptees, and I have not softened the edges of an often painful history. This work is in no way intended to pass judgment on the decisions of adoptive or birth families, especially mothers who found themselves in impossible circumstances. Instead, the aim is to understand the confining social and economic structures within which Guatemalan women made choices. One of the surprises of working on this book has been discovering a wide gap of information about where adopted children came from and where they were going between Guatemalans on the one side and North Americans and Europeans on the other. This is not to mention the sharply differing interpretations about what international adoption meant and means. Families abroad often knew little about circumstances on the ground in Guatemala. In some cases lawyers, social workers, or adoption agency workers deliberately kept information from both adoptive and birth parents. In the worst cases, ignorance opened the door for paying to adopt kidnapped children, or unwitting participation in the forced disappearances of children during a genocide unfolding in Guatemala. For their part, Guatemalans tended to know very little about the motives of families who wished to adopt. They could be forgiven for wondering if North Americans really wanted a stranger's child in their home—and from so far away. Suspicion and miscommunications helped fuel mob violence against foreigners wrongly suspected of child theft for adoptions in Guatemala in the 1990s.

I never imagined that I would have occasion to meet, speak on the phone, and exchange messages with so many adoptees over the years. Their attempts to create a connection with a country and families that are unfamiliar to them, along with their activism and scholarship and art, will undoubtedly continue to expand and revise our understanding of this history for many years to come. In the end, this book is really for the adoptees, whose attempts to find out more about the past run parallel to my own, and are charged with even greater urgency.

1

The Lie We Love

In the photograph a white woman pushes a brown toddler in a red baby carriage along the edge of a frozen lake. The boy is wearing a white snowsuit and
winter hat. The woman looks away from the camera toward the ground, nav-
igating the waterline. The photograph is taped into an adoption file dated 1972.
The toddler was one of the very first group of Guatemalan children to be
adopted by foreign parents through a new program at the Ministry of Social
Welfare run out of a Guatemala City orphanage. Two years earlier, police had
dropped the baby off at the orphanage, saying his parents were "awaiting capture" for an unspecified crime.[1] The baby remained in the institution, called
the Elisa Martínez Orphanage, for eight months, after which staff noted that
no family members had visited to claim him. Then the family judge assigned
to the case declared the boy legally "abandoned" and eligible for the orphanage's new adoption program.

Around the same time, a Swedish couple filled out a form provided by the
orphanage stating the reason they were requesting a Guatemalan baby: "we
don't have and we can't have children of our own."[2] Theirs was one of a packet of
eleven requests put together by a Guatemalan journalist in Quetzaltenango who
was married to a woman with family in Sweden. The journalist acted as go-
between and translator, writing first to the orphanage to see if foreign families
were allowed to adopt. International adoption programs already existed elsewhere. He wanted to know: could such adoptions be arranged in Guatemala?

A social worker named Georgina de Gaitán responded that, yes, foreign
families could be considered for a match if they filled out the same paper-

work provided to Guatemalan families. The forms provided to the Swedish families remained standard over the next four decades. Those who wished to adopt filled in their names and addresses and listed their incomes. They were required to provide copies of their marriage certificates and three letters of recommendation attesting to "financial and moral fitness."[3] The forms reveal both what the Guatemalan government considered a suitable family and the desires of adoptive parents. Couples—and occasionally single women, who were also permitted to adopt—were encouraged to note preferences at the end of the forms, which had spaces for "Age," "Gender," and "Other Details." Although there were no indications about how to fill out "Other Details," applicants most frequently used the space to make requests related to the race, age, gender, or health of children they might consider adopting.

It seems likely that the Swedish couple filled out their form in consultation with the Guatemalan journalist. Unlike most other forms submitted by foreign families, it showed familiarity with racial divisions and categories in Guatemala: Indigenous *(indígena)* or, in documents from the period, sometimes *indio* or *natural,* and *ladino,* a term used only in Guatemala to mean non-Indigenous. The couple requested a child of "1–6 months, girl or boy." Under "Other Details" they noted, "We do not care if we will have a girl or boy who is *natural* or *ladino,* we only want a little child who is in good health in view of the trip to Sweden."[4]

Social workers, most if not all of whom were *ladina* women as far as I could tell from archival records and interviews, filled out adoption forms as if the categories of *ladino* and Indigenous, and, less frequently, Afro-Caribbean *garífuna,* were self-evident. But these labels were and remain deeply subjective and have changed over time, based variously on language spoken, family histories and bloodlines (real or imaginary), hometown or city, clothing, and self-identification, to name just a few considerations.[5] Often the label "Indigenous" only came into play during contact with *ladinos* eager to label for the purposes of discrimination or exploitation. Mayas might only be called Indigenous when they moved to Guatemala City for work, or appeared in a file written by a *ladino* social worker.[6]

Social workers matched the Swedish couple with the baby, whose race they did not record. Since his birth parents were allegedly on the lam, the officials did not attempt to consult them before approving the adoption. Neither did they try to find other living family members. (In other cases, the Ministry of Social Welfare sometimes published photographs of children in the Guatemalan newspapers in an attempt to find relatives.) Work demands prevented the couple from traveling to Guatemala to pick up the child, as they explained in a letter to the social worker in charge of the new adoption program. They asked a local lawyer to make arrangements in Guatemala on their behalf and chaperone the baby on a flight to Sweden. The family paid for these services, and social workers noted, "economically they live well." Many adoptive parents took brief trips to Guatemala to pick up babies over the coming decades, but this was not required by an international adoption program that emerged more ad hoc than by design. The photograph of the Swedish adoptive mother pushing her new child around the frozen lake, along with other photographs—meals with the extended family, toy blocks in his new home—were included in the child's adoption file as "positive evidence of the results of family placement."[7]

International adoptions may have been new to Guatemala, but they were not new to Sweden. The country had stayed neutral during World War II, and Swedish families had taken 650 Jewish refugee children and 70,000 children from neighboring Soviet-occupied Finland into foster homes. Over the next decades, Swedes adopted a large number of children from Korea and elsewhere. With over 50,000 international adoptees to date, Sweden has the highest proportion of internationally adopted children as compared to the native-born population in the world. One would-be adoptive mother wrote in a letter to the Elisa Martínez Orphanage in 1972, "Here in Sweden we feel a great obligation towards those who suffer more than us." She added that Guatemalan children "would never feel foreign. We have here in Sweden children from Korea, Japan, China, India, of every race who are now speaking Swedish and go to school to learn and play like all children."[8] Sweden became such an important destination country for Guatemalan children that a social worker from the Ministry of Social Welfare, Yolanda Rodriguez, visited in 1974.[9] To complete the early case of the toddler in the red baby carriage, Swedish social workers, practiced in sending follow-up reports, visited him in his new home. They noted that the boy lived in his own room in an "agreeable area of villas with gardens and parks all around."[10] The adoption was deemed a success and the case closed. Ten other requests by Swedish families, including one from a single woman, submitted together with the help of the lawyer in Quetzaltenango, were all also granted. Eleven newly minted Swedes began very different lives.

Our Little Orphan Daughter

The new adoption program was centralized. Even if children were first housed in other orphanages throughout the country, those placed in adoption by the Ministry of Social Welfare first passed through the Elisa Martínez Orphanage in Guatemala City. This marked a sharp change from how child placements had previously worked in the country, often by informal agreement between families. The policies and practices established by orphanage staff for this new program endured: near absolute discretion of social workers to place Guatemalan children with foreign families, comparison of economic conditions between birth families and adoptive families to justify adoptions, and—a disturbing aspect of the files—finalizing the adoptions of children with living birth parents, some of whom did not give meaningful consent for relinquishment. In the adoption file of the toddler who ended up in Sweden, social workers did not note the nature of the alleged crime of the parents, or whether they might wish to collect their child at a future date.

Orphanage records show that birth parents were sometimes confused by the new adoption program, especially by the fact that placements were final and permanent. Adoptions in Guatemala long predated the orphanage's new international program. As part of informal adoptions, sometimes babies were inscribed directly into the Civil Registry with the names of their adoptive parents. This way, they do not appear as adopted in records at all. Domestic adoptions could be approved locally through an *acta*, or legal document signed by birth mother and adoptive mother. For example, in the municipal archive of Tactic, a town in the coffee-growing region of Alta Verapaz where Spanish and the Mayan languages Poqomchi' and K'ekchi' are spoken, there are *actas* recording adoptions from the 1950s. One *acta* from 15 November 1957 records that a twenty-two-year-old woman "without schooling, single" and with no form of personal identification had three children "but because she is extremely poor and lacks resources for the sustenance of her aforementioned children she has arranged to give the first two to *Doña* [name redacted] . . . as adopted children."[11] The *acta*, in which the adoptive mother vowed to care for and feed the children, and in which no men were mentioned in any capacity, was signed by both parties with thumbprints. Someone had written in their names over the top of the curves of the thumbprints, indicating that both women were illiterate. The *acta* refers to the birth mother as *mujer,* woman, and the adoptive mother as *señora* and *doña,* indicating higher social status. Though the *acta* does not mention race, the birth mother's last name is recognizably Maya. The document is in Spanish, and it is unclear which language or languages the birth mother spoke. It is also impossible to know, though tempting to guess, whether she had an ongoing relationship of any kind with the children after their adoptions.

Other children were simply "gifted" without any paperwork, usually to a wealthier family in the same or neighboring community. Parents might choose to "gift" children to others for a variety of reasons: to cement ties with a powerful godfather or godmother *(compadres),* to provide company for a childless relative, or to secure shelter and food for a child they could not afford to keep. Gifting children is one way of creating what anthropologists call "fictive kinship," a strong social tie without a relation through blood or marriage. Jessaca Leinaweaver, in a study of similar practices in the Andes, refers to informal placements as "child circulation," and notes that placing children informally is often considered temporary, described using the verb *prestar* (borrow and loan) or *mandar* (send). The most common terms in Guatemala are *niños regalados,* referring to children "gifted" to other families, or *entenidos,* referring to children "kept" by other families, closer to what Aymara speakers in Peru call *wila wawat uywasta* ("raised since birth").[12] In Guatemala, the experiences of such children ran the gamut from fully adopted and beloved to semi-enslaved. Informal adoptions, often involving girls doing unpaid domestic labor and boys doing artisan work in unpaid apprenticeships, dated back to the colonial period in Latin America. One frequent arrangement was for the child to cook, run errands, and clean house, for which they were "paid" in shelter and food, not cash.[13] Nara Milanich found that adoption was so commonly a labor relation that for many adopted boys in Chile the passage from childhood to adulthood was the first wage paid to them by their adoptive family for work they had already performed for many years.[14] Children, especially Indigenous children, were trafficked for both adoption and labor or a mix of the two as early as the "Conquest of the Desert," which drove Indigenous peoples out of their land in what became Argentine Patagonia in the 1870s.[15] Adoption as a formal institution through which the adoptee gained the legal rights of a birth child was unknown in Latin America until the nineteenth century, and only formalized in Guatemala with the 1877 civil code. In the United States, it wasn't until the 1930s that children became, in the words of sociologist Viviana A. Zelizer, "economically 'worthless' but emotionally 'priceless.'"[16] In some parts of both the United States and Latin America where child labor remained common, the transition came later, if at all.

Aside from work, some early informal adoptions, especially of Indigenous children, were for the purposes of religious conversion. White Protestant missionaries living and preaching in Central America took in children in the hope of saving their souls. Indigenous communities were and remain the focus of mission work by many Protestants who believe the Second Coming of Christ can only occur when, quoting Acts 1:8, the word of God has been spread "unto the uttermost part of the earth." A series of letters to the *Central American Bulletin,* sent to donors from the mission base Disciples of Christ in Dallas, Texas, beginning in 1919 described one such informal adoption.[17] A missionary named Ms. Townsend and her husband spent their honeymoon evangelizing among Guatemala's Maya Kaqchikel population, and then settled in Antigua, Guatemala's former colonial capital. Townsend wrote:

> On September 29th (1919) one of our Indian believers from a far off place in the mountains came to us with his two daughters. Their mother had been dead some eleven years, and so these two girls have been living with their father away off in no man's land, making tortillas and staying in their little hut. He asked us if we could not take one of the daughters in the home to teach her to sew, cook, read, etc. His chief idea seemed to be that his daughters needed a mother's care. The oldest girl had already been accepted by another family of believers, so we decided to take the twelve-year-old girl.

In a letter to the *Bulletin* the following year, Townsend described the girl as "our little orphan daughter."[18] The error is telling. Townsend wrote: "She is developing into a sweet, gentle little girl, neat and tidy, whereas when she came to us she was the dirtiest little creature you can imagine . . . How I would love to take in more such little, unloved, homeless girls. It pays." How quickly the memory of the girl's concerned father and his hut ("unloved, homeless") faded in the mind of this missionary![19]

Parallels between missionary adoptions and later wartime adoptions of Maya children are striking. Indigenous parents may have calculated: would their children be materially better off if surrendered to non-Indigenous people, particularly during dangerous times? In a 1920 letter, Ms. Townsend, the same missionary wife, wrote:

> Just yesterday some Indians came in from San Andres Itsapa *(sic)*, asking if we would not take in two of their little girls, one eight years old and the other ten. They are the only believers in town and because of the Gospel have suffered much persecution, even to having had their homes burned and many of their things broken into pieces by angry mobs of people. They say they cannot stand to see their children growing up among such people and in such total ignorance, so these two they wish for us to take. One of the Indian sisters has taken them into her home, we paying all expenses, and after a few weeks when I have been able to get away for a short rest, we will take them into our home.[20]

The Kaqchikel family's stated reason for offering their children may have been straightforwardly true or a canny move to convince the family to take in the children, maybe in a temporary fashion to ride out a difficult period—or some combination of both. Not recorded in the mission's bulletin was widespread Maya hostility to missionary presence all over Guatemala, expressed by lighting firecrackers outside a Presbyterian church to smoke out the congregation, selling missionaries food laced with ground-up spicy chiles and red ants, and what Virginia Garrard-Burnett describes as "belligerent crowds" trying to "drown out Protestant services with shouts and loud music as a matter of course."[21]

Another girl, Elena Trejo, who was adopted later by the Townsends from an orphanage they ran in a Kaqchikel town near Antigua, turned out to be extremely bright. In the 1930s, William Cameron "Cam" Townsend wrote to his parents in California. Would they take care of her if she attended high school there? They responded, "send her on up."[22] By that time, Cam Townsend was becoming a well-known missionary in the region. Frustrated by the meager fruits of his evangelizing, he translated the Bible into Kaqchikel and founded his own group, the Wycliffe Bible Translators, to make the word of God available in as many Indigenous languages as possible. The organization in turn funded the Summer Institute of Linguistics, which ran faith missions disguised as educational programs throughout the Americas. In later years, the group was frequently accused of working with the CIA, though without concrete evidence, and more plausibly accused by anthropologists of facilitating culture and language loss through "ethnocide."[23] Elena Trejo, the bright Kaqchikel girl, went on to earn a medical degree in the United States.

One aspect of earlier adoptions that was lost in formal adoptions, especially those to foreign families, was a certain flexibility and impermanence. Placement with missionaries or other families was one of a wide variety of strategies to sustain families in the face of extreme poverty. *Niños regalados,* who were "gifted" to another family without any paperwork or involvement of the state, might be later returned to their birth families. Although legal adoption had been an option in Guatemala since 1877, it was not centralized. Records could be found in municipal *actas* like those from Tactic in the 1950s, though many domestic, informal adoptions left no documentary trace at all. One adoption file held in the Ministry of Social Welfare noted that a Guatemalan family only consulted the orphanage in 1970 to begin a formal adoption process after a failed informal adoption because "they had a child that the mother had gifted but the mother changed her mind and took him back."[24]

Welfare against Communism

Compared to other Latin American countries, Guatemala was late to build even a skeleton welfare state.[25] When in 1968 social workers at the Elisa Martínez Orphanage assigned the first child to a foreign family, the Ministry of Social Welfare was only five years old. The new ministry was part of a counter-revolutionary regime that hoped limited social welfare provisions would make communism less attractive by making the poor just a little bit less poor.[26] This was not a new idea. In an 1850 speech, Karl Marx had criticized "welfare measures" as a "hope to bribe the workers with a more or less disguised form of alms and to break their revolutionary strength by temporarily rendering their situation tolerable."[27] In Guatemala, the welfare state emerged at the same time that international adoptions became common around the world. Adoptions from many places were a not-so-subtle Cold War–era transfer of children growing up in Communist countries or countries that looked likely to go communist to safely capitalist, Christian countries.

From 1944 to 1954, Guatemalans enjoyed a rare democratic opening: a chance to freely elect presidents, catch their collective breath after the depredations of the secret police and forced labor of the previous decades, and even attempt to rectify the underlying causes of some of the worst social inequality in the Americas through land reform.[28] Juan José Arévalo, Guatemala's first democratically elected president, promoted what he called "spiritual socialism," which emphasized moral and social values alongside a more equitable distribution of wealth. In his first speech to Congress, Arévalo announced that as part of his program of spiritual socialism, and "thanks to the work of self-sacrificing women," the first state-run daycare centers for the children of working women had opened in Guatemala. His wife, Elisa Martínez, an Argentine who admired Evita Perón's social welfare programs in her home country, led the project.

During what became known as the Guatemalan Spring, adoptions nearly took a very different turn. For a brief moment from 1949 to 1954, the government framed the best interests of the child—a formulation that would come to mean many different things at different times—in the context of a whole family, not just an individual child. In 1949, the First Lady pressed to legally reframe adoption as an institution of "social aid." Through what newspaper *La Hora* credited to her "initiative and enthusiastic persistence," Congress passed new laws governing minors, the Children's Code. The adoption law read: "every minor has the right to live with moral and material security and possess a home" and "the right to live always at the side of his mother." Most important, the new law stated: "A lack of economic resources is not considered sufficient reason to separate a minor from his parents."[29]

This law, along with its attempt to protect impoverished mothers from losing their children to adoption or foster care, was one of the many casualties of the 1954 CIA-backed coup in Guatemala. The coup overthrew the second democratically elected Guatemalan president, Jacobo Árbenz. A social democrat who idolized Franklin Delano Roosevelt, Árbenz embarked on a land reform, expropriating some of United Fruit's holdings. Thanks in part to the ministrations of Edward Bernays, who invented the job of public relations and was on the United Fruit payroll, officials in the U.S. government became wrongly convinced that Árbenz was a crypto-communist.[30] The coup, which installed a military dictatorship, helped unleash a long-running armed conflict from 1960 to 1996. It was part local struggle over land and other resources, part escalation of anti-Indigenous violence, and part Cold War proxy struggle. Leftist guerrilla groups tried for decades, unsuccessfully, to topple a series of U.S.-backed military governments. After the coup, land reform was rolled back right away. The immediate post-coup regimes were corrupt and authoritarian, but they maintained some hollowed-out versions of labor reforms and social welfare programs.[31]

In addition to undoing land reform, the 1954 coup also reversed legal justifications for adoption. Under a revised Children's Code, keeping children with their mothers in the face of economic deprivation was no longer stated policy, not to mention practice. Instead, adoption files show that extreme poverty was the most common reason for relinquishing children. The Guatemalan Spring–era provision of the right of the child not to be separated from their family for economic reasons would have disqualified many, if not most, of the children who passed through the Ministry of Social Welfare's adoption program. The new welfare state built in the aftermath of the coup reversed the logic of the earlier code, posing children's rights as individual and separate from the family. Post-coup, the best interests of the child were the greater opportunities and material privileges a foreign adoptive family might provide. This was in tune with much of the legislation on adoptions around the world throughout the twentieth century and beyond, which saw a child's rights as individual, not collective—making it easy to justify moving children from a poor family to a richer family through adoption placements, ignoring Indigenous and other notions of kinship and community in Guatemala and around the world. The main state-run institution, repurposed from an existing children's shelter, was named the Elisa Martínez Orphanage in 1968 in recognition of the former First Lady's role in pushing for welfare programs, though the adoption program begun during the counterrevolution operated by principles opposite to those she had championed.[32]

In 1954, Carlos Castillo Armas, the dictator handpicked by the CIA to lead the coup, created the National Committee of Defense against Communism, which added 10 percent of the Guatemalan population to a list of people considered suspect because of their political beliefs.[33] Previously, the meager assistance to women and children that was available had been provided through churches and private charitable organizations, not the government. This changed when Castillo Armas's wife formed the National Council on Welfare (Consejo Nacional de Bienestar), a predecessor organization of the Ministry of Social Welfare, whose bylaws specified that it "does not have activities of a religious, political, or sectarian bent." Still, according to minutes from a 25 November 1955 meeting, the group gave off more than a whiff of anticommunism: one stated goal was to "work for the prevention and elimination of the social conditions that cause problems."[34] A 1959 article in leading newspaper *El Imparcial* characterized the country's first child welfare programs as having its "embryo" in the first daycare founded by Elisa Martínez, but noted, "It is definitely a humanitarian social action and not political as many people believe."[35]

Throughout the early 1960s, welfare programs were promoted by the United States and its allies—moderate or right-wing administrations throughout Latin America—to wick away potential support from communists. Following the coup, Guatemala received US$130 million in economic aid with the intent of making the country a "showcase" for capitalist development in Latin America.[36] This was a spectacular flop. Meanwhile, between corruption and the reconcentration of lands in the hands of the elite after land reforms were rolled back, 70 percent of the country saw their income decline between 1954 and 1960.[37] In 1960, an academic turned community development consultant to the U.S. government named Richard Poston took a yearlong research trip around Latin America, the Middle East, and Asia funded by the Rockefeller Foundation. Poston wrote a book describing the "threat to freedom" poverty posed in Guatemala, arguing that "agents of Communism" were eager to "exploit that advantage cunningly and vigorously."[38] (The book was published with the unintentionally funny title *Democracy Speaks Many Tongues.*) He praised the first director of the Ministry of Social Welfare, Elisa Molina de Stahl, whose "personal attack on the ancient forces of poverty has become a demonstration of the kind of leadership that must be found and supported if democracy is to succeed in the under-developed world." Molina de Stahl had been appointed by a Guatemalan general turned president whom the CIA had originally considered to lead the 1954 coup.[39]

At his inaugural address on 20 January 1961, President John F. Kennedy announced: "To our sister republics south of our border, we offer a special pledge—to convert our good words into good deeds—in a new alliance for progress—to assist free men and free governments in casting off the chains of poverty." That "free" was aimed at Cuba, where the previous month Fidel Castro had declared in a televised address "I am a Marxist-Leninist and shall be one until the end of my life." The local anticommunist push to create a limited welfare program in Guatemala converged with the goals of the new Alliance for Progress, which sent 20 billion dollars to Latin America over the next twelve years. John F. Kennedy warned his Latin American allies in 1962: "Those who make peaceful revolution impossible will make violent revolution inevitable." In Guatemala, the U.S. Agency for International Development (USAID) emphasized that "'primitive' Mayan Indians, who comprised half the population, needed to be integrated into the national fabric lest they fall prey to Communism."[40] In 1963, falsely claiming that the government was once again lousy with communists, a defense minister overthrew the democratically elected president of Guatemala with Washington's blessing.

Another concern was the population boom. In 1953, a Washington, D.C.–based organization noted in a pamphlet called *Communism in Guatemala* that the population there had grown 120 percent from 1920 to 1951.[41] Amid fears that overpopulation would push people toward communism, John F. Kennedy, the first Catholic president of the United States, announced in 1963 that the nation would provide "technical assistance" in family planning to any country desiring it. In 1966, the USAID chief of human resources in Guatemala said at a university convocation: "The earth is populated by over three billion people, of whom almost 500 million live in the Americas . . . The deprived groups behave like hungry men. They strike, make war, disrupt social systems."[42] In 1968, both the U.S. Democratic and Republican parties endorsed nearly identical messages that population control was an urgent global threat. That same year, a USAID-funded academic conference at the University of San Carlos of Guatemala concluded that the increase in Guatemalan population did not pose a problem, and rather that persistent racism, hunger, and exploitation were larger problems.[43] Still, the United States led and funded the population control movement, which, according to Emily Klancher Merchant, "aimed to convince women that their poverty was caused by the number of children that they had rather than by the structure of the global economy," and which ran clinics that inserted IUDs in women and then closed, leaving no medical care for complications or the removal of devices if women decided they wanted more children.[44] For those who saw population growth as a kind of threat multiplier for communism, international adoptions could serve a potentially stabilizing role.

Adoptions were certainly cheaper than housing children whose parents could not afford to feed them over long periods of time in orphanages. As Donna J. Guy notes of a similar history a few decades earlier in Argentina, three years after a 1944 earthquake, President Juan Perón sent a message to Congress urging it to change the law to facilitate "philanthropic" adoptions. A law passed in 1948 relaxed adoption requirements, which, according to Guy, "meant that orphanages could be smaller and the cost of child welfare privatized."[45] In Guatemala, internal Ministry of Social Welfare annual reports stress a chronic lack of funding. One orphanage had a bakery where children were trained as apprentices, and the sale of bread helped pay to keep the institution running.[46] Placing children for adoption was a less expensive option than fully funding or expanding a network of state-funded orphanages.

After the revolution, military regimes supported some limited welfare programs, but mostly blamed the struggles of Guatemalan children on supposed flaws in the personal morality of parents, not on the poverty they had done so little to alleviate. Since its founding, the Ministry of Social Welfare was headed by successive first ladies. In 1963, Guatemalan-Honduran writer Augusto Monterroso published a cutting short story, "First Lady." The main character was modeled on the wife of the dictator installed by the 1954 coup. Monterroso imagines a fundraiser for children in which an education bureaucrat introduces the lightly fictionalized First Lady, saying she was moved by the predicament of "those unfortunate children who because of drunken parents or mothers who had abandoned them or for both reasons could not enjoy in their modest homes the sacred institution of breakfast which endangered their health and impaired their ability to take advantage of the education that the Ministry which we have the honor to represent here tonight was determined to give them."[47]

The Ministry's attempts to provide some social services to lessen the appeal of communism were limited by the fact that they were underfunded and concentrated in the capital. A 1964 article described a supposedly impromptu gesture by the mothers who worked in Guatemala City's biggest street market, La Terminal, showering the director of the Ministry of Social Welfare with flowers for "opening these centers that solve the problem of the abandonment of their children."[48] The daycare had a capacity for only 225 children.

Each daycare the Ministry of Social Welfare opened was celebrated in the sycophantic national press, with headlines often including the phrase "homage to mothers." But after 1954, alternatives to adoption grew fewer because the coup had foreclosed the possibility of social democracy meeting the basic needs of most Guatemalans. In other words, the coup blocked the possibility of improving the conditions of the poorest Guatemalans enough that they could keep and care for their own babies if they so desired. A 1966 article celebrating the opening of another small daycare center in the capital quoted one of the mothers who planned to drop off her child there during the day. She said that she must work to eat, so previously she would have been forced to "abandon" her children.[49] Given that the ministry had minimal coverage in Guatemala, worsening economic conditions forced many mothers to do just that.

Babylifts

The Swedish families' requests to the orphanage came at a time when North American and European families were increasingly interested in adopting nonwhite children from abroad, in large part because of later marriages and lower fertility. Highly publicized "babylifts" helped popularize the idea of adopting from overseas. After the end of the Second World War, orphan-rescue missions in Germany and Japan delivered hundreds of children to the United States. In 1975, a mass evacuation of at least 3,300 Vietnamese children during the fall of Saigon was called Operation Babylift. The operation ended with adoptions of the children in the United States, Europe, Canada, and Australia. Journalist John Seabrook noted that the babylifts following the Korean War, the Bay of Pigs ("Operation Peter Pan" spirited more than 14,000 Cuban children to the U.S.), and Vietnam were, "in part, political, fueled by a new superpower's desire both to demonstrate its goodwill to the rest of the world and to rescue children from Communism, but the press covered them uncritically, as humanitarian mercy missions."[50] Postwar and Cold War international adoptions were very much part of great power politics, though often misconstrued, then and now, as a family matter—private, and somehow apolitical.

South Korea was the first of the major "sender nations," a designation that later came to include Guatemala, Russia, and China, among other countries that dispatched children in large numbers to U.S. adoptive families. Nearly all these countries were either communist or, in the U.S. view, "threatened" by communist takeover or recently emerging from war. Arissa Oh writes that the original Korean adoptees were mixed race, with either white or Black American soldiers as fathers: "One drop of black blood made a person black in the United States, but in Korea a drop of white or black blood made a child American."[51] Given Korean notions about racial purity, the babies were considered a social problem. U.S. officials, for their part, concerned about the future of "their" half-Korean babies, began to speak of international adoption as repatriation. The mutual solution, found without consulting birth mothers, was adoption by white families in the United States, overseen by a cadre of newly professionalized Korean social workers. Oh notes that the for-profit adoption process created in South Korea in the 1950s came to structure international adoption elsewhere, as the same U.S.-based adoption agencies expanded business to new sender countries. U.S. couples who wished to adopt lobbied Congress for laws that allowed for more and faster adoptions by arguing that this would support Cold War objectives.

No one pushed harder for making international adoption widely available in the United States than Harry and Bertha Holt, an evangelical Christian couple. In 1954, the farmer and housewife attended a talk by a traveling minister from World Vision—then a new interdenominational group but today the largest Christian international relief and development organization in the United States—who showed a documentary film about mixed-race children abandoned by American soldiers in Korea after the war. The Holts decided to adopt eight Korean children to add to the family of six they were already raising on a farm in Oregon. The Holt family became a media phenomenon. The Korean adoptees' first breakfast in the Oregon farmhouse, everyone's heads bowed around the table to say grace, was featured in *Life* magazine in 1955. The *Life* story and the wave of publicity that followed framed the adoptions as an apolitical act of charity and Harry Holt as a latter-day Good Samaritan. This despite the fact that the Holts had lobbied for a special bill from Congress in order to adopt six more children than the legally allowed limit of two.

The Holts received so many letters from families wishing to adopt that they opened their own agency, which is now one of the biggest in the world: Holt International Children's Services. Harry Holt shuttled back and forth to Korea for over a decade, bringing hundreds of Korean babies in cardboard bassinets back to the United States. In order to take the babies out of Korea, Holt first adopted them all himself through power of attorney in "proxy adoptions" before putting them on a plane. According to Tobias Hübinette, "foreign individuals and voluntary agencies considered themselves to be the guardians of the country's children" based on a religious calling.[52] Holt International also arranged adoptions for Europeans, beginning with Swedish families in the 1960s.[53] Until 1964, the Holts arranged adoptions only for Christian families.

The Holts popularized international adoption among U.S. families, but the practice was not new. In the 1930s, Nobel Prize–winning author Pearl Buck adopted four children from the United States, Europe, and Asia. Buck

Harry Holt arriving with Korean children to be adopted in the United States in 1956.
Bettmann / Getty Images.

criticized the existing U.S. adoption practice of racially "matching" children to families. In a 1953 article, she wrote: "These are the citizens of the new world, the children without parents and the parents without children, pressing eagerly toward each other, and yet unable to reach each other. A barrier stands between, a high wall, and in the middle of the wall is a narrow gate, kept locked until a social agency unlocks it a little way and lets one child through at a time."[54]

The image was moving, but did not reflect reality: most children available for adoption were not "without parents." As Laura Briggs writes in *Somebody's Children*, the popular idea that adoptees were all orphans was flat wrong. The vast majority were the children of families too poor to feed them.[55] One journalist calls the orphan myth "The Lie We Love."[56] International adoption has been mixed with profit motives from the start. Historian Gonda Van Steen writes that at least 3,200 Greek children were adopted by U.S. families from 1949 to the 1970s, first orphans whose parents had died during a civil war there, then nonorphans to meet the increasing demand for adoptees.[57] The special bill passed in Congress in 1955 allowing the Holts to adopt eight children was called "Act for the Relief of Certain Korean War Orphans." The law's fine print defined "orphan" rather broadly, as a child who "has suffered the death or disappearance of, or abandonment or desertion by, or separation or loss from both parents or who has only one parent . . . and the remaining parent is incapable of providing care for such child and has in writing irrevocably released him for emigration and adoption."

Still, the story of mass international adoption consisted of the lowering of that "high wall," beginning in the 1950s. Over the next decades, the Holts continued to push for favorable legislation and drum up demand. They went on nationwide tours displaying images of Korean war orphans at churches, convincing couples that foreign children needed their love and support. Until 1961, all adoptees were legally categorized as refugees; after that, when the United States reclassified them as immigrants, they were never subject to national-origin quotas or any other numerical restrictions. In the 1970s, when birth control became more widely available, single motherhood less stigmatized, and abortion legalized, fewer babies were available for domestic adoption and the number of international adoptions climbed further. Several decades into large-scale adoptions from their country, many Koreans began to feel that they were a wound to national pride, especially when Korea was dubbed the "orphan-exporting nation" by international media during the 1988 Seoul Olympic Games. When Koreans began to relinquish fewer children for international adoption, Holt International started placing children from Ethiopia, Peru, Guatemala, Haiti, and other countries with families abroad.[58]

The pattern set by Korean adoptions, which eventually totaled an estimated 200,000, also included fraudulent paperwork. Agency workers keen to process adoptions quickly did not always verify information, including whether children relinquished by other family members while mothers were working really had the mother's consent. Mothers were generally not paid for their children, but, according to anthropologist Eleana Kim, were sometimes told that they would be selfish to keep children who could be raised in affluent U.S. homes.[59] One woman named Hyun Sook Han who worked for a Korean adoption agency in the 1960s recalled: "I misunderstood my job and thought I was supposed to make the birth mothers relinquish their children; I pushed those mothers to sign the papers. Of course, I did not walk into town and just grab the children. The way I tried was to convince those mothers that their children were better off coming with me and being adopted internationally . . . Believe me, I wasn't trying to separate mother and child; I really believed, in my youth and naïveté, that I was doing the best I could for these children." She recalled that she began the work "fresh out of college" and with "little instruction and training." Han wrote, "Back then, the area of social work was relatively new to Korea and so we had no models to follow."[60] Han later moved to Minnesota, where she helped place Korean adoptees with midwestern families. Interviews conducted by historian Yuri Doolan show that demand in the United States prompted Holt International to hire Korean women to convince mothers to relinquish their babies, including by entering "camptowns" where sex workers lived near U.S. military bases. Women working for Holt sometimes used coercion and lies to separate women from children. Rumors of birth mothers paid for children or babies stolen from hospitals, if impossible to verify decades later, demonstrate the fear some Koreans felt as adoptions became more common.[61] This is hardly the story of orphan rescue told in U.S. newspapers at the time.

The "lie we love" was exposed in other countries as well, as cracks grew in the early consensus that international adoptions were apolitical and purely humanitarian. Controversy followed "Operation Babylift," during which Holt International Children's Services, the Pearl Buck Foundation, and others collaborated with the U.S. government to evacuate thousands of infants and children from South Vietnam before the fall of Saigon. The first evacuation flight crashed shortly after takeoff, killing seventy-eight children. That same day, 4 April 1975, a group of professors of ethics and religion signed the "Statement on the Immorality of Bringing South Vietnamese Orphans to the United States," arguing that "even though they may be motivated by good intentions," those coordinating the airlift were in the wrong. "Many of the children are not orphans," they wrote, and "the only reason for bringing the children here is to salve our conscience and children should not be used that way . . . The attitude that 'we know how best to help them' is the same attitude that sustained our immoral involvement in Vietnam for so many years."[62] Most Vietnamese children who arrived safely in the United States had paperwork processed at the Presidio army installation in San Francisco, where Vietnamese-speaking volunteers were aghast to hear some of the older children insist that they weren't really orphans. The volunteers helped organize a 1975 class-action lawsuit, *Nguyen Da*

Yen vs. Kissinger, hoping to halt adoption proceedings by arguing that the children were held in the country against their will and that of their parents or guardians.[63]

Decades later, Babylift children who had been adopted by families abroad were found in some cases to have been separated from mothers without their consent or to have been placed by parents in institutional care only temporarily. Vietnamese mothers who had not voluntarily relinquished their children for adoption testified in *Nguyen Da Yen vs. Kissinger* that they wanted them back. Advocates for predominantly white, middle-class adoptive families argued that the children—war notwithstanding—had not been well cared for, citing poor dental health. At the trial, Joyce Ladner, a Black sociologist and civil rights activist, offered testimony that while "Asians may not experience as much hostility" in white-dominated parts of America as Black children, "they do experience subtler forms of discrimination." Ladner at the time was working on a book based on interviews with 136 families who adopted Black children in the United States. She concluded that while some families dealt well with their children's racial identities, others denied that their children were Black at all.[64] During her testimony in the class-action lawsuit against Operation Babylift, Ladner said of the Vietnamese children: "Even if the circumstances to which they return are less economically secure than the American homes they are presently in, emotional security must not be traded for a middle class life style where racial and cultural gaps are so broad and often ignored."[65] The judge eventually threw out the lawsuit, and children's adoption files were sealed. In the aftermath of the lawsuit, historian Allison Varzally found, only twelve children were reunited with their parents.

In Guatemala, too, economic justifications weighed strongly in favor of shifting from domestic to international adoptions. Social workers started to receive inquiries not just directly from families but from adoption agencies already active in South Korea, Vietnam, and elsewhere. Around the world, agencies worked with intermediaries in sender countries who had broad latitude over deciding which children were considered adoptable, including nonorphans. At the Ministry of Social Welfare, social workers had near-total discretion over deciding what was in the best interests of the child. As foreign demand rose and the revolutionary notion of a child's right to remain with their birth family was suppressed, the principle of the best interests of the child was defined in a straightforward way: material wealth. Foreign families could both pay for the process of adopting a Guatemalan child—fees for which rose even in early years into the thousands of U.S. dollars—and support a middle-class lifestyle most Guatemalan families could only dream of. As commodification of children faded in wealthy countries, the boom in international adoptions accelerated the dynamic in certain poor countries— where the "emotionally priceless" child gained a price tag.[66] In 1972, a Swedish woman wrote a letter to the Elisa Martínez Orphanage, questioning why social workers there referred her to a lawyer, Rafael Bugur, who charged 250 *quetzales* (US$250) for each finalized adoption. She hoped to adopt two children, and wrote: "Is it true that we have to pay Q500? For *el Señor Lic* Rafael Bugur? It's a lot! In Sweden it doesn't cost anything. It is the state that pays . . . It's not good that the paperwork is expensive, because that makes it impossible for many people to adopt orphans in the future. Not only rich people are going to have the opportunity, right?"[67]

Formal and informal adoptions had a long history in Latin America and globally, but from the mid-twentieth century onward they took on a new form and scale. International adoptions during this time are the only instance of a wholesale international transfer of children from South to North, poorer to richer families. The suspicious Swede was prescient. Adoptions would eventually transform into a for-profit industry.

2

Social Reports

As social workers organized the program for international adoption at the Elisa Martínez Orphanage, they began to write up stacks and stacks of paperwork. To see the adoption files, archived away at the Ministry of Social Welfare in Guatemala City, the process appears to have a given logic, even bureaucratic inevitability. But there is in fact a certain randomness, a personal element to international adoptions that comes through by reading the files with care and speaking to some of the people involved. For each adoption that was finalized, an unlikely group of people had to come together—an adoptive family, a birth family, a social worker, a lawyer, a family judge, workers at an adoption agency. Seen this way, the aspect of chance and even improbability comes more clearly into view, along with all the prejudices and inclinations of the people involved in the rather godlike act of radically changing the trajectory of a child's life.

Carlos Larios Ochaita, now well into old age, recalled in an interview in his Guatemala City office that he had recently graduated from McGill University, in Montreal, when he began working on adoption cases. Larios Ochaita, who later rose to become general counsel to a president, chief justice of the Supreme Court of Guatemala, and a well-known law professor, was in 1972 a young lawyer freshly returned to his home country. He noted that Guatemala had participated in international adoption previously, but as a receiver country. Wealthy Guatemalans had adopted Costa Rican children, because the adoption program there was longer standing and better organized, and, he allowed, because "the children were whiter." A psychologist who later worked on private adoptions also mentioned that she knew several wealthy

Guatemalan families who adopted from Costa Rica in the 1940s because the children had "lighter skin and lighter eyes." In 1972, one of Larios Ochaita's former classmates put him in touch with several Canadian families interested in adoption. Larios Ochaita remembers that he told them, "Come, come to Guatemala. We told them that there was nothing institutionalized but that there was an institution called the Elisa Martínez Orphanage." He recalled that a social worker named Blanca Morales, who later appeared frequently in the paperwork when she became the head of the adoption program, helped push to formalize the process once foreign families were interested. "It was very ad hoc, very unexpected, you see?"[1]

According to Larios Ochaita, starting in the 1970s he helped place about thirty or thirty-five children and charged a fee of the equivalent of US$500 per adoption. This was a point he wanted to emphasize most emphatically, because of later criticisms of how commercialized adoption had become. "I'm telling you 3,000 dollars was the most we ever charged, including expenses. You can publish that if you want. That was the maximum, I'm telling you." Expenses included airfare to Canada, as well as care and supplies for the child while adoption paperwork was processed. As I came to see over a series of interviews with lawyers who participated in international adoptions, it was common for them to be defensive even when talking about the earlier, less commercial period when lawyers worked with state-run orphanages. I found Larios Ochaita's name in several dozen adoption files in the Ministry of Social Welfare paperwork. Receipts for legal work were not included in his cases or in others. Larios Ochaita insisted that his participation in adoption "was never a business," but noted that it presented certain opportunities for his firm. "Namely, many Canadian and North American companies got to know us through adoptions and became our clients."

The first adoptions from the Elisa Martínez Orphanage, facilitated by lawyers like Larios Ochaita, involved families in Sweden, Canada, and the United States. As letters preserved in the Ministry of Social Welfare's archive show, early adoptions sparked interest among neighbors and family members, who then also contacted the orphanage, setting off a kind of adoptee chain migration. Once families contacted the orphanage, the most important decisions were taken by social workers, who made matches based on their training and, often, their desire to pair children with families based on appearance, which is to say race. In the early years of the program, domestic adoptions were still more common, and the requests of Guatemalan families are filed alongside those of families from abroad. Any family who wished to adopt had to present letters attesting to their "financial and moral fitness." As social workers received more and more applications from abroad, where adoptive families often owned homes or drew salaries that were almost unimaginable in Guatemala, they placed more and more children farther and farther away. According to the adoption files at the Ministry of Social Welfare, in the first four years of the program, only fifteen of forty-six adoptees traveled abroad, though several foreign citizens living in Guatemala adopted children. Over the next four years of the program, only eighteen of sixty-one children were placed abroad. Guatemalans who adopted were not uniformly wealthy, or even middle class. Though it is impossible to tell without receipts, it seems lawyers sometimes waived fees for helping with domestic adoptions. The program at the Elisa Martínez Orphanage was still small scale, and adoptions had not yet tipped overwhelmingly to the international market, as in later years. All adoptions had a probationary period of six months to a year, but social workers clearly regarded this as a formality. Children traveled abroad during probationary periods, but it was clear they would never return. The United States, and especially Harry Holt, had pioneered what were called "proxy adoptions." Adoptive parents never had to travel but instead granted power of attorney to an in-country lawyer.

Social workers in the early years sometimes went to great lengths to search for birth family members and fill out lengthy reports. To judge by the files they kept, the orphanage's social workers were punctilious. Social workers occupied a different social world than Larios Ochaita, with his relative wealth and privilege. They tended to be neither poor nor rich. Never Indigenous themselves, as far as I could tell from the files, they worked closely with Indigenous families. Social workers were professionals, but not always recognized as such. They were, without exception, women.

Social workers were required to complete academic training but did not have degrees. According to a commission tasked with restructuring social work education at Guatemala's leading public university in 1978—already deep into Guatemala's counterrevolution—formalizing a certificate program for social work was one of the "achievements of the so-called '44 Revolution."[2] Social work certificates were originally administered by the Guatemalan Social Security Institute and, in 1975, this program was absorbed by the prestigious public University of San Carlos.[3] By this time, every other country in Latin America, apart from El Salvador, had the equivalent of bachelor's degrees for social workers. Efforts to elevate the certificate to a bachelor's degree or "professional" degree were denied by university officials in Guatemala. The commission's report called existing programs for social workers in the 1960s and 1970s "unsatisfactory training": "Often social workers, since they work with economically marginalized sectors and were deeply familiar with the problems experienced by that sector, were regarded as not really workers and salaried employees; the lack of option for an academic degree limits the possibilities for social workers to be considered as a member of the public sector and earn a decent salary."[4] In 1978, social workers' monthly salaries ranged from 200 to 250 *quetzales* a month. This is a salary range that social workers categorized as middle class when evaluating prospective Guatemalan adoptive parents.

Despite low social prestige and relatively low pay, education for social workers was expansive. The student preparing for a certificate in social work, according to the University of San Carlos, must "through the area of Behavioral Sciences acquire sufficient capacity to understand the existing relationships between people." A variety of classes were required: sociology, including a class called "Class Struggle: Various Forms"; family law; the history of families, including separation, divorce, and legal recognition of children; custody law; political science; economics; psychology, including a course called "Evolution of the Family"; and children's psychology. Social workers in training were also required to take anthropology courses, including "Criteria for Racial Classification."[5]

We Got It in the Garbage

Once social workers were trained, those who were hired by the adoption program at the Ministry of Social Welfare or worked with the program as psychologists or nurses enjoyed an unusually freewheeling professional life for women of the era. Adoption files, as well as other casework files, record visits to slums in the capital and long drives out to rural areas to attempt to locate family members of abandoned children. Social workers at the Elisa Martínez Orphanage worked closely with social workers at the public hospital in Guatemala City. I met Barbara Reckenholder, a retired social worker who later became a psychologist, in her cozy office in Zone 10. The animated octogenarian, dressed in matching maroon from her turtleneck to heeled loafers, recalled with affection her work at one of Guatemala City's two largest public

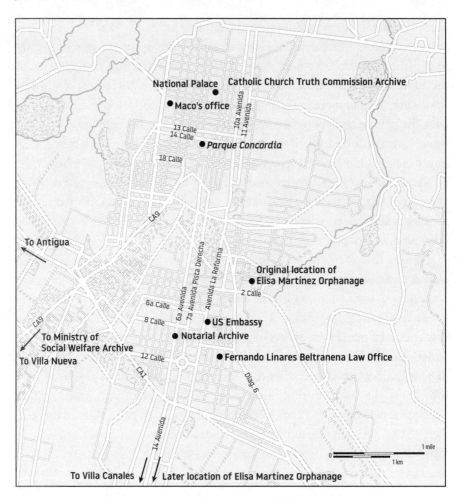

Guatemala City

hospitals during the first years of the Ministry of Social Welfare's adoption program.

Reckenholder was born in Guatemala City in 1937 to a middle-class family. Her father was an engineer, and she wanted to be an engineer, too. But she calculated that she had limited options, since she also wanted to marry. Social work was one of few choices. Reckenholder earned her social work certificate in 1955 and began work at San Juan de Dios Hospital, a cramped structure built to only one level for fear of earthquakes. It sat next to a bullring, which for a time was owned and run by the hospital. Profits from admissions were used to support hospital services. Reckenholder was the head of social work at the hospital from 1961 to 1967. Referring to Elisa Molina de Stahl, the powerful early head of the Ministry of Social Welfare, by an affectionate nickname, she recalled, "Doña Moli gave us the task to investigate where the abandoned newborns were from. We sent telegrams to the addresses the mothers had left, but often they weren't correct. When a few days had passed, the babies couldn't stay at the hospital. So we began the home visits."[6]

In addition to illiteracy and the vagaries of the Guatemalan mail system, Reckenholder explained that one reason families didn't respond to letters or telegrams was that they participated in the mass seasonal migration of poor families from the highlands to the coast to provide temporary day labor for coffee and sugar harvests. The majority of these families were Indigenous.[7] When enough families from one area were unreachable, Reckenholder would take one of the hospital's cars, along with a chauffeur and the secretary of the hospital's social work office, and travel to the highlands. She remembered that sometimes when the team from the hospital arrived, "almost the whole town had up and left" for a harvest elsewhere. In those cases, Reckenholder found a local authority, either a police chief, priest, or mayor, who could look up the child in the civil registry. Sometimes these authorities gave her a birth certificate and helped her find the parents. At other times, they would say that no one with that name lived in the village. Reckenholder and her colleagues took this to mean that the mother had given a false address, abandoning her child on purpose at the hospital. Those children were sent to the Elisa Martínez Orphanage and often placed in the adoption program. She was sad to see that some children were indeed abandoned, but remembered the trips to the highlands fondly, as an adventure. Some cases involved less running around, when mothers gave up children right there in the hospital. For example, one adoption file with Reckenholder's signature included a relinquishment form signed by an Indigenous woman in the capital working as a maid whose partner abandoned her when he learned she was pregnant. According to the form, she "refused to meet the baby" after giving birth.[8] By the time Carlos Larios Ochaita was fielding requests from friends in Canada, there were a growing number of children considered adoptable in the public orphanages. Many children were referred from hospitals. Others were found abandoned on the street, dropped off by needy parents at the orphanage, taken into custody when mothers were in mental hospitals, or separated from women sentenced to prison terms—often for prostitution or theft—who had been deemed "morally unfit."

Reckenholder recalled pressure by her superiors to clear unclaimed babies out of the hospital to make room for new patients. "We had the doctors breathing down our necks saying 'they must be discharged, they must be discharged, they must be discharged, they must be discharged, they must be discharged.'" I asked Reckenholder if the public hospital paid for her trips to the highlands to search for parents. She replied: "Oh, my dear, if you only knew where we got small change to pay for those trips. We got it in the garbage." Reckenholder meant this literally. Social workers used to sell off waste from the hospital to a man who kept pigs. In later years, the social workers opened a few *tienditas,* little stores, in the public hospital, stalls selling candy and cigarettes. They used this money to pay for the search trips, but also for hospital necessities that were always in low supply, like syringes and wheelchairs. One year, when the budget ran out early, the social workers pitched in money from the stalls for food for patients for the months of November and December. The 1959 annual report of the ministry's predecessor organization, the Association of Infant Welfare, discussed plans to build another orphanage since "demand for this service is so marked . . . that we have understood the need to expand in order to satisfy the requests for admitting children that we receive from the hospitals."[9]

While the ministry kept very complete adoption records, not all of its annual reports are filed or accessible. The 1966 annual report is the next to appear in the archive, and by then aims for the welfare program were changing. Funding, never very abundant, had dried up further. Even as Guatemala transitioned briefly to a left-of-center civilian presidency, foreign aid was redirected from welfare to a military buildup and counterinsurgency. Curtailing guerrilla insurgencies no longer seemed likely, or possible. In the 1960s, programs backed by Alliance for Progress and the Peace Corps in Guatemala, along with grassroots Catholic Action religious reformers, had formed agricultural cooperatives and community development programs, many in Maya areas. Not only did the United States withdraw funding from these groups, but it armed and backed counterinsurgency campaigns that, in a tragic repeat of the 1954 coup, did an about face, suspecting cooperatives of being crypto-communist or outright communist. Foreign priests and nuns who stayed the course with community development and created new education projects in the 1960s also found themselves vulnerable to violent repression or expulsion from Guatemala.[10] Increasingly throughout the 1970s, the Guatemalan government and its U.S. allies behaved as if the way to stop communism was to kill anyone suspected of being a communist. By 1973, the Organization of American States disbanded the "permanent" committee to disburse Alliance for Progress funds, and the United States ramped up counterinsurgency training for Guatemalan and other Latin American military officials at the School for the Americas and in the Panama Canal Zone.

The national and international political situation was changing, but social workers faced the familiar if ever more acute problem of too many orphaned children and too few resources to take care of them. The Ministry of Social Welfare funded itself in part using income from one-arm bandit slot machines installed around Guatemala City, the institutional equivalent of the hospital social workers' little stores and dumpster-diving expeditions. During the same period, the U.S. government started funding welfare programs by selling lottery tickets in reaction to a growing population, inflation, and the cost of the Vietnam War.[11] A lawyer who worked on adoptions from the Elisa Martínez Orphanage during the early years told me "you would enter and feel a blow to the heart because there were all those children trying to hug you. 'Mama, mama, I want to go with you. I want to get out of here.'" She recalled sometimes there would be as few as one or two babysitters for thirty children.[12] Guatemalan social workers noted in the Ministry of Social Welfare's 1966 annual report that despite a continued influx of abandoned children, foster homes had helped ease overcrowding in orphanages. Referring as well to another orphanage that oversaw a smaller number of adoptions of older children: "We express our wishes that this system of family placement will be extended in the future until the Orphanages 'Rafael Ayau' and 'Elisa Martínez' become transit centers for children with a family deficit."[13] The paperwork prepared by ministry workers never reflected on the many reasons that there seemed to be more "children with a family deficit" than ever. As the new adoption program started to place just a few children at first, then several dozens each year, the majority of adoptions were still domestic. But over the first decades of the program the orphanages did become transit centers—with new endpoints in North America and Europe.

Adoption Files

Flip open an adoption file and it begins at the end. First comes the finalization of the case. Then comes the follow-up report on how children adapted to new families during a trial period of six months. Then come the adoption request forms. Finally, the *informe social,* or "social report." The social report contains extensive detail, gleaned through interviews or sometimes hearsay, about the working life and background of the birth mother, the conditions of her pregnancy, and sometimes, though less frequently, about the identity of the birth father. The social report is the most important document in the adoption file, the account of how it all began. It is the record of how a child was abandoned, came loose, or was shaken loose from his or her birth family. For those children who were not abandoned or orphaned, the social report also served a bureaucratic function: to record why the birth mother relinquished her child for adoption, and in doing so to justify the adoption.

Adoption files show the back and forth between the desires of adoptive parents for certain kinds of children and the ever-changing circumstances of unwanted pregnancies, forcible separations, and fractured family life in Guatemala that landed children in state custody. Crudely put, social reports record supply, adoption request forms record demand. Together they show the extraordinary discretion of social workers to decide which children would be assigned to the adoption program and which families would be selected to receive them. Some social reports also show, in detail, the flimsy or sometimes nonexistent consent of birth mothers and fathers before adoptions went forward.

The very first adoption overseen by the new Ministry of Social Welfare adoption program was domestic, finalized in 1968. The birth mother had tuberculosis and was mentally ill. Her older child lived with an uncle, and the family dropped off her younger son at the newly named Elisa Martínez Orphanage in 1966. A sketch of building plans for a new orphanage from an earlier ministry report showed a sleek, futuristic three-story building with a rather sexy social worker out front surrounded by a ring of children holding hands.[14] The more prosaic orphanage built by the ministry wasn't completed until 1984, and, in the meantime, the Elisa Martínez Orphanage took over an old installation in Zone 5, near Campo Marte—a complex of fields with baseball and basketball courts, the obligatory soccer field, and a bizarre faux-castle military tribunal constructed in the 1930s. The orphanage had space for 250 children. The government spent 26.05 *quetzales,* roughly US$26, per child per month for their food and shelter.

The official reason listed for this first adoption case was abandonment after "hospitalization of the mother and irresponsibility of the father." The father had migrated to the United States. Some Guatemalans already traveled to "El Norte," often for seasonal work, though large-scale migration didn't begin until the 1980s.[15] The mother said that, at first, the father of her child had sent her fifty *quetzales* each week, then fifteen *quetzales,* then ten *quetzales,* then nothing. They fell out of touch. After an interview with the mother in the hospital, a social worker wrote, "since he went to the United States he has doubted the fidelity of the patient and in every letter he sends her he expresses his unhappiness with her hospitalization and supposed abandonment of the minors, which he thinks is because of her lack of love *[desamor]* for them."[16] In language that became boilerplate in adoption files, social workers noted, "The home is completely broken *[desintegrado]*." Neither aunts nor grandparents could take the child for more than a short time, according to the social report. They couldn't afford to feed him.

The social worker gingerly brought up the possibility of adoption with the mother:

> I asked her if she had ever thought about adoption, since it is completely impossible for her to have the minor. Immediately she responded, "Do you want him, ma'am?" ["Usted lo quiere seño'?"]

"Seño'," short for *señora,* is the deferential way Guatemalans refer to people of a higher social class. For example, a domestic servant would call the lady of the house *seño'*.

> I responded that it was not exactly for me, but that people come to the institution to look for children and that they can give them very good opportunities. I also told her that we never give a child in adoption without previous consent of the parents. She said that she would consult the father of the child and if he wasn't capable of helping her with the child, she would let us know. Because of the foregoing we note in *Señora* [name redacted] a marked detachment from the child.

Because the adoption program was so new, the birth mother assumed that the social worker was suggesting that she informally gift the child: a *niño regalado* rather than formal adoptee. She wrote to the father of her child, and he responded that he did not give permission, and that he would send her money to help support the child. The money never materialized. The social worker noted that while the boy remained in the orphanage as these letters were exchanged over several months "it was recommended to the mother that she visit with more frequency and try to desist from the idea of giving him to another person . . . She is depressed and cannot find a solution for her problems, but the letter from her husband cheered her up and she was grateful that he is writing to her again." Social workers monitored the behavior of mothers, noting when less frequent visits or willingness to consider adoption indicated what they saw as a lack of proper maternal interest in the child—including in situations, such as this one, when the social worker had suggested adoption to the mother in the first place. They sometimes included a bit of speculation or gossip, often about new boyfriends or partners. "Since the mother doesn't visit him it would seem that she leads an independent life and it is suspected that she has a new partner *[conviviente],* so the child could be a good candidate for adoption."[17]

Fathers had little say. In 1967, the father wrote to the orphanage that "with respect to my *hijito* [name redacted] while I am living I will not give him to anyone, and it is hard for me to believe that his own mother wants to give him in adoption when she is the person who should least think about giving away her son." Despite the birth father's objections, and contrary to what they had originally told the mother about requiring consent from both parents, social workers decided that the child was a good candidate for adoption. Around this time, an elderly Guatemalan couple put in a request at the orphanage. They wished to adopt, they wrote, to "contribute to the rearing of a child who at the same time will be company for us, since we have two children who are already adults." Social workers wrote to the birth father a few more times, and he did not respond. When the mother stopped visiting the boy at the institution for several months, they concluded that they could put up the child for adoption without further verbal or written consent.

It turned out that the elderly couple were really planning to be adoptive grandparents, not parents. Their eldest daughter wanted to adopt but was afraid she would be turned down because she was divorced. She need not have worried. The records show that social workers were quite flexible on this score, deciding in favor of both domestic and foreign adoptive parents who were single or divorced—especially when they were solidly middle class or wealthy, as this family was. In fact, most rejections were of people they considered too old to adopt, or, on rare occasions, families whose houses struck the social workers as too impoverished or chaotic. One file noted that a child was assigned to a fifty-year-old who social workers considered "of advanced age" but competent to raise a child. In 1972, one child was reassigned from a foster home to an adoptive family over the protests of the foster mother after the social workers noted that the family "does not provide acceptable conditions" since it is a "household made up solely of women, lacking the necessary presence of a man to perform the functions of a father." The foster mother lived with her sister in a house the social worker deemed "dirty and unhygienic" and, during a house visit, she observed a drunk cousin on the scene and worried that the child could "witness unpleasant scenes."[18] Still, social workers regularly approved the requests of single and divorced women who wished to adopt. Catholics, evangelicals, Mormons, Mennonites, Jews, and those who "practiced no religion" all adopted. There seemed to be no systematic rules about age or religion or minimum income, only the discretion of the social worker.

Even after social workers found out that the couple requesting a child in this case would be grandparents, not parents, they agreed to the adoption. The boy was placed in adoption, despite the fact that the mother had appeared as recently as that same year at the Elisa Martínez Orphanage to visit him. On that occasion, according to the social report, "it became known that the mother has a new partner . . . and lives a completely disorderly life." The child went to live with the other family, who social workers noted approvingly "were of white skin [de tez blanca]" and who "had a great physical resemblance to the child."[19]

Social reports contain constant references to the skin color and appearance of children. Matching children with parents of a similar race was a goal, however elusive, of the adoption program, especially during its early years when the majority of adoptions were still domestic. Would-be parents also made frequent requests for light-skinned children. As one couple wrote to the orphanage: "We hope that the skin color could be similar to ours to avoid future problems that might arise for the infant."[20] Racial matching was a goal— or fantasy, more than a reality—in Guatemala, since children available for adoption were generally of darker skin than the families who wished to adopt. Social workers, in their attempts to make matches, carefully described children on orphanage intake forms, down to eye shape and hair texture. The majority were *moreno* (dark) or *indígena* (indigenous), with a few children described as *moreno claro* (a lighter brown) or *blanco* (white). Social workers also described the racial characteristics of adoptive parents as well as their "cultural level," which they rated "high," "medium," or "low" based on nebulous and subjective judgments of education, income, and—of course—race. Even in cases for which racial matching was not possible, social workers noted the race of adoptive parents whom they interviewed with what they must have thought of as precision. A "white" Guatemalan woman and her husband with "brown skin *[tez morena]*" requested a "light brown-skinned *[morena clara]*" girl and were assigned a darker-skinned girl.[21] Another *ladino* family that requested a child with "white skin and light eyes *[tez blanca ojos claros]*" was assigned an Indigenous child.[22]

Indigenous children were not always explicitly identified in adoption files, and even taking into account clues like town of origin or last names it is impossible to give a full and accurate count of what percentage of adoptees had Indigenous mothers—other than to say it was high. The issue was further clouded by the fact that orphanage workers began changing children's names, a process that would continue throughout later years, during the war. Children who were found on the street took the last name Barrios. In at least one case, a recognizably K'ekchi' last name was changed to a common *ladino* last name before adoption—with the K'ekchi' name crossed out and rewritten by hand on the file.[23] Other children were put up for adoption with their recognizably Indigenous last names intact in the files.

Guatemala's racial politics, especially the unwillingness of non-Indigenous families to adopt Indigenous children, comes through clearly in the social reports. Though both foreign and local families often requested children based on race and appearance, Guatemalan families were more specific. A note by a Guatemalan family looking to adopt a child *"que sea blanquita,"* "white if possible," was typical.[24] A sense of what kinds of children were requested, by both Guatemalan and foreign parents, comes through in the "Other Details" box on adoption request forms. Girls were more frequently requested, by a small margin, as were younger children and babies. There was a litany of more specific requests, often having to do with race. A sampling from 1970s adoption files: "child of honest people," "of good color, skin light brown," "of the *ladina* race," "white skin," "brown (but not *mulata*)," a word still used in Spanish for mixed African descent, "healthy," "recently born baby," "a true orphan" (meaning no living mother or father), "preferably with my characteristics, that is light skin, light eyes, etc.," "light brown colored skin, should be orphaned on both sides—mother and father—if possible," "newborn," "light-skinned," "white race and normal." "I would wish that the child be somewhat blonde, affectionate, and that she be healthy," wrote one applicant: "preferably *ladina*." "White, curly-haired *[colochita]*, light eyes," "1–2 years, white," "born of healthy parents with good morals and a white complexion," wrote others.[25]

Sometimes poor or Indigenous Guatemalans who wished to adopt would instead be designated as foster parents, with social workers citing their economic status. A handful of Maya families did adopt from state orphanages during the early years. In a case finalized in 1971, one family received a child who was a "brown-skinned boy, black hair, black large and expressive eyes."[26] It is likely, though not spelled out, that the boy was of Indigenous origin. The social workers continue, "The child does not have good features *[bonitas facciones]* but is agreeable." Indigenous families were themselves of course not immune to Guatemala's profound color-consciousness. This couple had originally requested "a child who is perfectly healthy, of decent parentage, and in addition has light brown skin color."[27] The family earned relatively high wages and ran a small bakery out of their house. Of another child, a social worker wrote, "It seems that the child has taken all the characteristics of the adoptive family who are of the indigenous race, but who make the impression of very responsible people of good habits and very identified with the minor."[28] That "but" is telling. Social workers made judgments about the economic status of families based not just on income but on what kind of house they lived in, whether the house had a cement or dirt floor (negotiable) and whether it had running water and electricity (both considered a must). This Maya family was given the right to adopt the child only once they had made certain improvements to their property, including building a latrine close by and painting a thick layer of lime onto the adobe walls to protect the house from humidity. This was the only case I found in which the ministry required changes to a home before allowing an adoption to go through, though a social worker wrote of another house owned by an Indigenous family that it was comfortable "but arranged in a little bit of bad taste."[29] Another Indigenous couple who wished to adopt were assigned a child with "indigenous facial features" of which social workers elaborated "dark skin, black eyes and hair, snub nose, prominent mouth." In a rare case of a non-Indigenous child assigned to an Indigenous family, the child was described in the following way: "dark-skinned but *ladino* . . . In his physical aspect the minor makes a good impression, but his adoption might be difficult because of his mother's mental illness." Social workers also noted that this Indigenous family rather unusually lived in a three-story house with a garden "surrounded by luxury and comfort."[30]

More surprising were the numerous requests from white North American families looking to adopt "white" babies or infants from Guatemala. One of the first U.S. families asking to adopt from the Elisa Martínez Orphanage in 1973 sent the required family study assessing "economic and moral fitness" written by a North American social worker after a home visit. The report, with underlining in the original, noted: "<u>They don't wish to accept a child with handicaps, or of another race.</u> They feel that children are usually happier with those of <u>their own race.</u> Nevertheless, they would like to have a boy from a Latin America *[sic]* background if he is able to adapt to their family." In a later letter, the North American social worker wrote that the family had changed their minds:

> It seems that the family [name redacted] has not changed their desire to adopt another child, but one of the requests concerning the type of child they would like has changed. They now feel that they could easily accept a child of mixed blood; and they only prefer that he not be of black blood. They are also anxious to receive a child who is as young as possible. When asked about their change of heart concerning the bloodline of the child, they told me they had realized after submitting their original application the improbability of receiving a totally Caucasian child.[31]

In the end, the family submitted a request form for a child with the "other details" box filled out in both English and Spanish. The English text read: "No Negro Blood. But any other." This is an especially bald example of what several scholars have noted about the growing popularity of U.S. adoptions from Asia and other Latin American countries during this period: the children were desirable because they weren't black.[32]

For those who wished to adopt in the United States in the 1970s, there was a "white baby famine": declining birth rates, *Roe vs. Wade,* the rising use of contraceptives, less stigma surrounding single motherhood, and the rising age for both marriage and first pregnancies for women were all factors. Waits for domestically available white children rose from to three to seven years by 1975.[33] A 1979 letter of recommendation from a U.S.-based adoption agency to the Elisa Martínez Orphanage read "As you probably know, the adoption of an infant in the US is very difficult due to a lack of available children."[34] The couple that had at first sought a white child from Guatemala told the U.S. social worker that between her house visits they had met more people from other countries and enjoyed their company. "They said that they could love a child from almost any blood background," the social worker relayed to her counterparts abroad. The family was assigned a boy who in Guatemala was categorized as *moreno claro,* light-brown skinned. There is no record of his experience or adjustment to the adoptive family.

Adoption files record conversations and judgments about the attractiveness of babies and children of different races, according to both social workers and adoptive families, that are frankly painful to read. The files reveal a hierarchy of attractiveness, mostly based on race. Of an Indigenous child, one social worker wrote: "The child does not have good facial features but he looks healthy."[35] Another wrote of a different child: "white skin, dark straight hair, dark eyes, nice."[36] Another wrote, "he is of the indigenous type . . . he is not attractive."[37] Of another child: "The minor is dark-skinned with dark straight hair, indigenous features, but he is sweet and apparently mentally and physically healthy."[38] Guatemalan families were invited to visit children in person at the Elisa Martínez Orphanage before filing adoption requests for specific children, and the social workers' appraisals were in part based on their reactions to different children. A small minority of foreign families expressed a preference for Indigenous children, generally without saying why. In the original packet of requests from eleven Swedish families, for example, there were a variety of requests. One couple "prefers *mestizo (ladino)* but with dark eyes and hair," another "prefers indigenous," and for another couple, "it does not matter but if there is an indigenous child, that is the preference."[39]

Social reports included in adoption files give rare glimpses into the lives of birth mothers. But it is worth recalling that the files were not intended, nor should they be read, as a documentary record of what happened in the past. They should be read keeping in mind what they are: case files. Social workers were motivated by what they thought was in the child's best interest, by their desire to justify the adoptions that they had arranged, and by the need to close cases quickly. A network of orphanages and hospitals across the country fed the Elisa Martínez Orphanage in the capital, the central hub for the adoption program, and a very high volume of paperwork passed through the Ministry of Social Welfare's offices. The adoption files should be read less as recorded fact than what social workers thought they must write down in order to process adoptions, follow the law (in most cases), free up space in the orphanages, and keep the higher-ups in the ministry satisfied. Adoption files existed less as a narrative recording of fact, or to provide a reliable personal history to adoptees, than as a means of recording, justifying, and closing cases.[40]

Certain stories, especially stories about birth mothers, recur in the files so frequently that it is reasonable to wonder whether they are accurate in every case, or complete. Birth mothers were housewives, tortilla-makers, market vendors, prostitutes, and teenagers without professions. But by far and away the most common work listed for birth mothers in adoption files, when that information was listed at all, was domestic service. This remains true across decades and across the state orphanage and private adoption files I was able to consult. Many women who worked as maids relinquished children for adoption, or at the very least that was the story they told or that social workers recorded most frequently.

Since colonial times, young women from the countryside—especially Maya teenagers and girls—traveled to work as domestic servants in Guatemala City, and their numbers only increased as Guatemala urbanized in the twentieth century. In the colonial period, some domestic workers were called *indizuelas*, "little Indians," or, in reference to informal adoptions, *hijas de la casa*—literally "daughters of the house."[41] This arrangement was so ubiquitous that it can be almost invisible in archives. For example, a social worker's description of a Guatemalan adoptive family notes "they live alone, with the *muchacha*," meaning "girl" or maid. This was a job filled by women without children or women whose children lived elsewhere. Domestic servants were often fired if they became pregnant. Social workers' accounts tend to the elliptical on this question, but given high levels of recorded sexual violence against live-in maids throughout Latin America and the sparse details that the files do contain, at least some of the cases were likely rape.[42] One social worker wrote that a teenage Indigenous girl working for a *ladino* family in the capital "sustained relations with" the nineteen-year-old son of the family. When their son was born, and here the underlining is in the original, "she gave away the child because she did not want him."[43] Another case file is more explicit: it spells out that a teenager who worked as a domestic servant was raped, and "upon leaving the maternity ward she was offering her child to others." The teen said that even if economic support were available "she did not desire to keep her daughter."[44]

Girls and women who worked as maids faced a choice if they became pregnant: either leave their workplace and return to their place or village of origin, or place the child with another family or person by "gifting," informal, or formal adoption. Some sent their children to live with grandparents. Those who didn't have that option were more likely to relinquish their children. In fact, adoption files from the first decade of Ministry of Social Welfare adoptions show that the adoptive children weren't necessarily orphans. It was the *birth mothers* who were likely to be orphans.[45] One birth mother who worked as a domestic servant explained her decision to give up her child for adoption to a social worker who obviously changed some of the language if not the sentiment: "the minor prevented her from development because she was always fired from workplaces and is currently confronting serious economic problems."[46] Over and over, young women told social workers that they had no parents or relatives able to watch their children while they worked. The Ministry of Social Welfare's much trumpeted daycare centers only covered a fraction of the need. Family pressures and misogyny were also a concern. One K'iche' woman who worked as a domestic servant for fifteen *quetzales* a month in the capital visited the orphanage when she was still pregnant. According to a social report, she wished to "assert her desire to 'gift' her future child since she is a single mother in a deficient economic situation that prevents her from caring for him. Her greatest concern was her father, who lives in [home village redacted] and who had threatened her not to get into a situation similar to her state."[47]

Adoption files from state orphanages often contained mention of informal paid foster care. It was a common practice for working mothers to temporarily leave a child with a nonrelative in the capital, usually an older woman who was finished raising her own children. According to the social reports, leaving a child with a nonrelative for full-time care cost about ten *quetzales* a month in the early 1970s. Maids were paid at most between thirty and forty *quetzales* per month with food and housing included, though food was often inadequate and housing often meant sleeping on a mat rolled out on the kitchen floor or in a windowless room. By contrast, a standard wage for male workers was 100 *quetzales* per month. (One *quetzal* was exchanged for one U.S. dollar during this period.) Placing a child with a nonrelative could easily eat up a quarter or even a third of the mother's salary. Social reports contain many instances of a mother dropping off her child in such an arrangement, then ceasing payment and no longer visiting the child. The woman caring for the child then contacted the authorities or brought the child directly to the orphanage. Some of these women no doubt continued caring for abandoned children after mothers ceased to pay or visit, in yet another form of informal adoption. In one such case, the caretaker told a social worker that she wished she could care for the child for free but was "herself very poor."[48] Adoption files show that the majority of early adoptees were children of domestic servants and children left with paid caretakers whose birth mothers ceased payment and did not return to collect them. A small number of children were orphans or were found abandoned on the street or in churches, but most of the children in the adoption program were not orphans. Rather, the children were considered abandoned because birth mothers lacked the money or social support to care for them.

A small number of early adoptees were children whose parents had lost custody. In these cases, social workers sent reports to family court judges, who made decisions based on the concept of *patria potestad,* which dates back to Roman law and is broader than "custody," its usual translation in English. The category includes all rights that parents hold over their children. In the absence of a legally recognized father, the mother could exercise *patria potestad* unless she was deemed immoral by public authorities. Legally speaking, parents could lose custody for several reasons including, according to the civil code adopted in Guatemala in 1963: "For depraved or scandalous conduct by the parents, excessive harshness in the treatment of their children or abandonment of their family duties . . . or for abandoning their children."[49] At least one boy was taken away after his mother was put in prison for public drunkenness. In the files, the prejudice of social workers against Indigenous or poor mothers sometimes shows clearly. In one case, social workers debated whether putting up a child for adoption would be counterproductive, because it might free up the birth mother, whom they judged "irresponsible and thoughtless," to have another child.[50]

Though Our Laws Do Not Allow It

From the very earliest years of the adoption program, social workers at the Ministry of Social Welfare bent or broke the law, especially when it came to consent by the birth mother. In several cases, the ministry provided formal paperwork for adoptions that had been conducted illegally, either to cut down on their workload, to further what in their view was the best interests of the child. In a 1972 case, when social workers got in touch with a family to finalize an adoption after a probationary placement, they learned that the family had no plans to formally adopt the child. Rather, they had simply gone to a civil registry and paid for the child to be inscribed as their own—even though falsifying this paperwork was a crime.[51] Though it is difficult to track with any accuracy, this seems to have been a relatively common form of fraud. A decade later, a report from the U.S. Embassy in Guatemala sent to Congress as part of a 1984 hearing on adoption fraud noted: "The weakness in civil registration of births is that it is quite possible, and often happens, for a woman not the mother to present herself to the civil registry with a child to register the birth as her child. Hospital birth certificates are not always required and midwife certificates are far from reliable. Hence, one's nephew, or grandchild or a baby found on the street can be passed off as one's own, with little problem; it is of course against Guatemala law thus to falsify a birth registration, but it is done all the time."[52] In the case of the Guatemalan family in 1972, the social worker decided to accept the falsified paperwork, saying that it would entail "less trauma" for the child. In this case, the social worker decided that the child was doing well with the family: "In the face of the already resolved situation, as in the present case, nothing was to be done but accept what they had done themselves without prior consultation," she wrote, then closed the case.[53]

In one case, ministry workers checked on a Guatemalan couple to see if a child was adjusting well to a placement, and the couple admitted "with great embarrassment that they had not returned to the orphanage previously because they feared the reaction of the authorities at the institution." The couple said they had paid for a falsified birth certificate listing the child as theirs by birth. The social worker concluded, "Really, given the situation there was nothing to do other than accept what they had done because the outcome was ideal, but the laws of our country are not broad in that regard." The social worker wrote approvingly that "the minor had found some real parents." After checking with her supervisor, "under these irregular circumstances the case was closed" since, she wrote, "given the situation there was no other option."[54]

In 1972, one politically connected couple wrote directly to the First Lady explaining that they had taken in a child. They admitted that they had falsified a birth certificate for her, but now thought it best to draw up adoption papers. "Because she was an abandoned girl, we didn't think there would be any problems," they wrote. The First Lady referred the couple to social workers at the Elisa Martínez Orphanage, who at first explained that if the child was legally considered abandoned, she must pass through the orphanage and be assigned to the adoption program. If they followed the rules, the child would end up assigned to another family. But the family convinced social workers to accept the falsified paperwork and process a formal adoption. In the adoption file that they drew up, social workers wrote: "They made us see that given the situation there was nothing to do but accept, since if we hadn't accepted this situation, everything would have gotten complicated and we would have created problems that in the end could be damaging for the girl." Closing the case, they wrote, "Faced with this choice, we had to accept the document as proof to close the case, which was the best solution and is done in other countries, though our laws do not allow it."[55] These are cases from the period in which illegal acts are actually recorded in the paperwork, though it is easy to imagine social workers stretching or breaking the laws in other cases and in other ways.

In that very first case from 1968, it was the birth father who objected to the proposed adoption, and the adoption went forward anyway. But, more frequently, adoption files show that children were put up for adoption over objections by or without the consent of birth mothers. Some of these birth mothers spoke Mayan languages and may not have fully understood the proceedings. Adoption files record cases of illiterate or mentally ill mothers and those pressured by family members into relinquishing children. One woman who suffered a mental breakdown and was diagnosed with "post-partum psychosis" signed a release form for the adoption of her baby. "I'm not in the condition to take responsibility for my daughter, given my illness" read the form.[56] In another case, a child was put up for adoption after her mother entered a hospital for treatment for epilepsy. The social worker noted, "in addition to her mental weakness she speaks an indigenous language so it was impossible to obtain more information."[57] If social workers ever worked with Mayan language translators on these cases, the adoption paperwork left no record of it. Consent was assumed when it was not explicitly or meaningfully granted.

One Indigenous mother, accompanied by her brother to the Elisa Martínez Orphanage in 1972, left social workers with the impression that her family was coercing her into relinquishing the child. Her brother "intervened directly in our conversation . . . to make us see that she is not a responsible mother," the social worker wrote. The woman worked as a waitress, making twenty *quetzales* a month, and the father denied that the child was his. She already had four children, her brother said, and their mother couldn't help care for another. The social workers contrived to speak with the birth mother alone, but it was difficult, they wrote, since she was "timid, barely answers questions that are put to her, seems indifferent to her situation, but at the end of the interview she did tell the undersigned, crying, that it hurt her very much to surrender her girl." (Timidity and diffidence are clichéd ways of describing Indigenous affect that date back to colonial times, often due to miscommunication, distrust, or fear rather than the situation at hand.) Social workers did not specify how much Spanish this woman spoke and did not have an interpreter present. They decided to accept her child into the adoption program. The mother signed the relinquishment papers with a thumbprint, indicating that she was illiterate.[58]

In another case, a mother had left an infant with a paid caretaker in the capital to travel to a farm in the countryside, where she could work as a day laborer. The birth mother was illiterate and earned only seven and a half *quetzales* a month selling tortillas. She hoped to make higher wages on the farm to help her cover the ten *quetzales* a month she had promised the caretaker to look after her child while she was gone, but instead she fell out of contact. The birth mother later explained why, saying she had suffered a stroke and was immobile in bed for six months. In the meantime, the caretaker dropped the child off at the Elisa Martínez Orphanage. When the mother resurfaced and asked for her daughter, the social workers investigated her, traveling to the farm that the mother had left as an address. They found that the woman had not been working at that particular place, and the local doctor said he hadn't cared for anyone of that name. Nobody considered the possibility that the mother was using a false name to hide the pregnancy and birth, or that someone at the farm had reason to lie. Social workers wrote in the file: "We also investigated the current situation of the mother, establishing that she is an indifferent, cold person, she is not responsible, she does not have a fixed job, she has a new lover and it is not a formal relationship, this person gives her one *quetzal* a week to help her. In short, it is a very bad situation." The mother was not identified as Indigenous in the file, but her town of origin is majority Kaqchikel. It's impossible to know what the social workers meant by "not a formal relationship." This could have been anything from a casual relationship to the kind of common-law marriage to a partner who was called a *compañero*, or companion, that was typical among the working class. Social workers concluded that although the mother wanted her daughter back, an adoption by a couple abroad who was interested in the child should go forward. To justify going against the mother's repeated attempts to regain custody of her child, a social worker wrote, "Even if she is her mother, she hasn't known how to be a mother or love her. Even today she asks for her back, but without showing that missing her little girl has her depressed." In the social report, the social worker wrote disapprovingly that the relationship with her new partner was "apparently very irregular." Over the objections of the birth mother, the little girl was adopted by a foreign couple.[59]

Months after the child had already left the country, the mother reappeared at the orphanage and again demanded the return of her daughter. The Ministry of Social Welfare deemed the case "serious and delicate" and took it to a family court judge to see if they had been legally justified in finalizing the adoption. The judge ruled in favor of the social workers, finding that the orphanage was, he wrote, "as always looking out for the best interests of the girl." As far as the file shows, the ministry never communicated the birth mother's desire to reclaim her daughter to the couple who adopted her. In fact, the social worker in charge of the case later wrote to the adoptive parents about other matters without mentioning the birth mother's reappearance at the orphanage.

In another case, a foreign adoptive mother wrote to the orphanage in 1972 wanting to know precisely why her little girl had ended up in the adoption program: Was the birth mother poor? Had she rejected the baby? Did the birth father even know of her existence? The adoptive mother wrote that she was concerned about what to tell her daughter when she was old enough to understand. The director of the Elisa Martínez Orphanage responded on 8 February 1972:

> When doubts arise for children in similar cases like the one that you raise, we have guided the family to give a version that although not truthful allows a child to satisfy their doubts and concerns. Permit me to instruct you and it is you, with your deeper knowledge of the child, who will decide what best serves. At the right time so as not to hurt her, you might say that her mother died when she was very young and that you, in turn, so eager to give love to a girl and love her as your own daughter, went to an orphanage where you selected her out of all the little girls. As I repeat if you think it wise at the most appropriate time if she insists on asking, I hope this can help you so that everything goes smoothly and the girl can be eased of doubts of any kind and can be a happy child.

A copy of this letter was preserved in the Ministry of Social Welfare's archive of adoption files. Clearly the adoptive mother was never given a full copy, because right there in the file is the social report with all the answers. The birth mother, who was very much alive, had come looking for her daughter at the orphanage after the adoption had been finalized and the child had left the country. In a note never shared with the adoptive mother, the social workers wrote: "The mother presented herself to reclaim the minor." She was presumably told it was too late, because there were no further entries to the file.[60]

What the reams of bureaucratic paperwork produced by the Ministry of Social Welfare show is that even before the privatization of adoptions in Guatemala in 1977, there was an ad hoc quality to how families were matched to adoptive children. Social workers enjoyed broad discretion over decisions about which children went where. Their decisions, including a rising preference for international adoption at the expense of domestic adoption, reflected social workers' frequently racist and classist assumptions about who might make a good mother. Still more alarming, the consent of birth mothers—including those who were illiterate or who spoke Mayan languages—was often assumed, even in cases where they were quite obviously being coerced into giving up children. Family members seeking the return of children were sometimes turned away from state orphanages with the excuse that placement in adoption was in the best interests of the child.

3

Privatizing Adoptions

On 4 February 1976, at 3:03 A.M., a 7.5-magnitude earthquake hit Guatemala, shaking most of the country for forty-five seconds. Minor earthquakes rock gently, but this one began with a sharp sideways jerk. The quake did the most damage in densely populated areas: a small city called Chimaltenango and the capital. Adobe walls of older homes crumbled under the weight of heavy tiled roofs, trapping people inside. Major buildings half collapsed, hanging crazily to the side "like a counterpart to the leaning tower of Pisa," according to a national newspaper.[1] An estimated 23,000 people were killed, 77,000 injured, and more than one million made suddenly homeless—out of a population of fewer than six million. These numbers, circulated by the national and international press, are improbably round, but they give an idea of the loss and destruction. An estimated 5,000 children lost at least one parent to the earthquake.[2] Prompted by lawyers who seem to have sensed an opportunity, the Guatemalan government responded to what it deemed an "orphan crisis" by opening a new, privatized process for international adoptions.

Guatemala City looked and still looks like an inside-out Rio de Janeiro. Instead of building favelas up the sides of cliffs, Guatemala's poor built their adobe, wood, and *lámina*—corrugated iron sheeting—shacks down into forested gullies, which cut deep gashes into the city's surface. These homes clung precariously to the sides of ravines to begin with, and the earthquake dashed them down to the bottom along with their inhabitants. Outside the slums, known in Guatemala as *asentamientos,* there were many fewer casualties. Destruction was so concentrated in poor communities that the great natural disaster of 1976 became known as a "class quake."[3] By the mid-1970s, the

Wreckage after Guatemala's 1976 earthquake. *U.S. Department of the Interior, U.S. Geological Survey.*

guerrilla insurgency seeded by disgruntled military officials in the eastern part of Guatemala had spread to other parts of the country. One group, inspired by the Cuban Revolution, called itself the Ejército Guerrillero de los Pobres (Guerrilla Army of the Poor) and in a secretly circulated pamphlet wrote that 1976 had been a "tremor for the rich, an earthquake for the poor."[4]

Major earthquakes tend to shake people's political and religious certainties, their sense of place in the world. The 1976 earthquake hit Guatemala at a vulnerable moment, more than a decade into a war in the country with the most inequitable distribution of wealth in the Western Hemisphere. The earthquake set off a mass migration of suddenly homeless *campesinos,* or farmers, to the capital, where there was still no water and spotty electricity. Social inequality rooted in the inequitable distribution of land had already incentivized mass internal migration of the poor to Guatemala City to work in poorly paid jobs, especially as maids. This inflow into Guatemalan cities was hastened by the earthquake.[5] For the first few days, city dwellers slept in outdoor spaces for fear of aftershocks, which terrorized survivors for a whole week after the original quake. The capital suffered the most damage, but at least some emergency services were available there. The government officially recommended that people sleep in parks for the first few nights or "open places that allow for easy access and or evacuation" in case of aftershocks.[6] People from the countryside and the newly homeless of the capital set up improvised tents with sheets and ponchos.

The army used the earthquake and disaster response to ramp up their increasingly violent efforts to crush the guerrilla movement and root out anyone considered "subversive." President General Kjell Laugerud took advantage of the chaos to declare a state of emergency, and to disappear and murder a new round of political dissidents, mostly student leaders and trade unionists. General Romeo Lucas García, who later became president, first rose to prominence as head of the National Emergency Committee. Military brass understood the political importance of the emergency response for shoring up control. Guatemalan sociologist Edelberto Torres-Rivas wrote that the army sweep of the northern part of the country two weeks after the earthquake was two-pronged, intended both to repress the guerrilla movement and to force workers to accept lower wages during a worldwide economic downturn.[7] Counterinsurgency went hand in hand with economic exploitation.

In the face of inadequate governmental aid, Guatemalans formed neighborhood organizations to quickly rebuild homes. Some of these solidarity groups spilled over into support for the guerrilla movement. The stark difference between how the rich and the poor experienced the crisis aided consciousness-raising and mass organization, including the formation of the CUC (Comité de Unidad Campesina), Guatemala's leading peasant organization, which had close ties to one of the guerrilla organizations attempting to overthrow the military government.[8] This was a similar dynamic to the aftermath of the 1972 earthquake in Nicaragua, when the government's inadequate response and obvious theft of foreign disaster aid helped fuel the revolution there. As natural disasters often do, the earthquake made Guatemala's ongoing larger crisis—extreme social inequality—even more obvious to all.

For their part, Guatemala's military government seized the opportunity to use disaster relief for good press to counteract critical international coverage of its escalating human rights violations. The government tried to shift the discussion away from human rights toward their framing of humanitarianism. Guatemala's less-than-independent newspapers covered the earthquake as an apolitical humanitarian disaster. Seen from outside Guatemala, the politics of earthquake and disaster response were muted. News out of the country was of a humanitarian crisis seemingly unconnected to the war, despite the fact that the root causes of war were the same as those that had caused such massive loss of life and dislocation during the earthquake.[9] Newspapers played up an "orphan crisis," which no doubt existed, but was a small subset of the wider problem and had in any case already existed before the earthquake. Foreign coverage of a humanitarian orphan crisis in Guatemala also prompted hundreds of families in Latin America, Europe, and the United States to offer to adopt Guatemalan children.

It Is Not True That They Are Giving Out Orphans

After the earthquake, Guatemalan newspapers kept a rising tally of the dead, wounded, and displaced, along with the number of children orphaned. Journalists published heartbreaking photographs of children. In one example, an Kaqchikel girl of about four leads an even younger boy by the hand through rubble in the town of Sumpango, near Antigua. The caption reads: "Asked about the whereabouts of their parents, they reply 'We haven't seen them.'" A long spread in *National Geographic* noted, along with harrowing photographs: "Thousands of children are orphaned. Many will always suffer dreams of the living nightmare." In response to news stories, there was a surge in international aid, as well as offers to take in or adopt orphans.[10]

Natural disasters, along with wars, were prime invitations for families in wealthy countries to imagine a needy, faraway child. Not until the late 1970s did the Guatemalan war make international headlines, and then only because of mounting levels of violence against civilians and reports by human rights organizations like Americas Watch and Amnesty International. (The generals ruling Guatemala were aware of this dynamic, and frequently denounced human rights organizations as communist.) It was the 1976 earthquake, rather than the ongoing armed conflict, that focused wider international attention on Guatemalan children as readily adoptable. Foreign aid money and workers rushed into Guatemala after the earthquake in numbers never seen before. Protestant groups from the United States fanned out across the country to practice what anthropologist David Stoll calls "disaster evangelism," using the "opportunity" of natural disasters to spread the word of God. Missionaries travel to areas that have just faced a massive shock, because nonbelievers are more likely to convert under such circumstances. "If you want church growth, pray for economic and political devastation," said one missionary working in Central America in the 1980s. After the earthquake, missionaries forever changed the religious landscape in Guatemala, which—along with Peru and Brazil—now has among the highest rates of Pentecostal Christians as a percentage of the population in Latin America.[11] Protestants grew from about 7 percent of the Guatemalan population to over 22 percent by 1982, many of whom were Pentecostal (*evangélico* in Spanish).[12] One of the most famous, and later infamous, converts was Efraín Ríos Montt. North American evangelicals made connections in Guatemala that would later help facilitate private adoptions to evangelical families in the United States.

Humanitarian aid and terrified reactions to counterinsurgency pulled people toward Pentecostal churches in the aftermath of the earthquake. Many Guatemalans converted at least in part because association with local versions of Catholicism, particularly those that drew on liberation theology, became increasingly dangerous as the government started to associate them with guerrilla activity. Death squads began murdering catechists, lay Catholic teachers.[13] Army sweeps two weeks after the earthquake targeted farmers who had participated in reconstruction brigades or met with USAID representatives or Catholic Action groups—grassroots religious organizations that promoted cooperatives to rebuild homes and villages. The army disappeared and murdered some of these farmers. Communities in areas the army suspected of supporting guerrillas that accepted aid from the wrong kinds of people or in a suspiciously left-wing form found themselves in grave danger. As David Carey Jr. recorded in oral interviews, a small number of Canadians and other North Americans traveled to the areas around Chimaltenango ostensibly to do aid work after the earthquake. But they were also hoping to organize cooperatives and, in a few cases, make clandestine contact with guerrilla groups. A few meetings were enough to trigger repression. After attending gatherings where aid materials were handed out, some Kaqchikel men were added to the army's lists of subversives and massacred in a subsequent sweep of the area. Perversely, the army advertised their arrival for these operations in advance, saying they would offer post-earthquake humanitarian outreach. "You have to understand how it was," one Kaqchikel-speaking man from Tecpán told Carey. "We assumed the soldiers were going to help us, but they killed us."[14]

The National Emergency Committee, formed by the military government, coordinated the delivery of an enormous volume of international aid, much of it specifically earmarked for orphans and children. A week after the earthquake, Guatemala received 254,961 pounds of food, clothing, and medicine from the United States, Mexico, Venezuela, Costa Rica, and Canada. The United Nations donated US$3.5 million in cash and goods for reconstruction. An international organization based in Austria called SOS Children's Villages, originally formed to care for WWII orphans in "families" of eight to ten rather than in institutions, had arrived in Guatemala the previous June. Former Ministry of Social Welfare head Elisa Molina de Stahl served as president of the local branch, and after the earthquake, she rushed to open a new outpost in Chimaltenango.[15]

An outpouring of unexpected international interest in adopting local children turned out not to be entirely welcome in Guatemala. The government's response, and the unpleasant rumors that began to circulate, foretold later ambivalence about international adoption both as a solution to Guatemalan social problems and as an affront to nationalist pride. In his presidential address broadcast on radio and television following the earthquake, President Laugerud warned Guatemalans against becoming overly dependent on the help of foreign countries, calling for "more action and fewer tears."[16]

Guatemalans needed no encouragement to be suspicious about aid to Guatemalan children. "It's not true that Mater Orphanorum is giving away their girls," Cardinal Mario Casariego y Acevedo felt compelled to announce to the media just ten days after the earthquake, referring to the large Catholic orphanage in the capital. His words were reproduced as a headline in *Prensa Libre,* one of Guatemala's two biggest newspapers. Because of earthquake damage to the three-story brick orphanage, Mother Superior had set up a camp for her charges in outdoor tents. Some of the youngest girls were at risk of becoming sick in the cold, so she temporarily sent thirty of the eighty-five girls to a sister orphanage in El Salvador. This was enough to trigger gossip, though the girls only stayed in El Salvador for four days before provisional housing became available in Guatemala. The cardinal addressed panicky rumors that he said had been amplified by newspaper coverage, though only a record of his denials remains in the record. He restated that "it's not true" that the orphan girls of this Catholic orphanage "are being given away in El Salvador." His irritation was obvious. "I can't understand who spread this rumor," he added. When the girls returned, the nuns again stressed to journalists that "the publications that claimed that we were selling the girls held at the center are completely false."[17] It is easy to imagine the unsavory undertones of rumors about orphan girls given away or for sale.

Rumors also circulated that state orphanages like the Elisa Martínez Orphanage were giving away children, and that it would be an easy time to adopt. The 1977 annual report from the ministry showed the destruction of one of the two main state orphanages in the capital. It included pictures of the Rafael Ayau Orphanage, crumbled into a mess of rubble and twisted wire.[18] A provisional home was set up to receive 650 children at Hospital Roosevelt.[19] In the absence of emergencies or natural disasters, the Ministry of Social Welfare oversaw adoptions in Guatemala, but after the earthquake, adoptions briefly came under the purview of the social service branch of the military logistics command. The head of this organization requested that members of the public inform government social workers of any orphaned children so they could be "collected." The headline in *La Hora* read: "It is not true that they are giving away orphans."[20] The story clarified that the military logistics command "denied the news circulating that they were handing over orphans to those who asked for them," explaining that the usual bureaucracy and paperwork surrounding adoptions was still in place.

The ministry announced that it did plan to place earthquake orphans in foster homes but had to dispel rumors in this arena as well, announcing "the children they are sending to substitute homes are not those who had problems in previous placements, but rather those who were orphaned by this tragedy. That is to say that foster parents are not returning children, as has been speculated." The government requested that children orphaned by the earthquake be given to the ministry for care, but many families had other plans. People sent children to stay with relatives in unaffected rural areas rather than camp together in improvised tents and shacks in city parks, for fear of ongoing aftershocks. Extended families both in the city and in rural areas also took in many orphaned children on an informal basis.[21]

The military organization briefly in charge of adoptions felt compelled to respond to the international clamor for children, saying that the government would take things slowly before placing anyone abroad. As of two and a half weeks after the earthquake, not a single child had been given in adoption. Adoptive parents had to "fulfill various requirements, since children won't be handed over to be turned into servants, but rather as children with full legal rights." The same official spokesman hinted at families' resistance to turning over children to government workers, or possibly resistance to the idea of adoption by strangers. He complained that it was difficult to determine the exact number of children orphaned by the earthquake, because families "keep them in spite of the circumstances in which they live, especially in Chimaltenango," a poor, majority Indigenous area. The spokesman complained that there it was difficult to find affected children and convince the families currently caring for them to give them over to a state institution. He made a direct appeal to those sheltering orphaned children: "Send them to the capital."[22] Despite the government's call, local committees and religious groups set up private shelters in the highlands. The emergency committee of Quetzaltenango worked with the Catholic charity CARITAS and a local evangelical Christian group to shelter and care for earthquake orphans. The committee received many inquiries from families in that city "requesting children to adopt."[23] These groups didn't have the legal authority to give children up for adoption, but it is possible that they did so informally in some cases.[24]

News of the earthquake, and possibly rumors that children were available for the taking, circulated abroad. The Guatemalan embassy in Mexico received 293 requests by phone and mail from Mexican families wishing to take in earthquake orphans.[25] The Guatemalan government received requests to adopt "huge numbers of children" from families in Bolivia, Ecuador, Chile, Venezuela, and Peru. The Lion's Club International of Chile alone requested 1,000 children for placement, though the adoption files make it seem this request went unmet. Guatemalans from the low-lying tropical regions and the highlands, two areas less affected by the earthquake, also submitted requests to adopt earthquake orphans. If the government also received a spike in requests from the United States, Canada, or Europe, it was not reported in the newspapers nor did it appear in the Ministry of Social Welfare's annual report from that year.

The earthquake surfaced national and international demand for Guatemalan children, and with it, Guatemalan fears about adoptions. The Guatemalan press tried to address rampant rumors, and in doing so likely amplified them. In a country where the press was known to be controlled by the government and individual reporters were often paid bribes for favorable coverage, headlines of "it's not true that . . ." likely conveyed the opposite impression to some readers.[26] Various sports teams, including the Guatemalan Olympic Committee, announced that they would fund programs for orphans, and felt the need to specify that "the children to be aided will remain in Guatemala, since it would be illogical to send them abroad considering that they will live in a better way in their own land given customs, foods, etc."[27]

Only once the immediate crisis had passed and rumors died down did Guatemalan lawyers, and then Congress, begin to regard international adoption as a potential solution to what was now posed as the country's orphan problem. While it seems many Guatemalans would have preferred that orphans stayed in their home country, the reality was that their government didn't have the resources to care for so many children—or, more to the point, in the context of an escalating war, the government didn't choose to allocate their resources to social welfare. The year before the earthquake, the Elisa Martínez Orphanage housed a rotating group of 1,059 children. The ministry approved only 122 adoptions and 63 foster families that year.[28] In 1977, the ministry still employed only one social worker working full-time on adoptions.[29] Adoption files from those years show delays in the family courts for full approval of judicial adoptions from six months to two years, without counting the probationary period. Prompted by the very real crisis of the earthquake and a show of international enthusiasm for adoptions, a powerful lawyer's guild came up with what they considered to be a solution to what newspapers persisted in calling an orphan crisis: to privatize adoptions.

Humanitarianism, Not Human Rights

The Bar Association (Colegio de Abogados y Notarios), founded in 1810, is one of the country's oldest and most powerful professional organizations. In Guatemala, all lawyers are notaries and all notaries are lawyers—an important and powerful role since colonial times. Like lobbying groups in the United States, the Bar Association often put together draft bills, which were sometimes passed in Congress with the very language the group had proposed. On 10 September 1976, seven months after the earthquake, the Bar Association presented Congress with a draft bill called "Law Regulating the Notarial Procedure for Matters of Voluntary Jurisdiction." Despite its modest-sounding name, the bill was a major grab for influence over legal family affairs, proposing that lawyers—in their capacity as notaries—take over full responsibility for uncontested procedures previously overseen by a judge. When the law based on the draft bill was passed in 1977, the Guatemalan government created a second, faster path for adoptions. Lawyers could sign off on adoptions representing both the adoptee and adoptive families without the oversight of a judge. This type of private adoption process does not exist and has never existed in any other country in the world.[30]

The draft bill presented by the Bar Association covered a variety of procedures, not just adoptions: provisions for the goods of minors; recognition of pregnancy or birth in the case of an absent, separated, or dead father; corrections to inscriptions in the civil registry. The bill proposed that only "uncontested" family affairs be governed by this new procedure. Any disagreement and it would revert from a notarial to the usual judicial process. If a family member of a potential adoptee objected to an adoption underway, the procedure would lose status as a notarial process and a judge would have to review the case.[31] The president of the Guatemalan Bar Association included a letter to the president of Congress to accompany the draft bill, writing that it would "reduce the voluminous work of the courts, it will permit the notary, as a subsidiary of the judicial branch, to more rapidly settle matters that traditionally have required judicial intervention."[32] Congress found that the existing adoption program, run by the Ministry of Social Welfare, was too slow and inadequate to meet the upsurge of humanitarian demand for Guatemalan children. This bill, which ultimately served to privatize and open the way to speedier adoptions, was discussed in Congress in terms of its "humanitarian" potential at a time when the Guatemalan government was trying to fend off criticisms of its violations of "human rights," a term that was becoming increasingly popular around the world in the 1970s.[33]

Congress's debate over the law relied on a locally significant interpretation of the concept of humanitarianism. The terms of political debate had changed radically since 1963, when discussion of what to do with orphans and the founding of the Ministry of Social Welfare shifted solutions from private, often Catholic charities to the public realm. During debates in Congress, some representatives pointed out downsides to this new approach. Any savings obtained by outsourcing decision making and care might be outweighed by the disadvantages of introducing more commercial interest or corruption into the adoption system, they said.

The debate in Guatemala over the new law coincided with the global rise of the idea of human rights. Legal historian Samuel Moyn pinpoints 1977 as the year when human rights rhetoric gained international purchase, following a first effort after World War II when the phrase failed to catch on.[34] In 1977, the U.S. Congress amended the Foreign Assistance Act of 1961 to require the Department of State to submit an annual report to Congress evaluating the human rights practices of any foreign country receiving aid. According to Kathryn Sikkink, President Jimmy Carter "never engaged in the same kind of high-level arm-twisting" he and his cabinet used on Argentine generals during the dirty war in Guatemala. But when the State Department did release its first report on human rights abuses on 12 March 1977, it included a four-page section on Guatemala's forced disappearances and killings. The Guatemalan government joined El Salvador, Argentina, and Brazil in claiming that the report violated national sovereignty and rejected further U.S. military aid.[35] Carter faced opposition at home, too, where the army feared alienating allies against communism. Chairman of the Joint Chiefs of Staff General George S. Brown told the *New York Times* he hoped that human rights could be respected "without losing our friends in the process."[36] Still, the United States cut off military aid to Guatemala altogether the following year, citing human rights violations. Lack of support turned out to pose a less serious problem than intended for the Guatemalan government, since some of the aid was simply rerouted through Israel, but it was still the subject of discussion and consternation.[37]

Strangely enough, the 1977 U.S. human rights report that so offended the Laugerud regime mixed praise with criticism, and the government's humanitarian earthquake response was singled out for approval. The report credited the government for "restraint" in response to guerrilla provocations and for "reducing markedly" high levels of state violence, particularly in the run-up to the 1978 presidential elections. This was largely inaccurate; the regime was brutal but more skilled at hiding its brutality from outsiders than its predecessors. The report noted that Laugerud's was the first administration in recent history to complete three-quarters of its term without imposing a state of siege, suggesting that this was to be applauded.[38] But Congress's new strictures meant that military aid could not be sent because of ongoing human rights abuses. The earthquake cut the Gordian knot: the United States could send supposedly apolitical humanitarian aid to the military dictatorship instead, as could other countries in Europe that also on paper deplored Guatemala's human rights record. The 1977 report noted: "The Government's handling of problems created by the 1976 earthquake has been a major success. With the assistance of the US and other donor countries, the Guatemalan Government has worked effectively to restore shelter and basic social services to the hardest-hit highland areas."[39] Meanwhile, the government siphoned off humanitarian aid for military spending. Deborah Levenson-Estrada has shown that the military took ambassadors from Western European countries on helicopter tours of areas affected by the earthquake in order to request humanitarian aid, then used the aid, which was intended to build new homes for the displaced, for military infrastructure projects.[40]

Guatemalan politicians cannily promoted their own humanitarian efforts following the earthquake. While the international media was covering the earthquake, they didn't cover the "classquake"—that is to say the structural reasons for the disproportionate numbers of poor and Indigenous people killed and maimed by the natural disaster. Decades later, the first line of Laugerud's *New York Times* obituary was not about the brutal killings and repression during his presidency, but rather: "Kjell Eugenio Laugerud García, a former president of Guatemala who is credited with helping to rebuild his country after a devastating earthquake in 1976, died Wednesday at his home."[41]

Guatemalan politicians may have been furious about the inconveniences posed by the new international fixation on human rights, but they were happy to promote humanitarianism, which they laid out in explicitly apolitical terms. As members of Congress discussed the adoption bill, they repeatedly spoke about orphans as a humanitarian matter, even as children and the idea of "family" were both becoming increasingly politicized. Right-leaning politicians throughout Latin America threatened that Marxists were "anti-family" and would take children from their parents or force parents to raise children in collectives. From 1960 to 1962, in what became known as "Operation Peter Pan," Cuban families had secretly sent 14,000 unaccompanied minors as young as six to the United States, alarmed by unfounded rumors that Fidel Castro was planning to terminate parental rights, confiscate children, and place them in communist re-education camps. Many Guatemalans feared that a Cuban-style guerrilla communist takeover was imminent in their own country—with a breakup of families to follow. On the suggestion of First Lady Helen Losi de Laugerud García, Congress declared 1977 the "Year of Guatemalan Childhood." The stated goal was to "Raise consciousness among parents, authorities and the population at large about the importance of caring for children, and that this should be a priority to avoid future societal problems."[42] The solution to the "orphan crisis," then, was to speed up adoptions as much as possible, in line with a limited and avowedly apolitical vision of humanitarianism: removing barriers and delays for those who wished to adopt from abroad.

Something That Could Be Damaging to This Society

The Guatemalan Congress formally put the new bill up for discussion on 1 March 1977. It had received immediate support from the president of Congress and was first distributed and read during sessions on 10 September and 21 September 1976.[43] As was common, the bill was tabled for several months before final discussion. Stretching over many sessions, attempts to debate the bill ranged from contentious to measured to farcical. Out of a total of fifty-four delegates, thirty-one were necessary to form a quorum. The debate records are full of accounts of the quorum falling apart and remaining members of Congress sending each other out to prowl the halls to pull anyone left in the building back into the discussion.[44] Ahead of a holiday, representatives left early and could not be convinced to return.[45] After long delays, a final heated discussion raised both humanitarian concerns related to the earthquake and perceived orphan crisis, but also worries about the possibility of creating a market for children in Guatemala. The bill explicitly mentioned the expanded powers of lawyers to oversee adoptions. Both the wider powers and increased earnings lawyers would enjoy under the new law were apparent to all. Many powerful members of Congress were themselves lawyers who were allowed to continue to practice during their time as public servants. Those members of Congress who were not lawyers did raise the issue of a conflict of interest during the debate. Nevertheless, lawyers serving in Congress managed to successfully argue that the bill was "humanitarian," and push it through despite the chaos of numerous recesses and power outages. In the end, the language of the draft bill was reproduced almost exactly in the final version of the law.

The debate over whether to privatize adoption occurred during a period of extreme political polarization in Guatemala, of splits within the left and election fraud on the right. On the left were bitter arguments between reformists who believed that change could come through democratic channels and those who believed that violence was necessary and ended up joining the revolutionary guerrilla movement. Many on both sides believed that General Efraín Ríos Montt, candidate of the Christian Democratic Party, had been the real winner of the 1974 presidential election. The military government's chosen successor, General Kjell Eugenio Laugerud García, had stolen the election in such a brazen fashion that it was obvious to everyone at the time, "complete with darkened television screens, patriotic music on the radio, and reprinted newspapers."[46] Arguably the country's most important political party was the Movement of National Liberation (Movimiento de Liberación Nacional, or MLN), formed by Carlos Castillo Armas, the U.S. puppet installed as dictator after the 1954 coup. By the 1970s, the MLN was closely associated with violent repression of the left and had even called itself the "party of organized violence." The MLN joined Laugerud's party in a governing coalition, and there were only four political parties represented in Congress at the time.

When the bill that would privatize adoption came up for substantive discussion, Representative Armando Bravo López, from a small party in coalition with the MLN, introduced it as a matter of apolitical bureaucratic expediency:

> Mr. President, my fellow Representatives, the bill of voluntary jurisdiction presented by the honorable Guatemalan Bar Association isn't supposed—as has sometimes been misinterpreted—to only and exclusively benefit lawyers; the truth is that every litigious issue, as the very word suggests, will be exclusively presented before the courts, still, they currently see a number of situations where there is no litigation and there is no controversy and the task is doubly harmful: first, it lays an unnecessary amount of work on the courts, which accumulate excessive work; and second it damages those who brought the case when they wish a resolution, when they wish the administration of justice to be rapid and prompt.[47]

López continued by saying, "I won't say that the law is perfect," and noted that he would introduce some amendments himself, though his objections had to do with provisions for divorce and separation, not adoptions. Requiring judges in family courts to consider each adoption case, he said, was "to steal time from the courts, to fill them up with work."

The debate pitted lawyers against nonlawyers in Congress rather than breaking down along party lines. The nonlawyers were aware of the money-making possibilities presented by the lawyers' proposals and protested that the lawyers were trying to strong-arm them into passing the law. One congressman said that "it is urgent to take into account that the vast majority of the Representatives in the Congress, who are not lawyers and notaries, have our serious doubts about the issue." Vincente Eduardo Cano Ponce, representing the MLN, acknowledged fears about "some ingrate notaries" but suggested that these issues would be resolved by the lawyers' own Bar Association, who might mete out punishments for any who erred—a wildly optimistic if not cynical prediction.[48] On the matter of adoption, Cano Ponce warned, "we don't want to back something that could be damaging to this society." He proposed requesting a professional evaluation from the University of San Carlos and other universities before ruling, but no other representatives backed this suggestion.[49]

The provisions for adoptions were among the least controversial of any in the bill—indeed, they were used to justify the rest of expanded powers for lawyers. The president of Congress, Luis Alfonso López, a far-right politician who supported Laugerud, said:

> There are doubts about whether this law is socially beneficial. I'm going to demonstrate that it is, and why I support its immediate passage. When an orphan, a nameless child, is abandoned to penury without even a last name, and a humanitarian person who is able to do so wishes to adopt, they must begin a very lengthy adoption trial. The child is completely legally helpless. There are humanitarian parents who wish to adopt the child, but with this whole cumbersome legal process many people don't do it. So to benefit these abandoned children who are in need, the law establishes the notarial system of adoption.[50]

There was no discussion of or debate over the core part of the new law, Article 33, which privatized adoption: "Adoption as regulated in the Civil Code may be formalized by a notary public, without prior judicial approval of the proceedings being required."[51] Two representatives proposed adding another requirement for a notarial adoption: "notice of a favorable opinion taken under oath by a social worker employed by a Family Court in their jurisdiction."[52] Representative Cano Ponce, the MLN representative who was one of the few to raise doubts, said that he didn't necessarily agree with or fully understand the role of social workers in the proposed amendment. He mentioned a recent law school thesis written at the University of San Carlos to suggest that social workers' reports "left doubts in respect to the investigation, which often was superficial." Another representative added that if social workers were to be involved, "wouldn't it be advisable to include the Ministry of Social Welfare of the Presidency of the Republic, which does this type of work, namely, that which has to do with matters of adoptions?"[53] Even at this late stage of discussion of the law, if Congress had decided to involve the Ministry of Social Welfare in the process, the new private and old state-run adoptions might have been folded into one process. But no one responded to this suggestion because the quorum had fallen apart once again. By the time members of Congress searched the halls for their colleagues, reconstituted the quorum, and re-entered the debate, the issue had been forgotten or dropped from discussion. A vote on adding a social worker's report from a family court to the new private process passed unanimously, a step that did not involve the Ministry of Social Welfare at all.

Only the president of Congress raised the possibility that expedited private adoptions might encourage a commercial market for children, especially if foreign families were involved. López complained that his fellow members of Congress were not taking adoption seriously enough. He said, "We would spend a long time if we were to point out all the possible dangers, and thus the formalities that should be required." He added, "I beg you to think hard about the fact that we should protect the adoptee, as well as those who adopt."[54] Having worked in the attorney general's office before joining Congress, he recalled:

> We stopped about ten adoptions which had been completed without the legal requirements. These Guatemalan children were going to Sweden to be adopted in Sweden on a trial basis, which is to say that the little Guatemalan, our countryman, would leave the country. There he would be tested, and if he adapted to the environment, there would be an adoption and if not, not . . . There was money in the middle, señores Diputados, there was a little business in which they were charging to find kids to send them to other countries.[55]

This speech touched on two items that later made adoption such a hot political issue: a perceived affront to Guatemalan nationalism and payment for "finding" children and making a business out of what should be child welfare. It was also an early acknowledgment of corruption in the adoption process, even in the state system run through the Ministry of Social Welfare. The process López described with outrage—allowing a Guatemalan child out of the country for a probationary period—was common practice at the time. These ten cases do not distinguish themselves in any obvious way among other adoption files, though it is easy to imagine only certain forms of illegality were recorded. However, when I got in touch with a social worker who worked at the Ministry of Social Welfare in the adoption program during this period, she refused to give an interview, saying she had never taken money but was afraid of being associated with corruption at the ministry. So it is likely that some money may have changed hands even for adoptions moving through the state orphanage with greater oversight. Still, in the end López was willing to be swayed by humanitarian arguments in favor of fast adoptions. And he dismissed his fellow congressmen's concerns about arbitrary judges and potentially corrupt lawyers, saying, "if all the laws that this Congress passed were to have as a foundation the deficiency of human conduct, I think we wouldn't be able to pass a single law, because in any case there will be those who disfigure them."[56]

Doubts about meaningful consent by poor and Indigenous women only came up in debates over the possibility of expedited notarial divorce, not privatized adoption. Divorce had not been included in the Guatemalan Bar Association's draft bill as among notaries' new duties, but it was proposed for addition as a new provision on 23 February 1977. As with adoptions, the idea of assigning divorces to lawyers was intended to speed up the process. But while representatives acknowledged the snail's pace of family courts, they did not wish to accelerate divorces, protesting that to do so would be a disastrous sign of "social laxity."[57] Congressmen objected to speedier divorces on the grounds of paternalistic protection of the honor of Indigenous women. One congressman, Julio Hamilton Noriega Natareno—a member of the Christian Democrat party from the majority-Indigenous Quiché department—objected to the divorce law, saying that it might allow Maya men to hire unprofessional lawyers to take advantage of their wives: "Especially in rural areas, often women don't have the sufficient capacity, and may not even be able to speak Spanish, and they could be deceived; it's true that we have to rely on professional ethics, but unfortunately there may be one single case in which professional ethics may fail, and the exception confirms the rule. In this case, with even a single Guatemalan who could fall victim, this is already problematic." Natareno asserted that "peasant women [campesinas]" would suffer most from quick divorces, which would contribute to "family disintegration." He continued: "We are worried exactly when we turn our attention to a peasant woman who neither knows how to write nor read and who often needs a translator to manage many events in her life. We know of the torment faced by women, particularly those women who can be bamboozled and who don't have sufficient education to defend her rights and those of her children."[58] Congress voted down the divorce provision, which did not appear in the final version of the law. No one in the debate extended this preoccupation with *engaño*, or deception, to adoptions—though later cases show that Indigenous women were indeed pressured into giving up their children, their consent assumed without translators, and in some cases, women without command of Spanish were tricked into giving up children.

Congressmen tended to see the issue of adoption in reverse: speedy adoptions, they argued, would *better* protect vulnerable children. This despite the fact that the president of Congress during the debates acknowledged a history of child trafficking in Guatemala. One congressman tried again to introduce the Ministry of Social Welfare into the discussion, pointing to the role it had previously played in placing earthquake orphans. He said:

> Nowadays an adoption isn't accomplished just by filling in the paperwork, but undoubtedly by now there are institutions that do socioeconomic and psychological studies of the whole process . . . This leads me to ask the question again, Mr. President, why not present an amendment proposing that in addition to the attorney general's office, it would also be suitable to hear from institutions like the Ministry of Social Welfare of the Presidency of the Republic, which right now has a very similar function? They have adoption programs, which were increasing exactly in the post-earthquake period.[59]

According to the record, this was followed by a "pause." Then another representative picked up an entirely different thread of conversation. No one addressed this proposal, presumably since it would lead right back to the slower processes the congressmen were trying to avoid. Finally, they agreed on a compromise, adding the phrase: "If the attorney general's office objects, the case will be sent to the respective court."[60] This meant that if the attorney general's office rejected an adoption because it was flagged for fraud or other irregularities, a private adoption could become a state adoption, overseen by the Ministry of Social Welfare. The representative who presented the solution emphasized that this would allow for speedy enough adoptions to still be "in accord with the humanitarian rationale of the law."[61] And in that way, with the addition of a small caveat that was rarely, if ever, used, Congress approved private adoptions.[62]

The 1976 earthquake unexpectedly opened the door for the Bar Association, aided by lawyers pressing their advantage in Congress, to privatize adoptions in Guatemala. The response to a "class quake" that laid bare social inequalities and prompted coverage of an orphan crisis triggered not an expansion of social welfare but rather a turn to privatized international humanitarianism to fill the void left by a lack of state services. The bill was made law in November 1977. Afterward, some lawyers maintained connections with the evangelical Christians who had flooded into Guatemala after the 1976 earthquake, and together they helped get the nascent private adoption business off the ground. In 1979, the *Washington Post* published a story with the headline "U.S. Demand for Adoption Spurs Baby Trade in Guatemala." It noted: "The number of available U.S. children—especially the newborn, white and healthy ones who are often most sought—has diminished to the point where even the most desirable potential adoptive parents may have to wait years for a baby. For those with the right information, or right connections, a child can be legally adopted in Guatemala and taken to the United States in two months to a year." The *Washington Post* noted that many of the informal nurseries set up to care for children whose paperwork was underway for private adoptions were allowed to run "because there is no law that says they cannot." "Nearly all" had opened since the earthquake "triggered publicity about homeless children" three years earlier.[63] Guatemalan lawyers hired women to run these nurseries, which adoptive parents paid for as part of a package deal. The lawyers had found a novel, lucrative type of client: foreign adoptive parents. And adoptions began a new phase as a legal, for-profit business.

4

Adoption Rings
and Baby Brokers

On the morning of 9 June 1983, a group of kidnappers prepared a piñata party in a safe house in Guatemala City. They had held a three-year-old for several months in Zone 11, a working-class area of the city, while arranging papers to fake his mother's relinquishment and allow his adoption by a foreign family. The mother, a woman named Blanca Luz López, had most certainly not given her permission for adoption. In fact, like many other women who had to work, she dropped off her young son with a caretaker in Guatemala City whom she paid by the month. It was her tragic bad luck that the caretaker worked with an adoption ring, and turned over the boy to its leader, Grace Larrad de Quan, who owned the house in Zone 11.

When Blanca Luz went to visit her son, she was aghast to find that he was no longer there. She managed to learn the address of the safe house and went there several times to confront Larrad de Quan, demanding him back. Larrad de Quan at first seemed to relent, saying she would return the boy to his mother. But, she said, she had become fond of him, and wanted to celebrate the handoff. She invited his family to a party with lunch, gifts, and a piñata at one o'clock in the afternoon of June 9.

Blanca Luz arrived at the house with four other people, including the young son of a relative, one hour after the appointed time. According to a police report, "On arrival they were received in a seemingly cordial and attentive manner." Larrad de Quan sat her guests down around a table and offered them a bottle of liquor. Then her accomplices, who had been hiding upstairs, set upon the family with knives. They killed all four adult guests and spared the child, whom they "immediately hid in a room on the property thinking that they could do illegal business with him at the next opportunity."[1] Larrad de Quan and her accomplices wrapped the bodies of their victims in bedsheets and waited for night to fall before loading the corpses into the trunk and backseat of a blue Mitsubishi and dumping them in several locations around Guatemala City. Blanca Luz's son was not in the safe house at all that day. He was already living with a new adoptive family. The adoption had been arranged by a private lawyer, who gave a cut of his fee to Larrad de Quan. She was working a job that was new to Guatemala: *jaladora,* or baby broker.

Larrad de Quan had turned to violence, which was unusual for the job. Most women who worked as baby brokers—the job was dominated by women— used coercion or persuasion instead of outright violence. Hired by lawyers or other middlemen, or, more commonly, middlewomen, their job was to locate children who would be attractive on the private adoption market in Guatemala and convince mothers to relinquish them. What became known as the Piñata Case was the only adoption fraud scheme I found that involved murder. Other cases involved kidnapping, or—much more frequently— falsified relinquishment papers.

After the privatization of adoptions in 1977, lawyers in Guatemala learned that they could charge between US$7,000 and $15,000 per adoption arranged. Fees varied widely but rose further, sometimes more than doubling during the following decades. These sums were understood as lawyer's fees and expenses by adoptive families, but represented enormous profits in Guatemala, where expenses were low and lawyers could organize many adoptions each year. For private adoptions, lawyers didn't work with state orphanages and had no existing pool of children to draw on. Instead, a small group of powerful, well-connected lawyers organized new ways to locate adoptable children.[2] Adoption rings formed during the years after privatization involving one or several *jaladoras.* Their job was to "pull" *(jalar)* children away from their birth mothers and make them available to lawyers for adoption.

When adoption rings turned to crime and were caught, lawyers were rarely prosecuted or punished for their participation. Instead, women who worked for lawyers as nurses, babysitters, or baby brokers were more likely to appear in news accounts of adoption-related crimes, and they were more likely to be investigated and sometimes prosecuted.[3] Mothers who either accepted money in exchange for relinquishing their children or were suspected of doing so were the subject of occasional criminal investigations and panicky press accounts.

As soon as private adoptions were legalized in 1977, they began to outstrip adoptions organized by the Ministry of Social Welfare through the Elisa Martínez Orphanage. In the three decades during which private adoptions were legal, from 1977 to 2007, about 40,000 Guatemalan children were placed with families in the United States, Canada, and Europe—the vast majority through the private adoption system.[4] Most of these adoptions were processed legally, though laws were very permissive in Guatemala at the time. Private adoptions proved more appealing than adoptions from state orphanages because they were faster. Private adoptions were often completed in six months, from initial expression of interest by foreign families to the arrival of a Guatemalan child abroad. Private adoptions also gave would-be adoptive parents more control over the age, sex, and race of the children they adopted. Lawyers tended to hire *jaladoras* or to find other means of locating adoptable children, rather than dealing with state orphanages. This was perfectly legal.

As far as it is possible to ascertain—the process did not leave easily accessible public records—it seems the majority of children given in private adoption were the sons and daughters of desperately poor Guatemalans, many of whom worked as maids or sex workers around the capital city. Court cases at the time, and the frustrated searches of many adoptees, who are now adults, have shown over and over that the private system often involved falsified paperwork: fake names, fake addresses, and relinquishment papers signed by someone other than the birth mother. The Piñata Case, together with other police reports, court cases, and press accounts from the early 1980s, shows that criminal and semi-criminal rings cropped up to serve the international adoption market almost immediately after privatization.

Finding an Adoptable Child

After enactment of the 1977 law, lawyers developed a process for private adoptions that anthropologist Silvia Posocco described as a "peculiar form of state-sanctioned legal exceptionalism."[5] This system was unique to Guatemala. Every other "sender" country processed adoptions through a state organization of some kind.[6] Adoption agencies in the United States, Canada, and Europe contacted lawyers in Guatemala, while elsewhere they worked with state or religious orphanages.[7] Adoptive families agreed to pay a flat fee for the entire adoption and were required to submit a stack of paperwork: authorized social worker reports describing their fitness as potential parents and noting yearly income, two sworn statements by friends or colleagues attesting to their "moral and economic solvency," medical reports, and criminal background checks. Some adoptive families came to Guatemala to pick up children. Others designated legal representatives, often colleagues of the primary adoption lawyer, to sign papers for them, and arranged for adults to accompany the children on flights to the United States, Canada, or Europe—sometimes in groups of several children adopted by different families. Lawyers in Guatemala City specializing in this service worked with various foreign adoption agencies for years, even decades.

In this new private adoption system, it was lawyers who enjoyed near total discretion. They were in charge of finding the right child, hiring a babysitter to take care of him or her while the adoption paperwork was drawn up, requesting the necessary studies of the adoptive families and birth families by a social worker, and arranging international transportation for children to their new homes. Because of the last-minute additions to the law before privatization, lawyers were legally required to run the paperwork by the Ministerio Público, the attorney general's office. Social workers employed by family courts were required to provide a supporting report. Both critics and promoters of private adoptions as quick and easy described this step as a rubber stamp.

Social workers employed by family courts were notoriously overworked. Their reports ranged from detailed narratives of visits to birth mothers in their homes to a few lines of boilerplate saying the mother agreed to relinquish her child, without any indication the social worker had met with her at all. From paperwork I was able to consult, these reports seemed much less complete than social reports produced for the Elisa Martínez Orphanage. Birth fathers were rarely mentioned here, or anywhere in private adoption paperwork, except to note when they had abandoned the birth mother before the child was born. This circumstance was common, and social workers attached to family courts considered abandonment by the father persuasive justification for putting up the child for adoption. Single motherhood was common, but still frowned upon.[8] Gender roles were changing in Guatemala during the conflict, not least as a result of political violence as women took on community leadership roles when men were killed or went missing, or themselves participated in guerrilla warfare. Misogyny still remained widespread, and was reflected in reports written about women considered less-than-ideal mothers, sometimes merely because they had been abandoned by a man.

Any lawyer in Guatemala could oversee a private adoption. By the time the 1977 law was passed, all lawyers were authorized to perform this role by virtue of their status as notaries. (This is the Latin notarial system; in the Anglo-Saxon system, notaries need not be legal professionals, nor are all lawyers necessarily notaries.) A 1980 Guatemalan law school thesis on private adoptions noted the lack of regulations:

> Without a doubt, the primary risk is posed by the moral grade of the lawyer, which if it is not of the highest caliber will manifest in a lack of impartiality, abuse of the public's faith, and other aberrations that only solid moral principles and a serious scientific and technical training can avoid. Another danger derived from the former would be a lack of diligence on the part of the lawyer in following procedure, since the notarial process can be and should be faster than the judicial process.

The same thesis noted, just three years after the passage of the 1977 law, that private adoptions "have in some circles caused uneasiness . . . because in some cases—few, but significant—the lawyer has made adoptions lucrative, receiving 'honoraria' for 'acquiring' a child to be adopted."[9]

Once adoptive parents paid a flat fee, it was at the lawyer's discretion to divide the money between all the different players in emerging adoption networks. The law was quite permissive in Guatemala, but it did not allow paying birth mothers outright for their children, which was illegal under both national and international law. Payments to birth mothers tipped some adoption rings over from legal to illegal behavior. Most private adoptions in Guatemala were carried out in a gray area between the two.

Adoption networks—legal, illegal, and gray—brought together networks of people from disparate social classes: the lawyer who arranged the adoption paperwork; the lawyer with legal power of attorney who represented the foreign adoptive parents, usually a close associate of the adoption lawyer; women hired as nannies or caretakers for children who remained in the custody of the lawyer while the adoption paperwork was finalized; and, finally, the most crucial job: *jaladora*.[10] Finding the adoptable child was the most complicated aspect of private adoptions, and this new job was perceived as criminal by Guatemalans growing increasingly concerned about international adoptions. Baby brokers were then and are now vilified in Guatemala both because of their activities and because they were more visible than the mostly male politicians and lawyers in the higher rungs of the same business.[11]

Baby Brokers

Lawyers hired *jaladoras* to locate children who might be available for adoption and pull them into the orbit of adoption rings. They were also sometimes called *enganchadoras,* those who pull, rope in, or hook. The word derives from the same verb as *enganchadores,* male intermediaries who found and transported laborers to Guatemala's sprawling sugar and palm oil plantations and who often informally described their work as *jalando gente,* or "pulling people." (*Enganchados* is the more familiar term outside Guatemala, because this is what the more than 4.6 million Mexicans who worked as short-term agricultural guestworkers in the United States as part of the Bracero program from 1942 to 1964 called themselves, after the way that they were recruited or "hooked" by U.S. growers in Mexico.) *Jaladoras* who "pulled" children for adoptions were paid a flat, per-child fee that varied widely. Lawyers, as a general rule, did not inquire too closely into their methods—or if they did, they were unwilling to say so in interviews. *Jaladoras* appear relatively rarely in archives, but it was possible to build up a picture of their work from interviews, police records, private adoption files, and news articles—while taking into account the sexism and hysteria that permeates some of these accounts. *Jaladoras* worked by approaching poor, often Indigenous women who were visibly pregnant—at home, at bus stops, in hospitals, or in marketplaces. Baby brokers sometimes also worked as midwives, maids, nurses, obstetricians, civil registrars, or they ran nurseries or daycares. As part of their approach, they asked if the mother-to-be had money to raise a child, or if the child would be better off with a foreign family in a country with more opportunities. Some *jaladoras* carried photo albums and flipped through them with pregnant women, showing them Guatemalan boys and girls in the comfortable homes of middle-class families abroad. Many of the women they approached already had young children they were struggling to feed.

According to Guatemalan and international law, a birth mother must consent to relinquish her child for an adoption to go forward. But in a context of extreme economic pressure and inequality, what constituted meaningful consent was not at all clear—especially if the possibility of adoption was originally presented to the birth mother by someone else, often of a higher social class. Clouding the picture still further is the question of what was actually discussed with birth mothers before they signed papers. Despite the reassuring clarity presented by official documents after the fact, it is impossible to know: did some mothers have a temporary or reversible arrangement in mind? As in other parts of the Global South, new forms of permanent international adoption, certified with paperwork, were at odds with older forms of informal adoption.

Informal child circulation in Guatemala was often temporary. Poor mothers placed children with relatives or acquaintances as a stopgap measure when they could not afford to feed them and picked them up again when their material circumstances improved. Some unknowable proportion of mothers may have agreed to relinquish their children for adoption believing that they would get them back. Anthropologist Jessaca Leinaweaver shows how, in the Peruvian context, child circulation is understood differently by the state adoption office, anti-child-trafficking NGOs, children, their birth families, and international players. Examples of adoption from Andean Peru and Ecuador offer a useful comparison to Guatemala because in all three places birth mothers may speak Indigenous languages, speaking Spanish either as a second language or not at all. Bureaucrats and lawyers arranging adoptions are usually monolingual Spanish speakers, and opportunities for misunderstandings or coercion are rife.[12] In Guatemala, illiterate birth mothers frequently signed adoption paperwork with a thumbprint. Even when mothers provided these "signatures," which counted as legal consent, it is difficult to ascertain from the documents what they understood of this procedure. Did they think they would eventually see their child again or get their child back?

From what can be gleaned from interviews and the spotty archival record, *jaladoras* played a role in the lives of birth mothers that ranged from threatening to helpful. In the best case, *jaladoras* offered a way out for women with unwanted pregnancies at a time when abortion was illegal and unsafe in Guatemala. One often-repeated scenario was that of a woman from the countryside, often Indigenous, who came to work as a domestic servant in the capital. She became pregnant. Sometimes it was a consensual relationship, and sometimes it was sexual violence. The pregnancy threatened her plan to return to her home village with some money after a short-term stint working in the capital, and to return to a partner, get married, or start a family. The story could have been true. It was frequently told in private cases, where there was less investigation by social workers. Or it could have been a convenient cover story for cases that involved coercion or exploitation before a relinquishment. Everyone, including lawyers and *jaladoras,* must have known it was a common, convenient story.

A private adoption file from 1989 held in the archives of Fernando Linares Beltranena, the lawyer turned congressman who allowed me to read his files, included one such case. It described an Indigenous woman from a small town in the department of Quiché who met the father of her child in the capital, but only ever learned his first name. In this instance, there is a relatively complete report by the family court social worker assigned to the case. She wrote: "He tricked her telling her he was single, but when he found out she was pregnant he abandoned her. Before he left, he told her that she should give the baby in adoption when it was born. Through a woman named Herlinda Ajú, she delivered it to a lawyer named Arenales for adoption after the birth in Hospital Roosevelt, and she does not regret it." Herlinda Ajú almost certainly worked as a *jaladora,* though the paperwork did not explicitly identify her this way. Arenales worked in the same law firm as Linares Beltranena, who made the match with the adoptive family. The birth mother worked as a maid in a poor section of the capital, making 100 *quetzales* per month and sending half to her family. (By this time, the *quetzal* had lost parity with the dollar, and this was roughly US$40.) She already had one child, who lived with her mother. Relinquishing her second child for adoption, so long as it remained a secret, allowed her to return home as planned, according to the paperwork. "She did not regret it," such a definite-sounding line, was written by a social worker in a file justifying the adoption. After at most a short interview with the birth mother, it is impossible to know exactly what she thought or felt. This may have been the social worker's overly definitive judgment in order to close the report and get this particular file off her desk. Or it may have been entirely true.[13]

A second common scenario that appears in adoption files was the result of increasing numbers of Guatemalans, generally men, migrating to the United States starting in the 1980s. Some were fleeing violence; some were looking for a regular paycheck during an economic crisis at home. Unemployment in Guatemala rose from 25 percent in the mid-1970s to more than 40 percent by the mid-1980s.[14] If women who became pregnant in Guatemala had husbands or long-term partners (*compañeros*) who were absent, usually working in the United States, giving up the child for adoption meant they did not have to explain the pregnancy. This way, they could continue to receive remittances that sustained whole families. The omission also protected birth mothers from possible abandonment or domestic violence after their partner returned home.

Other cases in the private lawyer's adoption files record birth fathers migrating to the United States and abandoning pregnant women without resources to raise a child.[15] For example, in one case from 1989, the birth mother was nineteen years old, unmarried, and working as a domestic servant when "the birth father left her and left Guatemala—heading probably to the United States." The teenager gave up her child for adoption because she had no support either from the birth father or from her own family, since she was an orphan, and because it was impossible for her to both keep the baby and work to support herself. The social worker wrote, "no one would give her work with him along."[16]

In adoption cases involving migration, extreme economic inequality between Guatemala and the United States and the growing flow of Central Americans migrating north was important to the end result of adoptions, with social workers or lawyers organizing the transfer of children from poorer families in Guatemala to wealthier U.S. families. Extreme economic inequality was also important to the beginning of the process, creating family structures fragmented by migration that were more likely to produce adoptable children in the first place. Outside scholarly work by sociologists and demographers, it is rare to consider adoptions a form of migration. But adoptions became an unrecognized, though much smaller, parallel migration of Guatemalans to the United States alongside undocumented workers and asylum-seekers. Adopted children, of course, had visas and access to citizenship, and migrant adults usually did not. But adopted children had no choice about where they went. In 1984, demographer Richard Weil wrote that international adoptions were "the quiet migration."[17]

While contact with baby brokers sometimes gave pregnant women an element of choice in circumstances that were otherwise extremely constrained, it is difficult to judge either from interviews or adoption files how many birth mothers saw their presence as helpful rather than coercive. Only a few adoption lawyers were willing to talk openly about the role of *jaladoras*. One lawyer told me that her "best" *jaladoras* were Indigenous birth mothers who had relinquished their own children, then returned to their home villages or cities to convince others to do the same.[18] The lawyer posed this as proof that adoptions had been a useful option that these birth mothers had wished to share with other women, an argument that is obviously self-serving. Still, accepting work as a *jaladora* was undoubtedly a way for some women, Indigenous or not, to make money in the absence of other opportunities for paid work.

Since baby brokers were paid a set fee per case, they had a clear economic incentive to be aggressive in convincing birth mothers to relinquish children. All available sources make clear that the single most common reason for relinquishing a child was extreme poverty. One birth mother, who sought me out because she was looking for her child in the United States, told me that she had been approached by a *jaladora* in her home village when she became pregnant as a teenager. She did not really want to give up her child for adoption, she said, but the *jaladora* made an agreement with her mother and accompanied the two of them to the hospital for the birth to ensure that she really would relinquish her child.[19] Many such stories came out later in investigations before the closure of adoption in 2008, but it is of course rare to read them recorded in adoption files or hear anything about this sort of behavior from lawyers.

In the worst cases, *jaladoras* outright tricked or coerced birth mothers into giving up their children. According to a study carried out by several human rights organizations before the closure of private adoptions, one strategy was to pretend to offer educational grants in rural communities to the children of illiterate and Indigenous women. Birth mothers brought their children to the capital to claim the grant by signing blank documents with a thumbprint that could then be turned into consent forms for adoption relinquishments.[20] One woman in a tiny town called Aldea Güisiltepeque in the department of Jalapa told me that she had been the only parent to sign up her child for a program providing free school supplies, because everyone else feared it would end with strangers taking the children out of the country. (In this case, the aid was real.) The woman turned to her young son, who was hanging around us listening, and said to him, in what I hoped was a joking tone, that he had better not go away with me or I would "turn him into soap."[21] A Guatemalan man in his thirties who I met in the capital recalled that he grew up in a rural area where he heard rumors that North American evangelical missionaries traveling nearby were not there to proselytize but to steal children. He said his father dug a hole in the family's yard and covered it with a wooden lid. When they spotted the missionaries, he and his siblings were hustled into the hole and the lid closed over their heads.

There were also cases of women being told by nurses moonlighting as *jaladoras*—usually in rural areas—that their children had died in childbirth. This tactic is used in the (fictional) Guatemalan film *Ixcanul* to steal a baby for adoption.[22] The director, Jayro Bustamante, said in interviews that the film was based on a real story told to him by his mother, who worked as a doctor in Indigenous communities around Lake Atitlán. Mariela Sifontes Rodríguez, adopted as a baby by a Belgian family, found her birth mother in Guatemala in 2018. When they were reunited, her birth mother told her that nurses at the hospital said she was stillborn, and that they had refused to let her see the body, claiming to have already buried it. Sifontes Rodríguez, who also uses her adoptive name, Coline Fanon, wrote a memoir called *Mother, I Am Not Dead*, in which she observes, "A human being, living or dead, has no price. But demand creates supply."[23]

In some cases, *jaladoras* paid birth mothers outright for their children, which was illegal under Guatemalan and international law. An adoptive mother who happened to be a Spanish-speaking journalist quite unusually wanted to keep in touch with her son's birth mother. Even more unusual, she later interviewed the birth mother with the help of a Tz'utujil-language translator. The birth mother told her matter-of-factly that she had been offered 300 *quetzales,* about US$40, along with a promise from the *jaladora* to pay her back for bus fare to go to the capital to sign papers. The birth mother told the journalist, "I'm poor. I don't know how to read and write. People could bring anything to me to sign. I don't know what it means." The journalist Laurie Stern and her husband had paid US$25,000 for the private adoption of her son.

Stern also interviewed the *jaladora* who worked on their case, Rosa. She found Rosa in 2002 at her middle-class home in Chimaltenango, the closest city to where the birth mother lives along Lake Atitlán. "Look, Laurie," Rosa told the adoptive mother, "a lot of people look down on it, they look at me like I did something wrong." Rosa considered being a baby broker the "hardest job in adoption," because it involved traveling all over the country to make sure birth mothers showed up to their appointments. She was paid 3,000 *quetzales* (roughly US$500) per case. "I feel very satisfied with my work," she told Stern.[24]

Some of the best-documented information about baby brokers comes from later efforts by human rights organizations to interview birth mothers and denounce abuses in the system. One study defined *jaladoras* as "the link between the mother and child and the 'adoption workers.'" It added, "The majority of them are women between 20 and 40 years old. When it comes to *jaladoras* or mediators in rural areas, they belong to the same community as the mother." In rural areas, some midwives would broach the subject with mothers for a fee. *Jaladoras* were most prized by lawyers if they were poor, or at least lived in poor communities or had frequent contact with poor women. Working as a *jaladora,* in other words, offered the possibility of making money from something that was otherwise rarely valuable in Guatemala: proximity to poor people. (Lawyers were white-collar workers who rarely visited the dangerous or poor neighborhoods or rural areas where baby brokers operated.) Based on police reports, the study described a range of tricks, payments, and varying forms of coercion:

> The only way to approach pregnant women or women who had recently given birth was when they were alone. The *"jaladoras"* and mediators would do so after investigating the conditions of the woman they planned to approach. As long as there are lawyers or other people interested in the purchase of the child, they will approach her as soon as the opportunity arises. In any case, they take advantage of the mother's state of mind, her needs, or her educational and socioeconomic condition. The main argument is the opportunity for the child to live abroad and in better conditions, and that at the same time the woman will be able to take advantage of the benefit offered by remuneration for the child. It is precisely at this point in the process that the adoption turns illegal . . . Other arguments used to convince birth mothers include: help with medical costs in order to be able to give birth in hospitals or clinics, offering medical care for children so that the mother must sign blank documents or documents that they don't understand [which could later be used to "prove" consent for relinquishment], or asking them to agree to give blood samples which can be used for DNA testing or offering them work as maids.[25]

Blank documents signed by birth mothers could later be repurposed into consent forms faking legal relinquishment. Another ruse was to tell birth mothers that the adoption was temporary or that they would be allowed to see their children on a regular basis. Yet another was to offer to cover medical expenses or take in young children during periods of economic crisis for a mother, and then demand repayment—a practical impossibility—and confiscate the child as collateral. In at least a few cases, *jaladoras* outright kidnapped children.

One of only two lawyers who agreed to speak with me about *jaladoras* was Susana Luarca, the only lawyer who went to prison for adoption-related crimes. Susana Luarca, whose full name is Susana Maria Luarca Saracho de Umaña, was arrested in 2009 for child trafficking and falsifying paperwork for adoptions. In 2006, she helped arrange the adoption of a two-year-old girl who was reportedly kidnapped from her parents' patio in San Miguel Petapa, south of Guatemala City. Before her arrest, Luarca was a prominent defender of privatized adoptions. Three years before she was detained, she was "one of the busiest adoption lawyers in the country," according to the *New York Times*. "We're rescuing these children from death," she told a reporter for the newspaper. "Here we don't live—we survive. Which would a child prefer, to grow up in misery or to go to the United States, where there is everything?" It sounds like a line one of her baby brokers could have used on a birth mother. In 2015, Luarca was sentenced to eighteen years in prison for child trafficking for adoption.[26]

I met Luarca in 2016 at the women's prison in Guatemala City. We spoke first in the courtyard, and later in her private cell—a rare luxury—where she keeps three formerly feral cats, one of whom is named after a reggaeton star. She recalled that she arranged her first adoption in 1984, for friends—a childless American couple. Luarca had been previously married to a Guatemalan Supreme Court justice, and the North American couple, friends of her husband, visited them in Guatemala. The couple didn't have children because the wife was infertile, Luarca said, "and they were dying for a little girl." The couple asked Luarca to help them adopt. "I told them it is super-easy, of course, with pleasure. Without knowing anything about how to do it." Luarca's sister-in-law said she knew a woman who could help get them a baby, and they found a child they considered suitable in an arid town near the border with El Salvador. "Not even cactus grows there," Luarca recalled. "The man was married and when his wife found out, she said she was going to accuse him of adultery." Luarca paused to scoff at the idea of a man getting in trouble for cheating on his wife. "And the man believed her!" The couple agreed to relinquish their child.

I asked how lawyers without family connections found women like the one who helped her find this first child for a private adoption. Luarca answered with a phrase in English, "Word of mouth." She continued, "Do you remember when abortion was illegal? Women traveled from one place to another. From Madrid to London, for example. People know how to find people who can provide." (The United Kingdom legalized abortion in 1967, Spain in 1985. In Guatemala, abortion remains illegal except to save a woman's life.) Another lawyer who organized private adoptions, Dina Castro, wanted to avoid the topic of *jaladoras* in our interview in her modest law office in Guatemala City. But she also said she arranged adoptions as "something among friends, operating by word of mouth." (Castro acknowledged that other lawyers oversaw cases with "irregularities," but, like every other lawyer I met, insisted she had "always behaved in a most correct manner.")[27]

After Luarca's divorce, she told me, she made a living facilitating hundreds of adoptions through the private system. Eventually she opened a nursery for the children whose adoption paperwork she was processing. "The fact that I adopted two children myself is not considered a mitigating circumstance. Neither is the fact that I had the most beautiful nursery where the children were the best cared for," Luarca said. At its peak, her nursery, in the capital's upscale Zone 10—four blocks from the US Embassy—had been staffed by uniformed maids and held up to a hundred babies at once. "Children don't need much space," she said.

Luarca did confirm that she worked with *jaladoras,* whom she paid for their services, though she told me she did not scrutinize their methods. On my second visit to the women's prison, I asked if the baby brokers she worked with had ever paid birth mothers. She replied that she didn't know. Luarca drew me a diagram on a piece of paper to illustrate how the system worked. (She was extremely open, maybe because she was already in prison, or maybe because she seemed to view me as somewhat dim.) The lawyer needed a child—one dot. She contacted someone, maybe a friend or a relative or a *jaladora*—a line connecting to another dot. That woman got a sum of money from the lawyer. Luarca wouldn't say how much. She might find a child herself or contact another middlewoman—another line connected to another dot. And so on until someone knew a possible birth mother, the last dot. Luarca said she didn't know how the money was distributed down this series of links in the chain: "That was not my concern." When I last saw her, Luarca told me she was angry not to have more company inside. Other lawyers, she said, did the same things as she did.

The only other lawyer willing to talk about the work of *jaladoras* in an interview was Fernando Linares Beltranena, the conservative congressman who allowed me to read his entire archive of private adoption files. I first met Linares Beltranena in his fancy office down a bougainvillea-lined drive in the same area of the capital where Susana Luarca formerly ran her nursery. Linares Beltranena's reputation precedes him, and not in a good way. He is sometimes called an *abogangster*, combining the words for lawyer and gangster, for his defense of narcotraffickers. In Congress, he introduced a bill proposing blanket amnesties for crimes against humanity committed during the armed conflict, including forced disappearances, torture, and sexual violence. (The bill, which did not pass, would have revised Guatemala's 1996 amnesty law, which excludes genocide and crimes against humanity.) Linares Beltranena is an outspoken advocate against gun control and was part of the conservative coalition that pressured to oust CICIG, the UN-backed anti-impunity commission. He was a prominent supporter of Donald Trump's presidential campaigns and said that Trump should build the wall not on the U.S.-Mexico border but on the border between Guatemala and El Salvador because "it would be cheaper."[28]

Welcoming me to his law office, Linares Beltranena was at his ease and expansive, settling in to speak in excellent English. He was keen to have me know that he earned a master's degree in economics at the University of California, Los Angeles. (He received his law degree from Rafael Landívar University, in Guatemala City.) The lawyer wore his trademark bowtie, which set off what can only be described as a Hitler moustache. Linares Beltranena began arranging adoptions in the 1980s and eventually oversaw hundreds of cases. He was and remains one of the most insistent defenders of adoptions from Guatemala, even as crimes and abuses came to light. In our interview, he called *jaladoras* "intermediaries," recalling:

> We worked through intermediaries who had contact with mothers who most likely would want to give up their children. The profile of a mother who wanted to give up her children was usually that she was one, poor, and two, socially concerned with getting pregnant as an unwanted pregnancy ... Intermediaries would sometimes approach these women. And where would they find them? Very many times in houses of prostitution, or through connections with hospitals where the mothers would go and have their children. .... In a hospital, you had intermediaries for attorneys who would speak with nurses and tell the nurses, "Look, if you find a mother who is not content with her child and wants to give it up we know how." It's the same as how newspaper reporters would give a commission to those who work in

mortuaries, or would give cops a commission to call them if something happened on the street.

Linares Beltranena said that other lawyers paid *jaladoras* a few hundred *quetzales,* equivalent to about US$150. He said he paid *jaladoras* a "premium fee," between 1,000 and 3,000 *quetzales,* equivalent to between US$170 and $500. He also said that he would sometimes "help the mother," hastening to clarify, "which was not paying her to sell the child." Linares Beltranena said, "You give her a payment of maybe 2,000 *quetzales* [US$330], for example, to ease her way to make a life again."[29]

Police records dating back to the early 1980s confirm that baby brokers at least occasionally paid birth mothers. They also show that birth mothers, many of whom appear to have been Indigenous, were sometimes investigated by the police for "selling" their children. The weekly police report for Guatemala City of 14–20 November 1983 reads:

> HERLINDA REYNA ESCOBAR, ROSA ADELA MORALES OVIEDO and MARIA LUCILA YOOL SUNUC, arrested and referred to the suitable Court. It was learned that the minor GLADYS ARACELY YOOL of five months of age disappeared under unknown circumstances. She was located with the *señora* Adela Morales Oviedo, to whom the mother Lucila Yool Sunuc had given the child in exchange for the sum of Q50.00 [US$20]. Oviedo served as an intermediary for the *señora* Herlanda Reyna Escobar. For the commission of the crime, they falsified and altered documents, obtaining a new birth certificate for the abovementioned minor, on which she appeared as daughter of Rosa Adela Morales Oviedo.[30]

The last names Yool and Sunuc are most common among Maya Kaqchikel families, and the higher-up intermediaries mentioned by the police have names that are likely *ladino.* (The latter is less reliable as a hint about identity, since many Indigenous people have last names like Escobar or Oviedo.) Though the wording is somewhat confusing, it seems that the mother (Yool Sunuc) turned over her daughter to a woman (Oviedo) who was working as a *jaladora* for another woman (Escobar), who may have been either a lawyer or yet another intermediary. The *jaladora* was prepared to pose as the birth mother to "consent" to the child's adoption, a relatively common way to falsify paperwork. This sometimes meant that the baby was stolen. But in this case a woman identified as the mother (Yool) was also arrested, presumably for accepting payment. No further information was available about this case. Another account appears in a police report marked "confidential" in 1984: "Along the side of the soccer field in the village Boca del Monte, BDM school, lives a *señora* who cares for children. They are provided by a lawyer who buys them for Q100 [US$40] each and after some time has passed sells them to foreigners, arranging passports and the rest of the paperwork."[31] This is the clearest reference in the police records to lawyers buying children directly from baby brokers or birth mothers.

Members of adoption rings could be prosecuted for abduction or kidnapping of minors, or for falsified paperwork. But at the time there was still no legally defined crime of child trafficking for adoption.[32] In a police report from 1982 that lists crimes by gender of the perpetrator, kidnapping and prostitution were the only crimes committed more often by women than men.[33] Rarer to find in archives are cases in which lawyers were arrested or even investigated for adoption-related crimes. Adoption crimes, as investigated and prosecuted, tended to be poor women's crimes.

Adoption rings and the work of *jaladoras* created a reliable supply of adoptable children and also served as protection for the upper rungs of those rings in the event of a criminal investigation. The lawyer could claim he or she had been given to understand that the birth mother consented to the adoption and thus the proceeding was legal; the nurse could claim she was just being paid to care for a child and had no idea the birth mother was coerced; the *jaladora* could claim she had not paid for the child, so she had done nothing illegal. Short of outright kidnapping by *jaladoras,* proof of illegal payments to birth mothers, or forged or falsified documents, adoption rings often operated just inside the newly permissive laws. When a crime was committed, the sheer number of people involved in any given adoption could provide protections to lawyers and the more powerful members of adoption rings. Despite the unusual aspects of the Piñata Case, it is worth returning to take a closer look, since the case offers some clues about how impunity worked in the event of adoption-related crimes, how the Guatemalan press covered this new type of criminal activity, and how private adoptions fit into a wider world in which poor people, and Indigenous people especially, often distrusted or feared the police—leaving space for manipulation and coercion by those seeking to profit from the new market for children.

Caso Piñata: A Closer Look

When she was invited to a *piñata* lunch by her son's kidnappers, Blanca Luz, the mother of the boy, made no move to contact the police. In fact, the police had no idea that Larrad de Quan's adoption ring existed at all until after Blanca Luz's body was found. In 1983, two decades into the war, many working-class Guatemalans had good reason to be wary of the police, who were better known for collaborating with the army and death squads than for enforcement of the rule of law.[34] Widespread public distrust of the police and the claim by lawyers that facilitating adoptions was a humanitarian act—aided by the plausible deniability established by subcontracting to baby brokers—combined to create an atmosphere of impunity for the higher-ups in adoption crimes. After arrests, newspapers tended to print only the names of women working in the lower rungs of adoption networks.

The Piñata Case attracted a type of press coverage that later became relatively common, even for more minor adoption crimes. After investigating the quadruple murder, police presented their findings to the press in a lurid report. They had not managed to locate Larrad de Quan, the ringleader, but they arrested twenty-three other people implicated in the crimes. Police also seized twenty-eight children, from newborns to twelve-year-olds, who they said had been on the verge of being adopted by foreign families. The confiscated children were placed in orphanages while authorities tried to contact their birth parents and checked their adoption paperwork. The children were all determined to be held illegally, but none of their parents could be immediately found, so they were sent to the Rafael Ayau Orphanage, the Elisa Martínez Orphanage, and a private orphanage called Casa Guatemala Canada. The children do not appear in the list of children given up for adoption through state orphanages, making it impossible to find out what happened to them. In its case report, the police's public relations department crowed in all capital letters: "CAPTURE OF KILLERS, KIDNAPPERS, AND ILLEGAL TRAFFICKERS OF MINORS, CRIMES WHICH HAVE STIRRED THE GENERAL PUBLIC."[35] Newspapers picked up the story, repeating its moral judgments on the ringleaders: this was not a normal but an "inhuman" crime.

Journalists reported extensively on the Piñata Case during the very same year, 1983, that they maintained a deafening silence on the scorched-earth massacres perpetrated by the army in Indigenous villages in the highlands of Guatemala. Newspapers at this time were rarely independent. Journalists relied on government sources and often accepted bribes, called *la fafa,* and those who attempted to write more freely were targeted for death threats and murder.[36] In the 1980s, because most newspapers did not cover the highlands, many Guatemalans remained ignorant of massacres until after the war unless they had access to foreign press. In a time of censorship and willful ignorance, the Piñata Case was a useful story for both the press and the police. It was sensational but, on its face, unrelated to the armed conflict. The politics of the story were safe to write about: international, not domestic. Police and newspaper reports narrated the Piñata Case as capitulation by a few greedy, unnatural, unfeminine, and even unpatriotic Guatemalans to insatiable *gringo* demand for children. According to the police report, Larrad de Quan's "macabre banquet of blood" was "guided by her blind ambition to enrich herself, even at the cost of the life and sale of her fellow citizens."[37] Newspapers described the crime in even more florid terms. *El Gráfico* compared the "hair-raising scene" to that of "the Manson 'family' in the infamous case of the actress Sharon Tate."[38] Headlines called Larrad de Quan and her accomplices *robachicos,* "child-stealers," invoking a long folklore tradition in Guatemala of tales of baby theft.

According to the police report, Larrad de Quan's adoption ring kidnapped children "with the purpose of selling them abroad, which they have done before, since they have been dedicating themselves to these illicit and inhumane activities for months." The kidnappers, "for the sale of each child earned fat proceeds" of between 3,000 and 5,000 *quetzales* (between US$500 and US$830). It was to protect these earnings, according to the report, that ringleader Larrad de Quan, "with the rest of the group planned in cold blood to murder the mother of the minor to avoid accountability and to remove the dangerous annoyance posed by the mother's pleas. She managed to convince the anguished mother to come to her residence by inviting her to a piñata lunch, in this way setting the unbelievable mortal trap."[39]

The police report is undoubtedly inaccurate in some respects. Twelve-year-olds, for example, were rarely put up for adoption. The full count of children picked up by the police may have included some older children who happened to be in the homes of the women involved in the adoption ring, but who were never intended to be put up for adoption. Women who worked as babysitters were attracted by above-market rates lawyers paid for their services, about 100 *quetzales* (US$17) per month, and often cared for children whose adoption paperwork was underway in their homes alongside their own children. The children of these babysitters may have also been caught up in the raid, though it is impossible to say for sure.

Laying aside the triumphant police report and hysterical news coverage, a longer police report offered more details than the original press release, helping explain why Blanca Luz agreed to show up for a party at the house of a woman she knew to be holding her child effectively hostage. Like many adoptions in Guatemala, the longer story began with a woman who did not have enough money to care for her child without working, and did not have the kind of work where she could bring him along. The police wrote of Blanca Luz that "this *señora* being of scarce economic resources on May 10 1982 handed over said child to the *señora* MARIA BERNABELA MURALLES DE LOPEZ so that she could take care of him in a special way, in her house, where the mother of the aforementioned minor indicated that she would come to see him periodically and pay the woman entrusted with his care."[40] As adoption files show, this was a relatively common arrangement among working mothers. Police records did not say how often Blanca Luz visited her son while he lived with Maria Lopez, the woman entrusted with his care.[41]

In this case, Maria Lopez had been subcontracted by a *jaladora.* She dropped off the boy at the house of Larrad de Quan, the leader of the ring, who paid her 500 *quetzales* (US$83) for the child, according to the police report, "given that her goal was to send him abroad for a greater sum of money."[42] Larrad de Quan in turn earned between 3,000 and 5,000 *quetzales* (US$500 to $830) per child, according to what other members of the adoption ring told the police. Lopez's behavior diverged from how *jaladoras* and those they worked with usually operated. They might leverage the fact that the child was already living with them in order to pressure a birth mother into giving the child up for adoption, but adoption rings generally secured some form of permission—coerced or not—from birth mothers before finalizing the paperwork with an adoption lawyer.

Blanca Luz presumably only realized something was wrong when she attempted to visit her son at Lopez's house on 10 February 1983 and Lopez told her that he was no longer there. According to the police report, Lopez said the boy had been "handed over" or "entrusted" *(entregado)* to Larrad de Quan "for his greater safety." Lopez did give Larrad de Quan's address to Blanca Luz, indicating that perhaps she was not aware of the purpose of the adoption ring. The police report continues, "given the desperation caused by news of the disappearance of her son, she appeared repeatedly at the house of *señora* LARRAD DE QUAN. . . . to inquire about and, as of course as was in her rights, to DEMAND THE IMMEDIATE HANDOVER OF HER SON."[43] This appearance and request "exasperated Larrad de Quan to an extreme," making her "afraid of being reported to the police."[44] Still, by the time she lured Blanca Luz to the house with the lie that she would give back the boy, his adoption was already finalized. He had gone to live with his adoptive family, "sent abroad in exchange for an appreciable amount of money."[45]

The police's description of Larrad de Quan's work as a baby broker is the most complete available contemporary account of how they worked. It includes a description of the two-story home where she kept children:

> Taking advantage of its spaciousness, she had renovated her house as a NURSERY, not for the purpose of providing charitable assistance, but rather with the objective of fooling mothers of low economic resources and nothing bad in mind with regard to the safety of their children, enticing them to leave their children in that place trusting the insincere promises of the accused LARRAD DE QUAN. Once the children were in her power and under her effective physical control she seized the children in an IRREGULAR manner, without the consent of the mothers, despite the fact that, according to the law, they exercised representation and custody of their own children.[46]

This very confusion between humanitarianism and commerce, in the appearance and reality of the nursery, was what the few members of Congress who tried to block private adoptions in 1977 had feared. It's not clear whether other babies and children had been relocated before the piñata party, or if the nursery was for show and babies were always cared for elsewhere by women hired as babysitters.

The crimes were committed by several people: the babysitter who accepted the child with false promises, Larrad de Quan, the murderers, and the lawyer who signed off on adoption papers without the consent of the real birth mother. The police report listed several crimes committed by Larrad de Quan and her associates: "abduction of minors," "inducement to abandon the home," and "wrongful surrender of a minor." Larrad de Quan individually was accused of "falsifying paperwork," kidnapping, and, of course, murder.[47]

While the violence of the case was unusual, the Piñata Case is typical in one important respect: the involvement of unnamed Guatemalan elites who escaped responsibility for their criminal activities. *El Gráfico* wrote, "Lamentably, the police report indicates that among the group of child-stealers and killers there are various university-trained professionals. Little by little their names will be revealed, even if they belong to high social strata."[48] Police wrote in their report, "It is worrisome that among the Band that committed these horrendous crimes appear professionals, including prestigious members of our society, whose names will appear in accordance with the degree to which the investigation implicates them—regardless of the social class to which they belong."[49] Neither the newspaper nor the police followed through on these promises, or threats. Of the twenty-three people arrested, thirteen were women, most of whom worked as nannies and babysitters. No lawyers were arrested. This was an enduring pattern in the prosecution of adoption crimes: police arrested only the lower rungs of the adoption rings, and the names that appeared most frequently in newspapers connected to adoption crimes were women paid to care for children, not ringleaders or adoption lawyers. Newspapers routinely published the sums of money working-class women were offered to care for future adoptees, supposedly as proof of their guilt.[50]

Women intending to give up their children for adoption also could find themselves under investigation. In the Piñata Case, like in other cases, birth mothers were accused of selling their children or abandoning them.[51] As early as the 1930s, police and journalists began describing mothers who harmed their children as *madres desnaturalizadas*, "denatured" or "unnatural" mothers.[52] In the 1980s, women who relinquished children for adoption, especially those accused of accepting payment, were labeled the same way. The police report on the Piñata Case indicated that many of the children in Larrad de Quan's care were the children of prostitutes, but does not offer further information. Two of the women arrested were in their ninth month of pregnancy. According to the police report, "both said they were in that property with the purpose of giving birth and later selling those newborns to the owner of the property, MURALLES DE LOPEZ and to her husband ENRIQUE ORTIZ LOPEZ." The two women were arrested for "irregular conduct."[53] One was temporarily released to give birth in Hospital Roosevelt.

It is doubtful that these women told police that they wished to "sell" their children. At least one had a recognizably Indigenous last name, Coc, adding the possibility of discrimination to some already dubious interpretations by the police. (Were all the other children really born to prostitutes, or women who worked as domestic servants or in other roles?) It is impossible to know from the existing paperwork whether these women really did intend to relinquish their children in exchange for some form of compensation. As the later human rights reports showed, some *jaladoras* offered pregnant women free accommodations, food, or medical care rather than cash in exchange for a promise to give up their baby for adoption.[54]

The two pregnant women arrested in connection with the Caso Piñata were living in what Guatemalans had taken to calling *casas de engorde,* "fattening houses." Sounding like something out of the Brothers Grimm, these houses were so named because nurses and lawyers were supposedly "fattening up" birth mothers and then children to put them up for adoption. But these houses also offered a possible solution for pregnant teenagers, who could leave their homes or villages to live in a *casa de engorde* for a longer period of time, in order to hide the fact that they were pregnant. The term fanned panic about adoptions, but, again, it is impossible to know whether these particular women had been coerced or had reasons of their own to live in a "fattening house" before giving birth.

The lawyer who hired Larrad de Quan as a *jaladora* was never mentioned in any of the records of the case, and Larrad de Quan herself escaped arrest in Guatemala. She only surfaces briefly in the archival record again in New Orleans, Louisiana, this time facing deportation proceedings. In 1983, the Immigration and Naturalization Service and the U.S. Department of Justice received several telexes from the U.S. Embassy in Guatemala and from the Guatemalan office of Interpol. According to the case records, "These telexes relayed an accusation from the Guatemalan government that Mrs. Quan had engaged in baby smuggling and had ordered the murder of four people in Guatemala." The government initially "expressed an interest" in extraditing her but did not complete a formal request.[55] In 1985, Larrad de Quan petitioned to avoid deportation, claiming that she and her husband faced "political persecution" in Guatemala.

A Rare Arrest

On rare occasions, crimes were so egregious that lawyers were prosecuted, even if they were never sentenced. The most infamous case was that of

Edmond Mulet, a well-connected lawyer investigated for falsifying paper-work to speed up adoptions for Canadian families in 1981. This was the unusual case in which the press did print the name of the lawyer involved, creating a scandal that continues to reverberate decades after the events.

Mulet was a young lawyer and rising star of a new political party when the scandal erupted. He had signed five requests for tourist visas for babies to travel to Canada, skipping the already light requirements of the law that their cases be considered by a social worker and approved by the attorney gener-al's office. Using tourist visas was illegal, since the Canadian families of course had no intention of returning with the babies to Guatemala. Mulet was ar-rested for falsifying paperwork in 1981. A police detective squad in plainclothes also raided suite number 338 of the fancy Camino Real hotel in Guatemala City. They arrested four Canadian women about to take five Guatemalan children back to their home country, including a newborn.[56]

At the trial, birth mothers testified to how Mulet and his adoption ring op-erated. One *jaladora* who worked with Mulet was of unusually high social status: Ofelia Rosal de Gamas was the sister-in-law of a prominent general. At the trial, one of the birth mothers, identified as Evelia R., testified that she met Rosal de Gamas when she was pregnant and worked at a beauty salon where she did not earn enough to support her family. Rosal de Gamas ap-proached her at a street market "and we kept chatting on various occasions and she even sometimes brought me bread or tortillas as a gift. Finally she asked me if I would give him [the baby] to a person who could support him and that's how everything started."[57]

Rosal de Gamas approached another birth mother, identified at the trial as Delia D., who earned 45 *quetzales* (US$7.50) per month working as a maid. She testified that she was desperate when she discovered she was pregnant. The father said he wouldn't recognize her child, and she was worried that her employers would throw her out. She was walking in a park in the center of Guatemala City when a stranger asked about her pregnancy and offered to introduce her to Rosal de Gamas. When they met, she said, the *jaladora* brought along albums of photos of adopted children in order to convince her that it would be best to relinquish the child. Some birth mothers said they had read documents before signing them. But Delia D. said that when she went to Mulet's office to sign relinquishment papers, he was not there, and two señoritas, or young ladies, rushed her along. The judge asked whether "be-fore signing the aforementioned papers you read them or if they let you know about its contents?" The birth mother answered "No. I did not read it and they did not read it to me. I did not find out what it was that I signed. The *señorita* told me I had five minutes to sign those papers."[58] Despite Rosal de Gamas's participation in this adoption ring, she was not investigated or arrested in this case, possibly because of her army connections, though she was later arrested for child trafficking in a different case. Mulet was briefly in jail while under investigation, but the case came to an abrupt end when Mulet was released from prison.[59] An internal police report noted that Mulet "obtained his freedom because of political pressures."[60]

Mulet continued to organize private adoptions. Police investigated him yet again in 1984, but he was never sentenced. At a hearing in the 1984 case, two women from a poor neighborhood who worked for Mulet as babysitters explained to a judge that Mulet "bought" the children from "single women who were pregnant and also from prostitutes." He paid the caretakers 50 *quetzales* (less than US$10) a month to care for the babies while adoption paperwork was finalized. To their knowledge, his employees testified, Mulet had done this for at least a year. (They were unaware of the 1981 arrest.) The police report from 1984 read:

> Trafficking of minors from our country to other countries continues. The people who perform these operations are well-organized and have been operating for years. They have contacts abroad, with organizations dedicated to the adoption of minors who leave our national territory . . . Lawyer Edmond Mulet Lessieur *[sic]* candidate for the National Renewal Party (*Partido Nacional Renovador,* PNR) for Congress representing the department of Guatemala City to the National Constituent Assembly, is the lawyer in charge of doing the paperwork for the processing of this traffic. This Legal Professional was already tried for the same thing in 1981, and his case was heard by the Eighth Court of First Instance of the Criminal Branch (*Juzgado 8o de 1era Instancia del Ramo Penal*). The Fourth Chamber of Appeals ordered his release, so that he could participate as a Candidate for Congressman for the same party and department that he currently represents in Congress.
>
> His arrest at the time was said to be politically motivated, but through political pressure he regained his freedom. History repeats itself.[61]

The police investigated Mulet but did not arrest him in 1984, bringing in only the women who worked for him as babysitters. Mulet went on to enjoy a very successful political career, becoming president of Congress and later Guatemalan ambassador to the United States (1993–1996). He was appointed to various high-level roles at the United Nations, including chief of staff for Secretary-General Ban Ki-moon (2015–2016).[62] When journalists Sebastián Escalón and Pilar Crespo published a story in 2015 in the investigative news outlet *Plaza Pública* about his arrests for trafficking children for adoption in the 1980s, it circulated widely in Guatemala. Mulet wrote a reply, duly posted by *Plaza Pública,* stating: "I emphatically reject the accusations contained in the article that I was part of a[n] 'international adoption network.'" He noted that the "bias" of the article "begins with the title, which speaks of 'exporting' children as if they were fruits or vegetables." Mulet wrote that "my professional actions were always within the laws in force at the time and cannot be evaluated in light of current legislation" and that "there were many lawyers and prestigious law firms that, according to the law and procedures in force 34 years ago, performed these types of procedures." In 2019, he told Grace González of *Telemundo* in an interview that adoptions "saved children's lives" and "there are no victims here."[63]

Mulet first ran for president of Guatemala in 2019. Despite the reporting on his past arrests, and despite Guatemalans frequently calling him a *robachicos,* or child stealer, on social media, he got 11 percent of the vote and narrowly missed advancing to a runoff vote. Before running for president again in 2023, Mulet published a campaign memoir in which he describes himself as a fighter against dictatorship and corruption. He does mention the investigations of his adoption crimes, but says that they were part of a campaign of "social death" led against him by his political opponents because of his activism. It is striking that Larrad de Quan, slated for deportation in the United States, used the same defense: that she was the victim of political persecution. While it is true that the Guatemalan police were involved in repression in the 1980s, court documents and even Mulet's own description of the events in his memoir make this an unlikely explanation at best. Mulet writes that he relied on tourist visas for adoptees because the system in Guatemala was too convoluted and corrupt.[64] "Since in Guatemala it was increasingly common for officials to slow down processes to demand bribes," he wrote, "we made it possible for adoption processes to be completed in the destination countries, which had more solid institutional frameworks." While he may be quite right about bribes, Mulet uses legalistic language to describe issuing tourist visas to avoid the laws in one country and shift an entire adoption process over to another country. This not legal anywhere in the world.

Mulet's impunity is in line with those of other cases. Every leader of an adoption ring other than Susana Luarca walked free. What was unusual was that Mulet was investigated at all, and that police themselves at the time acknowledged the impunity enjoyed by lawyers who arranged private adoptions. Though babysitters and birth mothers were occasionally arrested, impunity for the wealthy and politically powerful helps account for the longevity of adoption rings in Guatemala. When a crime was discovered, lawyers simply hired replacements to reconstitute the lower rungs of their adoption networks. The business marched on.

5

Children for Export

Adoption rings swung into full operation during the most violent phase of the Guatemalan war. In 1983, the same year that the Piñata Case made headlines, Guatemala was in the throes of a massive campaign of state terror in response to a continuing leftist insurgency that Efraín Ríos Montt—the dictator in power from 1982 to 1983—saw as an existential threat to society. Under his regime, guerrilla fighters he called "subversives" and child traffickers were tried in the same military court system. On 1 June 1982, Ríos Montt's government created "Special Courts," military courts that sidestepped due process and supplanted the Supreme Court.[1] These courts were best known for attempting, and failing, to provide a veneer of legality to the extrajudicial killings of guerrilla leaders by firing squad.[2] However, the courts had a second function. Judges also heard cases on adoption crimes as part of a new, moralizing phase of the war.

From 1982 to 1983, adoption-related crimes and the women who committed them were singled out, alongside the guerrilla movement, as threats to the nation. Ríos Montt was a Pentecostal Christian who gave Sunday television sermons to the nation and created the military courts to hear cases of crimes against the state, or what scholars later categorized as "any aberration considered morally objectionable."[3] In practice, the courts heard only two kinds of cases: people accused of guerrilla activity, and women involved in adoption-related crimes—including, eventually, some of the women accused in the Piñata Case. While Ríos Montt was publicly moralizing about the depravity of for-profit adoptions, his administration was quietly ushering mostly Indigenous children—orphaned, forcibly disappeared, or displaced by his own policies—

Efraín Ríos Montt speaks shortly after leading a military coup to install himself as dictator in 1982. *Courtesy of Jean-Marie Simon.*

through the adoption programs at state and religious orphanages. The Special Courts tried 598 people during their year of existence, before they were discontinued under international pressure when Ríos Montt's regime was overthrown in 1983.[4] His regime's attention to adoption crimes failed to eradicate them in the face of growing demand for Guatemalan children abroad. Over the following decades, the national press, Guatemalan congress, and foreign embassies in Guatemala all contributed to selective punishment for a few people and widespread immunity for many others for adoption-related crimes. The U.S. Embassy in Guatemala, in particular, pointedly ignored adoption fraud that was becoming ever more obvious.

My Job Is to Clean House

Judges for the Special Courts, secretly selected by Ríos Montt, presided over trials with their faces covered to protect their identity, supposedly to prevent assassination attempts by guerrillas. The courts had no connection with the existing legal system and were run from the Palacio Nacional, the headquarters of the presidency, under the auspices of the Ministry of Defense. Judges were not necessarily trained as lawyers—they could be military officers, for example. The courts consisted of a three-member trial court and a five-member appeals court, and their jurisdiction extended to the entire country.

Later, the UN-backed truth commission report would call the Special Courts an "attempt to legalize political repression."[5] A colonel who helped set up the courts told anthropologist Jennifer Schirmer that they were a "personal invention of Ríos Montt" intended to overcome the "inefficiency of the common courts," a striking parallel to the creation of a private adoption system as an alternative to the allegedly inefficient state adoption system.[6] Judges were required by executive order to give doubly long sentences or severe punishment in all cases. Ríos Montt ordered the death penalty for several crimes, including kidnapping—of which both guerrilla fighters and members of adoption rings were accused—and "terrorism," the generic term for both insurgency and trafficking in explosives. Most of those who came before the Special Courts didn't have defense lawyers. Even lawyers who tried to defend clients weren't sure where the seat of the tribunal was located and communicated with the faceless judges only through writs delivered to the Ministry of Defense.[7] When the Inter-American Commission for Human Rights arrived in Guatemala in 1982, members expressed concern to Ríos Montt about the clearly illegal Special Courts. According to notes taken by the commission's secretariat, "the actual words of General Ríos Montt's response were: 'I am the one who makes the laws.' I guarantee the people a just use of force. Instead of bodies on the streets, we are going to shoot those committing crimes. I am President, although, *de facto:* but I say that I am a butler, because now, my job is to clean the house.'"[8]

At least forty-seven of the 598 people tried before the Special Courts were women, according to a study by Ana María Méndez Dardón and Juan Pablo Muños Elías.[9] Women were tried for two kinds of alleged crimes: involvement with the guerrilla movement and moral crimes against society, including at least fifteen cases of child trafficking for adoption.[10] Ofelia Rosal de Gamas, the general's sister-in-law who worked as a baby broker for Edmond Mulet, among others, was arrested on 17 June 1983, with her arrest record reading, "this person was mentioned as implicated in the case of abduction of minors."[11]

It is sometimes possible to find court records for cases that passed through the normal justice system, but the Special Courts are a different matter.[12] The fact that the Piñata Case, too, was referred to the Special Courts has made it impossible to find out what happened during the prosecution.[13] It is not clear which of the twenty-three people arrested in connection with the crime were tried and which were sentenced, nor is it possible to find out the outcome of the other fourteen cases of trafficking for adoption heard during the short operation of the Special Courts.

Special Courts were just one element of Ríos Montt's plan to remake Guatemala as a guerrilla-free and sin-free nation. He had been converted to evangelical Christianity by missionaries from the Church of the Word— founded in Eureka, California—who traveled to Guatemala after the 1976 earthquake.[14] In his televised Sunday sermons to the nation, Ríos Montt connected the guerrilla movement, which he saw as an expression of national disorder, directly to family dysfunction. "Misery and ignorance are the fruits of this family disequilibrium," he preached.[15] The family was the most important unit of society, he said in the sermons, and exhorted men to be faithful to their wives, women to be obedient, and couples to have no more children than they could afford to raise. Improving the moral fiber of Guatemalan families and restoring mothers, fathers, and children to their proper gender roles was one front of Ríos Montt's war on what he saw as deviance of any kind.[16]

The irony is that Ríos Montt turned out to be too moralistic even for his comrades-in-arms. Assigning adoption-related cases to the Special Courts had the unintended effect of letting perpetrators off the hook due to an unforeseen political twist. On 8 August 1983, Ríos Montt's Minister of Defense, General Óscar Humberto Mejía Víctores—the general who was Ofelia Rosal de Gamas's brother-in-law—staged a successful coup against his boss, claiming that Guatemala had been taken over by "religious fanatics." Mejía Víctores disbanded the Special Courts three weeks later. Aside from the new dictator's personal connections, there was international pressure to get rid of the Special Courts.[17] In the end, of the 598 cases assigned to the Special Courts, only seventy saw full trials. Of those seventy people, fifty were acquitted and twenty found guilty.[18] The rest of the pending cases, including all of the adoption-related cases, were transferred to the normal, nonmilitary court system in a return to due process. The following year, in

1984, the junta issued a general pardon to those prosecuted by the Special Courts.[19] It is likely, though difficult to confirm, that the accused in the Piñata Case were freed and pardoned. Records do show that Ofelia Rosal de Gamas was released.

The transition from the Ríos Montt to the Mejía Víctores administration offered little concrete change for most people. One dictatorship preached about morals, accompanied by massacres; the other engaged in barefaced corruption, accompanied by massacres. Guatemala's military and economic elite had used the war as a pretext to enrich themselves throughout, especially by grabbing Indigenous, communally held lands where oil had been discovered in 1971. Economist Luis Solano noted that various military dictators oversaw handouts of land and cattle farms stolen from Indigenous groups to long lists of people, "including the last names of famous Guatemalan families."[20] The Beltranena and Mejía Víctores families were among those who received land in the 1970s.[21] Elites protected and extended their privileges during the war, often through various forms of corruption like kickbacks on contracts or outright land grabs. These groups saw Ríos Montt as a threat, since he had advertised his 1982 coup as a strike against corruption. The moralistic tone of his antigraft campaign, not to mention his hectoring Sunday television sermons, soured many politicians and generals on the evangelical Christian dictator. (Corruption was still rampant, if better hidden, during his regime.) In an often-repeated, possibly apocryphal story, when Ríos Montt was thrown out of the National Palace, members of his former escort mocked his anticorruption slogan, "I don't steal, I don't lie, I don't abuse privilege," to explain why his own generals had turned against him. They supposedly told him, "The government that doesn't steal doesn't govern."[22]

Mejía Víctores's administration represented a return to openly corrupt business as usual. Adoptions remained an area of illegal and borderline illegal activity, but the new regime showed no interest in investigating entire adoption rings after the closure of the Special Courts. Still, cracking down on individuals, especially women who worked as babysitters for adoption lawyers, was a useful story for the government. Newspapers that were otherwise censored ramped up coverage of adoptions. As Guatemalan concerns about adoption crimes grew, lawyers and politicians who benefited from the adoption industry consolidated impunity by suppressing some press coverage, blocking reforms in Congress, and benefitting from the blind eye turned by foreign embassies to the increasingly egregious abuses in the adoption industry.

Scandal

Ofelia Rosal de Gamas may have been freed from the clutches of the Special Courts in 1983, but she was soon back under investigation for child trafficking. Her name pops up like a persistent ghost in the archives and in interviews. Many of the children whose adoptions she arranged for Belgian, French, and Canadian families were from Malacatán, a town near the Guatemala-Mexico border. A former public prosecutor who worked on adoption cases told me that she was likely active there because the border zone sees a lot of prostitution. Malacatán, the largest town in the area, was and remains a crossing point for migrants into Mexico on the way to the United States. "Many Central American women migrating to the United States ran out of money and stayed," he told me.[23] A courtly Belgian priest I met in the rectory in Malacatán, Father Juan María Boxus, had lived in the town for several decades. He recalled Rosal de Gamas visiting the town frequently in the 1980s and inquiring about children on behalf of the Belgian adoption agency, Hacer Puente. (The agency organized Dolores Preat's adoption among many others.) Father Boxus said Rosal de Gamas was "persistent," though it was not clear at the outset that she was involved in crimes. An adoptive mother recalled her as "tall, a little cold."[24]

Rosal de Gamas's first arrest in 1983 did not appear in the newspapers, so the police booking is the only available information.[25] The second time she was arrested, four years later, there was coverage in the press, helping fan a growing panic about for-profit adoptions in Guatemala. By the time of her second arrest, Rosal de Gamas's brother-in-law, de facto president of Guatemala until 14 January 1986, had presided over the return to at least nominal civilian democratic rule. Rosal de Gamas was arrested for trafficking for adoption a second time the year after her brother-in-law turned over power. On 3 March 1987, police raided a house where sixteen children aged one month to two years were held. They accused Rosal de Gamas of being the "intellectual author" of falsifying paperwork for an adoption ring involving seven women and one man. Police found adoption files at her home as well as receipts for childcare and birth certificates. They noted that she paid babysitters 100 *quetzales* a month (US$40) and adoptive parents paid between US$20,000 and $30,000 per adoption. Even if this may have been an exaggeration, prices were clearly going up.[26] The next day, *Prensa Libre*—the nation's largest newspaper—printed the news that Rosal de Gamas had been arrested under the headline "Police Locate Another 16 Children Ready for Export."

That same week, *El Gráfico* published a bombshell of an article by Carlos Rafael Soto, a columnist and political analyst, titled "Orphans of the High-lands: Booty of War?" Soto wrote openly about two issues usually unmentioned in the press: army massacres, and powerful people's involvement in commercialized adoptions. His 1987 article read: "The national police's discovery of storehouses of children for export has unveiled one of the most painful facets of the dirty war staged in Guatemala for many years: the exploitation of orphans as a valuable byproduct destined to enrich a few people."[27] Soto connected murderous state terror in the highlands orphaning Indigenous children at a high rate to lawyers and members of the elite profiting from adoptions. He wrote that it was both a business and a way to cover up war crimes. Soto identified Rosal de Gamas by name as someone enriching herself through selling babies. He included a phrase that had just come into use to describe international adoptions in Guatemala: "children for export."

Soto traced the connection between massacres and adoptions to 1982. There had been confrontations between guerrilla and army before, he wrote, "but it was not until the rise of Ríos Montt that the policy of eliminating the peasant base in support of the guerrillas led to the emergence of the phenomenon of 'the orphans of the highlands' and their eventual use by civilians linked to the government."[28] He calculated prices as 100 *quetzales* (US$38) to buy a child, similar to the fees mentioned by police sources from the time. Soto wrote that orphans were "sold" to foreign families for between US$15,000 and $30,000. He concluded that Guatemala's war had been taken advantage of by "civilians who, by virtue of their relationship with the strongman in power, have made themselves rich quickly at the cost of selling much of the future of our country: its children."

It is a mystery why even an usually independent journalist like Soto was able to publish an article like this in an atmosphere of censorship and repression. Still, the article appears not to have had much impact. Court records for Rosal de Gamas's 1987 case are unavailable, though it seems she was arrested, investigated, but never sentenced for any crime. Her name continued to surface in connection with adoption crimes until her death in 2014. Adoptees who are now adults looking into the circumstances of their own cases have found Rosal de Gamas's involvement in adoptions involving kidnapping, fraud, or falsifying paperwork to change identities.[29] Her brother-in-law, who may have helped defend her from proper punishment, was himself later investigated for war crimes. After the war, General Mejía Víctores faced charges of crimes against humanity and genocide for the murder of 264 unarmed civilians in the Massacre of Plan de Sánchez, which took place in an Indigenous Achi area called Rabinal. He was also charged with massacres in the Ixil region of Quiché that resulted in more than 1,000 deaths. Notably, he was one of the intellectual authors of the infamous counterinsurgent military plans—"Plan Victoria 82," "Plan Firmeza 83," "Plan Sofia," and "Operación Ixil"—which ordered scorched-earth campaigns in the highlands. It's a small country: Mejía Víctores was defended in a war crimes trial before the Guatemalan courts by none other than Fernando Linares Beltranena. In 2013, he was declared unfit for trial due to dementia and the aftereffects of a stroke.

Soto's article was very unusual in linking rising adoptions to ongoing massacres. But the phrase "children for export" began to appear frequently in Guatemalan newspapers in the mid-1980s.[30] Coverage of for-profit adoptions accompanied and fanned growing outrage and fear. In the first few months of 1988 alone, the police raided eighteen private nurseries suspected of being part of adoption rings, generating extensive press coverage.[31] A former judge, Olga Lucy Rodríguez Fernández, used the phrase in an interview with *Prensa Libre:* "In our country unfortunate events happen, such as the sale of children, who are surreptitiously taken abroad, as if they were a product for export, as if they were bundles of cargo."[32]

Rumors about adoptions spread beyond the reach of the capital-based newspapers, through regional press, radio, or word of mouth. The first attempted attack on a foreigner suspected of stealing children for adoptions, of which others later followed, was in 1987. The headline on the front page of *Prensa Libre* was, "They were going to lynch a North American." The spokesman for the national police said that a man named Bill Blair was attacked in a bus terminal in Quetzaltenango by "furious locals" who accused him of being a child kidnapper. The police intervened and transported Blair to police headquarters, where he showed his passport, said he was a tourist, and denied any connection to child theft for adoptions. No one showed up to formally accuse him of any crime, so he was released.[33]

Press coverage focused on the commercial aspect of adoptions and on kidnappings. Typical headlines from 1988 included "Little Child Made Away With," "Baby of Two Months Stolen," or "Small Boy Kidnapped."[34] One article recounted that a newborn went missing from the capital's largest public hospital while her mother slept. The nurse was under investigation because she was the last to handle the baby. The mother said she was probably drugged since she "never slept that well."[35] The names of lawyers were left out of these stories, but their fees were included: "Police investigations show that the small children were being sold for sums between US$10,000 and $15,000 in foreign countries, where couples incapable of having their own children adopt them."[36]

A 1988 *La Hora* editorial stated that crimes related to private adoptions had created an "enormous controversy" and called for more stringent control. It offered a reflection on private adoptions a decade into their legalization:

> Adoption is a noble institution of Civil Law, whose purpose is to provide replacement homes for orphaned or abandoned children and, at the same time, permit married couples without children to turn their love towards the small victims of misfortune. It is completely distorted when traffickers put economic interests before any other kind of situation. The quality of so-called replacement homes matters little as long as they have enough money to pay the price that has been assigned to each one of the objects of what has become a disgusting business.
>
> We have nothing against foreign homes welcoming Guatemalan children into their bosom; on the contrary, we know of many cases in which they are given love, care, and the kinds of comforts that could never have been offered in their own homeland. But there are also cases that proceed in a different way, and Guatemala, as a State, cannot sidestep its responsibility to act in protection of the rights of children.
>
> Many of the children for export do not undergo legal adoption, but rather by falsifying documents they are made to appear children of foreign couples. There are many professionals who undertake the procedure, assured that it secures high dividends.[37]

The word "mother" does appear in the editorial. Even early limited calls to reform privatized adoptions did not propose addressing the needs of impoverished birth mothers as a potential solution.

The circumstances under which journalists worked in the 1980s in Guatemala go a long way toward explaining why powerful people were only rarely mentioned in newspapers in connection with adoptions, and—like Mulet and Rosal de Gamas—only after committing egregious crimes. A conversation with the journalist who covered adoption crimes most frequently in the 1980s, for *El Gráfico,* certainly offered me a new way to read the stories about "children for export."

Ricardo Gatica Trejo, a slight, energetic man, met me in an old-fashioned café frequented by journalists in Guatemala City. If he hadn't been born in the 1950s, Gatica Trejo himself might have been a candidate for international adoption as a child. He was the son of a single mother from Jutiapa in eastern Guatemala whose family threw her out "because they didn't want a whore in the family," he told me.[38] He moved to the capital and found work as a fireman. Since he was often first to disaster scenes, beating tabloid reporters, *El Gráfico* offered him a side job taking photographs. He eventually started working full time as a journalist.

Gatica Trejo explained that adoptions were an attractive subject in the 1980s because police fed information directly to the press. Unlike war-related crimes, if journalists followed certain unspoken rules, they could safely report on adoptions. Gatica Trejo described a general atmosphere of fear that worsened during the Ríos Montt years. After receiving a black funeral wreath in the mail—not a very subtle death threat—his boss, Jorge Carpio Nicolle, director of *El Gráfico,* was forced to leave the country for a few months. Carpio Nicolle was a well-known journalist and editor who later became a politician before he was assassinated in 1993. According to Gatica Trejo, his boss was the one who came up with the phrase "children for export," which became ubiquitous in the news coverage of adoption.[39]

Gatica Trejo explained that he regularly left out information or even changed names in his articles in order to stay safe in an environment where journalists were murdered with perfect impunity. He told me, "Look, there were two types of journalists during the war." He counted them off on his fingers. "One, journalists by vocation. Two, journalists by hunger [*de hambre*]." Gatica Trejo said that he was trying to feed his family and stay out of trouble. Journalists by vocation ended up dead. Before I met him, I had read many of his articles about police raids on nurseries and "fattening houses," where babies were held before adoption. He told me that his only sources were the police and army, and he certainly didn't call lawyers for comment. He did not attempt to contact members of adoption rings at all, though he said he suspected that they paid other journalists to keep quiet about adoptions. Rival newspapers rarely published on the topic despite the ready availability of information from the police. Still, newspapers had to print something, and the subject of massacres and atrocities was clearly off limits. Police could instead provide reports of rolling raids on nurseries, and journalists could report on them.

Gatica Trejo said that the most important rule to stay safe during those years was to leave the names of important people out of the newspaper. If he had to put powerful people in his stories, he changed their names to protect himself. The names he did record correctly, he said, were those of the women who cared for the children, babysitters who were caught up in police raids. When I asked why, he replied, "because it was official information." These were names he got straight from the police that wouldn't get him in trouble. "And Ofelia Rosal de Gamas?" I asked. "We never wrote about that," he said. "There wasn't proof."

Gatica Trejo wasn't just accusing his colleagues of falsifying the news. He was saying that he had done it himself. I told him that historians often used news articles as the basis for our accounts of the past. He laughed a hearty laugh, then said, "I don't recommend that you do that. [*No te lo recomiendo.*]"

U.S. Embassy Turns a Blind Eye

Foreign embassies were the last stop for adoption cases, since they granted exit visas for children to travel abroad to adoptive parents. Though many early adoptions had been to Canadian and European families, beginning in the 1980s the majority went to the United States. According to government documents, the U.S. Embassy in Guatemala City became aware of adoption crimes as a problem at least as early as 1988. The embassy could have halted or slowed the flow of children out of Guatemala when it suspected fraud. But fraud was not their main concern. Instead of worrying about birth mothers who were scammed or coerced, embassy workers wrote internal memos about the potential risks of a kidnapping-for-adoption scandal. The embassy was less worried about adoption crimes than about a possible public relations disaster.

Guatemala was not the only country with an adoption fraud problem. In September 1988, a cable signed from U.S. Secretary of State George Shultz to the embassy in Guatemala ("Post") read:

> The problems expressed by Post are not limited to Guatemala or Latin
> America. The number of questionable cases reported throughout the

region is, however, in proportion to traditional adoption patterns . . . Many adopting parents have invested a tremendous amount of time and suffered emotional strain in order to achieve a highly laudatory end. Being so emotionally committed, these parents are prime candidates for exploitation and in some instances are willing accomplices.

Emotional strain on children or birth families is mentioned nowhere. The U.S. Embassy in Guatemala wrote back to Washington to ask what level of fraud should trigger further investigation. In other words, what might be considered within the realm of normal, or as the original cable oddly put it, "traditional"? The State Department replied:

What criteria would you use to determine which cases will be investigated? It is unlikely that we could sustain a position that all cases need further investigation simply because the Post is a high fraud country. Profiling in general is not well received. From a practical point of view, we need an understanding of just how long you expect these investigations to take. We and the INS [Immigration and Naturalization Service] will be under extreme pressure to bring these cases to conclusion.[40]

Other cables mention letters sent by adoptive parents to their representatives complaining about delays in adoptions and urging the U.S. government to press Guatemala to speed up adoptions further. Adoptive parents ranged from carpenters to farmers to teachers to lawyers, but some were rich, well-connected constituents.[41]

U.S. officials did investigate some issues. In March 1988, U.S. Consul Philippe Homes met with the civil registrar in Quetzaltenango, Guatemala's second-largest city, to take a look at his real signature so as to more easily identify falsified paperwork. He also asked to look through the records at the civil registrar and found, according to *Prensa Libre,* that "two sheets of each of them had been removed," likely to be used later for falsified paperwork. This satisfied the consul that "the illegal trafficking of minors to the United States isn't a news item created by the media."[42] A 1989 cable read: "We occasionally spot an American woman attempting to register as her own a baby actually born to someone else. However, we are concerned that there is more fraud in both passports and FBU [Federal Benefits Unit] than we have been able to detect."[43]

Embassy officials requested more staff to work on adoptions, but Washington denied the request. Despite many cables about fears of fraud and scandal, the U.S. Embassy in Guatemala imposed no further controls on adoption until instituting mandatory DNA testing in 1998.

In August 1989, the U.S. Embassy sent a cable to the secretary of state that captured the imbalance of power between U.S. and Guatemalan families, the crux of the matter. It read:

> The adoption of Guatemalan children by U.S. citizens constitutes a sensitive issue in both countries. The consular section often finds itself caught between anxious prospective U.S. parents and an unreliable and sometimes fraudulent Guatemalan adoption system. The combination of the urgency of parenting instincts of the relatively wealthy Americans and the failure of the Guatemalans to put their legal house in order concerning adoptions sometimes has yielded scandalous journalism regarding sale or theft of babies and their rumored export to be adopted . . . Our attempts to control the situation by investigating individual adoption cases often result in floods of congressional inquiries triggered by distraught prospective parents.[44]

The cables make abundantly clear that the "urgency of parenting instincts of the relatively wealthy Americans" won out. The embassy continued to send cables to Washington about individual cases of fraud but did not change their own system of vetting.

Someone with Very Large Interests

The Guatemalan backlash built slowly, starting about a decade after adoptions were privatized. In a 1988 interview with *Prensa Libre,* Director of Migration Arturo Chur del Cid laid out some of the problems he had found in an official investigation. He said, "In some cases we have found false documents, names of non-existent lawyers, false addresses, and a series of anomalies that reflect the sophistry used by some people to remove children from Guatemala. There are also deplorable issues like notarized paperwork that documents were signed in the presence of certain lawyers. Our investigations established that the lawyers who signed either don't exist or were out of the country." Chur del Cid raised the possibility of sending the Guatemalan Bar Association a list of lawyers to be suspended for infractions. Of course, this was the same professional organization that had written the draft for a bill privatizing adoptions a decade earlier. But the politician also pointed out that a lot of the anomalies in adoptions that he had found were, strictly speaking, legal. "The truth is that all this can't properly be called trafficking," Chur del Cid told *Prensa Libre,* "because it only reaches that extreme when done through a completely illegal process. In this case, the detected anomalies should serve as a base to impose drastic new rules for the exit of children from the country.[45] The only solution to prevent "anomalies" would be to change the law.

By the end of the 1980s, several members of the Guatemalan Congress had become concerned and proposed new bills to address corruption in adoptions. Among them was Hilda Morales Trujillo, a lawyer who had arranged adoptions both through the Elisa Martínez Orphanage and the private system; Nineth Montenegro of the Group for Mutual Support (GAM), the leading organization demanding the return of family members disappeared during the war, including children; and Mario Taracena Díaz-Sol, president of the congressional Commission for the Protection of Minors. Taracena Díaz-Sol told Mexican newspaper *El Día* in 1988 that the "trafficking of children in Guatemala makes an organized mafia profits calculated at a minimum of 10 million dollars per year."[46] In 1989, he told *Prensa Libre* that the adoption industry "weeps blood," adding, "There are many people who are wolves in sheep's clothing, who seem to do works of charity but who actually devote themselves to exporting children. At the moment, there is an atmosphere of psychosis among Guatemalan mothers, caused by the robberies and kidnappings of children, who are then sent abroad."[47] Another congressman called adoption a "business that blackens the reputation of the country."[48]

All of these attempts to reform adoptions were blocked in Congress. When reading through the private papers of Fernando Linares Beltranena, I found a set of letters archived together with his adoption files, seemingly by chance. The correspondence is from 1987, when Edmond Mulet—the lawyer investigated for trafficking children in both 1981 and 1984—had seen his political star rise. He was by then a congressman. Linares Beltranena wrote a letter to Mulet on 22 October 1987 to complain about one of the reform bills presented by Morales Trujillo, observing, "The bill wouldn't permit direct adoptions at all and would allow for semi-open adoptions," in which birth families stay in touch with children. He went on:

> The bill is better than that of Taracena, but the Executive Committee . . . is even better. That bill, from the Executive Committee, has already been completed, and will come before Congress shortly. It allows private adoption and only considers full adoption and not semi-open adoption (better, in my view) and only modifies the Civil Code and the Civil and Commercial Procedural Code, without making a new law.
>
> I recommend that you wait for the bill from the Executive Committee. We had some participation, because we attended a meeting and they took some suggestions from us.
>
> Let me know when this bill makes its way to the Executive and how the matter shapes up.[49]

Mulet responded with an undated note, signed by hand, using Linares Beltranena's nickname:

> *Dear Skippy,*
>
> Upon returning from our trip to China (Beijing), I found your thoughtful note in relation to that S.O.B. Taracena.[50] Thank you so much . . .
>
> In addition, congratulations on the arrival of the heiress [the birth of Linares Beltranena's daughter]. We owe you a visit, which I promise we will arrange in mid-July when we get back from another visit to the USA.
>
> I have attached photocopies of the two plans to modify the Civil Procedure Code and the Civil Procedure Code *[sic]*, put together by Gabriel Larios [Ochaita], in relation to the process of adoption. The Commission in Congress now seems more inclined in that direction than in creating a separate entity. Let me know your opinion.
>
> The situation in the UCN [Unión del Centro Nacional] is becoming complicated . . .
>
> Hugs,
>
> *Edmond*[51]

The two men use the second person *vos,* which is even more familiar in Guatemalan Spanish than the informal *tú. Vos* is used among close friends. Gabriel Larios Ochaita was the brother of Carlos Larios Ochaita, both of whom were lawyers who facilitated adoptions. These letters are a reminder that many of the lawyers performing private adoptions in a small country were close associates or friends. By the late 1980s several, including Mulet, had risen to political prominence and were actively involved in blocking reforms to private adoptions. The Guatemalan Bar Association and several magistrates on the Supreme Court came out against modifying adoption laws.

In July 1989, the U.S. Embassy in Guatemala cabled Washington: "Hopefully better controls will emerge in the new law." After the bill failed yet again, in August 1989, the U.S. Embassy cabled: "Several congressmen on the committee considering the bills ... are involved directly or indirectly with private adoptios [sic]. The private interests of these persons and some of their friends have until now been sufficient to fojestall [sic] an effort to tighten adoption procedures."

Not all lawyers who had overseen adoptions were in agreement. Morales Trujillo, who helped put together one of the failed reform bills, is now a well-known activist for women's rights and professor of family law. She told me that while she had performed a number of adoptions for acquaintances or when she thought circumstances merited, she disagreed in principle with the idea of private adoptions. "The law says that the idea is to offload some of the judges' work," she told me of the privatization of adoptions in 1977. "That law is a law that I don't see as really human."[52]

After discussions dragged on for two years, Congress opted for editing the various legal codes, exactly as Linares Beltranena had suggested in his 1987 letter, instead of changing the private adoption system or creating a centralized body to oversee them. The new head of the Commission for the Protection of Minors, who was in favor of these cosmetic changes, made an argument that was familiar from the original debate over privatizing adoptions. He said, "The process of private adoption, as it is fixed by our bill, speeds up and shortens the process to avoid corruption due to intentional and indiscriminate delays." Never mind that corruption could work the other way, too, speeding up adoptions through falsified paperwork. Taracena Díaz-Sol, the most vociferous proponent of reform, was accused by other members of Congress of trying to slow down the processing of private adoptions. He retorted that the president of the republic should "detain these illegal proceedings, because it seems that there is someone with very large interests who is meddling in the situation."[53] His protests were in vain. By 1994, fifteen bills to reform the procedure for private adoptions had been proposed in the Guatemalan Congress. All failed.[54]

6

Disappeared Children

In April 1983, Guatemalan army officers stationed at the Mariscal Gregorio Solares military base were patrolling the jagged green mountains near the municipal capital of Huehuetenango when they came across a group of five children wandering without adults.[1] The soldiers brought the children down from the mountains and consulted a family court, where the judge assigned the eldest two of the group to local families. The other three entered a public orphanage in Quetzaltenango, Guatemala's second-largest city and center of urban Indigenous life. The children were young: aged one, one and a half, and three years old. "Personal characteristics: color of the skin is brown, black eyes dark brown hair," a social worker wrote by way of description on the orphanage's intake form. "Ethnic group: indigenous *[indígena]*."[2]

Orphanage social workers listed the youngest boy's name as Daniel, but it is unclear whether that name was given to him by his birth parents, other children in the group, the army officers who found him, social workers, or the judge at the family court. Social workers noted only that it was "an assumed name, given to him before entering the Quetzaltenango Orphanage." Family court paperwork recorded Daniel's parents as deceased, but social workers noted that "documents to prove that situation are lacking."[3]

By 1983, it must have been self-evident to orphanage staff in Quetzaltenango that Daniel came from an area where Indigenous families were under attack by the army. In the early 1980s, the military was engaged in large-scale atrocities, genocidal mass murder, and scorched-earth massacres in the highlands. Since the end of the armed conflict, two truth commissions have established the disastrous death toll of at least 200,000. The UN-sponsored truth commission found that fully 93 percent of the violence was perpetrated by the army, police, and state-controlled community patrols, and 83 percent of the victims were Indigenous. Of that number, an estimated one-fifth of victims were children. According to the Catholic Church's report on minors, "Until I Find You," one-third of the bodies found in mass graves after the war belonged to children.[4] Forensic anthropologists have uncovered their small skeletons alongside adults, including at a military base in the highlands city of Cobán called Creompaz, where eighty-four mass graves were found.

A Maya survivor from Huehuetenango recalled, "What we have seen has been terrible. Burned bodies, women with their bodies pierced by stakes and buried as if they were animals ready to be cooked . . . children massacred and stabbed with machetes." The UN-backed truth commission concluded that "killing children was not an excess or accident; these were premeditated assassinations."[5] After witnessing these atrocities, many survivors fled to Mexico or, in smaller numbers, to the United States. Some survivors, including those who lived in villages that had previously rejected guerrilla presence, began to join or support the insurgency, to which the army responded with further fury.

Some of the most wrenching crimes of the armed conflict were large-scale forced disappearances, with army officials and police hauling away men, women, and children in trucks and helicopters, never to be seen again. (Guerrilla fighters forcibly conscripted people into their ranks, though on a much smaller scale, and kidnapped wealthy Guatemalans for ransom.) The vast majority of the estimated 40,000 adults who were forcibly disappeared by the army or police were murdered, their bodies later found in mass graves or never seen again. By contrast, the estimated 5,000 children who were forcibly disappeared met varying fates. Many were killed, while others endured coerced work as domestic servants. Reliable numbers are difficult to come by, but modest estimates suggest at least 500 of the disappeared children were put up for adoption. These children were presumed to be orphans or made to seem so through paperwork.[6]

Figures give a sense of the scale of forced disappearances. But telling the story of disappeared children by the numbers is somehow fundamentally wrong, since each child is not just an individual, but surrounded by a web of family and community. Numbers fail to convey the tearing of entire social fabric around the forced disappearance of a child. These estimates are based on individual cases that various commissions and the workers for two truth commissions were able to track. So despite being grounded in thorough research, the estimate of 500 disappeared children placed in illegal adoptions is likely a substantial undercount.[7] Maco Garavito, the director of the organization that seeks to reunite families with children disappeared during the war, told me that roughly 60 percent of people who contact his organization searching for lost loved ones never gave testimony to either of the two truth commissions, and so their children were not counted.[8] Family members may not have testified for several reasons. Many lived in very remote communities that were difficult to access. Others were afraid to share their stories soon after the war—the truth commission reports were published shortly after the end of the conflict—but have since approached Garavito's organization. After Guatemalans converted in large numbers to Pentecostal Christianity during the war, some were reluctant to give testimony to a truth commission run by the Catholic Church. (Roughly 40 percent of Guatemalans are now Pentecostal, which they call *evangélico,* rather than Catholic.) Indigenous people gave testimony in lower numbers than non-Indigenous people, according to Garavito: commissions did not always have translators for all Mayan languages. While many Indigenous people live in cities, others live in villages accessible only by steep footpaths. Another reason for the undercount is that adult victims of the war, especially women, regarded lost or stolen children with intense feelings of shame and guilt. Even when they reported other crimes, they did not always report a stolen or disappeared child.[9]

Anthropologist and columnist Irma Alicia Velásquez Nimatuj wrote in *El Periódico* on 24 March 2018, "It is surprising that in Guatemala there are no more or less exact numbers of the children who were disappeared during the 36 years of the internal armed conflict." But, she noted, "it has come to light that the army and repressive forces of the state, as well as kidnapping the children of multiple indigenous communities, also took children from the capital, making adoption one of the most profitable businesses for the military and lawyers."[10] A postwar report based on adoption files noted that "The disappearance of children in the context of war has been generally achieved through adoption. Either members of the repressive forces of the state keep the children or give them away, or they are dropped off at orphanages that arrange these types of things. The goal very probably was to erase more evidence of the violations of human rights that had been committed and take advantage of the booty of war." The report also observed that the number of children collected, adopted, or given away by the military "is not even close to appreciated, since many were given to other houses of which there are no registers, including religious and private orphanages."[11]

This last point helps explain why it is impossible to trace each disappeared child through the existing records. To give just one example, California-based Pentecostal Church of the Word (Iglesia de la Palabra), which converted dictator Efraín Ríos Montt before his rise to power, ran an unknown number of adoptions out of Casa Bernabé, its orphanage in Guatemala City. This orphanage, along with other private orphanages, which were often run by Catholics or Pentecostals, has never opened its doors to truth commissions, agencies searching for disappeared children, or any researchers at all. The Ministry of Social Welfare's adoption files show that 445 children passed through state orphanages before their adoption from 1981 to 1987. The majority were not Maya war orphans—indeed, dozens, not hundreds, seem obviously to have been disappeared children. A much greater proportion of the hundreds of disappeared children passed through private orphanages, adopted in processes handled by private lawyers, or were informally given away to families loyal to the army, who falsified birth certificates instead of filling out adoption paperwork. (Given the thorough records kept by the Ministry of Social Welfare, it seems possible, though not likely, that the Elisa Martínez Orphanage placed more disappeared children off the books.)[12] Available records and interviews show that social workers from the Ministry of Social Welfare were called in by the military after massacres or presented with children dropped off at orphanages by police or soldiers in some cases. These, along with testimonials by families and children themselves, provide the best and indeed only available evidence of what happened to forcibly disappeared children during the war.[13]

Military officials collected Daniel, one of the five children found wandering in the mountains, along with many other children from an area near the border with Mexico, home to two Indigenous groups, the Chuj and Q'anjob'al. These are two of twenty-two Maya groups in Guatemala, all of whom speak distinct, mostly mutually unintelligible languages. Claiming—often wrongly—that Indigenous families provided food and support for guerrilla forces in the highlands, the Guatemalan army singled out particular communities for extermination. The Chuj and Q'anjob'al were victims of at least nineteen documented massacres of civilians beginning in 1982. The army claimed that civilians in Huehuetenango harbored at least 20,000 guerrilla fighters, while interviews with members of the Ejército Guerrillero de los Pobres—the leading guerrilla

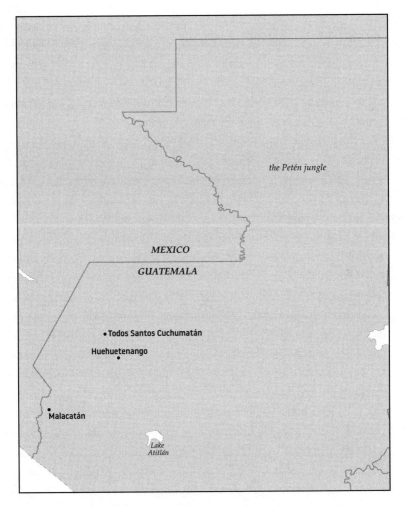

the Petén jungle

MEXICO

GUATEMALA

• Todos Santos Cuchumatán

Huehuetenango

Malacatán

Lake Atitlán

Mexico-Guatemala border

organization in the area—suggested there were never more than fifty-two armed men in the region. In retaliation for a largely imagined guerrilla presence there, soldiers murdered men, women, and children.[14] Many rank-and-file soldiers were themselves young Indigenous men who had been forcibly recruited. The UN-backed truth commission report later named massacres in Huehuetenango among "acts of genocide" committed against the Chuj and Q'anjob'al by the Guatemalan army from 1982 to 1983.[15] It also found genocidal acts to have been committed during this period against other Indigenous groups, including the K'iche' and Ixil. At the time, there was a near-total news blackout in Guatemalan newspapers about the army killings, though organizations like Amnesty International reported extensively on the escalation of violence. While people in the capital could plausibly still claim ignorance of the genocide as it unfolded, those in Quetzaltenango were closer to and more interconnected with the massacre areas.

Despite the lack of documentation of Daniel's origins, social workers at the state-run orphanage recommended "integrating the boy into society through the program of adoptions" overseen by the Ministry of Social Welfare.[16] Daniel was transferred to the Elisa Martínez Orphanage, which by that time had developed a more substantial adoption program since it opened in the capital in the 1960s. The program grew still larger with the influx of orphans and disappeared children during the most murderous phase of the war. One adoption file notes of a two-year-old girl in 1981: "According to obtainable information, this minor was taken to the Ministry by elements of the army who did not provide any information about her origin. It is believed she is originally from the West," a reference to the highlands, "and that she is possibly an orphan, since her features are of the indigenous race." The toddler spoke no Spanish. She was assumed to be an orphan and adopted by a French family some years later.[17]

Racial lines in Guatemala are both rigidly defined and possible to cross with a change in clothing worn or language spoken.[18] The distinction between a person considered Indigenous and a person considered *ladino* often had and has less to do with skin color, height, hair, or facial features than with cultural markers, such as living in a non-Indigenous community or city, speaking Spanish rather than a Mayan language, or dressing in jeans and a t-shirt rather than a handwoven *huipil* (blouse) and *corte* (long wrap skirt cinched with a woven belt)—an outfit called *traje*.[19] Fixation on racial distinctions and virulent racism were common even before the genocide. After a short-lived experiment with promoting Mexican-style *mestizaje* and *indigenista* policies in the 1930s that never gained popular traction, the Guatemalan government turned to what historian Arturo Taracena Arriola described as "fostering segregation while dreaming about assimilation."[20] During the early 1980s, those dreams of assimilation curdled into racial terror, further hardening distinctions between the Maya and *ladino* Guatemalans. Maya adults still had the option of appearing *ladino* by leaving their village, wearing jeans, and speaking Spanish. This was a choice, however coerced and overdetermined. Another route out of Indigenous identity for babies and infants, involuntary and dictated by social workers and private lawyers often without consent from Maya parents, was placement in adoption with a *ladino* family in Guatemala or with a family abroad.[21]

The Ministry of Social Welfare matched Daniel with a couple from the United States. If the couple was aware of the difference between Indigenous and non-Indigenous Guatemalan children, they did not indicate so on the paperwork they filled out. The couple traveled to Guatemala to pick up Daniel. According to follow-up reports by a social worker in the United States, Daniel quickly learned to speak English and refused to speak Spanish, which he likely only learned at the orphanage. According to his adoptive parents, he occasionally mentioned a woman who cared for him at one of the orphanages in Guatemala, but he never spoke about his earlier life in an Indigenous community, if he remembered it at all.[22]

Remove the Water from the Fish

While the history of the war in Guatemala has been written mostly about male protagonists—guerrilla fighters, student leaders, intellectuals, and trade unionists squaring off against the army and police—documents from the Ministry of Social Welfare and the few accessible or leaked army plans from the 1980s illustrate a total war against certain Maya families that extended far beyond a military standoff between mostly male combatants.[23] During the first phase of the war, 1960 to 1978, the police kidnapped and murdered university students and trade unionists in the capital and fought a relatively small guerrilla movement in the eastern part of the country.[24] After the 1978 Panzós Massacre, during which the government killed dozens of K'ekchi' villagers as they protested abuses by local plantation owners, repression shifted to Indigenous communities in the highlands in departments like Sololá, Quiché, Quetzaltenango, Huehuetenango, Alta Verapaz, and Baja Verapaz.[25] Greg Grandin called the events in Panzós "the last colonial massacre" to capture the paranoid fear of those who descended from colonial authorities or imagined they did. The international context had changed, with the success of the Sandinista socialist takeover of Nicaragua in 1979 frightening many in Washington to advocate for more military aid and unquestioning support for regimes committing atrocities in both Guatemala and El Salvador. Frustrated at its failure to wipe out the guerrilla leadership, the army started attacking not just combatants, but also Indigenous civilians suspected of giving the guerrillas food and shelter. Some Indigenous communities sided with the army, either out of real allegiance or fear. The army identified others, entire Indigenous communities, as an "internal enemy." Army leadership, citing a Maoist principle of fighting guerrilla insurgency, vowed to "remove the water from the fish" through wholesale destruction of these communities.[26] This meant an attack on entire families, including children.

Adoption through the Ministry of Social Welfare was just one of several possible fates for Maya children orphaned or displaced by the war or forcibly disappeared by the army. Other children were murdered in massacres, fled into the mountains with their parents or neighbors, or were taken as "mascots" or "pets" (*mascotas*), domestic servants, or informal adoptees by soldiers. The war affected vast numbers of Indigenous children by undermining or cutting off modes of transmission of Maya culture from one generation to the next. Even for children never separated from their families or communities, the fear created by the genocide in Guatemala caused many Indigenous families to raise their children in the 1980s as *ladino* for their own protection— not teaching them Mayan languages, for instance, or dressing them in jeans rather than *traje*, the traditional handwoven clothing that had already fallen by the wayside for most Indigenous men but was widely worn by Indigenous women.[27]

Daniel's story is just one example of how adoptions changed during the early 1980s. Previously, the Ministry of Social Welfare had mostly overseen the adoption of poor Guatemalans living in and around Guatemala City. Social workers were non-Indigenous, did not speak Mayan languages, and did not work with translators, as far as I could tell from the records. Social workers placed a few Maya children for adoption with Maya families during the first years of the program in the early 1970s, and records show they were still doing so, though infrequently, through the next decade. In one unusual file from 1980, for example, a social worker named Rosa Amanda de Wannam describes a Kaqchikel adoptive family as "people of good customs" who feel "very happy and proud to be of the indigenous race" and whose community offers "mutual aid, where one's own problems are shared by other members of the community."[28] Still, in the context of escalating genocidal attacks, evidence of obvious racism and lack of meaningful consent from family members for placements—which already appeared in some earlier adoption files—came ever more strongly to the fore. Many files contained reference to "irresponsible" birth mothers. While the moralistic tone of social workers' reports and their judgments about who constituted a "fit" mother remained mostly consistent from the 1970s to the 1980s, the biggest change was the geography of origin and ethnicity of the children whose fates they were deciding. The children in the adoption program were still often from the capital, but increasingly came from the predominantly Indigenous highlands, rural areas where the state expanded its counterinsurgent presence during the 1980s. As the war entered its genocidal phase beginning in 1981, the Ministry of Social Welfare began to process cases like Daniel's and those of other Indigenous children from the highlands, which had become the primary battlefields of the war.

Adoption files from the period show that social workers at state orphanages presumed without proof that disappeared children were orphans, chose to forgo the consent of birth parents or extended birth families, and guessed at or falsified the children's identities or origins to declare them in a "state of abandonment," making them eligible for the adoption program. While the disappeared children who passed through official channels at the state orphanage are a fraction of the whole, their intact adoption records provide the most information about the fates of any of the disappeared children who were adopted. Private adoptions, which left a spottier and mostly inaccessible paper trail, are more difficult to reconstruct and analyze. Complicating matters further, even the records for state adoptions through the Elisa Martínez Orphanage, though seemingly complete, are highly unreliable. Some information in the adoption files was falsified or obscured, as in the case of Daniel, the boy allegedly found wandering in Huehuetenango. What is clear from existing sources is that many of the children presumed to be orphans by soldiers and social workers were not really orphans at all. During sudden army attacks, Indigenous families who managed to flee often grabbed any children they could, whether theirs or the children of other members of their community. Guatemalans re-encountered children and other family members they had assumed were long dead at refugee camps in Mexico throughout the remaining period of the war, and even after the signing of peace accords in 1996.

Terminate the Seed

Throughout the twentieth century, governments and international organizations have drawn up laws and treaties defining genocide, as well as designating specific acts as genocidal.[29] Then, there is the understanding that comes from people under siege, in their testimonies and their denunciations of what is happening even as the violence is ongoing. In Guatemala, the two converged. As the army continued to raze whole villages in the highlands, Maya survivors—particularly those who managed to flee the country—told those who would listen of the devastation that was underway. When a Catholic organization in southern Mexico arranged a letter-writing campaign to gather testimony from Guatemalan refugees, the letters followed a standard format, answering questions including "Why did the army come to your village?" In response, a farmer named Pedro Ramírez, seeking refuge in Campamento de Nuevo Mexico, wrote: "because they wanted to kill all of us to finish off us indigenous people" ("a querernos matar a todos nosotros para terminarnos los indijenas").[30] It took another decade and a half for any official designation of genocide in Guatemala to follow—most notably in the 1999 UN-backed truth commission report, then later in the 2013 trial for genocide of former dictator Efraín Ríos Montt. During

Efraín Ríos Montt at his 2013 trial for genocide. *Hiroko Tanaka / Alamy Stock Photo.*

the war and after, Maya families have continuously asserted in human rights trials, testimonies for the two truth commissions, and in requests for asylum in the United States and Mexico that in addition to massacres and sexual violence, forcible separation of children from their families was part of the violence suffered during the genocide.

Well before the Guatemalan genocide took place, forcible adoptions were already part of the internationally accepted definition of the crime. In December 1948, the UN General Assembly adopted a resolution that legally defined genocide for the first time. The definition included five acts "committed with intent to destroy, in whole or in part, a national, ethnical, racial, or religious group."[31] The fifth act deemed constitutive of genocide was: "Forcibly transferring children of the group to another group."[32] Guatemala ratified the convention on 13 January 1950.[33] Also in 1948, the Universal Declaration of Human Rights asserted that "no one shall be arbitrarily deprived of his nationality." Historian Tara Zahra argued that together these two resolutions represented the emergence of a "new international norm" that the denationalization of children was an abuse of human rights.[34] International adoption fit uneasily into this paradigm: it stripped one national identity and conferred another.

When Efraín Ríos Montt was tried for genocide and crimes against humanity committed during his 1982–1983 dictatorship, the bulk of the evidence presented in court was accounts of mass killings of men, women, and children from particular Indigenous groups. But testimony also included other methods of attempting to dismantle communities targeted by the army, including kidnapping children who were later placed in adoptions. Marco Tulio Álvarez, former director of Guatemala's Peace Archives (Archivos de la Paz), formed after the war, testified that the army kidnapped children in "unknown numbers" for adoption.[35] In a report based on the Ministry of Social Welfare's adoption files, at that time still held at the Peace Archives, Álvarez wrote that he and his staff had found evidence of two types of wartime adoptions. The first was political. An increase in adoptions during the war coincided with the rising number of children orphaned or displaced by the army. Survivors who gave testimonies to both truth commissions often repeated the phrase "terminate the seed" to describe the Guatemalan government's wartime approach. Álvarez wrote, "Adoptions in this instance were a mechanism of forced disappearance, a way for children to survive but with another identity and knowing little or nothing of their origin." The second type was economic. "It became a source of rapid enrichment for actors who, taking advantage of the legal weaknesses of the process, turned it into a source of large revenues by giving priority to international adoption," wrote Álvarez.[36]

After the conflict, the National Commission for the Search for Disappeared Children in Guatemala was formed to reunite family members. In its final report, the group asserted that disappearing children served four main objectives of the Guatemalan state during the war: to "terminate the seed of future guerrilla fighters"; "obtain information" about suspect communities; "attract parents to military centers to capture them"; and find "children for adoptions." The report noted that the majority of disappeared children were Indigenous, which coincided with the first objective. The result of removing Indigenous children from their families was to "create general terror" and to "make a profit from the sale of children."[37] Low estimates for the number of children orphaned during the war hover around 250,000—though most of these children were informally adopted by family or community members, many of whom fled to Mexico as refugees.[38] The army's own publicity materials boasted that they destroyed over 440 rural communities in the highlands.[39]

A survivor from Huehuetenango told truth commission interviewers, "The army's plan was to leave us without seeds. Even if it was a little boy [*patojito*] one year old, two years old, they were all 'bad seed,' so it was said."[40] After massacring the inhabitants of a village, the army burned surrounding cornfields, which were the primary sustenance of most poor communities and of spiritual significance to the Maya, whose creation myth is of gods fashioning men and women from corn. Killing or disappearing children was another way to attempt to destroy a community and to make regeneration impossible. Testimonies also mention children who survived or were spared. A group of survivors described a scene of horror after a 1980 massacre: "There are babies lying under the sticks, they died all over the place. There are babies tied up on the branches of trees, like how they do it when they are at home, tying them up in a sling from the ceiling, that's how they are left hanging from the tree branches. And the babies are alive but you can't pick them up anymore. Where are you going to leave them if you don't know where their mothers are?"[41]

Some of the testimonies given to truth commissions mention babies left behind and thought later to have been adopted.[42] Others died in flight. During and after massacres, people fled to surrounding mountains, and in many cases were too fearful to return to their villages for years or even decades. Babies represented a grave risk to adults attempting to flee. Survivors recounted accidentally suffocating babies to death after filling their mouths with dry leaves to silence their cries, which they feared would attract the attention of soldiers combing the area.[43] Guatemala's mountainous highlands are dense with trees and cloud cover. They can be a good place to hide, but also an easy place to lose people, especially children. In the fear and chaos of escape, some children were lost in the mountains. Adults who fled didn't know if they died or were found and killed or captured by soldiers.

Most army documents from the period of the war were classified, hidden, or destroyed. Those that remain and are accessible to researchers show that the army regarded the Indigenous family in suspect communities as a threat, as a breeding ground for what dictator Efraín Ríos Montt's government called "bad seed," a term survivors remembered all too well.[44] In a 1980 counterinsurgency manual, the Guatemalan army identified the family, not the individual, as the "smallest unit" of counterinsurgency.[45] In April 1982, a U.S. defense attaché report informed the State Department that in areas where subversives operated, "unconventional warfare" would apply. The strategy: "Guerrillas would be destroyed by fire and their infrastructure eradicated by social welfare programs."[46]

Previously, social services were available to such a small number of Guatemalans that they were largely symbolic. Welfare institutions were confined mostly to the capital and a few large cities. In 1982, the Ministry of Social Welfare mobilized as part of the war effort, extending services to areas of Guatemala suspected of harboring guerrilla fighters. The ministry's internal annual report noted a new program called "Plan of Attention to Conflict Areas," which created ten new centers in places including Nebaj and Chajul, sites of infamous massacres during the war.[47] In its 1982 internal annual report, the ministry recorded that it offered "integral care to orphaned and/or abandoned minors at physical and moral risk."[48] Ministry bureaucrats complained constantly in their reports about chronic underfunding and described efforts to reduce the per-day cost of housing war orphans in state orphanages.[49] Tight budgets were yet another incentive to place children out quickly with foster or adoptive families.

The same year that the Ministry of Welfare expanded into the highlands, a military magazine published a "Social Plan" for an area it labeled the Ixil Triangle. This was a military designation for an area of the Guatemalan highlands that obsessed the army because 98 percent of the population was Indigenous.[50] Under "Courses of Action," the first step was to "complete the

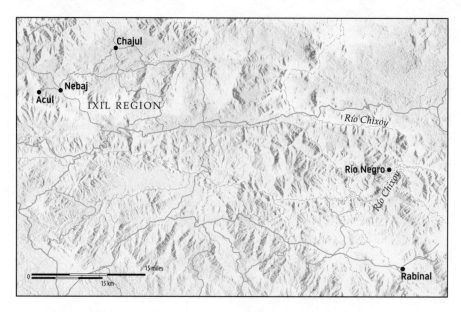

Areas of genocidal attacks by the army on Indigenous communities.

assigned mission intensifying the *ladinización* of the Ixil population in such a way that they disappear as a cultural subgroup alien to our national way of being."[51] The national way of being, which Ríos Montt promoted as "Guatemalan-ness *[guatemalidad]*," was a nationalist, non-Indigenous identity. The army perpetrated a large number of massacres and the massive reorganization of Ixil civilians into surveilled encampments that were euphemistically called "poles of development."[52] Many Ixil children ended up in orphanages.[53] The Social Plan, which was eventually used as evidence at the 2013 genocide trial, laid out a variety of strategies in an innocuous tone: reestablishing the rule of law, opening a bank and making credit available, and protecting private property, for example. Reducing infant mortality was cited as a counterinsurgent strategy, as was "extending the benefits of the Ministry of Social Welfare to the Ixil population."[54]

Social welfare provisions, including adoptions, were intended to improve poor Guatemalans' material lives such that they would be less tempted by the promises of forging a new society through guerrilla warfare. Another army manual from 1982 describes actions proposed to counter what the state identified as political, social, economic, military, and psycholog-

Women from the Ixil Indigenous group, which was targeted during the Guatemalan genocide, listen at Ríos Montt's 2013 trial. *Courtesy of Daniele Volpe.*

ical causes of rebellion. Under the category of "economic," the army suggested: "reach a level of life that satisfies the necessities and aspirations of the collectivity, *propounding a fair distribution of wealth.*" Under "social causes," it proposed: "eliminate the social injustices that foment 'class conflict,' procuring the well-being and spiritual and material progress of the collectivity."[55]

Government reports and survivor accounts show glimpses of how these programs were implemented, and how Maya families resisted army efforts to kill, kidnap, or disappear Indigenous children. Informal adoptions are always hard to trace, but they were hidden on purpose during this period when it was dangerous for Indigenous families to take in children. According to a human rights report from the late 1980s:

> It is also hard to be certain about the exact circumstances of these orphans. During the Ríos Montt government, there were reports that a number of orphans had been handed over as servants to high-ranking military families, or to childless couples to bring up the orphans . . .

Many children, who have lost both or one of their parents, have been adopted by their community and are being brought up by one or more families. In many cases, those looking after the orphans have enormous financial problems, but they do not request help from the church or relevant institutions, for fear the children will be taken away. Generally these families live in the countryside far from municipal capitals and without government services of any kind.

The report noted that the children are "tremendously fearful of strangers, especially of non-indigenous people."[56] Children who remained in Guatemala under the care of extended families or neighbors were subject to intense army surveillance. A decade later, former defense minister General Héctor Gramajo recalled: "I was watching the widows from the destroyed villages: how many there were, how much they ate, who gave them food, where the orphans were and who took care of them."[57] The government feared that children raised by Maya families would become the next generation of guerrillas. The "bad seed" would sprout.

In debriefs and plans, army officials referred to Indigenous children as "chocolates." Plan Operation Sofía, a notorious military document that called for "exterminating the subversive elements in the area," referred to eighteen adults and twelve "chocolates" captured after a massacre in Nebaj.[58] A small number of Indigenous children stolen by the army remained as "mascots," children who lived on army bases and performed small tasks, like shining shoes. Others were taken in by military officials either as adopted children or unpaid domestic servants. This is part of a historical pattern dating from before the twentieth century. Historian Nara Milanich wrote that the Argentine "Conquest of the Desert" in the 1870s was characterized by the widespread capture, enslavement, and circulation of Indigenous children, which, "in addition to a labor practice" was "a systematic state strategy for incorporating and assimilating vanquished peoples."[59]

A boy named Marcos Choc Maquín was one of six children in a Maya K'ekchi' family living in a village called Chiax Balamté, near Cahabón, Alta Verapaz. After an army massacre in 1982, Marcos fled his home village, and in the confusion was separated from his family as he recounted later in a testimonial. He and another child hid in the forest and covered themselves with dried leaves, but soldiers still found them.[60] An official gave the order to kill them, but two soldiers asked instead "that these two be gifted *[regalados]*." Marcos was taken in by one of the soldiers, who raised him as a servant in San Pedro Carchá, Alta Verapaz. He was forced to go hungry and sleep in the passageway of the soldier's house, and to gather firewood and do other housework without pay. The family told Marcos he would be killed if he tried to escape. But when he was twelve years old, a neighbor helped smuggle him out to her parents' house, and he enrolled in school for the first time. On 19 July 2003, more than twenty years after Marcos was disappeared, he was reunited with his father, who had survived the massacre by fleeing on foot into Mexico. They found each other after both approached a postwar committee involved in the search for disappeared children. The girl Marcos hid with under the dried leaves, along with two of his siblings who also fled, remain missing. Marcos's disappearance meant that he now struggles to communicate with family members, since he does not speak K'ekchi'.

As in Argentina and Spain, some stolen children in Guatemala were not told they were adopted. Guadalupe Boton García was disappeared in the Ixil region when she was just thirty days old. Days later, on 18 January 1982, an army lieutenant called a town meeting in the small town of Cunén, in Quiché, to warn the community against cooperating with guerrillas, and he asked who in the community wished to have a child. A *ladina* woman named Antonia González Santay decided to adopt a girl, and the lieutenant gave her Guadalupe Boton García. Santay falsified paperwork at the civil registry to register the girl as her own child, instead of going through an official adoption procedure. At first, she and her husband did not tell the girl she was adopted, but later they decided to reveal the truth. Boton García later said that though her adoptive parents sympathized with the military, they treated her well and raised her like a daughter. After she learned that she was adopted, Guadalupe got in touch with investigators who ascertained that she was from Nebaj, because of the clothing she wore when she was separated from her Ixil birth family. She later reconnected with her parents through a call put out via a community radio, Radio Ixil.[61]

Disappeared children who were placed with families abroad of course knew they were adopted, but may have not known their whole story. Denese Becker, who was raised in Iowa, knew that she was from Guatemala. But only when she was twenty-nine and returned to her country of birth did she learn the full truth of her past: she used to be called Dominga Sic Ruiz and she had been a victim of one of the most infamous army massacres of the war, which took place in Río Negro, a Maya Achi community. A documentary about her life recounts that she was nine years old on 13 March 1982, when the army attacked her town, soldiers killed both her mother and father. In the chaos, her mother managed to tie her baby sister to her back in a shawl and told her to "run." Sic Ruiz eventually made her way to a convent in Rabinal, a nearby town. The nuns brought her to a private orphanage in Guatemala City, which placed her for adoption with a Baptist minister and his wife in Iowa.

As a child in Iowa, she did have memories, not to mention nightmares, of what had happened. She remembered wandering the Guatemalan country-side alone with her baby sister, who grew weak. "I remember burying her under a really, really big tree on a hill." But for a long time she thought she must have made up these memories—nothing real could be so terrible. As an adult, she revealed her memories to an adoptive cousin, who did research online, matched Becker's story with what had happened in Río Negro, and started emailing people in Guatemala to learn more. Becker later got a phone call from another Río Negro survivor, who said, "I know you. I knew your dad, I knew your mom. You have aunts and uncles and cousins who have been looking for you for years." When Becker flew to Guatemala, her whole

A procession in Nebaj to bury remains of people killed in army massacres during the war, later found by forensic anthropologists. *Courtesy of Daniele Volpe.*

town turned out to meet her in a gathering in front of the church. She had memories of what happened to her parents and baby sister, but had no idea that hundreds of people had been killed by the army in the Río Negro massacre. Becker spoke neither Achi nor Spanish, and communicated with her family through a translator. In the documentary, she says "I wish one day I would wake up and remember all the Achi and totally surprise my relatives here." She tries on *traje* in the market, recalling that her mother loved to shop for new fabrics, and says, "I want so much to be a normal Achi Maya woman." Becker feels she is torn between being Dominga Sic Ruiz of Guatemala, where she attends Achi mourning rituals for the dead, and Denese Becker of the United States, where she works as a manicurist and raises her two children. She does not fully belong to either place.[62]

Available sources do not show a concerted plan on the part of the army to use adoptions as part of the genocide. What they show—between massacres, forced disappearances, and forcibly transferring children to another group—is not intent but adoptions as part of a genocidal outcome. Even detailed records of atrocities indicate that there was no overarching plan linking adoptions to the ongoing genocide, though this was often the result, if not the intent. A civil patroller who found a baby attempting to nurse from a dead mother's breast after a massacre in 1982 convinced his superior that he wanted to take him in. He was granted permission, "if and only if he personally took responsibility for the child since the mission was to attack the guerrilla and not to transfer children."[63] Complicating the picture still further is the fact that rank-and-file soldiers, who were themselves Indigenous, also took in an unknown number of disappeared children, either from their linguistic group or others.

The majority of disappeared children were Indigenous, just like the majority of the war's victims in general. But non-Indigenous children were also forcibly disappeared in army attacks. The case of Oscar Alfredo Ramírez Castañeda became known in the United States through a documentary, executive produced by Steven Spielberg, called *Finding Oscar*. Oscar was one of a group of five children who had wandered away from the center of his town, Dos Erres, in the Petén jungle, just before the 1982 massacre of 250 men, women, and children. Without evidence, the army suspected the poor community of harboring guerrilla fighters. After the killings were over, the children found their way back to the town center, where they were discovered by soldiers. The group of children included two young boys and three teenage girls. Soldiers raped and killed the girls and spared the boys—one of whom was a toddler with light skin and green eyes. An army lieutenant took him home and renamed him Oscar Ramírez, and never told him he was adopted. (His real name was Alfredo Castañeda.) Oscar was raised to believe that his "father," who died soon after stealing him, was a hero who protected Guatemala from communism.[64]

Oscar was thirty-one years old when he learned the truth. He was living undocumented in the United States, near Boston, when he received an email from a human rights prosecutor investigating the Dos Erres massacre. She strongly suspected he was the disappeared toddler. "I know that you were much loved and well treated by the family in which you grew up," the prosecutor wrote to him, but "although you don't know it, you were a victim of this sad event." Ramírez's real father happened to be away from Dos Erres on the day of the army attack, working in the fields of a nearby town. He had spent decades mourning his wife and nine children, all of whom were presumed dead. A DNA test matched Oscar to his father in 2012, and the two reunited later that year.

The other boy who survived the Dos Erres massacre, Ramiro Osorio Cristales, was a bit older. Unlike Oscar, he had dim memories of the killings. He was taken as a servant by a lower-ranking soldier who physically abused him. Both boys, now men, appear as witnesses at human rights trials in Guatemala. Ramiro Osorio Cristales has given testimony against his adoptive father, who received a 5,000-year sentence for war crimes—30 years each for the 172 deaths and forced disappearances for which he was found responsible for at Dos Erres.[65] (He took the stand accompanied by a psychologist.) Oscar has no memory of the events themselves, but says he has given testimony at trials because he considers himself "living proof" of the war crimes committed by the Guatemalan army.[66] He was granted political asylum in the United States after his lawyers argued he could be in continued danger of persecution in Guatemala, where the military retains significant political sway behind the scenes.[67] Even before the prosecutor contacted him, Oscar had an inkling that he may have been a war orphan. But his adoptive family convinced him that the idea was "preposterous, a leftist fabrication."[68]

Long before the situation in Guatemala was internationally recognized as genocide, massacre survivors and refugees pointed to the loss of Indigenous culture among children as one result of the violence, and demanded the return of children disappeared from villages targeted by the army. A 1984 report by a Guatemalan organization led by Maya refugees noted that both internal displacement and the mass exodus to Mexico spelled the "division and destruction of entire families." Separation from lands and family meant a permanent loss of Indigenous identity. "Above all among children, over the years we see uprooting and forgetting customs, culture, language; in a word, they are losing their cultural identity."[69]

Children from villages targeted by the army who escaped forced disappearance during the war often ended up living as refugees in Mexico. From 1981 to 1983, an estimated 200,000 Guatemalans fled to Mexico, taking an unknown number of orphaned children with them.[70] Most stayed in Chiapas in southern Mexico, but some were relocated by the Mexican government up the coast to Campeche. A 1985 fundraising appeal from the Guatemala Relief Project recorded that refugee camps were broken down by ethnic group to retain some semblance of Maya life, but the refugees had not been assigned enough land to provide for themselves by growing corn, beans, and vegetables. Weaving and other projects were important in the camps to "help provide an income for widows and aid the support of the many orphans."[71] The same organization noted that "Guatemala is now a country of orphans." A United Nations analysis showed that adult refugees were often caring for several orphans in addition to their own children.[72]

Orphans were a ubiquitous presence in Guatemalan refugee camps in Mexico. In workbooks published for use in camp classrooms in 1984, the second-grade social studies unit had a lesson called "The Family" that included a section on orphans. It instructed second graders to read the following text out loud along with their teacher and classmates:

> There are many children who don't have their father, or their mother, or either of the two because they already died. These children are ORPHANS.
> The people who live with orphan children are their family now. These are the people who should care for, attend to, love, and raise the children and work so that they don't lack for anything.[73]

Starting almost as soon as the first wave of refugees fled to Mexico in 1981, the Guatemalan government lobbied hard for their return. The government cynically wanted the families, along with orphans, to return as a signal to the international community that conditions were improving in Guatemala at a time when human rights abuses were so rampant that they threatened the continued receipt of foreign military aid.[74] In 1985, the Guatemalan First Lady went so far as to visit refugee camps in Mexico in an attempt to convince families to return. Before her arrival, refugees wrote letters outlining their conditions for even considering a return to Guatemala. Their demands included a "return of stolen children."[75]

7

Best Interests of the Child

The history of disappeared children in Guatemala recalls the theft and adoptions of Native Americans in the United States, First Nations children in Canada, and Aboriginal children in Australia as a means to forcibly absorb Indigenous children into white-dominated societies. Politically motivated adoptions also occurred in Francoist Spain, Nazi Germany, and Argentina during the 1976–1983 dictatorship. Forced assimilation alongside mass killings is familiar from many other colonial and neocolonial contexts. Less familiar is the simultaneous overlay of the two patterns in 1980s Guatemala: an army campaign against an "internal enemy," and—because the state designated that enemy as particular Maya communities—a continuation and massive escalation of anti-Indigenous violence that had been perpetrated in waves since the Spanish Conquest. Colonial and Cold War violence marched in lockstep in Guatemala.[1] Taking children is integral to both political violence and anti-Indigenous violence. It plays out in similar fashion: certain children, presumed to be assimilable or "salvageable," are forcibly separated from the group.[2]

Disappeared children in Guatemala met with many fates. Even among those who were adopted, records only remain for a small subset of the cases: those put up for adoptions through state orphanages rather than through private or religious orphanages working with lawyers. The Ministry of Social Welfare adoption files from the 1980s do contain records of children who were likely disappeared. But they also show the lies and omissions that characterized many adoption cases from Guatemala. Reading the Guatemalan adoption files gives us a rare chance to glimpse the omissions and rewritings of forcible adoptions. The case files are less reliable than they may seem on a first read.

The case of Daniel, a child the military claimed to find without parents in the hills near Huehuetenango, shows how even the best documentation could also be riddled with falsifications and possibly with outright lies. The case shows some features common among adoptions from the period of genocide: the immediate decision to put Daniel up for adoption with a foreign family, rather than to match him with a Guatemalan family or conduct a search for living relatives in Guatemala; uncertainty over whether he was really an orphan; and the rapidity with which the adoption was finalized. But the files created in order to document and justify adoptions obscure as well as clarify. Adoption files in general must be read with care, since they may give an account of the child's birth family that casts as negative a light as possible in order to justify an adoption that was already underway.[3] Adoption files contain a large accumulation of paperwork, from records of how a child entered into state custody to notarial documents and social reports to documentation of placements with adoptive families. What is most striking about reading full adoption files is to see how social workers changed or omitted details over time. Information that appears in early parts of the record disappears in later parts. In some files, these changes over time gradually erased, either partially or fully, the original identities of adoptees. The final versions given to adoptive parents—usually a fraction of the number of pages of the total adoption file—downplayed, evaded, and sometimes concealed the government's role in orphaning or disappearing children.

Even the fullest version of adoption records, like those preserved at the Ministry of Social Welfare, are a form of official story. It is worth returning in greater detail to Daniel's story to see how these official stories were put together. The earliest documents relating to Daniel's case date from 15 April 1983, when a family court judge in Quetzaltenango sent a letter to a social worker at the Ministry of Social Welfare's orphanage requesting that she prepare to receive three children aged one, one and a half, and three years old "for whom last names are unknown by virtue of the fact that their parents have died and there aren't other persons responsible for said minors." The judge suggested that the social worker should "try to place them in homes deemed appropriate."[4] The two older children found with Daniel in the mountains of Huehuetenango had already been placed with local families at the discretion of the court. This was technically illegal, since only social workers at the Ministry of Social Welfare were allowed to oversee family placements.

On 15 April 1983, social workers in Quetzaltenango noted that Daniel was dropped off at the state-run orphanage there. "Today the minor [redacted] without another name or last name entered [the orphanage] . . . the minor lacks family and persons who know him—since he was located with other minors in the mountains of Huehuetenango when the zone was patrolled by military troops." The social worker who wrote this report repeated the story told by military officials as the truth of Daniel's origins. In July 1983, social workers noted that Daniel was approximately two years old—one instance of ongoing confusion over his age—and had "hair made reddish by malnutrition." (Children who fled attacks with their families or alone often suffered from malnutrition while hiding in the mountains.) Social workers described him as a normal child, but "still he doesn't talk or babble . . . possibly because of the change of language, that is to say from his native language to Spanish."[5] Because he was "found" in Huehuetenango, Daniel likely came from a Chuj- or Q'anjob'al-speaking family and first learned Spanish at the state orphanage.[6]

In the context of the war, the military officials' account of "finding" the children in the mountains should be cause for skepticism. The area where Daniel was "found" suffered extensive military repression and massacres.[7] The oldest child apprehended in the mountains with Daniel's group was thirteen years old, and neither he nor any of the other children were able or agreed to give the army or social workers at the orphanage information about the location of their parents or names of their home villages. This could have been trauma, a language barrier, or simply a wise decision. Soldiers were known to force captured teenagers or children to lead them back into the mountains to hideouts of massacre survivors or guerrilla fighters. Soldiers then massacred the whole group, along with the child guides. Children, even those who spoke Spanish and were old enough to communicate, had good reason not to name their parents to soldiers. If their parents survived attacks, in many cases they could not or would not dare search for their children in state-run orphanages. Adoption files regularly note that "no relative has appeared to claim the child," as if this were strange during a war that was in large measure conducted as state terror. Both children's reticence or traumatized silence and parents' inability to or fear of attempting to recover their children are cited in adoption files as the legal bases for declaring children in a state of abandonment and thus eligible for Guatemala's international adoption program.

There are further peculiarities in the story army officials told about Daniel, at least as recorded by the social workers. If the children were truly abandoned in the mountains, why would such a large group have remained together? Even nuclear families often separated after an attack, in the panic of flight. Why would older children, who by all accounts were not siblings, carry around one-year-olds? Why were military officials never named in any of the documents included in adoption files, when the names of each social worker, judge, and orphanage director involved in each case was carefully recorded? One alternative to the narrative of abandonment provided by the official documents is that military officials brought children they spared to orphanages. Even if the particular soldiers who dropped off infants were not directly responsible for orphaning or separating those children from their families, army officials almost certainly were. Dropping off babies and infants with social welfare bureaucrats was then a second step in their forced disappearance.

The Ministry of Social Welfare was in close contact with the army throughout the war, especially as it expanded services and facilities into conflict areas beginning in 1982. Contacts went beyond what is recorded in the ministry archives, as I learned by interviewing a social worker named Licette Morales. Morales, a forthcoming and pleasant person, welcomed me into her office in the family courts in downtown Guatemala City. As a young woman in the early 1980s, Morales landed a job as a social worker with the Ministry of Social Welfare in Guatemala City. Like most of her colleagues, she was trained at the school of social work at the University of San Carlos, Guatemala's leading public university. Morales was utterly confident in her ability to distinguish which families were capable of taking care of children and which were not. She checked to see if there were dirty dishes in the sink when she arrived for unannounced home visits, and she talked to neighbors. "In a visit one observes not just the economic level but also how they live, if the house is hygienic, if it is neglected. The job was noticing a lot of detail." She acknowledged that house visits were "delicate" because "we had in our hands the future of the children." I asked if she used the same standards to judge Indigenous and non-Indigenous families. "Everyone has their dynamic and their way of life," she answered. "In San Martín de Jilotepeque," a Kaqchikel community, "they sleep on the floor and they are fine like that. They have always lived that way." Morales said that the war interrupted the usual practice of house visits for children being considered for foster or adoptive homes and made documenting the adoption process difficult. "They burned civil registries," she recalled. "There were no documents or anything." Because she lived in the capital during what was essentially a media blackout, Morales was mostly insulated from knowledge of massacres in the early 1980s. She only realized the extent of the violence through trips she made to the areas surrounding Guatemala City on behalf of the Ministry of Social Welfare. In San Martín Jilotepeque after a massacre, for example, a woman told Morales that she only survived the army sweep by hiding under her bed with her children.[8]

Morales surprised me by mentioning something that did not appear in ministry files. After massacres, the army called the Ministry of Social Welfare to pick up babies and children in more remote areas, like the Petén jungle. She did not go on those longer trips, she said. She heard about them from colleagues, especially a social worker named Irma Mijangos. Morales recalled, "Irma said that they flew to an encampment on military planes after a massacre because the soldiers had picked up children. They didn't have any way to bathe and slept in tents. And then they came with some children."[9] Morales said she did not remember how many children the ministry's social workers picked up, or if they ended up in orphanages, foster homes, or placed in adoption. She recalled Mijangos telling her about one trip to the Petén, an area of extensive army massacres. (Mijangos died shortly before I interviewed Morales, so I was unable to confirm this account.) One person who has been very forthcoming on this point is former army chief Benedicto Lucas García, who has since been sentenced to fifty-eight years in prison in several war crimes cases—including cases involving disappeared children. He is the brother of former president Romeo Lucas García, who escalated the violence of the armed conflict in the highlands during his time as president, 1978 to 1982. In an interview for a documentary film, Lucas García recalled that the army "collected children [recogió niños]" for "humanitarian" reasons.[10] Disappearing children was a war crime that hid in plain sight, in the sense that some military officials openly bragged about "saving" children.[11]

In Daniel's case, army raids were carried out near Quetzaltenango, where there was a state orphanage to which military officials could bring the children directly, without calling on social workers to transport them. He passed instead from a local orphanage into the adoption program in the capital. In order for Daniel to be adopted, he had to have a birth certificate. The bureaucratic steps for a child to be legally adopted were not changed or simplified during the war, though the wartime unavailability of documents and impediments to travel were likely a further incentive to falsify documents or otherwise cut corners. In July 1985, a social worker from Quetzaltenango requested a birth certificate under the name Daniel "(without last name)." The birth certificate did not list any information about his parents and provided a fabricated date for both his birthday (1 October 1981) and place of birth (Quetzaltenango). The paperwork also stated that Daniel's was a single birth rather than twins or triplets, which the social worker had no way of knowing. The social worker also made up a birth weight for Daniel, though in the space to fill out his hour of birth she wrote "unknown."[12]

For the adoption to proceed, Daniel had to be declared in a state of legal abandonment by a family court. Given wartime conditions, the standard of proof necessary to prove that a child was "abandoned" and without surviving family members was exceedingly low. In Guatemalan adoption files, social workers disapprovingly designated any arrangement in which a child did not live with both birth mother and birth father as a "disintegrated family." This term made the circumstance sound natural, perhaps the fault of the birth mother or other individual family members, although families as often as not "disintegrated" under the pressure of extreme poverty or violent attacks during the war.[13] Family courts and social workers even before the conflict interpreted "state of abandonment" with a great deal of discretion. As the war became more violent and chaotic, they no longer uniformly required the proof of consent that had provided some protections, however bare and frequently contravened, to birth parents.

On 26 November 1985, social worker Aura Maldonado Castillo wrote a petition to the family court about Daniel and one of the other children found with him. These petitions were formulaic and generally concluded with a category called "concept of the social worker" in which they made recommendations to family courts. Castillo wrote that since Daniel was "an abandoned child who lacked family members who could take care of him I consider it expedient that he be included in the Program of Adoptions of the Ministry of Social Welfare so that through that program he be integrated into the society to which he belongs, and his physical and emotional development occur within a family."[14] Castillo's bureaucratic boilerplate was darkly ironic given Daniel's disappearance from his Indigenous community. The court approved this petition, facilitating Daniel's passage from an Indigenous community in Guatemala into "the society in which he belongs," which turned out to be placement with a family in the United States.

On 18 November 1984, an "adoption consultant" for an evangelical Christian agency based in the United States had contacted the Ministry of Social Welfare on behalf of a couple who wished to adopt. The couple filled out a form called "Application for International Adoption," required as a first step. Under "motive for the application" the couple wrote, "For a 3 year old from Quetzaltenango."[15] An orphanage official had likely already identified Daniel to this couple as a potential match. The couple, like all would-be adoptive parents, were required to submit an application for adoption, along with a "social report" written by a U.S.-based social worker, a certificate of mental and physical health, birth certificates, criminal records, passport-sized photos, summary of income and goods, and three recommendation letters attesting to their "moral and financial fitness." The couple also filled out a form stating their gender and age preferences for the child they wished to adopt, which included the section for "other details." Like couples seeking children during the early years of the adoption program, both Guatemalans and foreigners continued to use the "other details" space to request children who were white or light-skinned, even though such children were in ever-shorter supply in Guatemalan orphanages as the genocidal violence escalated.[16] One Guatemalan couple wrote to the orphanage in 1984 that they would adopt a child of either sex "of light brown skin, who is not of indigenous origin." Also in 1984 came a request for a child "preferably of Spanish type rather than Indian."[17]

The couple interested in adopting Daniel completed the paperwork and began sending the orphanage photographs of themselves and their home in the United States in March 1985.[18] By the time the social worker requested that the family court declare Daniel abandoned, this family had already expressed their intention to adopt him. The adoption file can be read, at least in part, as an after-the-fact justification of an adoption that was already a fait accompli. The family court was slow to process Daniel's case, and Castillo took her request for a declaration of abandonment to several judges in Quetzaltenango. On 22 April 1986, her petition was successful, and Daniel was transferred from the orphanage in Quetzaltenango to the Elisa Martínez Orphanage.

Daniel's transfer paperwork contained slightly more detail about his past, but it seems the social worker filled out those details with what she imagined to be the case, or what she thought might speed finalization of the adoption, not through renewed contact with the military officials who brought Daniel to the orphanage. The social worker wrote: "[Daniel] lacks a family group, because the parents of the minor died during the time of conflict in the Department of Huehuetenango . . . During his stay at the Quetzaltenango Orphanage no family members or persons who knew him presented themselves for a visit."[19] Ministry of Social Welfare bureaucrats did, however, investigate further. In an undated recommendation for adoption—archived between other documents in a position suggesting it was written in 1985—another social worker wrote: "During his stay at the orphanage, no person has claimed the minor. In addition, the Social Worker who visited the places near where the child was found did not find any trail of family members or people who indicated the origin of the minor."[20]

Other case files also showed that social workers at the Ministry of Social Welfare did sometimes try to visit the places of origin of children they intended to put up for adoption, even in war zones. But Indigenous people often took several years to begin venturing back to villages that had been attacked, or to overcome their fear and approach military bases to search for their missing children. During the genocidal period of the war, the army created conditions of fear that made it extremely unlikely that older children would share whatever information they had, if any, about the names or locations of their parents. It is unsurprising that no kin presented themselves at the orphanage in Quetzaltenango, let alone in the capital, to reclaim Daniel. That social workers spoke only Spanish was an additional limitation to the searches, and the adoption file contains no further information about how the ministry's social worker might have searched for the family. Daniel's family had perhaps been killed, or fled: it is impossible to know from the existing records. After the Ministry of Social Welfare deemed Daniel officially abandoned, his adoption was finalized on 4 April 1986. He traveled immediately with his new adoptive parents to the United States. Despite initial delays in Daniel's case, the time elapsed between the application and finalization of the adoption was two years: from April 1984 to April 1986.

Other adoptions arranged during the same period show international adoptions going forward despite social workers acknowledging the existence of surviving kin in Guatemala or Mexico. In 1985, social workers deemed two Indigenous brothers, also from Huehuetenango, "abandoned" and thus eligible for adoption because their father was an "apparently disappeared entity."[21] This was bureaucratese for a massacre victim. In this case, unusually, the boys' grandfather did travel to the orphanage to collect them. But the director turned him away, saying that if he wanted to regain custody of his grandsons he would have to return with proof of kinship. Many Indigenous families, especially those who lived in remote areas, did not have the cash or means of transportation to travel to municipal capitals to request birth certificates. To fill out paperwork at a civil registry after a birth was the privilege of people who lived in larger towns or cities and who spoke Spanish. Either the grandfather did not have the necessary paperwork, or the war prevented him from safely returning to the orphanage. Either way, he was unsuccessful in reclaiming his grandsons. Their adoptions by a U.S. family were finalized on 3 June 1986. Another boy was given in adoption despite the fact that social workers recorded in his file that his birth mother was living in Mexico, likely in a refugee camp.[22] They made no attempt to contact her.

Family members had to back up a claim with official paperwork that Indigenous families were extremely unlikely to possess, but the word of an army official, however dubious, was sufficient to declare abandonment and place a child for adoption. The government approved adoptions even when reuniting a child with family members was a clear possibility. An infant girl from the area of Chajul—a notorious massacre site in the Indigenous Ixil region—was brought to a hospital in Quetzaltenango in 1983 with a bullet wound. A colonel visited her in the hospital and told social workers she was an orphan whose parents had died "in a confrontation with guerrillas." The parents may have actually died in a confrontation with guerrilla forces. Or the colonel may have lied to the social worker. It was much more likely in that time and place for the girl to have been orphaned in an army attack.[23] The social worker noted that "because of the young age of the minor it was impossible for her to provide any information about her family. No one claimed her during her time in the orphanage, and for this reason she is considered an abandoned minor." On the strength of the colonel's word, the Ministry of Social Welfare declared the girl abandoned and placed her for adoption with a U.S. family.[24]

Massacres continued, though they became less frequent after a return to civilian rule in 1985. The number of Maya children in state orphanages, and their representation in the international adoption program, accordingly dropped. Social welfare programs contracted in size and funding after the coup that removed Efraín Ríos Montt in 1983. Social workers, judging from adoption files, mostly returned to their original work of arranging the adoptions of the children of destitute mothers from areas surrounding the capital, rather than children from Indigenous communities in the highlands. The pattern of assigning children to foreign rather than Guatemalan families, however, continued, as did doctoring adoption files to justify outcomes social workers saw as desirable, even when meaningful consent from birth families, especially birth mothers, was lacking.

Every Repressive Regime

Novelist Margaret Atwood wrote of the many histories that inspired *The Handmaid's Tale:* "The control of women and babies has been a feature of every repressive regime on the planet."[25] Controlling reproduction and children takes different forms in different places and times, but some patterns are striking. Adoptions in Guatemala in the 1980s echoed two dynamics recognizable in other places and times as well. The first pattern was the forced disappearance of children during wars and their theft by dominant political or national groups. The second was forced removal of Indigenous children from their parents and communities, justified as in the child's "best interests."

The first pattern, of wartime forced disappearance of children to remake them politically, racially, or ideologically, was perpetrated by twentieth-century totalitarian regimes, including Nazi Germany, Francoist Spain, and dictatorship-era Argentina.[26] The Nazi regime kidnapped children considered "racially valuable" and arranged their adoptions by "Aryan" families.[27] The Nazi kidnapping project began as a social welfare program called Lebensborn, or "font of life." Founded in 1935, it provided services for unwed German mothers considered "racially pure" and arranged adoptions for their babies. Under the direction of Heinrich Himmler, Lebensborn expanded as Nazi Germany occupied countries across Europe. In 1939, the Nazis began kidnapping children from other countries for the program. Social workers assigned children German names, instructed them to forget their pasts, and placed them with foster or adoptive German families. The Lebensborn program ran orphanages, often in confiscated Jewish nurseries, in France, Austria, Poland, Norway, Denmark, Belgium, the Netherlands, and Luxembourg. Just before the end of the war, authorities burned the Lebensborn adoption files, so it is impossible to know how big the system was, though historians estimate at least 9,200 children passed through Lebensborn orphanages.[28] It is clear that Lebensborn was part of a wider eugenic plan to "Germanize" Europe. The postwar Nuremberg trials, which included evidence on Nazi kidnappings, helped shape the eventual inclusion of forced adoptions as part of the legal definition of genocide.

During the Spanish Civil War (1936–1939), government forces abducted thousands of children from imprisoned or murdered Republicans. The military's top psychiatrist, Antonio Vallejo Nájera, argued that Marxists had been infected by a "red gene" and were not fully Spanish in a racial sense.[29] Franco authorized medical experiments on prisoners of war to "search for a genetic susceptibility to Communism."[30] According to Vallejo Nájera, the only way to prevent the racial degeneration of Spain was to remove children from communist environments at an age when they were still malleable. In addition to this little-known fantasy of racial paranoia, the main purpose of appropriating Spanish children was to ensure their political loyalties and ideological orientation.

After winning the war, the Francoist government demanded the return of more than 30,000 Spanish children evacuated by the Republic to left-wing foster families in France, Britain, and the Soviet Union. Repatriated Spanish children were featured in Francoist propaganda about reclaiming the future of the nation.[31] Franco's government destroyed birth records and changed the names of repatriated children to give them new, noncommunist identities and prevent reunification with their parents or other politically suspect family members.[32] Changing Catalan or Asturian names to Castilian names also blotted out children's previous identities.[33] In Spain, some children were given in adoption to Franco's supporters, while others were housed in Catholic boarding schools administered through a welfare program called Auxilio Social, or Social Aid. "First the fathers are shot, then the children get charity," observed a political dissident at the time.[34] The process of illegal adoptions and child trafficking persisted after the Spanish Civil War throughout the 1980s, and took a commercial turn with children given or sold illegally into adoption in the tens of thousands.[35] As in Guatemala, Spanish adoptees searching for the truth of their origins may find that they were part of a lucrative business, the victims of war crimes, or both.

The best-known cases of disappeared children in the Americas were those forcibly disappeared by the military dictatorship in Argentina (1974–1983). Military officers stole as many as 500 newborns and young children from disappeared parents accused of "subversion," meaning support for the guerrilla groups attempting to overthrow the dictatorship.[36] The children's identities were erased or changed, and they were handed over or sold to childless military and police couples, or to those who supported the regime. "It was rare for a pregnant detainee to survive," wrote Marguerite Feitlowitz in a harrowing book based on survivor testimony. "Most were killed soon after giving birth, and their babies sold to 'proper' couples." "Proper" couples were noncommunist. According to the 1984 National Commission on the Disappearance of Persons report, "The repressors who took the disappeared children from their homes, or who seized mothers on the point of giving birth, were making decisions about people's lives in the same cold-blooded way that booty is distributed in war."[37] In language strikingly similar to that of Guatemalan military officials who called Indigenous children "bad seed," Argentine authorities described the babies they disappeared as "seeds of the tree of evil."[38]

When Argentina's former dictator Jorge Rafael Videla was sentenced to prison in 2012, it was not for the disappearance, torture, and murder of adults but rather for disappeared children placed in forced adoptions. Prosecution for the theft of children was a loophole left in a general amnesty for wartime crimes passed by the civilian Argentine government in 1983. The Mothers and Grandmothers of the Plaza de Mayo (Madres y Abuelas de la Plaza de Mayo)—an activist group famous for marching in front of the Presidential Palace in Buenos Aires wearing white kerchiefs embroidered with their missing children's names—created a DNA bank to match stolen children to their original families. The Abuelas have kept the issue of disappeared children at the center of postwar reckoning in Argentina, while in Guatemala a parallel history has mostly remained silenced despite the best efforts of activist groups.[39]

In Argentina, military officials kept captured subversive women alive in camps long enough for them to give birth to children who were then stolen, their mothers killed. In Guatemala, the army massacred men, women, and children alike without any temporary reprieve for pregnant women. Argentina and Guatemala's disappeared children met different fates in part because of the racial makeups of the two countries. In Argentina, the military dictatorship relied on domestic adoptions. The "white" (in Latin American terms) son or daughter of a murdered subversive could be more easily assimilated into a right-wing Argentine family than the Maya child of a Guatemalan *campesino* could be assimilated into a high-ranking military family in Guatemala. Children who might appear to be sons and daughters in Argentina would be perceived instead as domestic servants in Guatemala. Relatively light-skinned stolen children like Oscar Ramírez, who were raised by military officials pretending to be their real parents, seem to have been the exception rather than the rule in Guatemala.

In Nazi Germany, Francoist Spain, and dictatorship-era Argentina, children represented politically and racially salvageable future citizens who could still be valuable to the state or to "loyal" or "proper" families through domestic adoptions. In Guatemala, a proportion of wartime domestic adoptions followed this pattern. But larger numbers of children were killed, coerced into unpaid labor, or placed for adoption abroad. In this sense, wartime treatment of Maya children in Guatemala bore an even more conspicuous resemblance to the second pattern of adoptions: forced separation and theft of Native children in countries including the United States, Canada, and Australia, among many others.

In the United States, changing the identities of Native American children was also part of a broader genocidal attack.[40] Beginning in the late nineteenth century, the white settler government forcibly removed tens of thousands of Native American children from their families and placed them in boarding schools to teach them to be white, Christian, "civilized" citizens.[41] Children who resisted whitening re-education or displayed what schoolmasters considered "Indian" behavior were whipped.[42] When most boarding schools were closed in the early twentieth century, they were replaced by very high rates of foster care and adoption placements of Native American children with white families.[43] Social welfare theories of the time developed by white social workers held that separating Native American children from the poverty and "social pathology" of their communities was in the best interests of the child.[44] A similar history unfolded in Australia, where the so-called "Lost Generation" of Aboriginal children were removed from their parents and forced to assimilate into white Australian culture. Historian Margaret D. Jacobs showed that allegedly benevolent state policies of child removal in both the United States and Australia actually served settler colonial projects of consolidating control over Indigenous peoples and their lands.[45] Social workers' justifications for adoptions in Australia were similar to those in Guatemala: assumed deficiencies of families, especially when they were not structured as an intact nuclear family. In the United States, social workers also removed Native children at will from their families, with similar justifications. A woman named Mary Crow Dog recalled that Lakota children were placed with white families throughout the 1950s and 1960s, even in cases where parents or grandparents were willing and able to take care of them, "but where the social workers say their homes are substandard, or where there are outhouses instead of flush toilets, or where the family is simply 'too poor.'" Mary Crow Dog concluded, "A flush toilet to a white social worker is more important than a good grandmother."[46]

Canada's similar history shows that this was and remains a feature of settler colonialism and social work in many times and places, not an isolated set of abuses. The residential Canadian school system was designed by the Canadian government and administered by churches from the 1880s to 1996, a period during which the government separated 150,000 First Nations children from their families. Students were housed apart from siblings and prohibited from speaking their own languages or otherwise acknowledging their original cultures. Physical, sexual, and psychological abuse by staff was rampant. Children at some schools were punished with electric chairs. A 2012 Truth and Reconciliation Commission found the schools had perpetrated "institutionalized child neglect," and called the child separations a form of "cultural genocide." The commission wrote that the government feared that "if the children were not educated" into a white identity "they would be a menace to the social order of the country," attitudes sounding much like those expressed toward the Maya family in Guatemalan military records from the 1980s.[47] As in the United States, Canadian residential schools were gradually replaced by high levels of fostering and adoptions of First Nations children outside their communities.[48] In the early 1960s, the government granted white Canadian social workers jurisdiction over First Nations areas, where they began the systematic removal of at least 11,000 children from their birth families. Seventy percent were adopted by white, mostly middle-class families.[49] This was known as the "sixties scoop," and has only recently been acknowledged by the Canadian government as an attempt to erase Native identity.[50] Again, social workers were key players. First Nations scholar Raven Sinclair wrote: "The white social worker, following on the heels of the missionary, the priest and the Indian agent, was convinced that the only hope for the salvation of the Indian people lay in the removal of their children."[51]

Families in the United States, Canada, and Europe—even those acting with the best of intentions—were unknowingly complicit in anti-Indigenous violence in Guatemala that echoed these earlier patterns of political violence and colonial child separations around the globe. Forced disappearances of children involved webs of complicity, acquiescence, and ignorance that strung together army officials, social workers, adoption agencies, and Guatemalan and foreign families—extending well beyond the borders of Guatemala. Truth Commission workers, families of the disappeared, and Guatemalan activists have struggled mightily to document and raise awareness of the forced disappearances of children and their forced removal from Indigenous communities during the war. GAM, the Group for Mutual Support, was joined in 1992 by the Association of Family Members of the Detained and Disappeared of Guatemala (FAMDEGUA) in the work of denouncing disappearances and supporting exhumations and proper burials. But despite their best efforts, the forced disappearances of children and their theft from Indigenous communities are not crimes that can be easily reversed or redressed. Even when children are found, those who were adopted abroad or removed from Indigenous communities often lack the language skills to communicate with their families. A sad irony is that on their initial request forms for children, foreign families sometimes listed humanitarian concern for the war-torn nation of Guatemala as one reason for their wish to adopt. In a preliminary report, a U.S.-based social worker noted with approval that the couple who adopted Daniel planned "to equip him or her with a good sense of the adoption by sharing as much as they can of the child's cultural heritage by reading about Guatemala."[52] The family also planned to learn Spanish, unaware it was not Daniel's native tongue.

8

Inside Private Adoptions

Forced disappearances of Maya children as part of the genocide were the darkest chapter of adoption history in Guatemala. In Spain, decades earlier, forcible adoptions motivated by fascist ideology had also become a money-making proposition, and for-profit adoptions persisted even after the death of General Francisco Franco in 1975. In post-genocide Guatemala, too, demand for adopted children and the practices developed to facilitate forcible adoptions carried over, in somewhat different forms, into commercialized private adoptions.

Adopting with the help of a private adoption lawyer in Guatemala was much more expensive than adopting from a state orphanage, but vastly more popular. After legalization in 1977, private adoptions quickly outstripped their state-run counterparts. Adoptive parents preferred private adoptions because they were faster, and because lawyers were free to look for exactly the kind of child they wished to adopt. Nearly thirty thousand children were adopted to the United States alone through the private system before it was closed. The cost of private adoption varied wildly, depending on the lawyer, but rose sharply over time. In the early 1980s, one lawyer charged US$3,500 per child, though adoptive parents paid additional overhead costs to adoption agencies.[1] By 1997, the lowest fees were around US$13,500 per child and higher fees were around $21,500. By 2007, the year before private international adoptions were discontinued, adoptions could cost up to $40,000 per child—about $58,000 in today's dollars.[2] Private adoptions could take as little as three to six months to be finalized. Adoptions through the Ministry of Social Welfare could take up to two years. The speed of private adoptions, especially prized by non-Guatemalan families, helped crowd out slower adoptions through the state system. Adoption files show that the numbers of children adopted from public orphanages plummeted as private adoptions skyrocketed from the 1980s to the 1990s.[3]

Private adoptions are more difficult to trace than adoptions from state orphanages. Adoptions arranged through lawyers were notarial procedures, so they didn't leave a record like the state adoption files at the Ministry of Social Welfare. At the end of each year, Guatemalan lawyers are required to file the records of all their notarial procedures at the Archive of Notarial Registers (Archivo de Protocolos), a pleasant, plant-filled archive in downtown Guatemala City. Through an expensive and slow system of requests, it is possible to consult microfilm records of lawyers by year. It would be theoretically possible, though take several decades, to find out how many adoptions each lawyer performed if—and this is a big if—lawyers had followed the rules and filed their paperwork as they should. Many never sent their records to the archive, an infraction for which they are supposed to pay a minimal fine.

Archival records of private adoption are difficult to access but, to my surprise, many of the lawyers I contacted in Guatemala City—even those who had been investigated for adoption fraud—were willing to be interviewed. They admitted that there were problems with private adoptions, but insisted their hands were clean and the cases they had worked on "humanitarian." For proof, in our conversations many pointed to the difference in material circumstances between adoptive and birth families, presenting private adoption as necessarily a good deed, since it transferred a Guatemalan child from a poor home to a rich one. Some adoptions had, perhaps, been "just a business," but on the whole the lawyers shared, or at least expressed, the view that international adoptions as a whole had been unfairly maligned. The strong implication was that they had been unfairly maligned, too.

The sets of records I consulted at the Archive of Notarial Registers tended to be just a few pages of legal boilerplate finalizing adoptions, not the entire adoption file with a social report attached. During interviews, I asked lawyers whether they still had copies of full files, and whether they would be willing to show them to me. In every interview but one, the lawyers declined. Some said they had destroyed the files or turned over all copies to the archive. Others very reasonably cited privacy concerns. The only lawyer willing to show me his files, an archive of over ten thousand pages, was Fernando Linares

Beltranena.[4] He had worked on hundreds of adoptions, mostly from the late 1980s through the early 1990s. Linares Beltranena said he was fully confident about the legality of his adoption paperwork and happy to share. In fact, he said, he had been working on his own "investigation" of how international adoptions had been banned in Guatemala. So, he wanted to share not just his own adoption files, but also a large number of newspaper clippings from the years leading up to the closure of international adoptions. "I've always loved the topic of adoption," he told me. "It's an intellectual challenge to understand the alternative cost of forbidden adoptions," which he characterized as "kids out on the streets as burglars and prostitutes."[5]

Whatever our differences of interpretation of the set of events we both studied, Linares Beltranena generously said that I could spend as long as I liked reading his files. He explained that while the law required he file his notarial records at the archive, he felt they would be "safer" in his own law office. He said that many lawyers do the same, and that in his case the fine was never levied. Linares Beltranena only asked that I protect the privacy of the children and adoptive families and birth mothers by not using their real names.[6] Then he had an assistant drag four carefully labeled blue bins of adoption files into a conference room. For several weeks, his fancy law office in Guatemala City became my office, too, as I sorted through the files. Unlike the bare-bones private adoption paperwork I consulted at the Archive of Notarial Registers, these files contained a wealth of information: correspondence, U.S. social workers' reports on adoptive families, Guatemalan social workers' reports on birth mothers with varying levels of detail, and follow-up reports on cases.

Reading this set of private adoption files gave glimpses—however frustratingly partial—into the lives of and choices available to the people most frequently left out of adoption histories: birth mothers. Linares Beltranena was right: I did not find anything illegal in his paperwork. Birth mothers had duly consented to relinquish their babies. Or at least that's what the paperwork said. Consent was right there, on signed forms. But as I read, it became less and less clear what consent really meant, under conditions of grinding poverty. The picture that emerged from the files and interviews with lawyers was that Guatemalan children were adoptable above all because their mothers were poor. Even in adoption files that appear not to have been falsified or otherwise tampered with, and despite incentives for lawyers to characterize relinquishment as voluntary, it is obvious that "consent" was highly questionable in situations of extreme economic pressure. Consent was a form rather than an agreement.

Pressure on birth mothers aroused suspicions even among those who worked in the adoption industry as it became more and more commercialized through the 1980s and 1990s. In interviews, lawyers and a psychologist who worked with a private adoption agency described "good mothers," who gave up their children for adoption so they could have a better material life, and "bad mothers," who they suspected of selling their children to profit-seeking lawyers. It bears repeating that the choices of birth mothers in Guatemala were severely constrained by poverty, racism, and misogyny. Anthropologist Diane Nelson writes, "At the same time as they are accused of overproducing children and thus undermining national progress, they enjoy limited access to information, material methods, or the domestic relations of reproduction that would allow them control of their fertility." As women who are materially poor, they suffer the presumption of wealthier people in both their own country and abroad that, as Nelson pointedly puts it, their children are "available," that "of course it is better to be raised in the United States than to sell Chiclets in the streets of Guatemala City."[7] This was certainly Fernando Linares Beltranena's view. Though ideas of what is considered a "good mother" vary, most are run through with misogyny. In interviews conducted after the war, sociologist Cecilia Menjívar found that violence against women, rooted in inequality, exploitation, and rigid ideas about gender roles, remained so normalized and routine that it was often not even recognized as such. She met several women who were fearful about seeking help for their sick children, worried about being branded "irresponsible mothers."[8]

Prejudices about good mothers versus bad mothers still seem to dominate understandings of international adoptions in Guatemala and abroad. Still, the circumstances structuring private adoptions—very permissive laws, social inequality within Guatemala, and a wide economic gulf between families in Guatemala and wealthier families abroad—were more powerful in structuring the international adoption market than the personal morality or decisions of individual mothers. The broader circumstances in which mothers attempted to care for their children, or chose or were forced to relinquish them, remain for the most part invisible in the adoption files. Lawyers cited extreme poverty, but in a way that was depoliticized, stripped of its causes.

Maybe God Had Put Those Desires in Me for a Purpose

Like Carlos Larios Ochaita, the lawyer who arranged early adoptions for state orphanages, Linares Beltranena's education abroad opened doors into the adoption business. An adoption agency in McMinnville, Oregon, first contacted him in the 1980s, he said. "They were looking for attorneys who were fluent in English who had a reputation for reliability and for honorability, which is very important as well. Not fly-by-night attorneys, of which there were many."[9] Following the overall trend in adoptions from Guatemala in the 1980s and 1990s, Linares Beltranena worked mostly for families in the United States.

He kept good records. His blue plastic bins were filled with folders, and each folder held the adoption paperwork for one family. The inside flap of each folder had a form, with spaces for personal information about the adoptive family and the child to be adopted, dates for the opening and closure of each case, and other details. It looked very similar to the standard cover form for adoptions from the Elisa Martínez Orphanage, except for a section on payment that listed blanks to be filled in for "honorarium," "advance," "received for expenses," and "form of payment."

Another difference was that would-be adoptive parents were required to sign a "Letter of Acceptance of Terms" in which they agreed to "contract his legal services to find a child or children for me or us." The contract stated:

> We understand that if the adoption cannot be completed for reasons not attributable to the Attorney's work such as that the Law is modified, that the mother changes her mind or does not wish to sign the adoption papers, that the child has a health problem such that the adoptive parents no longer wish the adoption to continue, fees sent in advance will not be returned because of the legal work already done, and the incurred expenses must be paid by the adoptive parents.
>
> I understand or we understand that if the adoption were not completed, the Attorney will do his best to do another adoption for the adoptive parent or parents and find me or find us a new child.[10]

Linares Beltranena told me that in the hundreds of cases he had facilitated, birth mothers changed their minds only a handful of times.

The key phrase in the form was: "find a child for us." In public orphanages, adoptive parents would be assigned a child already in state care. In the private system, they would have more choice and more likelihood of adopting younger infants and babies. Adoptive parents could note preferences in either system, but they were more likely to be accommodated in private adoptions. In Linares Beltranena's files, adoptive parents expressed an almost universal desire for adoptions to be as fast as possible. They often requested children as young as possible, and, as in requests to state orphanages, as white as possible. Slightly more families requested girls than boys, though, unlike requests related to race, they did not generally give a reason for gender preferences. In many ways, the requests were identical to those made by families when they first contacted state orphanages looking to adopt. The difference was that private lawyers were in a position to meet these desires for their clients.

Social workers at state-run orphanages tended to write back to prospective adoptive parents that they would have to be willing to adopt older or darker-skinned children, because those were the children available. The private lawyers instead sourced children specifically based on the requests of would-be parents. Linares Beltranena "specialized in babies," according to a North American who worked at an adoption agency that contracted with him.[11] Not all lawyers who arranged private adoptions worked this way. Hilda Morales Trujillo, for example, told me that she only began working private adoptions after a personal request from a Swedish aid worker who came to Guatemala after the 1976 earthquake, who didn't have money to pay fees for a private lawyer.[12] Morales Trujillo, a well-known women's rights activist and professor of family law who worked on both private adoptions and adoptions through the state orphanage, told me, "I tried to find a family for a child, and not the other way around."[13] But her approach was unusual.

Linares Beltranena, who is Catholic, worked with several U.S.-based adoption agencies, but he collaborated most frequently with PLAN Loving Adoptions Now, based in McMinnville, Oregon. PLAN Loving Adoptions Now was a Christian organization that arranged adoptions for evangelicals as well as people of a variety of mostly Christian faiths. (The group also arranged adoptions for nonbelievers, including some single mothers.) The organization, formed by a couple who had adopted from Vietnam, worked with children from Liberia, Vietnam, Cambodia, Guatemala, Peru, Colombia, Honduras, Haiti, and Mexico. A number of evangelical groups that arrived to do relief work after the 1976 earthquake helped forge the connections that later facilitated adoptions. This echoed Harry and Bertha Holt's approach in South Korea.

Religious studies scholar Soojin Chung calls the Holts "adoption evangelists" after the way they both evangelized for adoption in the United States and "accomplished traditional evangelism through adoption." After their adoption of a baby girl was finalized, one family wrote: "Fernando, we greatly appreciate your help at each stage of the adoption process. We believe God is using you in His work."[14]

Most evangelical Christian couples who adopted lived in the United States, but some had traveled to Guatemala to do missionary work. Adoption lawyer Dina Castro told me the story of meeting a North American evangelical Christian couple who had gone for a walk in Concordia Park near her office in downtown Guatemala City. Concordia Park has been a gathering place for the homeless and street children since at least the 1980s.[15] The couple met a pair of children who lived on the street with their mother and offered to bring them home to the United States. The young children begged their mother to let them go with the tall foreigners, according to Castro. And, in a phrase that is not entirely illuminating about consent, Castro said, "the mother gave us permission."[16]

One constant refrain in letters from clients to Linares Beltranena was: could he please speed up the process? Many of the couples described spending several years trying to get pregnant before deciding to adopt. There was no age ceiling for couples wishing to adopt in Guatemala, but advancing age was a common reason for a feeling of urgency. On 28 February 1989, one family wrote a note to a U.S.-based adoption agency worker that said, "Enclosed is a don't forget us letter that we would like you to take to the attorney in Guatemala when you see him." The letter explained that the adoptive parents had already set up a room in their house with a crib. "As you know, waiting is hard and we like to feel that we are doing something to help move things along. We have faith in your ability and hard work. You have been highly recommended by PLAN." Linares Beltranena responded on 9 May 1989, "Thank you for your letter. We have not forgotten you and have you on our list. Sometimes, we get many offers of children but then again we may pass weeks without an offer. We always have a list of parents so that we can process the documents immediately when we get a child. We have two prospects for June so bear with us and we shall do our best to help you."[17] Most of Linares Beltranena's private adoptions took only six months after the first expression of interest, whether the adoptive parents planned to pick up the child themselves or have the child delivered to the United States by a person vouched for by the lawyer. Castro told me that her adoptions took up to eight months and that she vetted adoptive parents, down to whether or not they had traffic violations.[18]

A few adoptive parents caught wind of cases of fraud and asked questions. In 1987, one couple wrote to Linares Beltranena:

> In talking a few days ago with [another adoptive family] she told us about the scandal in Guatemala in regard to another attorney who falsified some documents. . . . Is there any way of telling how this is going to affect the adoption program in the future? Are <u>we</u> entering into a situation that is not going to be resolved for more than six months or a year? Do you have any way of telling? Since my husband and I are already in our forties, and are eager to get a child as quickly as possible under the normal time frame, is this going to delay our getting a child for more than a year?[19]

This couple didn't seem to draw any connections between speed of adoption, falsified paperwork, and lack of meaningful consent. Other adoptive parents, too, tended to express concerns about their individual cases rather than seeing them as part of a larger system.

As in the state orphanage system, foreign couples were required to document "moral and economic solvency" to adopt a Guatemalan child. In practice, the emphasis was on economic solvency. As long as a couple could prove they had the economic means to adopt a child and had no criminal record, they were allowed to do so. Guatemala became popular among adoptive parents mostly because of speed and ease in the private system, but also because couples that couldn't adopt in the United States or elsewhere because of age or sexual orientation could adopt in Guatemala. Divorced and remarried couples, single women, and gay and lesbian couples all adopted from Guatemala.[20]

Linares Beltranena worked often, though not exclusively, with evangelical Christians. One single mother who wished to adopt "considered medical assistance with getting pregnant, but her Christian values preclude that type of medical intervention."[21] When interviewed by U.S. adoption agency workers about their reasons for adopting, couples cited their humanitarian values or, more often, their Christian faith. Examples from the case files include:

They both have an abiding belief in Jesus as Savior and want to teach their children about God and about Christian principles.

Both have been attracted to the concept of adopting a child from another country, each having a "global view of the world, and the world's needs."

[Name of adoptive mother] has longed for a girl in which to share her interests, beliefs, and time, and after much prayer she came to the realization that "maybe God had put those desires in me for a purpose. Maybe there was a girl in the world who needed a home, a mother, love, that God had designed to be part of our family."[22]

Adoption files were thick with expressions of faith, but, as is clear from the correspondence, Linares Beltranena was not really interested in the motivations of adoptive parents. He was more concerned with how to meet the demands of a new clientele. After all, this was a for-profit business.

Don't Ever Ask Me to Babysit

Private lawyers tried to grant their clients' wishes, but there was little they could do to cater to unrealistic ideas about race. Request forms show that age was the most common specification, followed by race and gender. Requests for "healthy children" were also common. (Linares Beltranena asked clients if they felt able to deal with "correctible" or "non-correctible" disabilities.) Some adoptive parents gave fairly open-ended responses on forms, requesting a child as young as possible, or "healthy, of either sex."[23] Others were more specific: a little girl, healthy, between zero and six months, "particularly stressed one as young as possible."[24] Adoption agencies sometimes told people that their wait for a child might be shorter if they were willing to adopt a boy, since demand for boys was lower. One couple wrote to Linares Beltranena: "We are happy to adopt either a boy or a girl. We understand that many parents prefer girls. Therefore, we have been told to expect to adopt a boy, which is fine."[25] Specific requests were also common, such as a woman who requested: "1) a male sibling group of toddler and infant or 2) male infant or 3) male toddler, not over 18 months old."[26] Linares Beltranena did try to honor requests to keep siblings together, but some were separated and placed with different families.[27] (There was no law requiring siblings to be given in adoption together, and they were sometimes placed separately from state orphanages, too.)

Linares Beltranena's files show that it was easier for him to give adoptive parents what they wanted when it came to gender than when it came to race. Many parents specified to adoption agencies that they wanted a Central American or South American child, not a Black child.[28] The threat posed to adoptees by racism in the home communities of adoptive families or within the adoptive family itself was rarely mentioned, though it occasionally came up in reference to requests for the lightest-skinned children available. A 1987 request from a U.S. adoption agency reads: "The [adoptive family], who live in a rural community with few racial minorities, are willing to parent a bi-racial (black / white) child, but recognize that they would have limited opportunities to provide meaningful and extensive exposure to Black culture and people. Consequently, they wish to pursue adoption through a private attorney in Guatemala."[29] Historian Barbara Melosh recorded a similar process in the United States, where white families were open to adoptions that crossed race, but with limits. "When Mr. and Mrs. M came to the bureau in 1964 hoping to adopt an American Indian child, their case workers showed photographs and recorded reactions." The case worker wrote, "They responded with sincere delight over the appearance of many of the Indian children in the pictures and seemed equally related to the child with the darker coloring, not seeming to pick out just the light color Indian." The case worker, wrote Melosh, "was mindful of the limitations that these adopters had expressed: they had considered the possibility of applying for a biracial (white and African American) child, but decided that this was not something they could undertake." She matched them with a "medium complexioned copper toned Indian." In letters to Guatemala, couples frequently made requests related to skin color but seemed either unaware or unconcerned about the difference between Indigenous and non-Indigenous children. One U.S. social worker's initial report in 1989 reads: "[Adoptive mother] lives in a melting pot area where there are Black, Hispanic, Asian, and other racial groups. A Guatemalan child would be likely to be well accepted there . . . [Adoptive mother] isn't especially concerned about color; however, in the future, she may move from her present location. If this should happen, a lighter colored child may be better accepted than a darker child."[30] Another file, from 1987, noted, "[The adoptive father's] parents were very much against the adoption, and made it clear that they would have nothing to do with [name of adopted child]. 'She'll never be my granddaughter,' stated [adoptive father's] dad. His mother added, 'Don't ever ask me to babysit.'" According to the file, the grandparents came around once their son arrived home from Guatemala with a baby girl.[31]

Many adoptive parents wrote that they wanted to maintain a connection with their adopted children's home country. One adoption agency worker wrote, "They have pictures of the birth family and Guatemalan home and plan to take the kids there some day." Another family told a social worker: "They plan to spend their time in Guatemala learning as much as they can about the culture and getting arts and crafts that they can decorate her room with. They have already gone to their local bookstore and have sought books on Guatemala." A social worker wrote of another family that they "are anxious to learn about the culture and heritage of Guatemala and want to help their Guatemalan child gain a sense of cultural pride. They have contacted a local family who have adopted two Guatemalan children and are planning to get together with them."[32]

For nearly all adoptive parents, the trip to Guatemala to pick up a child was their first and often only experience in the country, and their understanding of what they saw and experienced was often limited by a lack of language skills. A U.S.-based social worker reported: "The trip to Guatemala was special for [adoptive mother]. She arrived Monday evening and got [adopted child] on Tuesday morning. They spent the week in Guatemala City and traveled on Saturday to visit the city of Antigua. She found while sight-seeing there that some of the women were interested in [adopted child] and she was able to communicate a bit with them to explain that she was adopting her, etc. She said that it was a special experience and that she felt support from these women for her and [adopted child]. They traveled home on Sunday."[33] This woman did not speak any Spanish. Adoptive parents rarely met birth mothers but sometimes met foster mothers or babysitters who had cared for babies while adoption paperwork was finalized. Families either went to Guatemala City to simply pick up children and return home or followed an itinerary including Antigua, the picturesque former colonial capital, Lake Atitlán, and even Tikal—the spectacular Maya archaeological site in the country's northern jungle. Some lawyers included tourist trips as part of their adoption package.[34] According to several adoption memoirs, adoptive parents perceived delays in adoptions as bureaucratic hurdles set by corrupt officials, rather than attempted controls on a system that was coercive or corrupt as a whole.[35]

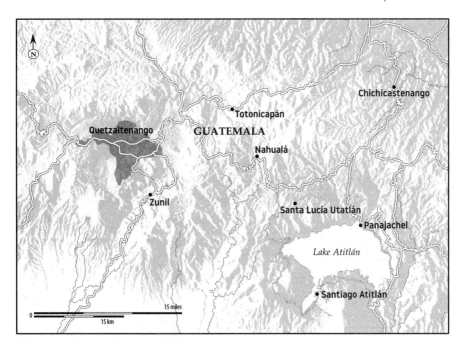

Lake Atitlán area, central Guatemala

She Cannot Fulfill the Obligations Imposed on Her

In Linares Beltranena's private adoption files, birth mothers are only mentioned in the social report put together by social workers on behalf of family courts in Guatemala. These reports were supposed to lay out the child's family circumstances and evaluate the birth mother's abilities to care for her child. They vary widely in their level of detail. But nearly all social reports make it clear that the decisive factor for relinquishments was poverty. Unlike children in state orphanages, children put up for adoption through the private system were only very rarely orphans or abandoned by their parents. Most birth mothers already had other children and did not have the resources to raise another child. Orphans were not an attractive proposition for lawyers. A birth mother could sign papers relinquishing her child for private adoption, but an orphan had to be declared abandoned by a judge, which would take longer. Privatized adoptions may have decreased the likelihood of true orphans finding adoptive homes by crowding out state-run adoptions.

What most unified the birth mothers was poverty, which was and is disproportionately suffered by Indigenous people. Linares Beltranena, in an interview, estimated that about 40 percent of the children he gave up for adoption were Indigenous. One of the few references to Indigenous children in Linares Beltranena's adoption files is this description of an adopted child: "Of Indian extract, his skin is olive."[36] The ethnicity of the birth mothers is not always clearly marked in private adoption files. But several indicators might roughly bear out the lawyer's estimate: name, town of origin, and occasionally photos of the birth mothers wearing *traje*—clothing typically worn by Indigenous women consisting of a woven patterned blouse tucked into a wrap skirt secured with a woven belt. (Not all Maya women choose to wear *traje*, since it is expensive and exposes them to discrimination.) Another adoption lawyer I interviewed, Jorge Armando Carillo Gudiel, also estimated that half of the children given in private adoption were Indigenous.

The notarial documents legalizing private adoptions contain minor variations on the same boilerplate explanation for why birth mothers relinquished their children. One reads: "The petitioner affirms that in spite of having done everything in her power, she cannot fulfill the obligations imposed on her by parental authority." This woman agreed to the adoption proceedings "so that her daughter has the opportunity to live in a home and to fully develop herself to become a person useful to society." The paperwork states that she is "completely confident in her decision to give up custody of her youngest daughter."[37] In this case from 1989, the Guatemalan social worker records that the child was assigned to a foreign family before she was born, because the father "didn't accept any responsibility" and the mother "also rejected her for economic reasons." The mother was Indigenous and worked as a maid, earning 100 *quetzales* (US$40) per month. She signed with a thumbprint. Though not all Linares Beltranena's adoption files contained invoices, this file did: the lawyer's fee was US$4,000. Room, board, and foster home care for a child as they awaited adoption was US$200 per month.[38] The total amount for this adoption was US$6,946.08. In other words, the total cost of the adoption was equivalent to what the birth mother could have earned working full time for fourteen and a half years.

Social reports in these private adoption files described extremely poor birth mothers, few of whom made more than the equivalent of US$2 per day. (Earning under US$1.90 in 2011 dollars is the most widely used global metric for extreme poverty.) In private adoption files, poverty appears as a problem for an individual or family, without political or social context. But even for those children who were not massacre survivors or war orphans, the circumstances of adoptions were intimately linked to U.S.-backed state terror—which caused a massive economic crisis in Guatemala in the 1980s—and U.S. support for the rollback of agrarian reform after the CIA-backed coup in 1954. For example, a social worker notes in a 1987 file that a birth father died as a result of malnutrition and respiratory failure. The birth mother was Indigenous, had not gone to school, and worked as a domestic servant.[39] This birth family was among several in Linares Beltranena's files who hailed from Santa Lucía Utatlán, a small, mostly K'iche'-speaking town near Lake Atitlán. (The number of adoptions from this town make it seem likely that he worked with a *jaladora* who either lived or had contacts there.)

A brief history of Santa Lucía Utatlán shows some of the circumstances structuring people's lives there that were not included in even the most scrupulously recorded adoption file. In 1978, a North American priest named Arturo Mertens came to preach in the village. He sympathized with liberation theology and helped found an agricultural cooperative to sell fish and wheat. People in the town later recalled the cooperative as a moment of possibility, their best chance to rise from extreme poverty. But the killings began soon after. The army accused the agricultural cooperative of being proto-communist. People in the town said that the Indigenous peasant organization CUC (Comité de Unidad Campesina) never had a base in the town but used it as a "waystation *[lugar de paso]*."[40] The CUC was separate from, but affiliated with, one of Guatemala's guerrilla groups—the Guerrilla Army of the Poor (Ejército Guerrillero de los Pobres). Such fine distinctions were lost on the Guatemalan army. The villagers' activism made them a target of the military, who viewed them as subversive, and unleashed scorched earth campaigns that destroyed corn and bean crops.

The army set up a permanent base in the town in 1980 and began borrowing the cars of some wealthier residents, returning them bloodstained after kidnappings and extrajudicial murders.[41] They forced the cooperative to disband in 1983, and people in the town were again plunged into extreme poverty. This pattern was repeated across Guatemala and Latin America—collectives were often suspected of being communist or proto-communist during the Cold War.[42] The army moved its base of operations to Chupol in 1983, ending the period of worst repression in Santa Lucía Utatlán, but not before it had destroyed lives and the economic hopes of many families.

Linares Beltranena's adoption file describes the town as "impoverished," without any further context. Despite severe poverty in Santa Lucía Utatlán, many people there chose not to give up their children for adoption despite the fact that this was known to be an option. One woman from the town, widowed when the army kidnapped and murdered her husband in 1983, was left with nine children. She recalled, "I suffered with my children. I was left without a cent, nothing, without even a cent." She began to take in laundry to wash at home to survive. She told an interviewer in 2003, "Now I am happy because my children are here with me. Two haven't married yet. One is a woman who doesn't have a husband, but now I'm not the one who is responsible for all of their needs anymore; now my children are responsible for the corn, our expenditures, and everything."[43]

Family Photographs

Unlike state adoption files, which usually just have pictures of babies or infants and adoptive parents, private adoption files sometimes contain photographs of birth mothers. These are very different kinds of photos. Couples from abroad are pictured, or staged, together. Birth mothers in Guatemala are shown pregnant, standing stiffly in front of bookshelves filled with leather-bound law volumes. They are turned to one side so their condition is visible, with their faces forward toward the camera. Many are in *traje,* the traditional Indigenous woven clothing. Some have frilly aprons on, the kind with deep pockets where women who work in markets keep their change.[44]

The gap between the relative wealth of adoptive families and deprivation of birth mothers is obvious from what is written in the reports, but even more so from the enclosed photographs. In Linares Beltranena's records, the photos tucked into adoption files are so similar that likely he or the U.S. agency told adoptive families what to send. Files usually contain a photograph of the couple, a family photograph including other children if they have them, and a few photographs of the family home itself, from the outside and inside. The couples are pictured in classic all-American situations, like sitting together at a picnic table on a front deck with their barbecue grill visible behind them. One couple sent a photo of the whole family out jogging together. Interiors feature bourgeois comfort. Pianos are a frequent fixture. One image is of a house with wall-to-wall plush carpeting, a fireplace, and a rocking chair in front of a window opening to a magnificent vista of Oregon mountains. The photos were an invitation to imagine a Guatemalan child in a luxurious place. According to testimony given by birth mothers at Edmond Mulet's trial, Ofelia Rosal de Gamas had a "viewer," a 1980s machine to show slide shows of photographs to women considering relinquishing babies.[45]

Adoptive families tended to be middle-class or rich, even by U.S. standards, which read as almost unthinkably rich in Guatemala. A Guatemalan social worker's reasoning for recommending adoption after visiting a birth family encapsulates the prevailing logic: the baby "comes from a home lacking everything, with few possibilities of being able to survive in the environment in which she was born, such that the opportunity that presents itself ensures her future in an advantageous way." While adoptive parents had resources—they were even wealthy beyond imagining in comparison to birth parents—the adoption itself could represent a significant financial burden. The follow-up report to this adoption recorded in oddly economic terms: "They appear to like both children and at this point feel very lucky to have them. The adoption was quite expensive for them and they had to sell some stock and take out a second mortgage on their home but they feel the children are worth it."[46]

Private adoption files usually included photographs of adoptees, and sometimes of birth mothers. These followed a different script. Babies, nearly always wrapped in white blankets, were held up by anonymous brown arms. The birth mother, foster mother, or babysitter holding the baby was almost always cut out of the frame. Birth mothers were usually photographed in Linares Beltranena's office. One of the only photographs I saw of a birth mother at home showed her standing outside a small wooden structure with a sheet-metal roof. Ears of corn hung over the lintel to dry, and two older twins—siblings of the child to be adopted—were in the background. Even seen from a distance, the twins were visibly malnourished. The mother was listed as Indigenous, and the social worker's report noted that she was "without schooling, domestic servant, and she is engaged in fieldwork like the planting and harvesting of corn and beans on a brother-in-law's land."[47]

Photographs of adoptive families served as a kind of visual enticement that lawyers and baby brokers used to convince potential birth mothers to relinquish babies. Linares Beltranena stayed in touch with adoptive families for years after adoptions were finalized, asking them for pictures of the adopted children. When one adoptive mother responded: "We thank God every day for being able to adopt this beautiful Little boy. . . . Please put this [photo] in [adoptive son's name's] file. Hopefully his birthmother can see this picture, and others we will send . . . as he grows up." Linares Beltranena wrote back: "Thank you for the pictures. They help us show the birth mother whenever she comes into the office how well her child is doing: they aid us in convincing other potential birth mothers that their children can be better off with an adoption and they also motivate us to continue doing our work with adoptions."[48] Birth mothers rarely returned to his office, Linares Beltranena explained to me. But he tried to stay in touch with them through *jaladoras* in case adoptive parents asked for their whereabouts later. He said that the best way to keep a current address on record was to send for them every once in a while, indicating that he would give them a bit of money if they showed up at his office. When you dealt with "people of that sort," he told me in an interview, "you have to give them a tip."[49]

Consent

For an adoption to take place, those who brokered it had to cross hard class boundaries in Guatemala, never mind crossing racial and class lines between the United States and Guatemala. Original contact was often made by baby brokers, or in situations that brought people from different walks of life into proximity, like domestic service. Linares Beltranena recalled adoptions as a useful option to "save" the children of women who did not want them:

> Sometimes the owners of the house where she is working call me up and say "Look, she is pregnant, and we know that you'll find a reputable home for the child, can you help her?" And so, we do. I'll tell you what I do. I take my album of photographs, and I show the photographs of kids, and say the child will be saved. We don't want to keep the child. If you send the child to your sister, back in El Quiché, we don't even know what's going to happen to the kid. Here, it would be adopted, have a much better life, and she says "okay, okay." But she is so embarrassed by having gotten pregnant that she just wants to give away the product. We take the child, as soon as possible, and usually arrange for her to go—not to a hospital—we usually arrange for a private clinic.[50]

He continued, "And then, once she signs all the papers, once it's set, she doesn't ask for any money. Then we give her money. Why? Because it's an act of charity.

It's not payment for the kid. We don't buy it. She had already made up her mind to give it."

More reliable than Linares Beltranena's memory, perhaps, were his adoption files, which don't necessarily tell of women eager to relinquish their babies for adoption. Instead, most were making a decision within the confines of acute poverty. Social workers' reports for private adoptions tended to be thin on details, but some had more information. One recorded that a birth mother lived in a dirt-road section of Villa Canales, a settlement on the outskirts of Guatemala City. She was *ladina* and could sign her name, shakily, in all caps. She recounted in detail to a social worker the story of why she relinquished her two youngest children for adoption in 1987. She already had two other children, eleven and eight years old, and they lived with a slightly better-off family member. Even so, the kids didn't go to school "because their extreme poverty hasn't permitted it."[51] The birth mother earned one *quetzal* a day making tortillas, and spent a third of her earnings to get from Villa Canales to the capital to sell them. The social worker recorded:

> She said that a passenger of the bus she takes every day told her that she could give her youngest children up for adoption, since the father flatly refused to recognize them, denying her any kind of help and leaving her. In the face of extreme poverty, she looked for a way to place the children, and was glad when she found a home interested in taking them in. She doesn't feel competent to feed them, dress them, or provide them with proper treatment in case of illness. She is proud of not having aborted them, which she could have done, she said. She gave them life, and now she is giving them the opportunity to grow up in a home that offers them a life of satisfactions. Her older children have suffered many limitations and, she said, "I don't want that for the little ones."[52]

Although her religion was not noted, the birth mother's view is in line with the views of many in Catholic and evangelical churches who see adoption as an excellent alternative to abortion, which in any event was neither legal nor safe in Guatemala.[53]

The social worker wrote that the birth mother's poverty was "sufficient reason" to approve the adoption. "Her situation reaches such an extreme that there were days that her children only ate tortillas. So she made the decision to give her third and fourth children up for adoption, because of their age. Therefore, it is considered that the adoption is favorable from every point of view." For the same reasons of extreme poverty, this birth mother wanted to give up her two oldest children for adoption, too, but learned that was impossible. It was difficult to place older children through the private adoption system, since most adoptive families wanted babies.

In some files, the anguish of birth mothers comes through strongly. A social worker wrote a report on one birth mother who had five children and was caring for them without the help of either of the two men who were their fathers. She consented to give up her two youngest boys for adoption. The social worker described the birth mother:

> —She dresses modestly, she wears discreet makeup. One perceives in her: physical and mental health. She can be considered of normal intelligence.

> —She states that she decided to give her children in ADOPTION, because what she earns is not enough to buy MILK FOR THE YOUNGEST CHILD. Since they are siblings, she thought they should remain together forever.

> —She appeared very TEARFUL, VERY TORMENTED, ASHAMED, but she recognizes that her decision will FAVOR HER CHILDREN because at her side they would have endured many hardships.[54]

If the social worker was disturbed by the birth mother's torment, she did not say so in the paperwork. She did write in her report that the children were in a position of "social disadvantage." In order to come to a decision about whether to formally recommend the adoption, she calculated what the birth families and adoptive families could offer in two lists. On the mother's side she listed: "extreme poverty; lack of family support; three other children to take care of; illiteracy; no work skills or training." On the adoptive family's side she listed: "parents; a home; protection; love and better opportunities in their life." The social worker recommended the adoption go forward. This happened to be one of the very few cases I consulted in which the birth mother was photographed holding her baby before the adoption. It is a disturbing and sad photograph to come across in the archive after reading about the mother's tears. When the adoption was finalized, she signed her consent with a fingerprint. This file contains a full invoice, dated 1 July 1987. The total expenses were US$3,392.65. Lawyer fees were US$3,500 per child. The total cost paid by a couple in the United States for the adoption of the two boys was US$10,392.65.[55]

Any thoughts adoptive parents may have had about birth mothers whose children they adopted are only rarely recorded in the adoption files. In one follow-up report for a different case, on the child's first birthday, one adoptive mother said "she felt great empathy for [name of adopted child's] birthmother, and wondered about her feelings on that day—was she sad, curious or remorseful?"[56] The two families, as was customary after private adoptions, were not in touch.

Resolving a Problem

Even a very complete archive cannot capture the dynamics that privatized adoptions introduced into Guatemalan life, as an interview with a retired psychologist showed. Ana María Moreno, an elegant and charming woman with short gray hair, worked at the Ministry of Social Welfare in the 1980s and then for a Swedish adoption agency that contracted directly with a private lawyer for several years in the early 1990s. As soon as a birth mother agreed to relinquish for adoption, the Swedish agency paid for a gynecologist, food, and a private hospital for the birth. The agency also provided pediatric care to the child as soon as they were born and paid a foster family to take care of the child until pickup.[57] (It was rare for adoptive families to claim a child directly from the hospital.) Moreno's job, she told me, was to visit birth mothers every month before relinquishment. Moreno recalled that of birth mothers she worked with, "the majority were domestic servants who had been raped. These are social problems you must be aware of." Her work also took her to brothels.

Moreno said that, at first, cases she worked on took five months "at the longest." She worked with the same agency for four years, until the Swedes decided to discontinue adoptions from Guatemala because of "distortions" in the process. Moreno recalled that around 1992 private adoptions "began to degenerate" as they became ever more commercial and corrupt. Other lawyers, she said, were able to use their connections or influence to speed up cases, "and ours went to the back of the cabinet." Moreno suspected that other lawyers were able to process private adoptions more quickly and easily if they were willing to pay bribes.

Moreno recalled one case from the late 1980s that, in her view, illustrated the change from humanitarian to commercial adoptions. A woman from an impoverished part of the capital had decided to give up her child for adoption. The Swedish agency paid for the birth in a private hospital. Moreno visited the birth mother regularly first at home, and then in the hospital. On her last day in the hospital, the birth mother changed her mind. "I regretted it," she told Moreno. Moreno said that she then "gave her the discharge papers from the hospital." The Swedish agency had the same policy as Linares Beltranena: if the birth mother changed her mind, she was entitled to stop the adoption and keep her child.

Some time later, Moreno said, "because of the human connection, I went to visit her where she lived." The mother was alone. The baby wasn't there. "She contradicted herself," Moreno said, when she asked what had happened to the child. "I was sure that someone had come up to her and said, 'Look, what are you doing? Why give it up for free when you can get money for that child?'" The mother never admitted it, but Moreno followed up—she wouldn't say how—and said she learned that the mother had "sold the baby" to a lawyer. "It was one of the irregular adoptions," she told me.

Moreno recalled other private adoptions in which she was proud to have participated. A woman from a city in the hot lowlands of Guatemala who worked as a maid in the capital had five children, all taken care of by her mother back home. In the early 1990s, she became pregnant again and felt she couldn't care for another child. She became even more worried when she found out she was expecting twins. "I can't do it," she told Moreno. "With the money I give my mother she can't support another child." When Moreno returned to visit the woman at the house where she worked as a maid, "They just about shut the door in my face." Moreno asked around in the neighborhood and found out that the woman was living two blocks away. ("People who work in *tiendas*," corner stores selling snacks and soda, "always know what's happening and where people are," she told me.) When Moreno knocked on her door, the woman said that her former employers had thrown her out, presumably for being pregnant. They threw her things out on the street, too. Later, the woman called Moreno to tell her contractions had begun. Moreno picked her up in a taxi and took her to the hospital, where she gave birth to twin girls. The adoption paperwork was swiftly finalized. Moreno noted proudly that the girls now belonged to minor nobility. She told this story to show how marvelous the adoption system could be when it "resolved a problem." But, according to Moreno, extreme economic differences could corrupt birth mothers even after the fact. When I asked if she stayed in touch with the birth mother, she said no. "We used to cut off contact with mothers because if not you opened yourself to manipulation of various kinds." She and her former colleagues worried that birth mothers might try to leverage their intimate connection with a foreign family for money.

Moreno also told me about the wild-card element that adoptions could introduce into Guatemalan family life. She said, "Now, I'm going to tell you a story," then took a long pause. "I won't say that it's beautiful, but it's interesting. A woman with a lot of money from the Guatemalan elite contacted the program." It was the late 1980s, and she told Moreno that recently she had "gone through some problems" with her husband, who was a doctor. She took her two daughters and went to live on their country estate. (Many of Guatemala's wealthy elite have a city home and a country home.) There she had an affair with a farmworker and became pregnant. She contacted Moreno and the Swedish agency because she was considering giving up the child for adoption. Guatemala is a small country, and Moreno said she knew perfectly well who the woman was. But, still, the woman insisted that they discuss the potential adoption together in the same room only if Moreno kept her back to her at all times, not looking her in the face. In the end, the woman found another solution. She gave birth to a baby boy, then called her husband and told him she was willing to reconcile with him, under one condition. A couple who worked the land, *campesinos,* had come to the country house, she said, and "given her their child [*regalado su niño*]."[58] She loved the child and would only reunite with her husband to rebuild their life together if he agreed to adopt the baby with her. A lawyer would arrange the paperwork. The husband agreed. A local couple who were farmers agreed to pose as birth parents at her request, to legally relinquish the child. And that is how, Moreno told me, a wealthy Guatemalan woman ended up legally adopting her own love child. If I had read about this case in an adoption file, rather than hearing about it from someone who was there, it would have been impossible to guess the truth.

Adoptions could introduce a sort of trapdoor into the family in Guatemala, obscuring certain truths about infidelity and premarital sex. Through both exploitation and expanded choice, adoptions allowed teenagers to return to school after extended absences, women to return from the capital to home villages seemingly child-free, the wives and long-time partners of absent migrants to appear to have been faithful. What kind of choice relinquishing children for adoption represented—and whether it was really a choice at all—depended on the realities of the lives of women dealing with unrealistic expectations about "good" motherhood combined with vulnerability to sexual violence and lack of access to any kind of reproductive health services—especially abortion. No doubt some women in Guatemala used adoptions to reshuffle their personal stories to tell a more convenient tale. These reshufflings were usually less dramatic than this last story recalled by Moreno, and undertaken by women in much more constrained circumstances. But it is a useful reminder that a birth mother was the protagonist of her own story, working within the possibilities—more or less coercive, more or less free—presented to her by the course of her life.

9

The Reckoning

It began with rumors. What if, instead of putting the children with foreign families for adoption the way they said they did, North Americans were actually cutting open the children, taking out their organs, and selling them off piece by piece? Starting around 1988, rumors of organ trafficking were on the radio, on television, in the newspapers. Neighbors were talking. A panic about *robachicos*, child thieves, spread hard and fast.[1] There were different versions of the "baby parts" rumor, but most featured foreigners said to run lucrative organ-selling rings. Maybe they even had help from Guatemalan government officials, according to some versions.[2]

There was never any proof that organ trafficking took place in Guatemala. But the rumor continued to circulate. It was entirely false, but plausible. Rumors can be false as fact, true as metaphor. For some Guatemalans, it was perhaps easier to imagine such violence than to believe that the children of poor, dark-skinned Guatemalans, lifted out of the country through adoptions, lived in middle-class white households as desired members of U.S. families. Guatemalans heard and read that children were disappearing when they sold snacks on city streets, when their mothers sent them out to buy tortillas, when they went out to gather firewood in the countryside, even when they were laid up in public hospitals. *Prensa Libre* reported that a newborn disappeared from its cradle in the Hospital Roosevelt while the mother slept. Police suspected the nurse, the last person to handle the baby.[3] The panic escalated into violent attacks on foreign travelers in Guatemala. Several tourists from the United States, Canada, and Japan wrongfully suspected of child theft were attacked by mobs.

Throughout the 1990s, Guatemala continued to climb the rankings of top sender countries in the world, easily surpassing—by number of children adopted—countries with much larger populations, like Russia and South Korea. Adoptions from Guatemala nearly doubled in the year before the attacks. From 1995 to 2005, U.S. families adopted 18,298 children from Guatemala, with the numbers going up nearly every year in that period.[4] In 2007, Guatemala sent more children abroad than any country in the world other than China. That year, one in 100 children born in Guatemala was adopted by foreign parents. Information about adoption fraud and abuses, especially in the private system—which had been common knowledge in Guatemala since at least the 1980s—had finally begun to appear in reports by international organizations and in foreign news outlets. International demand had helped keep Guatemalan adoption open for decades, but between newly enforced international conventions Guatemalan activism, the violent attacks, and several high-profile kidnapping-for-adoption cases, the Guatemalan government decided to definitively close international adoptions in January 2008.

Both false allegations of organ trafficking and real allegations of fraud focused attention and outrage on the private adoption system, not the government's history of forced disappearance of children. Still, without over-interpreting, much less justifying, the attacks, it is possible to read them as a sideways reckoning with state violence, exploitation of poor Guatemalans by local elites and North Americans, and the inability of the government to provide meaningful justice before or after the war. False rumors of organ trafficking spread at least in part because they expressed real dynamics of exploitation and impunity. The panic was one expression of what historian Deborah Levenson-Estrada called "inverse hegemony," an assumption that the Guatemalan government itself was "dangerous and alien," that it did not exist to protect citizens but to harm them.[5] If the officials said North Americans were adopting children, many might have had reason to assume they lied. Closing international adoptions ended some abuses, from kidnapping for commercialized adoptions to paying mothers for their children, but silenced rather than addressed other past abuses—providing impunity for those who stole children during the war.[6]

The baby parts rumor was false but seemed more credible because of real abuses in the adoption industry. Guatemalan-American journalist and writer Francisco Goldman, who lived in Guatemala City at the time, put it this way to the *Washington Post*: "Everything about the baby parts story is true, except for gringos and baby parts . . . Children get stolen all the time in Guatemala. But not for their organs and not by foreigners. The Guatemalans steal them for adoptions." Laura Briggs wrote of the panic, "children really had disappeared," but "perhaps the goal was to provide an alternative account about who was stealing children to the one many believed: that it was the military, government officials, and other illegal networks connected to them." "In a 'Third World country' like Guatemala," wrote anthropologist Diane Nelson, "how metaphorical *is* it to claim that a child has died because North Americans stole its organs?"[7]

From Rumors to Moral Panic

On 10 November 1988, one of the country's leading newspapers, *Prensa Libre,* published an article titled "Accusation in Europe against Guatemala for the Sale of Children: Children Found with Organs Extracted." It cited a European Parliament report on child trafficking that mentioned a police raid on *casa cunas,* private nurseries where children were held before adoptions were finalized. The newspaper used a phrase that sounded like it was lifted from Grimms' fairy tales: *casa de engorde,* or fattening house. The problem with the European Parliament report was that it only cited reports by local newspapers. And the problem with reports by local newspapers was that they only cited unverified gossip. At first, *Prensa Libre* reported that the police told them that two men who worked at the nursery said the children were bought from Guatemalan families for US$20 each and sold for US$75,000 to families in the United States and Israel whose children needed organs.[8] The two men may have been repeating what were essentially rumors, what they had heard or speculated might be the origin and fate of the children in their care. In any event, the police officer later retracted his statement—likely because there was no evidence of any kind. But to no avail. The false, scandalous original spread much farther than the correction. International news cited the European Parliament report, which cited local news, which cited the original discredited rumor, in a circle. The rumors gained credibility through repetition by local and international organizations—laundered into seeming true.

Rumors and reports of kidnappings for adoptions were not new, but organ-trafficking rumors were. The earliest they appeared in Central American archives was 1987. A Honduran newspaper quoted the head of welfare programs in that country, saying a raid on a house in San Pedro Sula found handicapped children from impoverished families. The families had been told the children would be given in adoption but instead were sold for $10,000 for organ transplants. The following day, the very same official issued a retraction, saying he had just repeated gossip heard from social workers. It was too late. This story and the story of the fattening house were frequently cited as official sources for the baby parts rumor, with the later denials omitted.[9] The story was picked up both in Central America and abroad, including by Soviet news outlets as a not-so-subtle metaphor for rapacious global capitalism. On 5 April 1987, a *Pravda* journalist wrote that "thousands" of Central American children were being transported to the United States, where their organs were removed for use by rich families. The Soviet state news agency TASS republished the story in various communist countries.[10]

Rumors move by word of mouth, but are also incorporated into written sources, jumping from the mouth to the page and back again. Even if rumors are entirely false, when they are considered credible by large numbers or powerful people, they can end up precipitating very real events, like the violent attacks on foreigners in Guatemala.[11] This is not to suggest that Guatemalans are particularly prone to rumors or in any way unusually "hysterical," as foreign reporting on the baby parts rumors often claimed. Violent responses to organ-trafficking rumors were no doubt shaped by recent experiences of an extremely bloody war and lack of access to meaningful justice. But this sort of reaction was not unique to Guatemala or Latin America.[12] On the contrary, rumors surface in archives and official reports all over the world. Headlines from the time described the atmosphere in Guatemala as a form of "hysteria" or "collective psychosis."[13] A longer view suggests it was a full-on moral panic.

The term "moral panic" was coined in 1972 by South African sociologist Stanley Cohen. He wrote that it is when "a condition, episode, person or group of persons emerges to become defined as a threat to societal values and interests."[14] The object of the moral panic does not necessarily present a threat proportional to the magnitude of the panic: "The 'thing's' extent and significance has been exaggerated a) in itself (compared with other more reliable, valid and objective sources) and / or (b) compared with other, more serious problems."[15] The object of the panic may be a substitute for another threat. Cultural theorist Stuart Hall showed these substitutions to be frequently racist: police drumming up a panic over muggings by young Black men in the United Kingdom, for example.[16] In Guatemala, "other, more serious problems" that did *not* cause moral panic included the forced disappearance of children during the war. A moral panic over organ trafficking was one way to address this still taboo, silenced history by highlighting the threat to children kidnapped around the capital—who tended to be *ladino*—rather than Indigenous children stolen by the government.

The moral panic may have been new, but rumors of child theft were at least as old as colonialism. Victor Perera, a Guatemalan author, wrote, "When Spanish conquistadors invaded the Guatemalan Highlands in the 16th Century, Mayan mothers believed the men with pale complexions and blond beards were anemic, and required the blood of brown-skinned infants to become well."[17] Army recruiters and plantation labor contractors who snatched children quickly became sources of fear. The baby parts rumor also echoed older rumors in Latin America and around the world about child abduction or ritual killing. The imagined bogeyman—or, often, bogeywoman—ranges from mythical creatures to real groups like Jews, as in the infamous blood libel, or Roma people. In Peru, a mythological figure called the *pishtaco* is a white man or a woman who steals children at night and sucks out their fat.[18] In some versions of the legend, the child fat is used to run machines in developed countries. A similar legend circulated in Mexico in the 1930s: children were stolen and killed, their "oil" used to run airplanes flown by North Americans.[19] Rumors of fat-powered machines draw on the gruesome and true history of conquistadors cutting up Indigenous bodies and using their fat to coat their own wounds and those of their horses, as told in Bernal Díaz del Castillo's chronicle of the Spanish Conquest.[20] White outsiders are a feature of many of these tales. Who might be considered "white" was a matter of local perspective. When dancer and civil rights activist Josephine Baker attempted to adopt an Afro-Colombian baby in the 1950s, there were angry demonstrations in the baby's home village. Her Colombian lawyer told Baker that, according to local legend, white people stole Black babies to drink their blood. Baker explained that she was Black, but the lawyer replied that in a rural Colombian context she was not. Her wealth made her white.[21]

Throughout Latin America, there have been allegations and rumors about child theft in Argentina, Bolivia, Brazil, Chile, Colombia, Costa Rica, the Dominican Republic, El Salvador, Guatemala, Honduras, Mexico, Paraguay, Peru, and Uruguay.[22] Rumors flared during moments of transition, economic downturns, and crises in international relations. In 1988, just as the baby parts rumor gained steam in Central America, a rumor circulated in Peru that men dressed like doctors were abducting children, removing their eyes, and selling them to pay off the soaring national debt. In 1995, a British traveler encountered another version of the *pishtaco* rumor, that the president of Peru was ordering the murder of Indigenous children, exchanging their fat to pay off the country's foreign debt.[23] The phenomenon was not confined to Latin America. As historian J. T. Way points out, the baby parts rumor exploded in Guatemala around the same time that panics about pedophiles, pornographers, and satanic ritual child abuse spread in the United States and Europe.[24]

The press helped fan the moral panic in Guatemala. In 1994, the largest newspaper, *Prensa Libre,* published a now-infamous graphic in the form of a butcher's chart. Modeled on a diagram of beef cuts, it showed what the newspaper claimed were prices in U.S. dollars for children's parts: liver for $100,000, kidney for $150,000, heart for $65,000, cornea for $2,500, set of heart and lungs for $125,000, pancreas for $90,000, bone marrow for $125,000, bones for $1,500. Such prices represented a fortune in a country where per capita income in 1994 averaged $1,300 and those in rural areas earned much less. *Prensa Libre* did not cite any sources or evidence, for the good reason that none existed. The newspaper claimed—again, without proof—that there was "considerable evidence" that organ traffickers were working with laboratories and private nurseries to extract children's organs "without fear of punishment or apprehension."[25]

Anthropologist Nancy Scheper-Hughes encountered a similar, if more localized phenomenon in 1987 in a shantytown in northeastern Brazil—a heavily Afro-Brazilian and marginalized region. After hearing rumors that children were being kidnapped for organ trafficking, she was assured by local coffin-makers and morticians that the rumors were false. Scheper-Hughes wrote that even if the details were unverified, or false, the rumors expressed deeper truths: "The people of El Alto," the shantytown, "can all too easily imagine that their bodies may be eyed longingly as a reservoir of spare parts by those with money." The rumors persisted and spread, she wrote, "because the 'misinformed' shantytown residents are onto something . . . refusing to give up on their intuitive sense that something is seriously amiss."[26] What they were "onto," wrote Scheper-Hughes, was that a market for medical transplants involved moving organs from the Global South to the Global North, from browner into whiter bodies and never the other way around. International adoptions from Brazil, though always on a smaller scale than in Guatemala, raised similar fears. Scheper-Hughes wrote that "by means of symbolic sub-stitutions," the rumors "confused the market in 'spare babies' for international adoption with the market in 'spare parts' for transplant surgery. Poor and semiliterate parents, tricked or intimidated into surrendering their babies for domestic and / or international adoption, imagined that their babies were wanted for fodder for transplant surgery."[27]

Politicians in Guatemala attempted to respond to the baby parts panic, but were divided over what it meant. Some members of Congress read the false rumors for indications of real abuses in the adoption industry while others saw them mainly as a threat to Guatemala's already damaged international reputation. Congressman Mario Taracena Díaz-Sol, who was involved in at-tempts to reform adoption laws, said that while "in regard to the adoptions of children . . . all kinds of anomalies have been discovered," for organ traf-ficking, "there is no proof that it is true." Taracena Díaz-Sol concluded that "what does exist is child-trafficking."[28] Other members of Congress denounced rumors as efforts to smear Guatemala's international image. Without refer-ring to the real genocide that had just unfolded in his own country, con-servative congressman José García Bauer said that organ trafficking, "like abortions," was part of "a worldwide genocide against children."[29] Another congressman, the independent Pedro Murillo Delgado, was more cautious. He argued both that the rumors were false, *and* that they should be further investigated because the European Parliament report about the fattening houses was a black mark on Guatemala's reputation.[30] The public prosecutor who was head of the government's anti-trafficking investigative team at that time surprised me by saying in an interview decades later that he knew the baby parts rumor was false, and that he thought it was spread to discredit the United States in a "communist conspiracy."[31]

While tales of organ trafficking were demonstrably untrue, they did draw attention to the very real issue of child trafficking for adoption. In 1988, a social worker named Olga Valenzuela who had worked in the two largest public hospitals in the capital wrote an article titled "Adoption or Trafficking?" for *Prensa Libre*. Valenzuela worried that a process that used to include years of follow-up visits had shrunk into a quick arrangement with little oversight. She wrote that lawyers were "unscrupulous delinquents who have found in infants a simple form of enriching themselves" with "trafficking disguised as adoption."[32]

A Highly Laudatory End

Part of the job of U.S. Embassy employees is to monitor the local press, especially for anything that might affect diplomatic relations or diminish U.S. prestige or power. In the 1990s in Guatemala, staff had their hands full. Cables from the U.S. Embassy to the State Department show that U.S. authorities had been aware of adoption fraud and kidnappings for adoption at least as early as 1987.[33] From 1987 to 1994, cables from the embassy to Washington show mounting concern, especially over potential damage to the reputation and prestige of the United States. But diplomats took no action until after the first violent attacks on North Americans.

In August 1987, the U.S. Embassy in Guatemala cabled Washington with the subject line "child trafficking in Guatemala," copying embassies in Mexico, Costa Rica, Honduras, and El Salvador. The cable read: "The recent confession of an alleged Guatemalan child trafficker revealed that at least two immigrant visas were issued by Embassy Guatemala to possibly stolen children based on falsified official Guatemalan documents. Further Post [embassy] investigation revealed an additional two cases which might be similar. Current revelations have caused Post to reconsider adoption procedures, especially with regard to required documents."[34] Embassy workers complained to their superiors in Washington that they were too understaffed to deal with widespread fraud. In September 1988, a cable to Washington noted that other countries like Paraguay and Honduras were also "high fraud," and continued: "Many adopting parents have invested a tremendous amount of money and suffered emotional strain in order to achieve a highly laudatory end. Being so emotionally committed, these parents are prime candidates for exploitation and, in some instances, are willing accomplices."[35]

Instead of addressing the concerns, or sending more staff to Guatemala, Washington started to spread rumors of their own—counter-rumors with a distinctly Cold War flavor. The Cold War lingered after the fall of the Berlin Wall in places like Central America, where Guatemala signed peace accords only in 1996.[36] Politicians in the United States claimed the European Parliament report that jumpstarted the panic by lending credence to false rumors of organ trafficking was politically motivated because it was authored by members of European communist parties. In a public statement, Richard Schifter— Ronald Reagan's assistant secretary of state for Human Rights and Humanitarian Affairs—wrote that the European Parliament report was presented by

French communist Danielle de March "to damage the image of the United States and Guatemala." He sent a letter of complaint to the European Parliament, calling the report "cynical lies" and claiming that the Soviet Union was behind it.[37] U.S. indignation notwithstanding, it seems that the report was just sloppily sourced.

As soon as adoptions were delayed in any way, would-be adoptive parents became extremely active constituents who continually contacted their representatives with pleas to speed up the process. In August 1989, the U.S. Embassy in Guatemala cabled the secretary of state:

> The consular section often finds itself caught between anxious prospective U.S. parents and an unreliable and sometimes fraudulent Guatemalan adoption system. The combination of the urgency of parenting instincts of the relatively wealthy Americans and the failure of the Guatemalans to put their legal house in order concerning adoptions sometimes has yielded scandalous journalism regarding sale or theft of babies and their rumored export to be adopted . . . Our attempts to control the situation by investigating individual adoption cases often result in floods of congressional inquiries triggered by distraught prospective parents.[38]

The embassy started to pay more attention when U.S. citizens were threatened with violence. By 1993, most foreigners living and working in Guatemala were aware of the baby parts rumor. A young North American human rights worker, Daniel Wilkinson, wrote that in 1993 he was invited by a soldier on leave to spend an evening with two German friends in a beach hut on the Pacific coast. In the morning "an angry mob from a nearby village marched out to the family's house and demanded to know why they had brought a *gringo robachicos* to the island." Luckily for him, the soldier was there to disperse the crowd, yelling that the men weren't baby thieves, and threatening violence if they were harmed. On a separate occasion, when Wilkinson first arrived in a small town, the baker's wife ventured to ask him "the question that so many others had never dared to ask: 'You're not a *robachicos*, are you?'"[39]

In 1994, *La Hora* reported that there was a generalized "psychosis" among the Guatemalan population over the trafficking rumors.[40] The embassy complained to Washington of a "prolonged baby parts hysteria."[41] The *New York Times* picked up the story: "Fed by rumors that Americans were coming to kidnap children, cut out their vital organs and ship them to the United States for transplantation, an extraordinary wave of panic has swept Guatemala."[42] The same year, in Zone 18, one of the poorest areas of Guatemala City, a group of women marched on the local police station to request more patrols to protect their children. They threatened to burn down the station if their demands were not met.[43]

Lynchings

The first highly publicized attack on a foreigner came in 1994. As the war transitioned into an unsettled and often violent "peace," lynchings had become common in Guatemala. Though the term is similar, lynchings, called *linchamientos,* are different in Latin America than in North America.[44] In Latin America, the word refers to collective vigilante justice, usually in the context of extreme social inequality and an absent, corrupt, or predatory state. These attacks, unlike North American lynchings, are not necessarily driven by racist hate.[45] Between 1996 and 2004 over 500 people were lynched. The vast majority of victims were Guatemalan. Most lynchings were vigilantes attacking men suspected of crimes ranging from murder to stealing a chicken, but attacks on foreigners suspected of trafficking children drew the most national and international attention. All of the attacks and near-attacks motivated by the baby parts rumor combined some of these elements: rumors of organ trafficking or child theft, visits by a foreigner, attacks on police stations or prisons, and the intervention of the army. Lynchings of foreigners created bad publicity of the kind the U.S. Embassy had feared for decades.[46]

The first was an attempted attack on Melissa Larson, a thirty-seven-year-old from New Mexico who went to Guatemala on vacation in 1994. Larson had no plans to adopt, and certainly no plans to kidnap any children. Intending to visit nearby Maya ruins, Larson stayed in Santa Lucía Cotzamalguapa, a majority *ladino* city in the hot flatlands of southern Guatemala.[47] Before she arrived, a rumor went around the city that the local morgue was holding nine bodies of children whose organs were missing, victims of organ-trafficking thieves. Local television and radio picked up the story. On 4 March 1994, the justice of the peace and local coroner invited people in to see for themselves that there were no children's bodies in the morgue. Still, even those who went to see remained suspicious. Perhaps the corpses had been removed just before opening it to the public. "Something must have been going on," one person from Santa Lucía later recalled. "People here are not crazy."[48]

An embassy cable from August 1994 recounted that Larson had been drinking pineapple juice in a market stall when some policemen asked for identification and searched her bags. The police took her into custody for her own protection and "later in the afternoon, a much larger crowd had formed in front of the police station, and their chanting and seemingly violent nature led police to believe that they intended to physically remove [redacted] from the police station and lynch her."[49] Larson protested that she had not gone near any children. Still, about 400 people remained gathered around the police station, some even sleeping outside to keep watch. Authorities transferred Larson to a prison in the municipal capital of Escuintla to keep her away from the crowds. The next day, a new false rumor spread: she had bribed police to get out of jail. Larson was said to have paid a bribe of US$10,000 to $35,000—eight to twenty times the Guatemalan annual GDP per capita. Perhaps not coincidentally, $35,000 was often cited by newspapers as the sum foreign families paid for adoptions. Although Larson had in reality paid no bribe and remained in custody in Escuintla, the idea of someone, whether a foreigner or Guatemalan, paying off the police was perfectly plausible. A car mechanic from Santa Lucía explained, "The only people in jail are those who can't pay—poor people."[50]

Embassy cables recorded that "in response to the false rumor" the crowd "became a violent mob, sacking and burning the police station, severely beating one officer, destroying ten vehicles, throwing stones and exchanging gunfire with the police. The police responded with a force of 500 from the riot control unit but despite hours of exhausting confrontation, were unable to control the mob until the arrival of army units with four armed vehicles."[51] In the end, soldiers dispersed the crowd. Fifteen police and thirty-four rioters were injured, and fifty-two people were arrested and taken to prison. Four days after the riot, 300 people from Santa Lucía—led by women—marched through the city's streets demanding the release from prison of their neighbors.[52] At the request of the embassy, Larson was transferred to a prison in Guatemala City. As she left the Escuintla prison, a group of more than thirty women surrounded the car, throwing rocks and beating the vehicle with sticks. News of the events in Santa Lucía spread rapidly as both news and rumors, catalyzing further panic. Larson eventually made it home safely.

The next outbreak of violence was not stopped in time. It took place in another small city, San Cristóbal de Alta Verapaz, on the other side of the country that same year. People there had heard about Larson, and panic in one small city helped make another city's fears seem more plausible. "After what happened in Santa Lucía, it was suddenly more than just a story," a missionary couple based in San Cristóbal told Daniel Rothenberg, who wrote a doctoral thesis on the baby parts rumors and attacks based on extensive interviews. The place is a town of 7,000 mostly Poqomchi'-speaking people in the highlands, on a lake ringed with pine forests and coffee plantations. It was Holy Week, and the town was more crowded than usual with people from outlying areas who had come to see the procession of saints. A young woman later said that, just like in Santa Lucía, rumors had spread beforehand: "They found the body of a child by the side of the highway, its stomach filled with dollars, the body missing eyes, with no heart, no kidneys, with a piece of paper, a note of some kind."[53] It was an unfounded rumor. There was no body, but still people believed it to be true. Locals told a reporter that, before the attack, someone had taped the *Prensa Libre* article with the butcher's price chart for different organs in U.S. dollars onto the wall of a store in town.[54]

June Weinstock was a middle-aged environmental activist from Alaska studying Spanish in Guatemala. An experienced traveler, she was aware of the baby parts rumor. Walking through San Cristóbal on 29 March 1994, she patted a small boy on the head. Or perhaps she took his photograph—accounts differ. Soon afterwards, the child's mother said he was missing. Rumors spread fast. In some versions, Weinstock had stolen the child, hiding him under her long skirt in order to later kill him and extract his organs. An ice cream vendor said, or perhaps joked, that the child was hidden in Weinstock's suitcase or backpack. What we do know for certain is that a crowd formed and began pushing Weinstock from all sides. A man from the town intervened and said she should be taken to the justice of the peace's office to be investigated. He escorted her there, and urged a North American missionary who lived in the town to join her for her protection. They hid in the office while the crowd continued to gather outside.

A tense standoff ensued. Meanwhile, the woman who said her son was missing had found him again. The child had merely wandered off to watch a religious procession. The justice of the peace asked the mother to speak to the crowd, saying, "Look, here is the mother and here is her son. It's all over.

It's not true. You can go home now."[55] Instead, the crowd only grew, swelling to hundreds of people. The bishop of Alta Verapaz, who had heard about the situation, arrived to help disband the crowd. Local newscasters' tapes show crowd members getting agitated, smashing windows, and trying to light the justice of the peace's office on fire. A group of men finally used a bench to break their way into the office. They beat both the missionary, who managed to run away, and Weinstock, who could not. The men dragged Weinstock out of the building, beat her in front of the crowd, and sexually assaulted her. She fell into a coma, and later only partially recovered.

The horrifying events were clear enough. There were many witnesses, even news footage. Fifty-seven men were arrested after the lynching and held in prison in Cobán. They were later released without charges. But what had caused the attack, and why those who tried had been unable to stop it, became a matter of national soul-searching. It also became a matter of international speculation, often ill-informed if not racist. *Reuters* explained the attack by citing a rate of 60 percent illiteracy and an atmosphere of "hallucinatory magical realism" in which "extravagant rumors are easily mistaken for reality."[56] A typical article, from the *Washington Post,* trotted out clichés about Latin America—particularly Indigenous areas—in which the words "dusty" and "timeless" never fail to appear:

> In her last conscious hours before the attack, the 51-year-old environmental activist from Alaska discovered the Guatemala of a traveler's dreams, the highland villages where the descendants of the Mayas grow moon lilies on the sides of dead volcanoes and time in the dusty town squares seems expanded and almost still. But this was not that Guatemala. This was the other Guatemala, the one travel guides do not speak of, the violent, unknowable Guatemala, where rumors have been circulating for months that there are gringos—evil longhaired hippies, their dusty backpacks filled with surgical gear—who roam the countryside, hunting.[57]

A reporter for the *Village Voice* was the one of the few foreign journalists to note that middle-class families in Guatemala City were also in a state of hysteria over organ-trafficking rumors—not just Maya communities in the highlands.[58] One of many strange things about the *Washington Post* article is that there *was* a violent, "unknowable," or at least silenced Guatemala: the Guatemala of army massacres, of disappeared children, of an ongoing war. Guatemalan journalist Jairo Alarcón came closest to naming this unacknowledged context, writing: "One begins to discover the latent explosive character of the Guatemalan. Living for such a long time in a society with an underlying culture of terror, where respect for life and the minimal conditions for humanity are utopias, has forged in part our personality as Guatemalans."[59]

Scholars have explained the outbreak of lynchings in Guatemala in a variety of ways: a response to impunity, mistrust of police and the government, a result of extralegal security patrols resembling and sometimes reconstituting the civil patrols that Maya men joined or were forced to join during the war, and—crucially—the replacement of "communists" with gangsters and criminal delinquents as the objects of fear and violence.[60] The most common and convincing explanation for the outbreak of lynchings is lack of effective justice. More than 75 percent of the population during the postwar period in Guatemala at least partially supported lynchings in the name of justice. Sociologist and human rights scholar Angelina Snodgrass Godoy writes that "virtually everyone told me lynchings happen because crime is out of control and the justice system is at a standstill."[61] Another useful clue to what was behind the lynchings lay in fears related to exploitation by outsiders. Historian Gema Kloppe-Santamaría connected earlier lynchings in Mexico with "the presence of foreign individuals" or "the appropriation of local resources by or for outsiders."[62] The attacks on foreigners were a small proportion of the lynchings in Guatemala during the last years of the war and in the transition to a nominal peace, but they received the lion's share of national and international attention. An Indigenous man told Daniel Rothenberg, the North American anthropologist, that perhaps he was interested for that very reason: "Your lives are worth more than ours."[63]

The attacks didn't stop. In 1994 alone there were at least half a dozen lynchings or attempted lynchings of foreigners traveling in Guatemala. Graffiti reading *"gringo robaniños"* and *"Yankis robaniños fuera"* ("Yankee child thieves get out") began appearing around Guatemala City.[64] Guatemala had one of the largest Peace Corps contingents in the world, and more than 200 volunteers were required to leave their posts and gather in the capital after the attack on Weinstock, the kind of security measure that usually follows in-country coups. The volunteers reported parents and children shying away from them in fear, and of children throwing rocks at North Americans to keep them away. The State Department warned U.S. citizens not to travel to the country unless strictly necessary.[65]

Some Guatemalans warned that the lynchings were not only dangerous to foreigners but could be the spark that set off a wider social upheaval, or "explosion," as in the Spanish phrase *estallido social*.[66] One of the few Guatemalan politicians to read the lynchings in a more subtle fashion was Nineth Montenegro, a prominent congresswoman and human rights activist involved in the continually failed push for adoption reforms. Montenegro said that "even if we do not agree with the violence," it was "the demand for justice and putting an end to impunity that forced the people to act in this manner." The attacks, she continued, "should stand as an example of what an angry population is capable of doing if they are not listened to."[67]

Counter-Rumor

After the original baby parts rumor caused the attacks, a counter-rumor began to gather force among journalists and nonprofit workers in Guatemala, and later appeared in the international press. It held that members of the Guatemalan army had invented or were at least circulating the original baby parts rumors for dark purposes of their own. In some versions, people said that the army had planted agents provocateurs in crowds during lynchings— making them essentially a false-flag operation. The closest any news outlet came to a source, though anonymous, was a front-page story in the *Los Angeles Times* in April 1994: "Informed sources said two members of military intelligence had been seen inciting the crowd in Santa Lucia, while police suspect that professional agitators were involved in the San Cristóbal riot."[68] According to the most pointed version of the counter-rumor, the panic served the army by demonizing foreigners and making Guatemala seem dangerous to outsiders who might otherwise get involved in solidarity and human-rights work. Lynchings allowed the army to swoop in and take over towns to restore order.

The softer version of the counter-rumor, to my mind more credible, was that the army had not originated the panic, but was profiting from it. According to the *Los Angeles Times* story, "Hard line factions of the Guatemalan military are believed to be exploiting visceral fears—perhaps even encouraging them—to undermine public security and to generate suspicion of foreigners." And a revealing detail: "The collective psychosis has been stoked by inflammatory reports in the local press of sightings of long-haired foreigners, driving Jeeps with tinted windows, supposedly hunting for children in remote villages."[69] During the war, jeeps with tinted windows were frequently used by police and military to disappear people. The jeep would pull up next to someone on the sidewalk, a door would open, hands would yank someone in, and that person would never be seen by their loved ones again. Here, the unnameable fears of the war and the nameable fear of the baby panic drew close together. The *New York Times* also took note:

> Diplomats and human rights advocates fear that the rumors are part of a campaign to destabilize the administration of President Ramiro de Leon Carpio by weakening the influence of the United States Government, which has been an important source of support for the embattled Guatemalan leader. The idea that there may be a political motive for spreading rumors of Americans eviscerating children reflects the deep insecurity felt throughout this country after years of a civil war in which more than 100,000 people have been killed, an estimated 40,000 disappeared, and the hold on power by civilian leaders is precarious.[70]

Neither newspaper fully endorsed the counter-rumor as true—confirming with sources would be difficult, to put it mildly—but neither did they dismiss it.

The febrile atmosphere for rumors carried over from the war. As anthropologist Linda Green wrote of the wartime atmosphere, "Fear thrives on ambiguities: denunciations, gossip, innuendos, and rumors of death lists create a climate of suspicion. No one can be sure of who is who."[71] Some observers noted that Weinstock was attacked on the same day, 29 March 1994, that the Guatemalan government signed the first of a series of peace accords with guerrilla groups that were highly unpopular among military officials. On 1 April 1994, the chief justice of Guatemala's Constitutional Court was assassinated, possibly because of several investigations he led into the operations of death squads connected to the army. Diane Nelson was one of several scholars who found the idea that the army had helped fan the baby-panic rumors plausible, but cautioned that the counter-rumor is "itself a rumor." Nelson wrote, "In fact, much of our understanding of Guatemala . . . is based on hearsay and rumor, on partial stories—both interested and incomplete."[72] Anthropologist Abigail Adams wrote that while news reports indicating that the army had helped to spread rumors appeared in the foreign press, solidarity groups' reports, and U.S. Embassy reports, these groups all tended to cite each other—a form of journalistic "cannibalism."[73]

It is tempting to despair of sorting through all the rumors and counter-rumors to get at the truth of what happened and why. Journalist David Grann, after attempting to investigate an unrelated case in which a lawyer possibly called a hitman on himself—arranging his own murder in order to frame the Guatemalan president—wrote that Guatemalan history is a "bewildering swirl of competing stories and rumors, allowing powerful interests not only to cloak history but also to fabricate it."[74] Francisco Goldman, in his book about the 1998 assassination of Bishop Gerardi, chronicles how military brass falsified evidence and cited fake witnesses in order to cover up the fact that it was the army that ordered the bishop killed. Rumors and misinformation promoted by the army—perhaps it was a robbery, or a gay crime of passion—swirled around the case. The truth about the bishop's death eventually was uncovered. Though it has been repeatedly proven that the army high command ordered Bishop Gerardi's assassination, people still repeat the false rumors the army helped spread to this day.[75]

The last infamous lynching of suspected child thieves was on 30 April 2000. A group of Japanese tourists traveled by tour bus to Todos Santos Cuchumatán, a picturesque town in the highlands near the Mexican border, unaware of rumors, spread in part by local radio, about foreigners coming to town to abduct children and extract their hearts in the local soccer stadium.[76] The town is somewhat remote, but it was a frequent stop for Japanese tourists at that time in part because the Mam-speaking inhabitants wear striking and distinctive *traje*. The visitors took photos in the town market, oblivious of a rumor that kidnappers took pictures to learn the locations and record images of appealing victims.[77] When one of the tourists gestured at a crying baby strapped to a mother's back, the mother started to scream. "Help, they are trying to kidnap my baby!" A crowd gathered to chase the tourist, killing both him and his son, who tried to intervene. More and more people gathered, and a rumor started that the tour bus was full of the corpses of children. When the Guatemalan bus driver tried to block the crowd from entering the bus to check, he too was killed.[78]

The traditional *traje*, handmade Indigenous Maya clothing, worn in Todos Santos Cuchu-matán. *Reuters / Alamy Stock Photo.*

Eleven years later, people in Todos Santos lynched a Guatemalan accused of extorting his neighbors, a crime that is on the rise as street gangs spread across the country. A reporter for Salvadoran news outlet *El Faro* traveled to the town and asked the mayor why people had taken matters into their own hands both times, instead of calling the police. The mayor answered, "because no one trusts the authorities."

> "Do you agree with the lynchings?"
> "Of course not! What we most wish is that what happened to the Japanese tourists had never, ever happened. Above all because the whole thing was a mix-up, a misunderstanding."[79]

Closure

The transition away from violence after the 1996 peace accords was difficult, with ongoing lynchings of Guatemalans suspected of crimes. Amnesty International by 2002 called Guatemala a "corporate mafia state," and the

Washington Office on Latin America chronicled the transformation of death squads into criminals for hire, including for assassinations of human rights workers with "little fear of arrest or prosecution."[80] Impunity reigned for adoption-related crimes as well.

The U.S. Embassy had put in place some limited safeguards after adoption scandals arose elsewhere, too, including in Romania. In 1984, communist dictator Nicolae Ceausescu decreed that abortion was punishable by incarceration of both women and their doctors and mandated that Romanian families produce at least five children or be penalized with drastic tax increases. Contraception was already banned. This was intended to increase the number of "pure-blooded" Romanians in proportion to the Romani population, known at the time by the racial slur "gypsies," who were considered undesirable by the state. Ceausescu's policies, together with the dissolution of social services, left more than 100,000 children in abusive or negligent state care.[81] When the regime fell in 1989, images of forlorn Romanian orphans flooded televisions in the United States and Europe, prompting a rush to adopt. After a widely viewed U.S. television broadcast on Romanian orphanages in 1991, the numbers of Romanian adoptees shot up, temporarily overtaking Guatemala.[82] This "rescue-adoption frenzy," as one journalist termed it, was followed by fears that the baby rush had been lawless.[83] Prospective parents visited Romanian orphanages, selected children, and left the country with minimal paperwork that indicated age, but not race, ethnicity, or special needs.[84] According to the *New York Times:* "Some prospective parents come on their own, referred to a lawyer who for a substantial fee may simply deliver a baby to their hotel. Others work through registered agencies and freelance adoption brokers in Romania. Fees range from $2,500 to $15,000 and increasingly include a payment to the birth mother."[85]

After Romania, the State Department requested that Latin American embassies check on adoption fraud throughout the region. The United States took two measures intended to address fraud without stopping adoptions altogether: mandatory embassy interviews with birth mothers and DNA tests. DNA testing sounds like it would be decisive, but after it became mandatory, there were allegations of adoption workers switching samples in order to make false matches. Internal U.S. Embassy communications acknowledged that "the whole thing that makes DNA allowable in court is that the chain of custody," meaning who has the sample at any given time, "can be verified and we can't do that here because we rely solely on the labs."[86] By 1993, the Canadian, French, and Swedish embassies also required interviews with birth mothers.[87] These turned out to be less effective than hoped. Duke Lokka, chief of American Citizen Services and Immigration Sections at the U.S. Embassy in Guatemala from 1993 to 1998, acknowledged in a 1996 interview that lawyers routinely falsified paperwork. The thirty-minute interviews with birth mothers were intended to minimize fraud, but power imbalances and language gaps meant that the interviews were not always reliable—not least because the embassy relied on freelance interpreters for conversations with Indigenous birth mothers. Lokka recalled:

> A very humble woman who may have never been to the capital before must go to the United States Embassy, which looks like a fortress, and go into a room to be interviewed by a person dressed in a suit who is more educated than she is. We have to try to make her comfortable and that's a real challenge . . . Also, often the woman won't even speak Spanish so we rely on interpreters that are brought in and you don't know what the woman is really saying.[88]

Susana Luarca, the lawyer I met in prison, told me that she brought her own translators to embassy interviews—not exactly a guarantee of impartial interpretation.[89]

Carmela Curup, a Guatemalan public prosecutor who worked on child trafficking cases in the 1990s, said women could be coerced into giving authorization for adoption in a way that looked perfectly legal on paper. "There are many intermediaries and many people who manipulated and coerced the poor mothers. These are women who come from marginalized areas. They are indigenous and poor. It is easy to trick them or play off their fears. Some are even told that after the child turns eighteen they can get the child back." Curup told Mexican journalist Karen Avilés that coercion and trafficking were common, but that the procedures were made to look aboveboard. "It was all—in air quotes—legal."[90] A November 1996 embassy cable reads: "Like the Dr. Seuss children's story 'Are You My Mother?' in which a little lost bird questions various animals in search of his true mother, natural mother identity riddles have long plagued the consulate's adoptions unit . . . While Post will continue to investigate each prospective adoption case, we have neither the authority nor the resources to attempt to locate the true birth mothers, nor to penalize unscrupulous adoption attorneys for their role in the fraud."[91]

Ongoing scandals in Guatemala and elsewhere pushed the biggest change in the international adoption market since its creation at midcentury. A new international agreement called the Hague Convention on Protection of Children and Co-operation in Respect of Intercountry Adoption came into force 1 May 1995. The Hague Convention explicitly banned baby brokers and payments of any kind for birth mothers, and in general mandated more stringent oversight for international adoptions.[92] Like many international laws, it only applied where countries both ratified and enforced it. And as with many other international agreements, the United States didn't enforce the Hague Convention right away. In fact, the United States waited fourteen years after signing to enforce the convention. But the international agreement did eventually contribute to the closure of adoptions from Guatemala.

Guatemala did not ratify the Hague Convention until much later, but it had signed the UN Convention on the Rights of the Child in 1990, providing a dress rehearsal of sorts for how poorly international limitations went over in the country. This convention stipulated, among other things, that children have the right to their own name and identity, to be raised by their parents "within a family or cultural group," and to have a relationship with both parents even when separated from them. The Guatemalan Congress dragged its feet on writing the laws to enforce it until 1996. Pentecostal Christians, by then over a third of the population and growing, ran a publicity campaign against the convention from a position of "Guatemalan family values" that echoed some of the language of the Christian right in the United States.[93] Former dictator Efraín Ríos Montt, who ordered the genocide in the early 1980s, reappeared at this time as the head of a new political party. Along with a conservative women's group called "Anguished Mothers," he condemned the UN Convention as an "assault on the traditional family." Adoption lawyer Fernando Linares Beltranena wrote in *Prensa Libre* that the UN Convention "breaks family values, handing family authority over to the state, to a great bureaucratic network," which he wrote had "foreign values."[94] Just because the Cold War was technically over didn't mean that its themes weren't still useful, and in use. The convention was never enforced in Guatemala.

After the war, there was a slight opening for new coalitions of Indigenous politicians, some of whom sought limits on adoptions of Indigenous children by non-Indigenous families.[95] Kaqchikel congresswoman Rosalina Tuyuc, a human rights advocate whose father and husband were disappeared and murdered by the army during the war, argued that international adoption was at odds with Maya practices. "Within the social system of each of the communities, and as a tradition within indigenous law, the Maya do not have the problem of children without protection or support for their development."[96] Before and during the war, if a child was orphaned or abandoned, *compadres* of the parents, godparents of the child, or other members of the community would take in the child, just as refugees in Mexico had taken in orphans. The Pan-Maya movement represented a major shift from emphasizing class consciousness to emphasizing ethnic identity, and the leadership was from the highlands rather than the capital. In 2010, the U.S. Embassy noted, "Some persons in the indigenous communities complained that the more developed countries were stealing their heritage and future by adopting their children."[97] Among many other demands, Indigenous politicians sought limits on adoptions of Indigenous children by non-Indigenous families.

Politicians proposed a new round of adoption reforms that would have involved establishing new courts to oversee private adoptions. In 1997, the Guatemalan Supreme Court ruled that this was impossible, since there were no funds available to create new courts. Luarca told me, "The Supreme Court magistrate at that time happened to be my husband. So it was said that he opposed the law so that I could continue processing adoptions."[98] (By the time Luarca went to jail a decade later, she was divorced.[99]) The courts never became a reality, but Guatemalans not involved in the industry became increasingly vocal about their discomfort with the volume and circumstances of international adoptions. A former member of the Guatemalan Supreme Court told a U.S. Embassy officer as early as 1990 that "many of the country's leaders wished international adoption would disappear—that they considered it a national embarrassment."[100] Still, a June 1997 cable noted that adoption lawyers were a "powerful lobby that has managed to kill all adoption law proposals, even during the height of the 'baby parts' scandal."[101] The embassy tried to reassure Guatemalan officials that South Korea and Russia had come into compliance with the Hague Convention and still had large international adoption programs, to no avail.

In 2000, the United Nations published a damning report highlighting the abusive behavior of lawyers in Guatemala toward birth mothers. It observed that too often children were "commercial objects to be offered to the highest bidders."[102] UNICEF commissioned a report from the Latin American Institute for Education and Communication that repeated many of the same findings just a few months later. The UNICEF-commissioned report, based on interviews and an analysis of ninety adoption files held at the attorney general's office awaiting approval, noted that state orphanages were full of children who were mostly not adopted, and that "those actually being adopted are, to a large extent, being 'produced' for this end." "Adoption," the report declared, "now routinely begins even before birth as there are individuals actively seeking out pregnant women in order to solicit the purchase of their unborn child."[103] The report noted that private adoptions by this time made up 99 percent of all adoptions from Guatemala, no longer even accompanied by the most rudimentary home visits by social workers, "and that the Elisa Martínez state-run orphanage had given up adoptions some time ago." The report also provided vivid stories of birth mothers pressured and coerced into giving up their babies.[104]

None of this was new information. These reports codified what had been common knowledge in Guatemala for quite some time. In fact, research for the UNICEF report, mostly based on interviews, took only eleven days.[105] But the imprimatur of recognized international organizations had an effect. Both Spain and the Netherlands stopped authorizing adoptions from Guatemala. The U.S. ambassador to Guatemala wrote in February 2002, "If we do not take action now, we run the real possibility of a scandal that could result in the USG [U.S. government] being accused in abetting child trafficking."[106] That year, the United States suspended adoptions from Cambodia, which were much smaller in scale, over similar concerns: baby brokers, fraud, falsified birth documents.[107] Guatemala remained open, and *Newsweek* estimated in 2002: "At an average fee of $20,000 per adoption, the Guatemalan adoption industry now brings in more than $50 million a year—or only slightly less than the country's growing textile-export industry."[108]

Under pressure to close private adoptions altogether, Guatemala instead signed the Hague Convention, on 26 November 2002. Several countries that had already signed—among them Canada, Germany, the Netherlands, Spain, and the United Kingdom—viewed Guatemala's participation as making a mockery of the Hague Convention and filed official objections to its accession to the Convention. The Adoption Council of Canada in 2004 warned that Guatemala would remain closed to Canadians because of "illegal and unethical practices" and "issues of child trafficking."[109] There was a six-month slowdown in adoptions as the Guatemalan government made minor revisions to adoption laws to appear to come into compliance. Two years after Guatemala signed, after a sustained round of lobbying by the same set of adoption lawyers that had sunk earlier efforts at reform, the Constitutional Court found that the Hague Convention violated Guatemala's constitution. Adoption numbers soared again. By this time, in 2004, the United States was one of the few countries that still allowed adoptions from Guatemala, since it had signed but not enforced the Hague Convention.

In Guatemala, pressure was building from another source, mothers of kidnapped children. Norma Cruz started hearing from them in the early 2000s. Cruz, a well-known human rights activist, had founded an organization called Fundación Sobrevivientes (Foundation for Survivors) to combat violence against women. Mostly addressing domestic violence and femicide, the group helps run one of the few victims' shelters in the country. Cruz is a petite, emphatic woman who has received multiple death threats for her work. We met in her tiny office in downtown Guatemala City, where she told me that she and her colleagues were reluctant to work on cases relating to adoption until she met with birth mothers and realized the extent of kidnapping and coercion. "We believed they were isolated cases, but when we began to accompany people, others started to hear we were working on those cases. We began to get into that world, saw that it was big business."[110] In 2007, Foundation for Survivors together with two other nonprofit organizations, Casa Alianza and the Myrna Mack Foundation, published a report called *Adoptions in Guatemala: Protection or Business?*[111] It was a careful study of the 230 cases of kidnapped children reported to the human rights office in the first half of 2007 alone. A second study, conducted by the Hague Conference on Private International Law in 2007, confirmed many abuses.[112]

Cruz took on ten cases of families whose children had been kidnapped, they suspected, for the purposes of international adoption. The cases filled her with rage, she said, because the police never investigated right away, always first accusing the mothers, all of them poor, of having sold their children. One of the families, who eventually helped send Susana Luarca and the rest of her

Loyda Rodríguez, mother of a toddler kidnapped in 2006 who was placed in adoption in the United States. *Reuters/Alamy Stock Photo.*

adoption ring to jail, was a pair of young parents named Loyda Rodríguez and Dayner Orlando Hernández. Cruz gave me their contact information, and I traveled to a rather remote part of Guatemala, where they now live, to meet them. Rodríguez, the mother, told me that they used to live in San Miguel Petapa, a working-class area south of Guatemala City. She recalled the worst day of her life: on 3 November 2006 she left her three young children playing downstairs in a fenced-off patio at their home. Rodríguez went up to the roof to hang some freshly washed laundry, then looked around in the bedroom for her children's jackets. It was afternoon, not yet dark. She still had time to take them out to the playground. But when she returned to the patio, one child was missing. Her two-year-old toddler, Anyelí, had slipped through the cracks of the fence out to the street. The daughter of the neighbor who sold tortillas across the way saw a woman lift Anyelí into a white car and drive away.[113]

After searching the neighborhood, Rodríguez and her husband filed a missing persons report with the police, then drove straight to the international airport downtown to hang up flyers with Anyelí's photo. "I thought that they might take my daughter out of the country," recalled Rodríguez, who had heard the baby parts rumors. Rodríguez and Hernández continued to visit the police station and courthouse every three days, hoping for news of their toddler. Eventually, a judge advised them to get in touch with Norma Cruz. The couple joined the Foundation for Survivors' campaign called "No More Empty Cribs," which included protests, and later a hunger strike. But they could not find Anyelí. Two years later, a newly formed governmental oversight body called the National Adoptions Council agreed to allow the families Cruz was working with into their office to review adoption files, to see if they could find their own children among the stacks of paper. Each adoption file had a passport-sized photo of the child attached to the front. On the eighth day of searching, Rodríguez's brother found three files with girls he thought looked enough like Anyelí to be her.

This launched the first criminal investigation of an adoption ring in Guatemala that was successful in netting players from top to bottom. It coincided with the country's one large-scale and, for a time, successful effort to address corruption in the form of the UN-backed International Commission against Impunity in Guatemala (CICIG). The United States strongly supported the idea, and, after at first balking, the Guatemalan government invited the commission to work alongside local prosecutors in 2006. Cruz asked the first head of CICIG, a well-known Spanish prosecutor, to "not leave me alone, right? Because it was a case that involved members of the Guatemalan state and criminal structures." He agreed, and CICIG supported the case, which was largely carried out by Guatemalan public prosecutors.

An extensive investigation showed that Anyelí had been lured from the patio, kidnapped, then sold to a baby broker, who in turn sold her to Susana Luarca. Working on commission for a Florida-based adoption agency, Luarca, with the help of a corrupt judge and notary, falsified documents in order to make the girl eligible for adoption. Anyelí became "Karen Abigail." An associate of Luarca's posed as the girl's mother in order to consent to her adoption. (Luarca denied all of this in court and during our interviews.) Authorities approved the adoption despite the fact that obligatory DNA tests matching the two came back negative. On 9 December 2008, "Karen Abigail" flew from Guatemala to Missouri with a set of adoptive parents—just three months before Rodríguez's brother found her photograph in the National Adoptions Council's office.

Rodríguez is shy, and she was nervous about taking the stand when Luarca and ten of her associates went to trial in 2012. Rodríguez told me that the adoption ring had been found to have ties to organized crime, which was on the rise after the end of the war, funding itself mainly through extortions. After strangers started showing up in San Miguel Petapa asking where Rodríguez and Hernández lived, they moved to a rural area, where I visited them. Despite threats and intimidation, the couple persisted with the case. Luarca's defense lawyer tried to argue that "Karen Abigail" was not really Anyelí, but independent labs in Spain and the United States returned a 99.98 percent positive DNA match between Rodríguez and the girl.

At first, Hernández and Rodríguez felt vindicated by the trial, they said. People had been quick to criticize them for being bad parents for "losing" their child. Police had even gone so far as to accuse them of selling Anyelí to an adoption ring and then having second thoughts. In 2011, a Guatemalan judge ruled to cancel the passport and birth certificate that had allowed Anyelí to leave the country and ordered her immediate return—a court order supposedly enforceable by Interpol. It soon became clear that the family had won their case, but only within Guatemalan borders. Karen Abigail's adoptive family, who live in Liberty, Missouri, responded with an appearance on the CBS *Early Show*. The adoptive mother said they would not send the girl back, that in Guatemala "DNA is sort of viewed as a title, and we strongly feel that Karen isn't property."[114] The couple retained Jared Genser, a well-known Washington-based lawyer, who argued that the Guatemalan judge's jurisdiction didn't reach the United States. The only contact between the two families has been a letter Genser sent to Norma Cruz with a series of questions. Genser has strenuously disputed everything about this account, posting a twenty-two-page response to reporting by Erin Siegal McIntyre about this case.[115] Rodríguez and Hernández told me they understood that the family in Missouri adopted their daughter without knowing she was stolen, and that the girl had "another life" now. While they are worried about the distress learning her full story will cause Anyelí, they wanted to speak to the adoptive family and come to some kind of agreement that would allow them to spend time with their daughter. Rodríguez told me, "The most difficult thing is that we know where she is, and they don't let us see her." When I visited her at the couple's new home, she showed me Anyelí's toddler clothing, which she keeps neatly folded and stored away.

In 2015, the Guatemalan court convicted eight people involved in Anyelí's adoption, including Susana Luarca and the woman who posed as "Karen Abigail's" birth mother. Luarca was sentenced to eighteen years in prison. Rodríguez and Hernández have lost hope that Guatemala will be able to pressure the United States to return their daughter and are waiting for her to be old enough that she might come looking for them. Some couples who heard or read about their story decided to stop pursuing adoptions and wrote letters to the U.S. Embassy in Guatemala in protest. An author and activist named Mirah Riben posted online in support of Rodríguez and Hernández: "Imagine if the girls stolen were American (and white)," she wrote. "Imagine the difference in response."[116] When I spoke with Norma Cruz about the couple's stalled attempts to get Anyelí back, she told me, "I know that one day will come when she will come to look for her roots in Guatemala and then she will learn the truth, that her parents did not stop fighting for her for a single minute."

By 2006, stories that had been familiar sights in Guatemalan newspapers since the 1980s began to appear in the international press. The *New York Times* wrote, "Critics of the adoption system here—privately run and uniquely streamlined—say it has turned this country of 12 million people into a virtual baby farm that supplies infants as if they were a commodity." It cited payments to birth mothers "from a few hundred dollars to $2,000 for a baby, according to interviews with mothers and experts."[117] Many news reports mentioned "baby hotels," where families lived for as little as a week to complete adoption paperwork and receive a child. Hundreds of families passed through the Marriott alone, and it sold diapers, wet wipes, and formula next to postcards in the gift shop. The Camino Real, another hotel in the upscale Zone 10 of Guatemala City, outfitted its rooms with cribs. Journalist Jacob Wheeler wrote:

> Until recently, almost every flight leaving Guatemala City for the
> United States had one: a tiny brown baby held in the arms of her white
> parents, many of whom were not able to have their own biological
> children . . . This beautiful yet strange scene of the foster mother and
> the Guatemalan attorney passing a baby to its new adoptive parents

in the sterile lobby of the Marriott or the Radisson or the Camino Real near the American Embassy became an everyday occurrence here.[118]

While everyone agreed on the high volume, the ethics were in the eye of the beholder. One adoptive mother wrote a magazine story called "Did I Steal My Daughter?" She included excerpts from her journal recording the trip to pick up the baby in Guatemala: "'I feel so sad for the pain your birth mother must be in since she is not able to raise you,' I wrote. 'But I believe now that I am your "real" mommy.' Reading those words now sparks a flash of shame."[119] In her book *Finding Fernanda,* Erin Siegal McIntyre documented in scrupulous detail another case of a kidnapped girl put up for adoption through a Florida-based agency, Celebrate Children International. The adoptive mother heeded signs that something was amiss with the paperwork, found out the truth, and dropped the adoption proceedings.[120] Norma Cruz, head of Foundation for Survivors, repeatedly brought birth mothers to meetings with U.S. officials. "We cannot act as accomplices to this," she told officials, adding that "Americans would not support children being stolen from their mothers."[121]

I met Julio Prado, a charming former public prosecutor who specialized in adoption cases, at a coffee shop in Guatemala City. He told me that he worked on kidnappings that still haunted him, including cases where newborns were stolen from public hospitals. In his view, the majority of private adoptions were what he called "gray," involving some form of fraud or coercion. In addition to his legal work, Prado was already a published poet. He later wrote a thinly fictionalized novel about adoptions called *The Night Comes Without You.* In our conversation, he recalled one case that had particularly obsessed him, of a baby girl who was kidnapped from Zone 6. They managed to find her through the review process that Norma Cruz had demanded for Rodríguez and Hernández and the other parents, in part because the girl had a recognizable characteristic: deviated fingers.[122]

Still, some adoptive parents and those who wished to adopt pushed to keep Guatemala open. On 4 September 2006, an adoptive father and author of the popular blog *Guatadopt,* Kevin Kreutner, wrote a post titled "What the **** Is Going On?" He described calls for the closure of adoption as "emotional terrorism" against Guatemalan children and adoptive families and called on the United States to ensure that adoptions would continue.[123] Laura Briggs analyzed discussion board posts and found that people in the United States, unlike their European counterparts, tended to minimize or deny allegations of kidnapping or fraud. These message boards were frequently cited as cause for concern in U.S. Embassy cables. On 21 February 2006, an embassy cable referenced "a message board where at least some adoptive parents very clearly understand that biological moms are selling their children. I would say it is getting harder for us to ignore this side of Guatemalan adoptions."[124]

Adoption lawyers tried to hold out. During the debate over the closure of adoption, the lawyer Linares Beltranena gave an infamous interview to the newspaper *Siglo Vientiuno* comparing children to the avocados sold in La Terminal, Guatemala's largest street market:

> It's good for lawyers to make money promoting adoptions. The more procedures there are, the lower the costs. It's the same as in La Terminal: those who sell avocados encourage people to eat avocados, and that way more people are going to plant avocados and they will be cheaper by the law of supply and demand. But if the production of avocados is restricted, the whole market suffers. If we restrict the adoption of children, those who are going to suffer are the children.[125]

By this logic, demand for Guatemalan children meant the market should expand to supply more of them internationally, which in Linares Beltranena's view would benefit more children. If Guatemalan children could pass from a poor family to a richer one, he thought, they should do so for their own good.

The avocado comments were controversial in Guatemala, to put it mildly. Longtime labor unionist and human rights activist Miguel Ángel Albizures wrote in *El Periódico* that "the avocado-peddling lawyer argues for his own interests. He would prefer things to be like in the old days of slavery, when we could find caged children in the markets, with a label out front with price, age, and origin and a guarantee of health."[126] Albizures wrote:

> Something needs to change in a society that, in the majority, remains unperturbed by the fact that its own children are objects to be sold abroad, and that the existing private nurseries—some with a veneer of legality and others operating illegally—have for a long time been functioning in Guatemala like factories *[maquilas],* where the raw material or the finished product are children that they find, or that they take, to be exported to the U.S., Canada, and Europe.[127]

In 2007, Josefina Arellano Andrino, a government official in charge of over-seeing children's rights, said baldly to the *New York Times:* "Babies are being sold, and we have to stop it." She went on, "What's happening to our culture that we don't take care of our children?"[128]

When change came, it came abruptly. A combination of pressure within the country, U.S. concern over bad publicity, and belated enforcement of international legal frameworks regulating adoption finally led to the closure of all international adoptions from Guatemala. In 2007, the United States fully enacted the Hague Convention fourteen years after signing. That same year, after decades of scandal and blocked reforms, Guatemala declared that it would also come into compliance with the Hague Convention. Guatemala definitively closed all international adoptions in 2008. This included adoptions that were already in process, leading families in the United States to protest that they were locked out before finalization. On 7 May 2008 Consul General John Lowell cabled Washington: "the Department (and Embassy) have been warning PAP's [prospective adoptive parents] since December 2006 of potential problems with Guatemalan adoptions, and since May 2007 basically warning folks not to start new cases at all."[129] One would-be adoptive father told the *New York Times* that his case, one of more than a hundred still stalled in 2012, had been "a torture." (All but a handful were resolved by 2023).[130] A 2010 report by CICIG found that of the 3,342 adoption cases underway at the time of closure, 60 percent had "serious irregularities."[131] These ranged from different names listed in abandonment documents and adoption files, to unmatched DNA tests, to uncorroborated accounts of children's birth families and pasts.

In 2007, the Guatemalan government formed a centralized body to oversee adoptions, the Consejo Nacional de Adopciones (National Adoptions Council). As a spokesperson explained to me at their office, the idea was to promote domestic adoptions in the absence of an international option.[132] The U.S. State Department website in 2023 read that the department "continues its effort to work with the Government of Guatemala on establishing procedures to resume intercountry adoptions."[133] But it seems unlikely that international adoptions from Guatemala will resume unless the country puts a wholly new process in place.

The moral panic of the 1990s didn't directly cause the closure, as is evident from over a decade of lag time. But, after Guatemalan lawyers had previously evaded all attempts at reform, it did create the conditions in which the closure became politically possible. In the end, it was crimes related to private adoptions, not a reckoning with forced disappearances, that led to the full closure of international adoptions from Guatemala.

By contrast, a reckoning with children disappeared during the conflict began quietly, is ongoing, and still does not command the level of public attention and activism as, say, in Argentina. The Truth Commission report called for the government to "urgently activate the search for children who have been disappeared" including "at the very least" the establishment of a national commission "to look for children who have been disappeared, illegally adopted, or illegally separated from their parents." It also called for "the implementation of a wide-reaching general information campaign in Spanish and all the native languages, across every region of the country and in refugee sites located in other countries, concerning the activities and measures connected with the search for these children." In reality, the search has mostly been conducted by small nonprofits operating on a shoestring.

Maco Garavito's organization, La Liga, mobilized a small staff that included Mayan language speakers to quietly search on behalf of families with disappeared children starting at the end of the war.[134] Garavito has a small team and a tiny budget. The work is slow and difficult. In Argentina, a DNA database has been the most important tool in helping to find children, but La Liga's irregular funding has meant that they are able to match stories more frequently than blood. (The private Guatemalan Forensic Anthropology Foundation has more recently launched a DNA matching program serving adoptees and victims of forced disappearance more generally, but they, too, are overstretched and operating on a shoestring budget.) La Liga's archives are full of testimony from parents, like a K'iche' couple whose child was disappeared in 1982 during an army attack on their village. La Liga had traced the son as far as a private orphanage called La Casa del Niño del Quiché, where staff changed his name, declared him to be in a legal state of abandonment, and gave him for adoption in the United States. "I just want him to know about everything I did to search for him," said the boy's father, Felipe Sosa Sarat, in testimony given to La Liga. "In spite of all the time that has passed, I love him just as much, if not more."

Birth parents and adoptees rarely speak the same language. Members of Garavito's team speak Ixil and K'iche', but he struggles to find regular translators for all twenty-one Mayan languages. Since the end of the war, he and his colleagues have traveled long distances by jeep and on foot to gather the testimony of those looking for disappeared children. Still, he told me in several interviews, sometimes he despairs that he cannot extend his reach to all areas affected by the war. "We haven't been able to get everywhere, so there are still stories that aren't known."

Despite national and international attention to the "children for export" trafficked and sold by adoption lawyers, the history of children disappeared during the war had stayed mostly silent, or was silenced. This is changing only slowly. The walls of downtown Guatemala City are plastered with the faces of the disappeared, with posters and murals calling for justice. The posters show the faces not of children, but of political activists and other adult victims of the armed conflict who were forcibly disappeared. These memorializations are often pulled down, plastered over with apolitical posters, or covered by stenciled graffiti declaring "there was no genocide." Then the faces of the disappeared reappear, hung again by groups like HIJOS, a Spanish-language acronym for "children." The longer name, Hijos por la Identidad y la Justicia contra el Olvido y el Silencio, means "Sons and Daughters for Identity and Justice against Forgetting and Silence." Argentine children of the disappeared

A poster of Ignacio Segura, who was adopted at the beginning of the 1980s and was attempting to find out if he was disappeared during the war in Guatemala. The poster says, "I'm looking for my family: I was one of the 5,000 children disappeared by the state." La Liga later helped Segura find his birth family, and he learned he was not among the forcibly disappeared. *Johan Ordonez / AFP / Getty Images.*

formed a group with this name in 1995, and Guatemalans formed a group of the same name in 1999 to ensure that the wartime past is not forgotten.

HIJOS was founded by children of the disappeared, but now works with children who were themselves disappeared, including Francophone adoptees from Canada, France, and Belgium—now adults—who are searching for their families. In 2022, HIJOS hung posters around the capital with two images. One is a child facing a wall, reading a sign that says "5,000 disappeared children. Where are they? Set fire to the genocidal state. We want justice." The second image, also posted online, was of two adults putting up a poster with more faces of the disappeared. The poster within a poster reads: "Where are our 5,000 families? Guatemala 1960–1996. *Nous sommes ici.*" Ignacio Segura, who returned to Guatemala from Quebec to search for his birth family, had helped form an adoptee collective the previous year called Nous Sommes Ici, We Are Here. The motto of the group is: "We are the seeds that the state tried to kill, but now we bloom in the morning light."[135]

Epilogue

The Search

Jean-Sébastien Hertsens Zune fields the same question over and over when meeting new people: where are you from? Zune lives in Jocotenango, a small town just outside the tourist-filled colonial city of Antigua. He boxes in a local gym and rides a motorcycle into Guatemala City to work in a call center. He goes by Alberto now, and has what social workers used to call "Indigenous features." But no one ever guesses that he is Guatemalan. They are misled by his Spanish with drawn-out, frenchified vowels. "Brazil?," they ask. No, he explains, and he tells his story one more time. He is always looking for help, for new leads.[1]

In 2013, Zune went looking for his birth parents on what he thought would be a brief trip. He was adopted as a baby from Guatemala by a Belgian church organist and his wife, who later moved him to France. When Zune was a teenager, his Belgian parents gave him his adoption file, holding back only receipts showing how much the process had cost. Most people pay little attention to their birth certificates, but for adoptees, these documents, along with paperwork about their relinquishment, tell an often patchy origin story.

The paperwork said that Zune's birth parents, Alfredo Gonzalo Cajas Barrios and Rebeca Natividad López Ramírez, lived in a small town near the Guatemalan border with Mexico. Alfredo had signed the consent form with his name, Rebeca with a thumbprint. The adoption file said Zune was born with a clubfoot and his birth parents could not afford medical treatment. But his adoptive parents told him that his foot had been fine when he arrived in Belgium as a baby. Why had Alfredo and Rebeca really given him up for adoption?

At the age of twenty-seven, Zune traveled to Guatemala and rented an apartment in Antigua, the former colonial capital laid out at the foot of a dormant volcano, with another two volcanos erupting in the distance. The city is popular among foreigners because it is a cheap and picturesque place to learn Spanish, with sixteenth-century church ruins and bougainvillea climbing the sides of adobe homes. Zune took intensive Spanish classes in a tile-roofed house with a courtyard filled with flowers and began to use his pre-adoption name: Alberto.

Zune has a restless energy that keeps him from staying in one place for too long. By the time he got to Guatemala, he had already worked as a brick-layer, pizza slinger, and airport information officer in Bosnia, Italy, Poland, and France. He already spoke a handful of languages and, after two weeks of Spanish classes, felt he could communicate fairly well. He was ready to set out for Catarina, the place listed in his adoption file as his birth parents' home. He convinced a new Guatemalan friend to accompany him by motorcycle on the eleven-hour trek.

The road to Catarina begins smoothly, rising from Antigua through pine forests where Maya families carry firewood up mountain paths on their backs with tumplines looped over their foreheads bearing the weight. Then it becomes dangerous, as trucks, cars, and motorcycles pass one another around blind curves. The worst offenders are "chicken buses," worn-out American school buses painted in bright colors and repurposed as intercity transportation. As the road descends from the mountains, the pines give way to banana trees and the heat of the border zone rises. Catarina is just a few streets crossed together in an area known for drug trafficking, where teenagers serve as lookouts for small-time narcotraffickers.

Before his trip, Zune had written to the Belgian Embassy, which put him in touch with a priest who had lived in the area for decades. The priest gave him the current address for his birth father, Alfredo, who was now married to another woman. At the address, Zune and his friend found a concrete-block house set back from the street. Alfredo, a slight man with an intense gaze, answered the door and welcomed them effusively, professing himself delighted to see Zune again. "I've always remembered you, my son," he said. "I never thought you would come back." Alfredo invited Zune and his friend to stay at his home in Catarina for several days. At family meals, Alfredo introduced Zune as his son, not mentioning adoption but simply saying "He's a son who went away." Everyone assumed Zune was the product of an affair, which would not be at all unusual. Alfredo didn't want to talk much about the past, but he was curious about Zune's life. How long did he plan to stay in Guatemala? What was his life in Europe like? Did he make good money there? Zune stumbled along in Spanish, and his friend did his best to translate and smooth the encounter.

At the end of his stay, Zune announced that he was going back to Antigua, but said he would return to visit often. Alfredo told him he was welcome anytime, but that it would be best not to seek out his birth mother. "She's a bad type of person," he said, insinuating that she might even be involved with the drug traffickers. "She won't want to see you." He would not say why.

Zune hadn't come all the way to Guatemala to meet only one of his parents. He returned to Catarina a few weeks later, alone on a chicken bus. Rebeca lived on a small ranch just outside of town. Her house was large enough only for a bed. The rest of her belongings—a table, a wood-burning stove—were arranged on the grass outside. Rebeca was home, and she invited Zune in. Here, finally, was his mother. His first thought was that she looked older than her years. "I was so happy," he recalled.

But Rebeca told him there had been *un error*, a mistake. "I'm not your mother," she said. Zune's Spanish was not perfect. Maybe he had misunderstood. "Look, ma'am," he said, "you are in my adoption file. It says here that you are my mother." But Rebeca was insistent. "I only signed for you," she told him, "nothing more." A long time ago, she said, a powerful neighbor had forced her to pretend to be Zune's mother. The neighbor brought her to a lawyer's office in Guatemala City, where she consented to Zune's adoption. She didn't know how to read or write, so she signed the papers with a thumbprint.

The neighbor who forced her to sign the paperwork was Alfredo Gonzalo Cajas Barrios. Rebeca told Zune that the man who was posing as his father was rumored to be a child trafficker. People in the area said he had earned money finding children for lawyers in Guatemala City who arranged international adoptions, the rare baby broker who was a man. His wife, whom Alberto had met, had been involved in the adoption business, too, as well as the illegal importation of cars from Mexico. Rebeca was religious, and what she had done had always bothered her. She said she had no idea who Zune's real parents were. She had only signed adoption papers that one time, but other women may also have done it for Alfredo. She was very, very sorry. Alfredo had threatened that if she ever told anyone what she had done, terrible things would happen. She warned Zune to be careful.

Rebeca spoke spontaneously, and Zune was inclined to believe her. After thinking it over for several weeks, he decided to confront Alfredo. He took Alfredo's whole family to Domino's Pizza at the shopping mall in Malacatán, in a nearby city. In the food court, next to the ball pit for kids, Zune told Alfredo that he had met Rebeca and asked for the truth. Alfredo claimed that Rebeca was lying. They had been together for a short while, he said, and this really was Zune's family. If Rebeca claimed that he was not the father, "maybe she had been unfaithful," he suggested.

Zune, confused and unsettled, went back to Antigua. He began contacting adoptee support groups for help and found that he was not alone in his predicament. He learned from lawyers working with a nonprofit organization that the adoption agency that handled his case was known to have placed children who were stolen from their birth parents with French and Belgian couples in the 1980s. (Zune was adopted in 1985.) This was Hacer Puente, the same agency that placed Dolores Preat for adoption. Zune was convinced that Rebeca was telling the truth. But if he wasn't from Catarina, where *was* he from?

Zune had always believed that his birth parents gave him up voluntarily, but now he could not be sure. "I think about them out there, looking for me," he told me. "I just want to talk to my real mother for one second, to find out if she gave me up because she wanted to or because she had to." Zune got in touch with Maco Garavito, director of La Liga. For the first time, he contemplated the idea that perhaps his adoption had something to do with the war, that he was one of the thousands of forcibly disappeared children. When the lawyers in Guatemala City asked him whether he wanted to open a criminal investigation into his adoption, Zune said yes.

Zune is part of the first wave of adult adoptees returning to Guatemala to face disconcerting revelations about their pasts. Many of the older adoptees are European and Canadian, though the younger wave of North American adoptees is coming of age and beginning to search. A few, including Osmin Ricardo Tobar Ramírez, have returned to live in Guatemala permanently. Tobar was seven in 1997 when social workers picked him up from a neighbor's apartment, where the neighbor was supposed to be taking care of him. There was no warning for his mother, who had drug abuse issues. He was taken to a private children's center, and a family in Pittsburgh adopted him when he was nine years old. "The gringos want babies," Tobar later said, but a younger boy at the center was very attached to him, so the family adopted both boys.[2] Tobar was initially excited that they had a room just for toys. But he had a hard time adjusting. "I only saw white people," he told a reporter from *Radio Ambulante*. He missed his mother, whose face he remembered. Three years later, his adoptive parents got a call from a journalist. An organization called Casa Alianza in Guatemala was working with Tobar's birth parents, who said that the family court had authorized his adoption without exhausting all the legal options for his family to keep him. Tobar got in touch with his birth parents via Facebook and learned that the abandonment process was based on anonymous testimonies from neighbors, without proper verification. The government had made no effort to contact Tobar's father before processing the adoption. Tobar's birth parents now suspect that the woman who was supposed to be taking care of him was a baby broker. The center where he was taken, Children of Guatemala Association, was run by Susana Luarca. When Tobar was twenty-three, he moved back to Guatemala permanently. Like Zune, he found work in a call center. In 2016, Tobar and his birth family brought a case before the Inter-American Court for Human Rights. The court found the government of Guatemala responsible for Tobar's separation, noting "The case happened within a broader context of serious irregularities in adoption procedures in Guatemala, which consisted of the absence of proper institutional oversight and inadequate regulation that allowed criminal networks to profit from international adoptions."[3]

I met Tobar and his birth father, along with other adult adoptees, in a café in Guatemala City. Only a few have returned permanently. Most adoptees who have found their birth parents or in other ways built a connection with Guatemala live elsewhere and visit frequently. But Guatemala may one day experience a larger return migration of adoptees, like South Korea. Journalist Maggie Jones wrote:

> Compared with Korea—a democracy and a developed country— Guatemala, China and Ethiopia may prove less welcoming, at least for now. But as adoptees grow up, Korean activists hope that they will demand more information about their histories and the adoption process from agencies and governments. Perhaps cities like Beijing, Antigua in Guatemala or Addis Ababa in Ethiopia—already popular destinations for adoptees and their families—may become their own

mini-adoptee communities and centers of activism against international adoption.[4]

An association of adult Korean adoptees called Adoptee Solidarity Korea at first called for banning international adoption, though they have since softened that position. The organization now attempts to call attention to coercion and ostracism of single mothers. Tobar is an outspoken opponent of international adoption.

Guatemalan adoptees have organized groups—Next Generation Guatemala, Racines Perdues–Raíces Perdidas, Adoptees with Guatemalan Roots, Estamos Aquí–Nous Sommes Ici, among others—for mutual support and to share information about how to search for birth families. Gemma Givens, who organized Next Generation Guatemala as a support group for over 900 adoptees in the United States, said that before she found out more about her birth mother and home country, "I felt like I was foundationless, or that I was floating, or I was a ghost." She has since reconnected with her Kaqchikel birth family and has learned some of the Mayan language along with Spanish. Other adoptees have also reconnected with their heritage, including Carlos Haas, who was raised in a small town in Germany and has since become a professor of Latin American history.[5] Many adoptees never search for their birth parents. Others feel the desire only upon becoming parents themselves.

Zune had intended to stay in Guatemala for only a month, but he skipped his return flight to help with the criminal investigation. When I met him, two years later, he said that the early days of his search had been the most difficult period of his life. But he wanted to see the investigation through. He had moved from Antigua to the less touristy neighboring town, Jocotenango, and decorated his new apartment with French and Guatemalan flags. Zune is what Guatemalans call *desconfiado,* someone who doesn't trust easily. Even before moving to Guatemala, he said, he had an odd habit of secretly taping conversations. At his apartment, Zune played me the recording of his confrontation with Alfredo at the mall. He had turned over copies to the Guatemalan attorney general's office and had given a statement to the Belgian police, who were working with Interpol to investigate the adoptions handled by Hacer Puente. He was obsessed by the investigation, researching his own story for hours each day.

Zune's problem was not just that he didn't know who his birth parents were, but that he didn't even know what type of adoption his might have been. Was he one of the children disappeared during the war? Had his mother been tricked or coerced? Zune's face, like that of so many Guatemalans, could be Indigenous or not. Without the clues of language or dress or community, it was hard to say where he came from. The only person who might have answers was Alfredo, and, for now at least, he wasn't telling.

Even once Zune was convinced Alfredo was lying to him, he continued to visit Catarina. He brought Rebeca little gifts, mostly food. Even if she wasn't his mother, he reasoned, she had the decency to tell him the truth. When Guatemalan investigators asked Zune to try to convince Alfredo to take a DNA test, Zune called him and said only "I need to talk to you." Several days later, Zune met him in the central park of Malacatán accompanied by two public prosecutors. Alfredo started to back away, but the public prosecutor convinced him to be swabbed. They drove Alfredo to the health center, and he was angry but also somehow wistful. "I'm going to lose you," he said to Zune. The test was negative.

Zune's Belgian parents hadn't believed him at first when he told them that he might have been stolen or coerced away from his family. But the DNA test finally persuaded them. They had known little about the armed conflict in Guatemala, but, as practicing Catholics, they had an idea they might save a child from a difficult situation.[6] The family had adopted a total of four children, each from a different country: Ethiopia, the Republic of Congo, Colombia, and Guatemala. Like many who adopted from Guatemala, the couple did not know how children were selected and matched to families. They simply paid a lump sum to a lawyer for the adoption. Zune's adoptive parents were naturally distraught to learn of the falsifications in Zune's adoption file, and have supported him in his search for his birth parents. The investigation into the adoption agency is ongoing. Hacer Puente's former treasurer was forced to step down as head of UNICEF Belgium in 2019. Several other official inquiries have been opened into illegal international adoptions in Europe. Under pressure from adoptee activists, the Netherlands froze all international adoptions in 2021 after a Dutch report found that children were stolen, sold, or given up under coercion. Sweden has also opened an investigation into its history of international adoptions, including calls for the transfer of all adoption files to a government agency to be checked. Two historians in France were granted permission in 2021 to review 9,600 pages of archives from diplomatic correspondence, much of it classified, relating to international adoptions. They found that illicit practices were common dating back to the 1980s in adoptions from Guatemala,

Vietnam, Mali, and seventeen other countries, and that nothing was done despite frequent warnings sent by French embassies around the world to the French Foreign Affairs Ministry. In 2022, the French government announced an internal investigation "to identify past alleged illegal practices to prevent them from happening again" and "to respond to requests from adoptees and civil society."[7] No such initiative has gained traction in the United States.

Zune had written about his search on Facebook, and other adoptees started to contact him for advice. Many did not have the time or money to travel to Guatemala, and Zune cautioned them that opportunities for Guatemalans to make money from international adoptions had not completely dried up when they were banned. A number of Guatemalans, including former baby brokers, now worked as "searchers," locating birth parents for a fee.[8] One searcher I interviewed, who asked not to be identified by name and emphasized that she had not worked as a *jaladora,* told me she found birth parents for a fee of about US$1,000 per case. She said that over more than a decade she had completed hundreds of searches. The searcher claimed to have a 90 percent success rate at finding birth mothers using information in adoption files but acknowledged that the approach was delicate. Sometimes she traveled to the last known address of a birth mother in Guatemala City, often in gang-controlled areas, and from there tracked her to a hometown outside the capital. "I've never found a mother who was not poor or desperately poor," she told me. Other times, she visited the parents of birth mothers in rural areas to find more recent addresses in Guatemala City. All she says at first is "I have an envelope from the United States," in case the adoption was secret. "Many families have family in the U.S., so that opens the door for me." Birth mothers often have an emotional response. "It always ends up with a lot of emotions, happiness among them," the searcher said. "Shame, too." After meeting hundreds of birth mothers, she said, she realized many of them never wished to relinquish their children. "I think that the most powerful coercion is poverty."[9]

One factor complicating adoptees' search is that some birth parents have joined the large-scale Guatemalan migration to the United States, pushed out by gang violence, climate change, political persecution, anti-Indigenous discrimination, and violence against women. The majority of Guatemalans in the United States live undocumented—making birth parents even more difficult to find. Other searches were complicated by the conditions of war: for example, a K'iche' woman who voluntarily relinquished her child for adoption in 1981 and then fled the violence to Mexico as a refugee shortly thereafter was difficult to contact. Even though there was no fraud or kidnapping in this case, her adoptive daughter only managed to track her birth mother to Mexico by a stroke of good luck.[10] Technological changes have made research and communication easier and have led to surprises for both adoptees and birth families. Some adoptees confronting dead ends in the form of falsified paperwork have seen unexpected breakthroughs in their own cases when half-brothers or half-sisters, often migrants living in the United States, get in touch through matches on DNA and ancestry websites like 23andMe. Adoptees regularly search for their birth parents using Facebook, which Guatemalans even in very remote areas tend to use. A private foundation of forensic anthropologists in Guatemala (Fundación de Antropología Forense de Guatemala) created a DNA bank modeled on that of the Argentine Mothers and Grandmothers of the Plaza de Mayo, and is collecting samples both in Guatemala and among migrants and adoptees in California, Massachusetts, and Washington, DC.[11] Despite successful searches and reunions, many adoptees still lack the most basic information, such as their mother's name, where exactly they are from, whether their families were Indigenous, or what language they speak.[12]

The Guatemalan government has thus far refused to acknowledge its history of disappearing and stealing Indigenous children during the war and arranging forcible adoptions. After the signing of Peace Accords in 1996, the UN-sponsored Truth Commission acknowledged that many of the disappeared children had been put up for adoption without the consent or knowledge of surviving parents or family members. It recommended that the government "urgently activate the search" for such children, and "promote extraordinary legislative measures that, on the request of the adopted person or his / her relatives, allow for the review of adoptions brought about without the knowledge, or against the will, of the natural parents."[13] But this search has mostly been conducted by underfunded nonprofit organizations like Maco Garavito's group, La Liga. Having relinquished a child for adoption, or even having lost a child during the war, is often considered a cause of shame—inhibiting those who would like to search. In an interview, Rudy Zepeda, spokesperson for the National Adoptions Council (Consejo Nacional de Adopciones), repeated to me a common reproach: "not even a dog leaves her pups."[14] The majority of the families of disappeared children were Indigenous farmers, many of whom could not pay the bus fare to the capital to begin a search that would necessarily be in Spanish, which they may speak with varying

Two posters stacked on top of one another on a wall in downtown Guatemala City read: "Where are they? Five thousand disappeared boys and girls." *(above)* and "Justice for the child victims of the war, terror, and impunity. Five thousand girls and boys detained, disappeared. Where are they?" *(below). Courtesy of Sebastián Escalón.*

degrees of proficiency, and involve a paper trail that they may or may not have been able to read.[15]

In Guatemala, private adoptions caused a moral panic. But contending with the disappearance of children during the war has for the most part been an exercise in collective suppression rather than collective memory.[16] This silence has left space for some in the United States to pressure for international adoption to be reopened. Some conservatives argue that reopening Guatemala to international adoption could help assuage the current political crisis over migration. Their implicit argument is that if Central American families had the option of sending their children for placement with adoptive families in the United States, the whole family wouldn't have to migrate. Fox News host Laura Ingraham, who adopted a child from Guatemala right before the ban in 2008, brought up the idea in the midst of the furor over family separation at the border during the Trump administration in 2018. Ingraham said: "We

A sign reading "They are not for sale #nototrafficking" in Guatemala City's airport, January 2023. © *Rachel Nolan.*

should make adoption easier for American couples who want to adopt these kids who are true candidates for adoption because our policies don't allow that. So let's put our hearts out there for the kids in the right way."[17]

Although the Trump administration claimed it was seeking to reunite families who were separated at the border, the Associated Press found in October 2018 that some children separated from Salvadoran mothers who were deported without them were at risk of being processed for adoption by families in the United States. The Associated Press investigation drew on immigration records, interviews, and hundreds of court documents to show that there are "holes in the system that allow state court judges to grant custody of migrant children to American families without notifying their parents."[18] In 2009, one undocumented Guatemalan woman in Missouri, who was arrested in an ICE raid, sued from prison to stop her one-year-old son from being adopted by a North American family. The judge on a Missouri Circuit Court found in favor of the adoptive family, writing about the mother that "smuggling herself into the country is not a lifestyle that can provide any stability for the child."[19] If Guatemala has not collectively reckoned with its history of child separation, neither has the United States.[20]

Zune's search for his birth family has come to a dead end, at least for now, but he has stayed on in Guatemala. He makes a good salary at the call center, since he can answer the phones in French, and commutes from Jocotenango to Guatemala City by motorcycle. Zune became friendly with Maco Garavito when he dropped off his paperwork at La Liga, in case he was a match with one of the families in their database. After reviewing Zune's file, Garavito thought it was unlikely that he was a victim of the war. The paperwork for disappeared children—even forms that have been falsified—generally locate the children's birthplaces in the highland regions, not on the border with Mexico. Zune told me it is impossible to know for sure.

When La Liga does manage to match a family with their disappeared child, the organization puts together ceremonies, often including elements of Maya spiritual traditions. There are candles, incense, and a spread of tamales. Adoptees have traveled from the United States, Mexico, and Europe for these reunification ceremonies. La Liga has managed to find the children of 527 families who were searching for children who went missing or were disappeared during the war. Thousands are still looking. Garavito started inviting Zune, too, who has understandably become something of a star at La Liga's ceremonies and meetings. Whenever he attends, Zune is surrounded by several rings of birth parents at all times. One family from Nebaj became convinced that Zune was their son who went missing after a 1982 massacre. Garavito had to break the news gently to both the family and Zune that it was not even worth doing a DNA test, since Zune was too young to be their son. "They still write to me every once in a while to see how I'm doing," Zune told me. He recalled that he sobbed openly while attending his first reunification ceremony, but now considers them the highlight of his time in Guatemala, because of all the affection shown to him by the parents. "They are all missing children," Garavito said, "and he is the one who came back. They like to imagine that he is theirs."[21]

Archives and Interviews

ARCHIVES

AFS	Archivo Fundación Sobrevivientes, Guatemala City, Guatemala
AGCA	Archivo General de Centroámerica, Guatemala City, Guatemala
AGT	Archivo General de Tribunales, Guatemala City, Guatemala
AGUSAC	Archivo General de la Universidad de San Carlos, Guatemala City, Guatemala
AHDSC	Archivo Histórico Diocesano de San Cristóbal de las Casas, San Cristóbal de las Casas, Chiapas, Mexico
AHPN	Archivo Histórico de la Policía Nacional, Guatemala City, Guatemala
ALC	Archivo Legislativa del Congreso, Guatemala City, Guatemala
AFLB	Archivo Privado de Fernando Linares Beltranena, Guatemala City, Guatemala
AP	Archivo de Protocolos, Guatemala City, Guatemala
AREMHI	Archivo del Proyecto Interdiocesano de Recuperación de la Memoria Histórica, Guatemala City, Guatemala
BLC	Biblioteca Legislativo del Congreso, Guatemala City, Guatemala
CIRMA	Centro de Investigaciones Regionales de Mesoamérica, Antigua, Guatemala
HI	Hoover Institution Archives, Palo Alto, California, United States
HN	Hemeroteca Nacional de Guatemala, Guatemala City, Guatemala
INE	Instituto Nacional de Estadística, Guatemala City, Guatemala
NSA	National Security Archive, Washington, DC, United States
SBS	Archivo de la Secretaría de Bienestar Social, Guatemala City, Guatemala
TN	Tipografía Nacional, Guatemala City, Guatemala

INTERVIEWS

All interviews were conducted with the author in Guatemala City unless otherwise noted. Some of these interviews were conducted jointly with research assistant Silvia Méndez, as noted below.

Elizabeth Bartholet, 14 February 2019 (conducted by telephone)
Father Juan María Boxus, 17 November 2016. Malacatán, San Marcos
    Department, Guatemala
Jorge Carrillo Gudiel, 31 March 2016
Doña Carmelita, 27 July 2018. Aldea Güisiltepeque, Jalapa Department,
    Guatemala
Dina Castro, 18 February 2016
Norma Cruz, 1 December 2015
Rodolfo Díaz, with Silvia Méndez, 3 March 2016
Marco Antonio (Maco) Garavito Fernández, 23 November 2015,
    28 January 2016, and 25 July 2017
Eduardo García 20 May 2016. San Salvador, El Salvador
Ricardo Gatica Trejo, 29 January 2016
Dayner Hernández and Loyda Rodríguez, 15 January 2016. Rural area of
    Guatemala (location withheld by request of interviewees)
Carlos Larios Ochaita, with Silvia Méndez, 22 April 2016
Fernando Linares Beltranena, with Silvia Méndez, 27 January 2016,
    18 March 2016; with author, 10 September 2017
Susana Luarca, 24 February 2016 and 6 April 2016
Licette Morales, 14 April 2016 and 12 September 2016
Hilda Morales Trujillo, with Silvia Méndez, 5 February 2016
Ana Maria Moreno, with Silvia Méndez, 24 February 2016
Claudio Porres, 22 March 2016
Julio Prado, 27 November 2016
Barbara Reckenholder, 9 February 2016
Loyda Rodríguez, *see* Dayner Hernández and Loyda Rodríguez
Susan (pseudonym for adoption agency worker), 10 April 2017 (conducted by
    telephone)
Teresa (pseudonym for Guatemalan birth mother "searcher"), 15 April 2016.
    Antigua, Guatemala

Rudy Zepeda, 9 October 2015

Jean-Sébastien (Alberto) Hertsens Zune, 11 November 2016, 7 May 2016, and 24 July 2017 in Antigua, Guatemala, and 21 November 2016 and 31 July 2018 in Guatemala City

Notes

INTRODUCTION

1. Expediente Dolores Preat, Archivo Fundación Sobrevivientes, hereafter AFS. Dolores Preat kindly confirmed the details of this trip with me by telephone.

2. For the history of race in Quetzaltenango, see Greg Grandin, *The Blood of Guatemala: A History of Race and Nation* (Durham: Duke University Press, 2000).

3. With the exception of a tiny number of Guatemalan elites who trace their imagined or real ancestry wholly to Spain, a non-Maya Indigenous group called the Xinca, Guatemala's immigrant populations from Asia and other regions, and a small African-descended population based along the Caribbean coast, everyone in the country has at least some Maya ancestry. Discerning who is Indigenous and who is not relies on fluid cultural markers that have changed over time, not on anything resembling the "blood quantum" the federal government used to restrict tribal membership in the United States and that some Native nations still use for citizenship requirements. The Guatemalan census counts about 40 percent of the population as Maya Indigenous, but this is widely viewed as an undercount.

4. Carol Smith, *Guatemalan Indians and the State 1540 to 1988* (Austin: University of Texas Press, 1995); and Marta Elena Casaús Arzú, *Guatemala: Linaje y racismo,* 3rd ed. (Guatemala City: F&G Editores, 2007). See also Jorge Ramón González Ponciano, "La visible invisibilidad de la blancura y el ladino como no blanco en Guatemala," in *Memorias del mestizaje: Cultura política en Centroamérica de 1920 al presente,* ed. Darío Euraque, Jeffrey Gould, and Charles R. Hale, 111–132 (Guatemala City: CIRMA, 2004).

5. "Llamado de la sangre." Expediente Dolores Preat, AFS. English translations of published or unpublished material quoted here are my own, unless otherwise noted.

6. Rodolfo Díaz interview, 3 March 2016. See the Archives and Interviews for the details of interviews I conducted; many, including this one, were conducted with the assistance of Silvia Méndez. Interviews took place in Guatemala City unless otherwise noted.

7. Juan Carlos Llorca and Julie Watson, "Guatemalan Adoption Raid Riles Parents," Associated Press, 16 August 2007. I first came across the statistic in Erin Siegel, *Finding Fernanda: Two Mothers, One Child, and a Cross-Border Search for Truth* (New York: Beacon Press, 2012),

34. For a statistical analysis, see Casa Alianza, Fundación Sobrevivientes, Secretaria de Bienestar Social, et al., *Adopciones en Guatemala: Protección o mercado?* (Guatemala City: Tipografía Nacional, 2007).

8. I use the unlovely phrase "sender countries," taken from export economics, throughout the book. It is a term frequently used by adoption agencies and adoption scholars.

9. Historians, anthropologists, and sociologists have all written about adoptions. See for example Catherine Ceniza Choy, *Global Families: A History of Asian International Adoption in America* (New York: New York University Press, 2013); Laura Briggs, *Somebody's Children: The Politics of Transnational and Transracial Adoption* (Durham: Duke University Press, 2012); and Karen Dubinsky, *Babies without Borders: Adoption and Migration across the Americas* (New York: New York University Press, 2010).

10. Carlota McAllister and Diane M. Nelson, eds., *War by Other Means: Aftermath in Post-Genocide Guatemala* (Durham: Duke University Press, 2013). I will use the terms *war* or *armed conflict,* rather than civil war, to avoid the misperception that this was a contest between opposing armies. Given mobilization into a variety of guerrilla groups and the onslaught by the army against the civilian population especially during the late 1970s and early 1980s, the term doesn't capture this history.

11. U.S. Department of State Bureau of Consular Affairs, Orphan Visa statistics. See https://travel.state.gov/content/travel/en/Intercountry-Adoption/adopt_ref/adoption-statistics-esri.html, accessed under "Adoptions by Country" and "Guatemala." The European statistics are more difficult to access, and this estimate is based on adoption records and news accounts. See, for example, Duncan Campbell, "Guatemala Babies Sold to Highest Bidders," *The Guardian,* 12 June 2000. Canada's records are spotty but show that 640 Guatemalan children were adopted from 1993 to 2001, when the country suspended adoptions from Guatemala. Government of Canada, Immigration Statistics accessed at http://web.archive.org/web/20070420210142/www.cic.gc.ca/english/monitor/issue03/06-feature.html. For 1979–2021, the French government recorded 1,970 adoptions from Guatemala. Yves Denéchère and Fabio Macedo, "Étude historique sur les pratiques illicites dans l'adoption international en France" (Laboratoire Temps, Modes, Société [TEMOS], UMR CNRS 9016, Université d'Angers, Angers, France, January 2023), 11. Some adoptee groups estimate as many as 50,000 Guatemalan adoptees worldwide.

12. Comisión para el Esclarecimiento Histórico (CEH), *Guatemala, Memory of Silence, Tz'inil Na'tab'al: Report of the Commission for Historical Clarification, Conclusions and Recommendations* (Guatemala City: United Nations Office of Project Services, 1999)—this is the UN-backed truth commission report. This war was one of the many Latin American conflicts in which Cold War pressures exacerbated local conflicts over land, resources, and social rights. See Vanni Pettinà, *Historia minima de la Guerra Fría en América Latina* (Mexico City: El Colegio de México, 2018); Patrick Iber, *Neither Peace nor Freedom: The Cultural Cold War in Latin America* (Cambridge, MA: Harvard University Press, 2015); and Gilbert M. Joseph and Greg Grandin, eds., *A Century of Revolution: Insurgent and Counterinsurgent Violence during Latin America's Long Cold War* (Durham: Duke University Press, 2010).

13. CEH, *Guatemala, Memory of Silence,* 23; and 2003 data from the Comisión Nacional de Búsqueda de la Niñas y Niños Desaparecidos (National Commission for the Search for Disappeared Children), cited in Casa Alianza et al., *Adopciones en Guatemala,* 24.

14. Laura Briggs, "Mother, Child, Race, Nation: The Visual Iconography of Rescue and the Politics of Transnational and Transracial Adoption," *Gender & History* 15, no. 2 (Aug. 2003): 179–200.

15. Karen Dubinsky noted the same repeated phrase, "just a business." Dubinsky, *Babies without Borders,* 112. Sarah Esther Maslin, "Home Alone," *Economist,* 6 August 2016.

16. "After Haiti Quake, the Chaos of U.S. Adoptions," *New York Times,* 3 August 2010; and "Eager to Adopt, Evangelicals Find Perils Abroad," *New York Times,* 31 May 2013. Controversies over meaningful consent from birth families after celebrity adoptions, including Madonna's adoption of a child from Malawi and Angelina Jolie's adoption of a child from Cambodia, have also raised awareness of corruption in international adoption.

17. David Crary, "Foreign Adoptions by U.S. Families Drop More Than a Quarter," Associated Press, 6 May 2020.

18. Arthur Brooks, "Let's Restart the Adoption Movement," *New York Times,* 17 November 2017.

19. Elizabeth Bartholet, "International Adoption: The Child's Story," *Georgia State University Law Review* 24, no. 2 (2007): 373, 344.

20. Rachel Nolan, "Destined for Export: The Troubled Legacy of Guatemalan Adoptions," *Harper's Magazine,* April 2019. Elizabeth Bartholet interview, 14 February 2019.

21. Expediente Dolores Preat, AFS.

22. Zunil was affected by violence, but not to the same extent as other areas of Guatemala, which saw larger-scale massacres. "31 muertos por violencia política en Guatemala," *El País,* 5 February 1982.

23. As Philippe Ariès argued in his classic work on the history of childhood, the category itself is socially constructed, not natural. Philippe Ariès, *Centuries of Childhood: A Social History of Family Life,* trans. Robert Baldick (New York: Vintage, 1962).

24. Deborah Levenson-Estrada, *Adiós Niño: The Gangs of Guatemala City and the Politics of Death* (Durham: Duke University Press, 2013), 15.

25. Vijay Prashad, *The Darker Nations: A People's History of the Third World* (New York: New Press, 2007).

26. Proyecto Interdiocesano de Recuperación de la Memoria Histórica (REMHI), *Guatemala: Nunca más!* (Guatemala City: Oficina de Derechos Humanos del Arzobispado de Guatemala, 1998)—this is the Catholic Church's truth commission report. For Gerardi's murder, see Francisco Goldman, *The Art of Political Murder: Who Killed the Bishop?* (New York: Grove Press, 2007).

27. CEH, *Guatemala: Memory of Silence,* 5.

28. The designation of "genocidal acts" in the UN-backed truth commission report was limited to the years 1981 to 1983 and certain regions of Guatemala, though residents of many more areas experienced race-based state terror and massacres.

29. See Maggie Jones, "The Secrets in Guatemala's Bones," *New York Times Magazine,* 30 June 2016; Victoria Sanford, *Buried Secrets: Truth and Human Rights in Guatemala* (New York:

Palgrave Macmillan, 2003); and Alexis Hagerty, *Still Life with Bones: Genocide, Forensics, and What Remains* (New York: Crown, 2023).

30. Kirsten Weld, *Paper Cadavers: The Archives of Dictatorship in Guatemala* (Durham: Duke University Press, 2014), 104. See also Diane Nelson, *A Finger in the Wound: Body Politics in Quincentennial Guatemala* (Berkeley: University of California Press, 1999), 159.

31. Diane Nelson, *Who Counts: The Mathematics of Life and Death after Genocide* (Durham: Duke University Press, 2015).

32. Ricardo Falla, *Masacres de la selva: Ixcán, Guatemala 1975–1982* (Guatemala City: Editorial Universitario, 1992), quoted in Levenson-Estrada, *Adiós, niño,* 34.

33. Greg Grandin, *The Last Colonial Massacre: Latin America in the Cold War* (Chicago: University of Chicago Press, 2nd edition, 2011), 3.

34. Gabriel Edgardo Aguilera Peralta and Jorge Romero Imery, *Dialéctica del terror en Guatemala* (San José: EDUCA, 1981).

35. Grandin, *The Last Colonial Massacre,* 2.

36. CEH, *Guatemala, Memory of Silence,* 23. See also Casa Alianza, *Adopciones en Guatemala.* The truth commission reports consider those under twelve years old children.

37. The Liga Guatemalteca de Higiene Mental, a nonprofit organization, has a subgroup called Todos para el Reencuentro that seeks to find adults and children disappeared or lost during the war and to reintegrate them into their families. Marco Antonio (Maco) Garavito Fernández interview, 25 July 2017. See also *A voz en grito: Testimonios de familiares de niñez desaparecida durante el conflicto armado interno en Guatemala* (Guatemala City: La Liga Guatemalteca de Higiene Mental, 2003).

38. Interview with Evelyn Blanco, head of the Centro Internacional de Investigaciones en Derechos Humanos (CIIDH), cited in Sebastián Escalón, "Los niños que el ejército se llevó (I)," *Plaza Pública,* 6 August 2013.

39. *Hasta encontrarte: Niñez desaparecida por el conflicto armado,* Oficina de Derechos Humanos del Arzobispado de Guatemala (ODHAG), Guatemala City, 2000, 40, 134, 133.

40. Convention on the Prevention and Punishment of the Crime of Genocide, General Assembly of the United Nations, Resolution 260, Articles 2 and 3. On the ideological underpinnings of the Convention, see Mark Mazower, *No Enchanted Palace: The End of Empire and the Ideological Origins of the United Nations* (Princeton: Princeton University Press, 2009). See also Universal Declaration of Human Rights, Article 13.

41. Emi MacLean, *Judging a Dictator: The Trial of Guatemala's Ríos Montt* (New York: Open Society Foundation, 2013), 7.

42. Marco Tulio Álvarez, *Las adopciones y los derechos humanos de la niñez guatemalteca 1977–1989* (Guatemala City: Secretaria de la Paz, Dirección de los Archivos de la Paz, 1999).

43. The definition and significance of the term genocide and whether it is applicable to various places and times, including before the 1948 convention, is a matter of continuing historical debate. See, for example, Benjamin Madley, "Reexamining the American Genocide Debate: Meaning, Historiography, and New Methods," *American Historical Review* 120, no. 1 (February 2015): 98–139.

44. A piece of the puzzle is still missing. No one has had access to records from private and religious orphanages, both Catholic and Pentecostal. Ríos Montt himself was a fervent Pentecostal Christian, and both the United Nations and Catholic Church truth commission workers were denied entrance to Casa Bernabé, an orphanage in Antigua advertised as housing war orphans. The orphanage was run by International Love Lift, an emergency aid group funded by Ríos Montt's church. Sara Diamond, *Spiritual Warfare: The Politics of the Christian Right* (Montreal: Black Rose Books, 1990), 168. See also Lauren Turek, "To Support a 'Brother in Christ': Evangelical Groups and U.S.-Guatemalan Relations during the Ríos Montt Regime," *Diplomatic History* 39, no. 4 (September 2015): 689–719. All Pentecostals are Evangelical Christian, though not all Evangelicals are Pentecostal. The terms will be used interchangeably throughout because both are called *evangélicos* in Guatemala, though usually in reference to Pentecostals.

45. Jo Marie Burt, "From Heaven to Hell in Ten Days: The Genocide Trial in Guatemala," *Journal of Genocide Research* 18, no. 2–3 (2016): 143–169.

46. The most notorious such organization is the Fundación Contra el Terrorismo, Foundation against Terrorism (referring to guerrilla fighters), founded in 2013.

47. Kirsten Weld, "Official Histories," *Guernica*, 3 March 2014.

48. Rachel Hatcher, *The Power of Memory and Violence in Central America* (London: Palgrave Macmillan, 2018).

49. Oswaldo J. Hernández, "The Case of Sepur Zarco: Beneath the Shawls, Justice Is Served," *Plaza Pública*, 23 March 2016, https://www.justiceinfo.net/en/26484-the-case-of-sepur-zarco-beneath-the-shawls-justice-is-served.html.

50. Chris Norton, "Guatemala, Charged with Rights Violations, Searches for Respect," *Christian Science Monitor*, 18 January 1985. Quoted in Jennifer G. Schirmer, "'Those Who Die for Life Cannot Be Called Dead': Women and Human Rights Protest in Latin America," *Feminist Review* 32 (Summer 1989): 14.

51. "Guatemala's Missing Children," *New York Times*, 20 August 2000. This editorial was in response to a publication following up on the 1998 Catholic Church's truth commission report, *Hasta Encontrarte*. The new publication chronicled the stories of eighty-six children forcibly disappeared during the war and listed hundreds more. *Hasta encontrarte*, ODHAG.

52. See, for example, Steve Stern's trilogy on historical memory in Chile. Steve J. Stern, *Remembering Pinochet's Chile: On the Eve of London 1998* (Durham: Duke University Press, 2004); Stern, *Battling for Hearts and Minds: Memory Struggles in Pinochet's Chile, 1973–1988* (Durham: Duke University Press, 2006); and Stern, *Reckoning with Pinochet: The Memory Question in Democratic Chile, 1989–2006* (Durham: Duke University Press, 2010).

53. See the advertisements circulated by a veteran's organization called Asociación de Veteranos Militares de Guatemala (AVEMILGUA) and the right-wing Foundation against Terrorism, including "La farsa del genocidio en Guatemala," insert in *El Periódico*, 5 May 2013.

54. Lawyers in Guatemala performed these adoptions in their role as notaries. All lawyers in Guatemala are notaries, and vice versa. While I will be using the word lawyer throughout, it should be taken to mean lawyer-notary.

55. "Adoption and the Rights of the Child in Guatemala," Latin American Institute for Education and Communication (ILPEC), for UNICEF, 2000.

56. Karen A. Balcom, *The Traffic in Babies: Cross-Border Adoption and Baby-Selling between the United States and Canada, 1930–1972* (Toronto: University of Toronto Press, 2011).

57. Sara K. Dorow, *Transnational Adoption: A Cultural Economy of Race, Gender, and Kinship* (New York: New York University Press, 2006), 17.

58. World Bank, *Poverty in Guatemala* (Washington, DC: World Bank, 2004).

59. Lawyers earned between US$3,000 and $7,000 of pure profit per adoption in early years. Fees later rose higher. Adoptions were a US$1.5 to $3 million business the year before they closed.

60. Casaús Arzú, *Guatemala: Linaje y racismo.*

61. Jim Handy, *Gift of the Devil: A History of Guatemala* (Boston: South End Press, 1984); and David McCreery, *Rural Guatemala 1760–1940* (Stanford: Stanford University Press, 1994).

62. John M. Watanabe, *Maya Saints and Souls in a Changing World* (Austin: University of Texas Press, 1992); Kay B. Warren, *The Symbols of Subordination: Indian Identity in a Guatemalan Town* (Austin: University of Texas Press, 1978); and Richard N. Adams, *Crucifixion by Power: Essays on Capitalist National Social Structure* (Austin: University of Texas Press, 1970).

63. Lucy Hood, "Adoption Brokers Prey on Guatemala's Poor," *South Florida Sun Sentinel,* 18 July 1988.

64. The most complete treatment of the history of CICIG is Sebastián Escalón, "El Experimento," podcast, *No Ficción,* 2021–2022, https://www.no-ficcion.com/project/guatemala-pide-auxilio-elexperimento. See Comisión Internacional Contra la Impunidad en Guatemala (CICIG), "Informe sobre actores involcrados en el proceso de adopciones irregulares en Guatemala" (Guatemala City: December 2010), 26, https://www.cicig.org/uploads/documents/informes/INFOR-TEMA_DOC05_20101201_ES.pdf.

65. Siegal McIntyre, *Finding Fernanda.*

66. Dubinsky, *Babies without Borders;* and Briggs, *Somebody's Children,* 179.

67. Carla Villalta, "De los derechos de los adoptantes al derecho a la identidad: los procedimientos de adopción y la apropiación criminal de niños en la Argentina," *Journal of Latin American and Caribbean Anthropology* 15, no. 2 (2010): 338–362. Karen Alfaro Monsalve, "Madres que buscan hijos e hijas: Adopciones forzadas de niños y niñas del sur de Chile 1973–1990," *Revista de Historia (Concepción),* December 2022, 2 (29).

68. Briggs, *Somebody's Children,* 168.

69. The activism of the Asociación Madres de la Plaza de Mayo is one reason so much is known about Argentina. Another is the success of the 1985 film *La Historia Oficial, The Official Story. La Historia Oficial,* Luis Puezo, dir. (Buenos Aires: Historias Cinematograficas Cinemania, 1985). In contrast, little is known about Guatemala or El Salvador.

70. *Finding Oscar,* Ryan Suffern, dir. (Santa Monica: Kennedy / Marshall, 2017).

71. Eduardo García interview, 20 May 2016, San Salvador.

72. Eduardo García interview, 20 May 2016, San Salvador. See also Sergio Arauz, "La red que exportaba niños," *El Faro,* 28 October 2014 and "Separated by War, Reunited through DNA," *New York Times,* 22 December 2006. One of the founders of the DNA bank, Elizabeth Barnert,

wrote a moving book about attempts to reunify Salvadoran families with their children. Elizabeth Barnert, *Reunion: Finding the Disappeared Children of El Salvador* (Berkeley: University of California Press, 2023).

73. "El Salvador's Military Not Opening Archives for Missing Kids," Associated Press, 27 February 2018.

74. Researchers who have gained access to adoption files usually work with a set of paperwork from a particular region or an earlier period. For example, E. Wayne Carp, *Family Matters: Secrecy and Disclosure in the History of Adoption* (Cambridge, MA: Harvard University Press, 2000); and Barbara Melosh, *Strangers and Kin: The American Way of Adoption* (Cambridge, MA: Harvard University Press, 2002). Donna J. Guy writes that she gained access to 50,000 adoption files from the Argentine Consejo Nacional de Niñez, Adolescencia y la Familia (formerly the Society of Beneficence), from the years 1880 to 1955 in Argentina. Donna J. Guy, *Women Build the Welfare State: Performing Charity and Creating Rights in Argentina, 1880–1955* (Durham: Duke University Press, 2009), ix.

75. I learned of the existence of these files in Weld, *Paper Cadavers;* Weld discusses the process of archiving adoption files on page 214.

76. "Cierran Archivos de la Paz," *Prensa Libre,* 31 May 2012.

77. In 2012 an anthropologist who was able to access many other sources on adoption also visited the ministry, where she was told, "There are no adoption documents, there is no archive." Silvia Posocco, "Substance, Sign, and Trace: Performative Analogies and Technologies of Enfleshment in the Transnational Adoption Archives in Guatemala," *Social & Cultural Geography* 16, no. 5 (2015): 576.

78. I use pseudonyms and case file numbers to protect the identities of adoptees, birth mothers, and adoptive families. I use real names for social workers, lawyers, politicians, and those who worked at adoption agencies. For example, SBS Adoption File 7-71 is the seventh case finalized in 1971, Archivo de la Secretaría de Bienestar Social (SBS), Guatemala City, Guatemala.

79. Sebastián Escalón and Pilar Crespo, "La increíble historia de Edmond Mulet y los niños que 'exportaba,'" *Plaza Pública,* 30 January 2015. See also Mulet's reply, "Edmond Mulet rechaza el contenido del reportaje 'La increíble historia de Edmond Mulet y los niños que "exportaba,"'" *Plaza Pública,* 26 February 2015.

80. Personal communication, Mary Evans, 6 July 2015.

81. "People Power and the Guatemalan Spring," *Al Jazeera,* 3 September 2015.

82. Whatever distortions of the facts these narratives may have involved are themselves worthy of interpretation. As Alessandro Portelli wrote, oral histories are "not always fully reliable in point of fact. Rather than being a weakness, this is, however, their strength: errors, inventions, and myths lead us through and beyond facts to their meanings." Alessandro Portelli, *Death of Luigi Trastulli and Other Stories: Form and Meaning in Oral History* (Albany: State University of New York Press, 1991), 2, cited in Daniel James, *Doña María's Story: Life History, Memory, and Political Identity* (Durham: Duke University Press, 2002), 124. James's analysis of the politics of narrative has influenced my use of interviews. I also learned from the sensitive approach by Ann Fessler, *The Girls Who Went Away: The Hidden History of Women Who Surrendered Children for Adoption in the Decades before Roe v. Wade* (New York: Penguin, 2006).

83. Next Generation Guatemala, "Between Two Worlds," Special Issue, *Maya America* 4, no. 1 (2022). For research on the outcomes of transracial adoptions more widely, see Eleana Kim, *Adopted Territory: Transnational Korean Adoptees and the Politics of Belonging* (Durham: Duke University Press, 2011); Heather Jacobson, *Culture Keeping: White Mothers, International Adoption, and the Negotiation of Family Difference* (Nashville: Vanderbilt University Press, 2008).

1. THE LIE WE LOVE

1. The phrase from the file is "estando pendiente de captura los padres." Ministry of Social Welfare Archive, Archivo de la Secretaría de Bienestar Social (hereafter SBS) Adoption File 23-72. I will use real file numbers but pseudonyms for children. As stated, the file numbers represent the case number followed by the year the case was finalized. Adoption File 23-72 was the twenty-third case finalized in 1972. Most children were allowed to leave the orphanage with adoptive families on a probationary basis at least a year before the paperwork was fully finalized.

2. "No tenemos y no podemos tener hijos propios." SBS Adoption File 23-72.

3. No forms consulted at the SBS described adoptive parents rejected for "moral" reasons, though family members were prevented from taking in children if social workers observed signs of poor hygiene, alcoholism, or extreme poverty.

4. SBS Adoption File 23-72.

5. Recent scholarship on Indigenous identity in Guatemala emphasizes the mutability of racial categories. See Charles R. Hale, *Más Que un Indio: Racial Ambivalence and the Paradox of Neoliberal Multiculturalism in Guatemala* (Guatemala City: AVANSCO, 2006); Irma Alicia Velásquez Nimatuj, *La pequeña burguesía indígena comercial de Guatemala: desigualdades de clase, raza, y género* (Guatemala City: AVANCSO-SERJUS, 2002); Marta Elena Casaús Arzú, *Guatemala: Linaje y racismo*, 3rd ed. (Guatemala City: F&G Editores, 2007); Arturo Taracena Arriola, *Etnicidad, estado y nación en Guatemala 1944–1985*, vol. 2 (Antigua, Guatemala: CIRMA, 2004); and Liza Grandia, "Back to the Future: The Autonomous Indigenous Communities of Petén, Guatemala," *Antípoda: Revista de Antropología y Arqeología* 40, no. 7 (2020): 103–127.

6. Since I am emphasizing racial categories throughout adoption history, I want to make clear that I'm writing less about race itself than about the perception of race that so sharply divided and continues to divide Guatemala. As Paul Gilroy notes, race is not intrinsic or immutable but imposed and often illusory. Paul Gilroy, *Against Race: Imagining Political Culture beyond the Color Line* (Cambridge, MA: Belknap Press of Harvard University Press, 2002), 37.

7. SBS Adoption File 23-72.

8. SBS Adoption File 26-72.

9. SBS Adoption File 9-76.

10. SBS Adoption File 23-72.

11. "Por ser sumamente pobre y carece de recursos para el sostén de sus mencionados hijos, ha dispuesto darles los dos primeros, de [nombres redactados], a Doña [nombre redactado] quien también está presente en este acto." Archivo Municipal de Tactic, Libro de Actas, November 1957. Many thanks to Sarah Foss for giving me photographs of these records.

12. Jessaca B. Leinaweaver, *The Circulation of Children: Kinship, Adoption, and Morality in Andean Peru* (Durham: Duke University Press, 2008), 3. Leinaweaver chose to study the subject because of the "frequency with which I was offered babies on one of my first trips to the region" (4). I had the opposite experience in Guatemala: people told me that it was no longer possible to adopt and that I should not try. Neither of us, it is worth noting, were engaged in research in an attempt to secure a baby.

13. Nara Milanich calls this arrangement "child tutelary servitude." Nara Milanich, "Degrees of Bondage: Children's Tutelary Servitude in Modern Latin America," in *Child Slaves in the Modern World*, ed. Joseph Miller, Gwyn Campbell, and Sue Miers, 2 vols. (Athens: Ohio University Press, 2010), 2:116. There are regional variations in the practice; for example, in Haiti live-in servant children are known as *restavèks*. On the practice of taking in orphans as servants in the Guatemalan context, see Greg Grandin, *The Blood of Guatemala: A History of Race and Nation* (Durham: Duke University Press, 2000), 36–37. Latin America was not the only region where children were placed for involuntary domestic service. Historian Marco Leuenberger brought to light the history of Swiss *Verdingkinder*, children separated from poor or single mothers deemed "unfit" by the state and placed with farmers for contract labor in a system that persisted from the nineteenth century until the 1950s. Marco Leuenberger, *Versorgt und vergessen: Ehemalige Verdingkinder erzählen* (Zürich: Rotpunktverlag, 2008).

14. Nara B. Milanich, *Children of Fate: Childhood, Class, and the State in Chile, 1850–1930* (Durham: Duke University Press, 2009), 209.

15. Diana Isabel Lenton, "Wounds of Indigenous Genocide in Argentina and Possibilities for Healing," presentation at University of Southern California as part of the conference Mass Violence and Its Lasting Impact on Indigenous Peoples—the Case of the Americas and Australia / Pacific Region," 24 October 2022. See also Lenton, "De centauros a protegidos: La construcción del sujeto de la política indigenista argentina desde los debates parlamentarios 1880–1970," PhD diss., Universidad de Buenos Aires, 2014, and Lenton, Walter Delrio, Diego Escolar, and Marisa Malvestitti, eds., *En el país de nomeacuerdo: Archivos y memorias del genocidio del Estado Argentino sobre los pueblos originarios, 1870–1950* (Buenos Aires: Editorial UNRN, 2018).

16. Viviana A. Zelizer, *Pricing the Priceless Child: The Changing Social Value of Children* (Princeton: Princeton University Press, 1994), 3.

17. Hoover Institution Archives, David Stoll Collection, box 18, Central American Mission folder, *The Central American Bulletin*, 15 November 1919.

18. Hoover Institution Archives, David Stoll Collection, box 18, Central American Mission folder, *The Central American Bulletin*, 20 May 1920.

19. Protestants also organized orphan trains in the United States. See Marilyn Irvin Holt, *The Orphan Trains: Placing Out in America* (Omaha: University of Nebraska Press, 1992) and Linda Gordon, *The Great Arizona Orphan Abduction* (Cambridge, MA: Harvard University Press, 1999).

20. Hoover Institution Archives, David Stoll Collection, box 18, Central American Mission folder, *The Central American Bulletin*, 15 July 1920.

21. Virginia Garrard-Burnett, *Protestantism in Guatemala: Living in the New Jerusalem* (Austin: University of Texas Press, 1998), 54.

22. Janet Benge and Geoff Benge, *Cameron Townsend: Good News in Every Language* (Seattle: Youth with a Mission Publishing, 2000), 106.

23. David Stoll, *Fishers of Men or Founders of Empire?* (New York: Zed Books, 1982). The leading Indigenous organization in Ecuador demanded the expulsion of the Summer Institute of Linguistics in 1990. See Deborah Yashar, *Contesting Citizenship in Latin America: The Rise of Indigenous Movements and the Postliberal Challenge* (Cambridge: Cambridge University Press, 2005), 146.

24. SBS Adoption File 6-71.

25. Many Latin American countries passed welfare legislation in the 1920s and 1930s, with Brazil the first to pass a Children's Code in 1927, followed by Uruguay, Costa Rica, Argentina, Chile, Mexico, Ecuador, and Venezuela throughout the 1930s. Donna J. Guy, "State, Family, and Marginal Children," in *Minor Omissions: Children in Latin American History and Society,* ed. Tobias Hecht (Madison: University of Wisconsin Press, 2002), 159.

26. "Como operará la Secretaría de Bienestar Social," *El Imparcial,* 18 June 1963.

27. Karl Marx, "Address of the Central Committee to the Communist League," London, March 1850.

28. Piero Gleijeses, *Shattered Hope: The Guatemalan Revolution and the United States 1944–1954* (Princeton: Princeton University Press, 1992); and Jim Handy, *Revolution in the Countryside: Rural Conflict and Agrarian Reform in Guatemala 1945–1955* (Chapel Hill: University of North Carolina Press, 2000).

29. "Codigo de menores: La revolucion de Guatemala y la proteccion a la infancia," *La Hora,* 19 June 1949.

30. Stephen Kinzer and Stephen Schlesinger, *Bitter Fruit: The Story of the American Coup in Guatemala* (Cambridge, MA: David Rockefeller Center for Latin American Studies, 1999). See also Nick Cullather, *Secret History: The CIA's Classified Account of Its Operations in Guatemala, 1952–1954* (Stanford: Stanford University Press, 2000). For the continuing political relevance of the 1954 coup, see Rachel Nolan, "No Bananas Today," *London Review of Books* 43, no. 23 (December 2021).

31. See Heather Vrana, *This City Belongs to Us: A History of Student Activism in Guatemala 1944–1996* (Berkeley: University of California Press, 2017); and Deborah Levenson-Estrada, *Trade Unionists against Terror: Guatemala City, 1954–1985* (Chapel Hill: University of North Carolina Press, 1994).

32. I translate *bienestar social* as simply "welfare," rather than "social welfare." Over the twentieth century, the connotations of the word "welfare" in English dramatically changed from positive to negative. See Linda Gordon, *Pitied but Not Entitled: Single Mothers and the History of Welfare* (New York: Free Press, 1994). Other Spanish-language terms include *asistencia social* and *prestación social,* referring to entitlements like welfare payments, benefits, or aid.

33. Kinzer and Schlesinger, *Bitter Fruit,* 221.

34. Archivo General de la Universidad de San Carlos (AGUSAC), Fondo: Universidad de San Carlos de Guatemala. Subfondo: C.S.U., Sección Rectoría, Serie: Documentos de Rectoría, Año 1955–1957, Folios 80, Tomo 32.26.5.1071.32C21.

35. Walda Valenti, "A.B.I.," *El Imparcial,* 13 January 1959.

36. Stephen Streeter, "Nation-Building in the Land of Eternal Counter-Insurgency: Guatemala and the Contradictions of the Alliance for Progress," *Third World Quarterly* 27, no. 1 (2006): 57–68, 58.

37. Stephen Streeter, *Managing the Counter-Revolution: The United States and Guatemala 1954–1961* (Athens: Ohio University Press, 2000), 156.

38. Richard W. Poston, *Democracy Speaks Many Tongues: Community Development around the World* (New York: Harper & Row, 1962), xiv.

39. León Aguilera, "The Most Cruzading [sic] Woman," *El Imparcial,* 12 November 1963.

40. Streeter, "Nation-Building," 59.

41. Sarah Foss, *On Our Own Terms: Development and Indigeneity in Cold War Guatemala* (Chapel Hill: University of North Carolina Press), 66–67.

42. Annika Hartmann, "'La familia pequeña vive mejor': Investigación demográfica, expertos transnacionales y debates académicos acerca de la 'explosión demográfica' en Guatemala después de 1945," *Mesoamérica* 57 (2015): 69–98, quotation on 74.

43. Hartmann, "'La familia pequeña'": 88–90.

44. Emily Klancher Merchant, *Building the Population Bomb* (Oxford: Oxford University Press, 2021), 6. See also Matthew Connelly, *Fatal Misconception: The Struggle to Control World Population* (Cambridge, MA: Harvard University Press, 2008).

45. Donna J. Guy, *Women Build the Welfare State: Performing Charity and Creating Rights in Argentina, 1880–1955* (Durham: Duke University Press, 2009), 173.

46. SBS Annual Reports, "Resumen de labores de la secretaria de asuntos sociales de la Presidencia de la República correspondiente al periodo presidencial 1966–1970."

47. Augusto Monterroso, *Complete Works and Other Stories,* trans. Edith Grossman (Austin: University of Texas Press, 1995), 23.

48. "Inauguración de Sala Cuna que Alojará a 50 y con Capacidad de 225; Acto emotivo desarrollado," *El Imparcial,* 16 May 1964.

49. "Mejor homenaje a madres: Sala Cuna," *El Imparcial,* 11 May 1966.

50. John Seabrook, "The Last Babylift," *New Yorker,* 20 May 2010.

51. Arissa H. Oh, *To Save the Children of Korea: The Cold War Origins of International Adoption* (Stanford: Stanford University Press, 2015), 68. See also Susie Woo, *Framed by War: Korean Children and Women at the Crossroads of U.S. Empire* (New York: New York University Press, 2019); SooJin Pate, *From Orphan to Adoptee: U.S. Empire and Genealogies of Korean Adoption* (Minneapolis: University of Minnesota Press, 2014).

52. Cited in Kathryn Joyce, *The Child Catchers: Rescue, Trafficking, and the New Gospel of Adoption* (New York: Public Affairs, 2013), 51. See also Tobias Hübinette, *The Korean Adoption Issue between Modernity and Coloniality: Transnational Adoption and Overseas Adoptees in Korean Popular Culture* (Köln: Lambert Academic Publishing, 2009).

53. Barbara Melosh, *Strangers and Kin: The American Way of Adoption* (Cambridge, MA: Harvard University Press, 2002).

54. Pearl S. Buck, "The Children Waiting: The Shocking Scandal of Adoption," *Woman's Home Companion* 33 (September 1955): 129–132.

55. Laura Briggs, *Somebody's Children: The Politics of Transracial and Transnational Adoption* (Durham: Duke University Press, 2012).

56. E. J. Graff, "The Lie We Love," *Foreign Policy,* 6 October 2009.

57. Gonda Van Steen, *Adoption, Memory, and Cold War Greece: Kid Pro Quo?* (Ann Arbor: University of Michigan Press, 2019).

58. Eleana Kim, *Adopted Territory: Transnational Korean Adoptees and the Politics of Belonging* (Durham: Duke University Press, 2010), 250.

59. Interviewed in Maggie Jones, "Why a Generation of Adoptees Is Returning to South Korea," *New York Times Magazine,* 18 January 2015. See also Kim, *Adopted Territory,* 69.

60. Hyun Sook Han, *Many Lives Intertwined: A Memoir* (St. Paul, MN: Yeong & Yeong Book Co., 2004), 100–101.

61. Yuri Doolan, "The Camptown Origins of International Adoption and the Hypersexualization of Korean Children," *Journal of Asian American Studies* 24, no. 3 (2021): 351–382.

62. "Statement on the Immorality of Bringing South Vietnamese Orphans to the United States," April 4, 1975, Viola W. Bernard Papers, box 62, folder 8, Archives and Special Collections, Augustus C. Long Library, Columbia University. Found in Adoption History Project, University of Oregon, https://pages.uoregon.edu/adoption/archive/SIBSVOUS.htm.

63. Rachel Rains Winslow, *The Best Possible Immigrants: International Adoption and the American Family* (Philadelphia: University of Pennsylvania Press, 2017), ch. 6.

64. Ladner is quoted in Allison Varzally, *Children of Reunion: Vietnamese Adoptions and the Politics of Family Migrations* (Chapel Hill: University of North Carolina Press, 2017), 56. For her book, see Joyce A. Ladner, *Mixed Adoption: Adopting Across Racial Boundaries* (New York: Anchor Press, 1977).

65. Varzally, *Children of Reunion,* 159.

66. Childhood itself was a social invention: "The ages of life did not correspond simply to biological phases but also to social functions." Philippe Ariès, *Centuries of Childhood: A Social History of Family Life* (New York: Vintage, 1962), 21.

67. SBS Adoption File 10-72. *Quetzales,* the Guatemalan currency, were exchanged 1:1 to the U.S. dollar until 1986.

2. SOCIAL REPORTS

1. Carlos Larios Ochaita interview, 22 April 2016. Ana María Moreno interview, 24 February 2016. A Guatemalan journalist told me that she had been working on a report about wealthy Guatemalans adopting Ukrainian children in the early 2000s when a few phone calls from influential businessmen quashed the story.

2. Archivo General de la Universidad de San Carlos (AGUSAC), Guatemala City, Coleccion de publicaciones impresas, Escuela de Trabajo Social, Caja No. 47, folder "Primer Congreso de Reestructuración de la Escuela de Trabajo Social."

3. For the history of this university and its outsized role in the political life of the nation, see Heather Vrana, *This City Belongs to You: A History of Student Activism in Guatemala 1944–1996* (Berkeley: University of California Press, 2017).

4. AGUSAC, Coleccion de publicaciones impresas, Escuela de Trabajo Social, Caja No. 47, folder "Primer Congreso de Reestructuración de la Escuela de Trabajo Social."

5. AGUSAC, folder "Primer Congreso de Reestructuración de la Escuela de Trabajo Social."

6. Barbara Reckenholder interview, 9 February 2016.

7. The majority Indigenous seasonal labor force moving within Guatemala was an estimated 200,000 people in the 1950s. By the end of the 1960s it was more than 300,000, and by the 1970s it was over 500,000 people. George Lovell, *Conquest and Survival in Colonial Guatemala: A Historical Geography of the Cuchumatán Highlands, 1500–1821,* 4th ed. (Montreal: McGill-Queen's University Press, 2005), 26.

8. Ministry of Social Welfare Archive, Archivo de la Secretaría de Bienestar Social (hereafter SBS), Adoption File 26-72.

9. "Ay, mujer linda si tú supieras donde encontrábamos caja china para pagar estos viajes. Lo encontramos en el desperdicio." Barbara Reckenholder interview, 9 February 2016. SBS, "Memoria de la Asociacion de Bienestar Infantil 1959–1960," 70.

10. Stephen Streeter, "Nation-Building in the Land of Eternal Counter-Insurgency: Guatemala and the Contradictions of the Alliance for Progress," *Third World Quarterly* 27, no. 1 (2006): 57–68; and Susan Fitzpatrick Behrens, "From Symbols of the Sacred to Symbols of Subversion to Simply Obscure: Maryknoll Women Religious in Guatemala, 1953 to 1967," *The Americas* 61, no. 2 (2004): 189–216.

11. SBS, "Resumen de labores de la secretaría de asuntos sociales de la Presidencia de la República correspondiente al periodo presidencial 1966–1970." See also J. T. Way, *The Mayan in the Mall: Globalization, Development, and the Making of Modern Guatemala* (Durham: Duke University Press, 2012), 109–110. Jonathan D. Cohen, *For a Dollar and a Dream: State Lotteries in Modern America* (Oxford: Oxford University Press, 2022).

12. Hilda Morales Trujillo interview, 5 February 2016.

13. SBS, "Resumen de labores," 5.

14. SBS Archive, "Memoria Anual del Bienestar Infantil 1959–1961."

15. Susanne Jonas and Nestor Rodríguez, *Guatemala-U.S. Migration: Transforming Regions* (Austin: University of Texas Press, 2015).

16. SBS Adoption File 1-68.

17. SBS Adoption File 1-68.

18. SBS Adoption File 2-72.

19. SBS Adoption File 1-68.

20. SBS Adoption File 9-73.

21. SBS Adoption File 18-72.

22. SBS Adoption File 6-73.

23. SBS Adoption File 3-73.

24. SBS Adoption File 2-72.

25. SBS Adoption Files 1-71, 4-72, 13-72, 14-72, 15-72, 19-72, 24-72, 28-72, 1-73, 3-73, 10-73, 11-73, 4-73, 13-73, 17-73, 4-74, 11-74, 13-74.

26. SBS Adoption File 2-68.

27. SBS Adoption File 1-71.

28. SBS Adoption File 2-71.

29. SBS Adoption File 19-74.

30. SBS Adoption File 27-72.

31. SBS Adoption File 3-74.

32. Catherine Ceniza Choy, *Global Families: A History of Asian International Adoption in America* (New York: New York University Press, 2013); and Arissa H. Oh, *To Save the Children of Korea: The Cold War Origins of International Adoption* (Stanford: Stanford University Press, 2015).

33. Oh, *To Save the Children of Korea*, 156; and Laura Briggs, *Somebody's Children: The Politics of Transracial and Transnational Adoption* (Durham: Duke University Press, 2012), 6.

34. SBS Adoption File 20-79.

35. SBS Adoption File 5-71.

36. SBS Adoption File 8-71.

37. SBS Adoption File 15-73.

38. SBS Adoption File 3-71.

39. SBS Adoption File 26-72.

40. My thanks to Linda Gordon for this useful insight on how to approach case files.

41. Catherine Komisaruk, *Labor and Love in Guatemala: The Eve of Independence* (Stanford: Stanford University Press, 2013), 123.

42. SBS Adoption Files 6-73 and 13-72.

43. SBS Adoption File 13-72.

44. SBS Adoption File 37-79.

45. SBS Adoption Files 11-71, 3-71, 10-72.

46. SBS Adoption File 3-71.

47. SBS Adoption File 6-73.

48. SBS Adoption File 5-73.

49. Código Civil, Guatemala 1963, Article 274, Ley 106.

50. SBS Adoption File 33-72.

51. SBS Adoption File 5-72.

52. Hearing before the Subcommittee on Courts of the Committee on the Judiciary, U.S. Senate, Ninety-Eighth Congress, Second Session, on S. 2299, A Bill Entitled "The Anti-Fraudulent Adoption Practices Act of 1984," 16 March 1984, 100.

53. SBS Adoption File 5-72.

54. SBS Adoption File 13-72.

55. SBS Adoption File 29-71.

56. SBS Adoption File 14-72. See also SBS Adoption File 9-74.

57. SBS Adoption File 12-73.

58. SBS Adoption File 19-72.

59. SBS Adoption File 9-72.

60. SBS Adoption File 32-72.

3. PRIVATIZING ADOPTIONS

1. "Grandes pérdidas en edificios de varios niveles," *La Hora*, 5 February 1976.

2. "Guatemala Earthquake: Hearing before the Subcommittee on Western Hemisphere Affairs and Subcommittee on Foreign Assistance of the Committee on Foreign Relations,"

United States Senate, Ninety-Fourth Congress, Second Session, 16 February 1976 (Washington, DC: U.S. Government Printing Office, 1976), 36. This estimate comes from the wife of President Kjell Eugenio Laugerud.

3. Instituto de Estudios Políticos para América Latina y Africa, *Guatemala, un futuro próximo* (Madrid: IEPALA, 1980), 169.

4. Kirsten Weld, *Paper Cadavers: The Archives of Dictatorship in Guatemala* (Durham: Duke University Press, 2014), 124.

5. David McCreery, *Rural Guatemala 1760–1940* (Stanford: Stanford University Press, 1994). For rural-urban migration see Kevin O'Neill, ed., *Securing the City: Neoliberalism, Space, and Insecurity in Postwar Guatemala* (Durham: Duke University Press, 2011); and J. T. Way, *The Mayan in the Mall: Globalization, Development, and the Making of Modern Guatemala* (Durham: Duke University Press, 2012).

6. "Diversos puestos de socorro ubica comité de emergencia," *El Imparcial*, 5 February 1976.

7. Edelberto Torres-Rivas, *Crisis del poder en Centroamérica* (Ciudad Universitaria Rodrigo Facio: Editorial Universitaria Centroamericana, 1981).

8. Greg Grandin, Deborah Levenson, and Elizabeth Oglesby, eds., *The Guatemala Reader: History, Culture, Politics* (Durham: Duke University Press, 2011), 314. For ties between the CUC and the Ejército Guerrillero de los Pobres, see Rigoberta Menchú Tum, *I, Rigoberta Menchú*, ed. Elisabeth Burgos-Debray, trans. Ann Wright (London: Verso, 1984); and Betsy Konefal, *For Every Indio Who Falls: A History of Maya Activism in Guatemala* (Albuquerque: University of New Mexico Press, 2010), 118–126.

9. There were exceptions. See Alan Riding, "Earthquake Relief in Guatemala Appears to Neglect the Stricken City Slums, and Politics May Be a Part of It," *New York Times*, 22 February 1976.

10. "Cauda," *El Imparcial*, 9 February 1976; "Earthquake Toll Put at 12,000," *New York Times*, 9 February 1976; and "3:04—Earthquake!" *Newsweek*, 16 February 1976. Bart McDowell, "Earthquake in Guatemala," *National Geographic* 149, no. 6 (June 1976), 823.

11. David Stoll, *Is Latin America Turning Protestant? The Politics of Evangelical Growth* (Berkeley: University of California Press, 1990), 11. See also Virginia Garrard Burnett, *Protestantism in Guatemala: Living in the New Jerusalem* (Austin: University of Texas Press, 1998). Some Christians use the term, like the Gideon Rescue Company, a self-described "Disaster Evangelism Ministry" based in Oklahoma.

12. Lauren Turek, *To Bring the Good News to All Nations: Evangelical Influence on Human Rights and U.S. Foreign Relations* (Ithaca, NY: Cornell University Press, 2020).

13. Virginia Garrard Burnett, *Terror in the Land of the Holy Spirit: Guatemala under General Efraín Ríos Montt* (Oxford: Oxford University Press, 2010), 125.

14. David Carey Jr., *Our Elders Teach Us: Maya-Kaqchikel Historical Perspectives* (Tuscaloosa: University of Alabama Press, 2001), 146.

15. "Corriente de víveres, ropa y de medicina llegando de varios paises," *El Imparcial*, 13 February 1976. Luisa Raggio, "International Response to Disaster in Guatemala," United Nations Disaster Relief Organization (UNDRO), *Disasters* 1, no. 2 (Geneva: Pergamon Press, 1977), 81. "Un lugar para niños sin hogar," *El Imparcial*, 19 February 1976.

16. President Laugerud's speech was televised and reprinted in *El Imparcial,* 14 February 1976.

17. "Reparar al Mater Orphanorum tendrá un costo de Q 70,000," *Prensa Libre,* 26 February 1976. "No es cierto que estén regalando a las niñas del Mater Orphanorum," *Prensa Libre,* 16 February 1976.

18. Ministry of Social Welfare Archive, Archivo de la Secretaría de Bienestar Social (hereafter SBS), "Memoria Secretaria de Asuntos Sociales de la Presidencia," Guatemala 1974–1978.

19. "Localizados 650 niños en la orfandad," *El Imparcial,* 12 February 1976.

20. "No están entregando los niños huérfanos," *La Hora,* 12 February 1976.

21. The USAID postmortem on aid efforts following three major Latin American earthquakes didn't list the equivalent numbers for Guatemala, but for the Peruvian earthquake of 1970 noted "20,000 orphans created by disaster, 200 orphans—not absorbed by local friends, relatives, etc." Robert Gersony, Lima Disaster Preparedness Report, Section 12, "Critical Abstracts from the Literature: A Field Perspective on Major Earthquakes, Peru 5-31-70, Nicaragua 12-23-72, Guatemala 2-4-76," for Office of U.S. Foreign Disaster Assistance, Agency for International Development, November 1981, http://pdf.usaid.gov/pdf_docs/PNAAT581.pdf.

22. "Llegan solicitudes para adoptar niños," *Prensa Libre,* 21 February 1976.

23. "Quetzaltenango: Planifican la ayuda para niños huérfanos," *El Gráfico,* 16 February 1976.

24. Sources on these private orphanages have been nearly impossible to attain. See the section on sources in the Introduction.

25. "Piden adoptar 293 huérfanos guatemaltecos: embajada de México recibe solicitudes," *Prensa Libre,* 17 April 1976.

26. Deborah Levenson-Estrada calls this unwillingness to believe what the Guatemalan government is saying "reverse hegemony." Deborah Levenson-Estrada, *Trade Unionists against Terror: Guatemala City 1954–1985* (Chapel Hill: University of North Carolina Press, 1994), 66–67.

27. "Campaña deportiva para ayudar a los niños huérfanos," *Prensa Libre,* 24 February 1976.

28. SBS, "Memoria anual de labores," Direccion de Bienestar Infantil y Familiar 1975, 11.

29. SBS, "Memoria de labores," Direccion de Bienestar Infantil y Familiar de la Secretaria de Asuntos Sociales de la Presidencia 1977.

30. For example, China has a private adoption system overseen by a central authority.

31. After the bill passed, I never saw any records of this happening, i.e., private adoptions reverting to state adoptions.

32. Archivo Legislativo del Congreso (hereafter ALC), Expediente del Decreto 54-77, 23.

33. Michael Barnett divides the history of humanitarianism into three phases; I use the term "humanitarianism" to refer to what Barnett describes as neo-humanitarianism. Michael Barnett, *Empire of Humanity: A World History* (Ithaca, NY: Cornell University Press, 2011).

34. Samuel Moyn, *The Last Utopia: Human Rights in History* (Cambridge, MA: Belknap Press of Harvard University Press, 2012). Among the critiques of Moyn's view of human rights is that it is U.S.-centric, but his timeline works well for the U.S.-Central American story told here.

35. This coalition was led by Argentina. See Patrick William Kelly, *Sovereign Emergencies: Latin America and the Making of Global Human Rights* (Cambridge: Cambridge University Press, 2018), 269–270.

36. "General Brown Concerned over Latin Stand on Aid," *New York Times*, 18 March 1977.

37. Michael McClintock, *The American Connection* (London: Zed Books, 1985), 192–193; and Manolo Vela Castañeda, *Los pelotones de la muerte: La construcción de los perpetradores del genocidio guatemalteco* (México D.F.: El Colegio de México, 2014). See also Leslie Gelb, "Israel Said to Step Up Latin Role, Offering Arms Seized in Lebanon," *New York Times*, 17 December 1982, and Cheryl A. Rubenberg, "Israeli Foreign Policy in Central America," *Third World Quarterly* 8, no. 3 (July 1986): 896–915.

38. U.S. State Department, *Country Reports on Human Rights Practices*, 1977, 165.

39. U.S. State Department, *Country Reports on Human Rights Practices*, 1977, 167.

40. Deborah Levenson-Estrada, "Reactions to Trauma: The 1976 Earthquake in Guatemala," *International Labor and Working-Class History* 62, no. 1 (2002): 60–68.

41. "Kjell Eugenio Laugerud García, Leader of Guatemala during '76 Quake, Dies at 79," *New York Times*, 11 December 2009.

42. SBS, "Memoria Secretaria de Asuntos Sociales de la Presidencia," Guatemala 1974–1978.

43. ALC, Expediente del Decreto 54-77, 42.

44. ALC, *Diario de Sesiones del Congreso de la República de Guatemala, Periodo Ordinario 19 de Abril al 15 de Junio 1977*, 5 May 1977, 30.

45. "All of the Representatives told us that they were going to prepare their cars for tomorrow's trip, so they couldn't return." ALC, *Diario de Sesiones del Congreso, Periodo Ordinario 19 de Abril al 15 de Junio 1977*, 20 April 1977, 24.

46. Garrard Burnett, *Terror in the Land*, 43.

47. ALC, *Diario de Sesiones del Congreso, 28 de Enero al 30 de Marzo 1977*, 20 May 1977, 20.

48. ALC, *Diario de Sesiones del Congreso, 28 de Enero al 30 de Marzo 1977*, 20 May 1977, 22.

49. Biblioteca del Congreso (hereafter BLC), *Registro de Servicio de los Diputados*. ALC, *Diario de Sesiones del Congreso, 28 de Enero al 30 de Marzo 1977*, 20 May 1977, 22.

50. ALC, *Diario de Sesiones del Congreso, 28 de Enero al 30 de Marzo 1977*, 20 May 1977, 23.

51. ALC, *Diario de Sesiones del Congreso, Periodo Ordinario 19 de Abril al 15 de Junio 1977*, 3 May 1977, 12–13.

52. In the original Spanish, the assumed gender of the social worker is female *("trabajadora social")*. ALC, *Diario de Sesiones del Congreso, Periodo Ordinario 19 de Abril al 15 de Junio 1977*, 3 May 1977, 13. This amendment was first proposed on 8 September 1976.

53. ALC, *Diario de Sesiones del Congreso, Periodo Ordinario 19 de Abril al 15 de Junio 1977*, 3 May 1977, 13–14.

54. ALC, *Diario de Sesiones del Congreso, Periodo Ordinario 19 de Abril al 15 de Junio 1977*, 3 May 1977, 20–21, 18–19.

55. ALC, *Diario de Sesiones del Congreso, Periodo Ordinario 19 de Abril al 15 de Junio 1977*, 3 May 1977, 22.

56. ALC, *Diario de Sesiones del Congreso, Periodo Ordinario 19 de Abril al 15 de Junio 1977*, 31 May 1977, 21.

57. ALC, *Diario de Sesiones del Congreso, 28 de Enero al 30 de Marzo 1977,* 23 March 1977, 17.

58. ALC, *Diario de Sesiones del Congreso, 28 de Enero al 30 de Marzo 1977,* 23 March 1977, 20.

59. Representative Elizardo Urizar Leal, representing Baja Verapaz for the MLN. ALC, *Diario de Sesiones del Congreso, 28 de Enero al 30 de Marzo 1977,* 23 March 1977, 18–19.

60. ALC, *Diario de Sesiones del Congreso, 28 de Enero al 30 de Marzo 1977,* 23 March 1977, 23.

61. Bravo López of the Partido Revolucionario (PR). ALC, *Diario de Sesiones del Congreso, 28 de Enero al 30 de Marzo 1977,* 23 March 1977, 22.

62. The attorney general's office did reject some files during the scandals of the early 2000s, especially if names of children or other identifying details did not match alleged birth mothers.

63. "U.S. Demand for Adoption Spurs Baby Trade in Guatemala," *Washington Post,* 17 April 1979.

4. ADOPTION RINGS AND BABY BROKERS

1. Archivo Histórico de la Policía Nacional, Guatemala City (hereafter AHPN), AHPN GT PN 99 DCS 33597.

2. This estimate of fees is based on interviews with private adoption lawyers in Guatemala City. Carlos Larios Ochaita interview, 22 April 2016; Hilda Morales Trujillo interview, 9 February 2016; Dina Castro interview, 18 February 2016; Jorge Carillo Gudiel interview, 31 March 2016; Fernando Linares Beltranena interviews, 18 March 2016 and 10 September 2017; Susana Luarca interviews, 24 February 2016 and 14 April 2016. I will cite the private archive of the one lawyer who allowed me to consult his adoption files as Archivo Privado de Fernando Linares Beltranena (AFLB). I have identified cases from this archive with the first initial of the adoptive parents' last name and year of finalization of the case.

3. Not all involved were prosecuted, and not just the elite lawyers. The taxi driver who transported the killers to Larrad de Quan's house at her request was arrested but not prosecuted. AHPN GT PN 99 DCS 33597.

4. Ministry of Social Welfare Archive, Archivo de la Secretaría de Bienestar Social (SBS) Adoption Files. While the numbers of public adoptions per year continued to climb after 1977, they rarely hit triple digits. The peak year for state adoptions was 1986, with 114 finalized adoptions. To compare to the conservative estimate of 40,000 private adoptions from 1977 to 2007, public records show that from 1968 to 1997, 984 public adoptions were finalized.

5. Silvia Posocco, "On the Queer Necropolitics of Transnational Adoption in Guatemala," in *Queer Necropolitics,* ed. Jin Haritaworn (London: Routledge, 2014), 76.

6. Sara Dorow, *Transnational Adoption: A Cultural Economy of Race, Gender, and Kinship* (New York: New York University Press, 2006); and Catherine Ceniza Choy, *Global Families: A History of Asian International Adoption in America* (New York: New York University Press, 2013). This is not to be confused with "independent adoptions," domestic adoptions in which adoptions are processed without the involvement of a licensed agency. These are prohibited in some states for fear of baby-selling.

7. For the history of these adoption agencies, see Barbara Melosh, *Strangers and Kin: The American Way of Adoption* (Cambridge, MA: Harvard University Press, 2002); Julie Bere-

bitsky, *Like Our Very Own: Adoption and the Changing Culture of Motherhood, 1851–1950* (Lawrence: University Press of Kansas, 2000); and Rachel Rains Winslow, *The Best Possible Immigrants: International Adoption and the American Family* (Philadelphia: University of Pennsylvania Press, 2017).

8. See Judith Zur, *Violent Memories: Mayan War Widows in Guatemala* (Boulder: Westview, 1998); and Linda Green, *Fear as a Way of Life: Mayan Widows in Rural Guatemala* (New York: Columbia University Press, 1999).

9. Maria Eugenia Berger Fernández, "Intervención del notario en los asuntos de jurisdicción voluntaria" (PhD diss., Facultad de Ciencias Jurídicas y Sociales, Universidad de San Carlos, 1981), 58, 96.

10. The structure of criminal adoption rings varied. Some involved public servants who faked birth certificates in various civil registries, or judges who were paid to give favorable rulings on judicial adoptions—sometimes in the absence of the necessary paperwork.

11. *Jaladoras* did not exist under the same name in other countries, but brokers were involved in commercialized international adoption rings elsewhere. See Lisa Swenarski, "In Honduras, a Black Market for Babies," *Christian Science Monitor*, 13 May 1993; Kathryn Joyce, *The Child Catchers: Rescue, Trafficking, and the New Gospel of Adoption* (New York: PublicAffairs, 2013); and Karen Balcom, *The Traffic in Babies: Cross-Border Adoption and Baby-Selling between the United States and Canada, 1930–1972* (Toronto: University of Toronto Press, 2011).

12. Jessaca Leinaweaver, *The Circulation of Children: Kinship, Adoption, and Morality in Andean Peru* (Durham: Duke University Press, 2008).

13. AFLB P 1989.

14. See Susanne Jonas and Nestor Rodríguez, *Guatemala-U.S. Migration: Transforming Regions* (Austin: University of Texas Press, 2015), 36.

15. AFLB J 1989. See also AFLB H 1987.

16. AFLB J 1989.

17. The original demographic work identifying adoptions as migration is Richard Weil, "International Adoptions: The Quiet Migration," *International Migration Review* 18, no. 2 (1984): 276–293. See also Kirsten Lovelock, "Intercountry Adoption as a Migratory Practice: A Comparative Analysis of Intercountry Adoption and Immigration Policy and Practice in the United States, Canada and New Zealand in the Post WWII Period," *International Migration Review* 34, no. 3 (Fall 2000): 907–949.

18. Susana Luarca interview, 24 February 2016.

19. As an ethical matter, I did not seek out birth mothers for interviews. I spoke to this birth mother on the phone at her request.

20. Casa Alianza, Fundación Sobrevivientes, Secretaria de Bienestar Social, et al., *Adopciones en Guatemala: Protección o mercado?* (Guatemala City: Tipografía Nacional, 2007).

21. Doña Carmelita interview, 27 July 2018.

22. *Ixcanul*, dir. Jayro Bustamante (Guatemala City: La Casa de Producción, Tu Vas Voir Productions, 2015). Gerardo Saravia and Patricia Weisse, "Jayro Bustamante: El guatemalteco no quiere verse representado por indios," *Revista Ideele*, no. 254.

23. Mariela SR-Coline Fanon, *Mamá, no estoy muerta: La increíble historia de Mariela, secuestrada al nacer* (Guatemala City: Piedrasanta, 2022), 7.

24. Laurie Stern and Aa Tiko' Rujuk-Xicay, *All Relative: Defining Diego*, podcast audio, Episode 2, 3 October 2022, https://podcasts.apple.com/us/podcast/all-relative-defining-diego /id1607121653.

25. Casa Alianza et al., *Adopciones en Guatemala*, 58. This study found that payments to birth mothers ranged between 3,000 and 15,000 *quetzales* (roughly US$400 to $2,040), much higher than the figures noted in police documents from the 1980s or cited by Rosa, even taking into account the weakening of the *quetzal* against the dollar. This was likely because the report was compiled later, when fees for adoptions had risen considerably.

26. Quotation from Marc Lacey, "Guatemala System Is Scrutinized as Americans Rush in to Adopt," *New York Times*, 5 November 2006. Susana Luarca interview, 24 February 2016. "Tribunal condena a ocho por adopciones ilegales," *Prensa Libre*, 17 June 2015.

27. Dina Castro interview, 18 February 2016.

28. "Recorrido por el gallero," *Prensa Libre*, 20 October 2016.

29. Fernando Linares Beltranena interview, 18 March 2016.

30. AHPN GT PN 30-01 S011. This police record doesn't note the tribunal to which this case was assigned, so this is all of the available information on the case.

31. AHPN GT PN 30-01 S020 33264.

32. The police bulletin occasionally mentions people charged with "illegal trafficking of minors." Forcible adoption only became a recognized variant of the crime of trafficking with reforms to the Guatemalan Penal Code in 2005.

33. AHPN GT PN 30-02 S021 50282.

34. See Deborah Levenson-Estrada, *Trade Unionists against Terror: Guatemala City, 1954–1985* (Chapel Hill: University of North Carolina Press, 1994); Kirsten Weld, *Paper Cadavers: The Archives of Dictatorship in Guatemala* (Durham: Duke University Press, 2014); and National Consultative Council of the Guatemalan National Police Archive (AHPN), *From Silence to Memory: Revelations of the AHPN* (Eugene: University of Oregon Libraries, 2013).

35. Capitalization in original. AHPN GT PN 99 DCS 33597.

36. See Mario Carpio Nicolle, "El negocio de la prensa" (BA thesis, Escuela de Ciencias de la Comunicación de la Universidad de San Carlos, 1979). Carpio Nicolle later became a prominent journalist.

37. AHPN GT PN 99 DCS 33597.

38. "Banda de robachicos acuchilló a familia," *El Gráfico*, 24 June 1983.

39. Underlining in original. AHPN GT PN 99 DCS 33597.

40. AHPN GT PN 99 DCS 33826.

41. I am following the spellings in the police records, which often lack accent marks.

42. AHPN GT PN 99 DCS 33826.

43. Emphasis in the original. AHPN GT PN 99 DCS 33826.

44. AHPN GT PN 99 DCS 33826. This part of the report is based on interviews with Larrad de Quan's accomplices.

45. Capitalization in the original. AHPN GT PN 99 DCS 33826. The archive offers no further information about what happened to this child.

46. AHPN GT PN 99 DCS 33826.

47. AHPN GT PN 99 DCS 33826.

48. "Banda de robachicos acuchilló a familia," *El Gráfico,* 24 June 1983.

49. AHPN GT PN 99 DCS 33597.

50. The usual pay was about 100 *quetzales,* ten times the monthly pay for domestic servants.

51. Archivo General de Tribunales, Guatemala City (hereafter AGT), Caso contra Aura Marina Morataya, Juzgado 110 de Paz Penal, 17 June 1983.

52. David Carey Jr., *I Ask for Justice: Maya Women, Dictators, and Crime in Guatemala 1898–1944* (Austin: University of Texas Press, 2013), 136. Carey chronicles cases of women defending themselves in court against accusations of abortion or infanticide during an earlier period.

53. AHPN GT PN 99 DCS 33826.

54. Casa Alianza et al., *Adopciones en Guatemala.*

55. *Raul Quan Young and Grace Larrad de Quan, Petitioners, vs. the United States Department of Justice, Immigration and Naturalization Service, Respondent,* 759 F.2d 450 (Fifth Circuit, 1985), https://law.justia.com/cases/federal/appellate-courts/F2/759/450/260040.

56. Sebastián Escalón and Pilar Crespo, "La increíble historia de Edmond Mulet y los niños que 'exportaba,'" *Plaza Pública,* 30 January 2015.

57. Declaración de Evelia R., AGT, Caso contra Edmond Lesieur Mulet, Juzgado 50 de Paz Penal, 25 November 1981. See Escalón and Crespo, "La increíble historia de Edmond Mulet."

58. Declaración de Delia D., AGT, Caso contra Edmond Lesieur Mulet, Juzgado 50 de Paz Penal, 25 November 1981.

59. "Revocan prisión a damas canadienses y padres guatemaltecos," *La Prensa,* 15 December 1981; and "En Libertad Mulet Lesieur y las damas canadienses," *El Imparcial,* 6 December 1981.

60. AHPN GT PN 30-01 S007.

61. AHPN GT PN 30-01 S007. Underlining in original. The correct spelling of Mulet's second last name is "Lesieur."

62. AGT, Caso contra Edmond Lesieur Mulet, Juzgado 50 de Paz Penal, 25 November 1981. See also AHPN GT PN 50 S001 F50279. See Escalón and Crespo, "La increíble historia de Edmond Mulet," *Plaza Pública,* 30 January 2015.

63. Underlining in the original, "Mulet rechaza el contenido de 'La increíble historia de Edmond Mulet y los niños que "exportaba,"'" *Plaza Pública,* 26 February 2015. *Los niños perdidos de Guatemala,* Grace González, dir., *Telemundo,* 14 November 2019.

64. Edmond Mulet, *El nuevo comienzo: Volver al pasado o construir el futuro* (Guatemala City: F&G Editores, 2021), 54–55.

5. CHILDREN FOR EXPORT

1. Gobierno de Guatemala Decreto Leyes 46-82, 111-182. See Jennifer Schirmer, "The Guatemalan Politico-Military Project: Whose Ship of State?," in *Political Armies: The Military and Nation Building in the Age of Democracy,* ed. Kees Koonings and Dirk Kruijt (London: Zed Books, 2002), 68. Jennifer Schirmer, *The Guatemalan Military Project: A Violence Called Democracy* (Philadelphia: University of Pennsylvania Press, 1998), 128. I follow Schirmer's

translation of Tribunales de Fuero Especial as "Special Courts," which is simpler than the more literal "Courts of Special Jurisdiction."

2. The Special Courts became internationally notorious after fifteen men accused of subversion were executed by firing squad right before the arrival of Pope John Paul II on a visit, even after the Pope's specific appeal for clemency for this group. Conrado Alonso, *15 Fusilados al Alba: repaso histórico jurídico sobre los tribunales de fuero especial* (Guatemala City: Serviprensa Centroamericana, 1986); and "Report on the Situation of Human Rights in the Republic of Guatemala," Inter-American Commission on Human Rights, Organization of American States, OEA / Ser.L / V / II.61, doc. 47, rev. 1, October 5, 1983, https://www.cidh.oas.org/countryrep /Guatemala83eng/TOC.htm. See also Edgar Alfredo Balsells Tojo, *Olvido o memoria: El dilema de la sociedad guatemalteca* (Guatemala City: F&G Editores, 2001), 169.

3. Juan Pablo Muños Elías and Ana María Méndez Dardón, *Mujeres ante los Tribunales de Fuero Especial* (Guatemala City: Instituto de Estudios Comparados en Ciencias Penales de Guatemala, 2013), 67. On the Sunday sermons, see Virginia Garrard-Burnett, *Terror in the Land of the Holy Spirit: Guatemala under Efraín Ríos Montt, 1982–1983* (Oxford: Oxford University Press, 2010), 59–66.

4. Gobierno de Guatemala Decreto Ley 46-82. The law went into effect on 9 June 1982, and the courts began hearings later that month.

5. Comisión para el Esclarecimiento Histórico (CEH), *Guatemala, Memory of Silence, Tzínil Natabál: Report of the Commission for Historical Clarification, Conclusions and Recommendations* (Guatemala City: United Nations Office of Project Services, 1999), vol. 3, 139.

6. Schirmer, *The Guatemalan Military Project,* 143.

7. Alonso, *15 Fusilados al Alba,* 32.

8. "Report on the Situation of Human Rights in the Republic of Guatemala," Ch. II, Part C, para. 4, https://www.cidh.oas.org/countryrep/Guatemala83eng/chap.2.htm.

9. Muños Elías and Méndez Dardón, *Mujeres ante los Tribunales,* 51.

10. Muños Elías and Méndez Dardón, *Mujeres ante los Tribunales,* 74.

11. The police records misspell her name as Ofelia de Gamez. Archivo Histórico de Policia Nacional, Guatemala City (hereafter AHPN), GT PN 50 S001 F60627.

12. It is difficult but not impossible to follow cases from this era from the police reports in the AHPN through to the Archivo General de Tribunales del Organismo de Justicia, an archive located in the basement of the Supreme Court. Sometimes their ledgers show that the full records are in an archive of one of the various courts around the Guatemalan capital, where they can be requested.

13. The Ministry of Defense is legally obligated to make this information public through the Law of Public Access to Information (2008). Unlike the Ministry of Social Welfare, the Defense Ministry did not honor my requests for access to information under this law, and very rarely if ever allow researchers inside.

14. See T. M. Luhrmann, *When God Talks Back: Understanding the American Evangelical Relationship with God* (New York: Vintage, 2012); David Stoll, *Is Latin America Turning Protestant? The Politics of Evangelical Growth* (Berkeley: University of California Press, 1990); and Virginia Garrard-Burnett, *Protestantism in Guatemala: Living in the New Jerusalem* (Austin: University of Texas Press, 1998).

15. Garrard-Burnett, *Terror in the Land of the Holy Spirit*, 65.

16. Other Latin American military dictatorships also had moralizing phases, often emphasizing proper gender roles. For example, see Ben Cowan, *Securing Sex: Morality and Repression in the Making of Cold War Brazil* (Chapel Hill: University of North Carolina Press, 2016). Long after the transition to democracies, many Latin American countries saw a right-wing backlash against "gender ideologies." In Brazil in 2017, as gender theorist Judith Butler gave a talk inside a cultural center in São Paulo, protesters burned her in effigy outside the building. See Masha Gessen, "Judith Butler Wants Us to Reshape Our Rage," *New Yorker*, 9 February 2020.

17. Schirmer, *The Guatemalan Military Project*, 144.

18. "De 70 casos, 20 condenado por Tribunales de Fuero Especial," *Prensa Libre*, 31 January 1983.

19. Gobierno de Guatemala Decreto Ley 64-84.

20. Luis Solano, "Development and / as Dispossession: Elite Networks and Extractive Industry in the Franja Transversal del Norte," in *War by Other Means*, ed. Carlota McAllister and Diane Nelson (Durham: Duke University Press, 2013); and Bayron Milián, Georg Grünberg, and Mateo Cho, *La conflictividad en las tierras bajas del norte de Guatemala: Petén y la Franja Transversal del Norte* (Guatemala City: FLACSO, MINUGUA y CONTIERRA, 2002), cited in Luis Solano, *Contextualización histórica de la Franja Transversal del Norte (FTN)* (Huehuetenango, Guatemala City: CEDFOG, El Observador, 2012), 22.

21. George Black, *Garrison Guatemala* (New York: Monthly Review Press, 1985), 95.

22. Virginia Garrard-Burnett, "Resacralization of the Profane: Government, Religion, and Ethnicity in Modern Guatemala," in *Questioning the Secular State: The Worldwide Resurgence of Religion in Politics*, ed. David Westerlund (New York: St. Martin's Press, 1996), 106. Witnesses in later corruption cases named Efraín Ríos Montt himself as having taken kickbacks during the corrupt administration of Alfonso Portillo (2000–2004). Bill Barreto, "De Moreno a la Linea: la huella militar en la defraudación aduanera," *Plaza Pública*, 22 August 2015. See also Rachel A. Schwartz, *Undermining the State from Within: The Institutional Legacies of Civil War in Central America* (Cambridge: Cambridge University Press, 2023).

23. Julio Prado interview, 27 November 2016.

24. Father Juan María Boxus interview, 17 November 2016. *Los niños perdidos de Guatemala*, Grace González, dir., Telemundo, 14 November 2019.

25. AHPN, GT PN 24-05 S004 223079; and AHPN, GT PN 24-05 138050.

26. "Otros 16 niños listos para ser exportados localizó la policia," *Prensa Libre*, 4 March 1987. The children were sent to the Elisa Martínez and Rafael Ayau Orphanages.

27. Carlos Rafael Soto, "Los huérfanos del altiplano: Botín de guerra?" *El Gráfico*, 8 March 1987.

28. Soto, "Los huérfanos del altiplano."

29. See Mariela SR-Coline Fanon, *Mamá, no estoy muerta: La increíble historia de Mariela, secuestrada al nacer* (Guatemala City: Piedrasanta, 2022).

30. See, for example, "Editorial: Tráfico de niños y adopción," *La Hora*, 23 November 1988; Ricardo Gatica Trejo, "Localizan más niños de 'exportación,'" *El Gráfico*, 19 June 1988.

31. Alvaro Gálvez Mis, "Acusación a notarios," *Prensa Libre*, 3 December 1988.

32. "Alto al Trafico de Niños: Es inhumano vender a los niños opina Licda. Rodriguez F.," *Prensa Libre,* 20 June 1988.

33. "Iban a linchar a norteamericano," *Prensa Libre,* 2 April 1987.

34. "Plagiaron a niñito," *Prensa Libre,* 8 March 1988; "Robaron niño de dos meses," *Prensa Libre,* 13 March 1988; "Pequeño niño secuestraron," *Prensa Libre,* 21 April 1988; "Aún sin saberse paradero de un recién nacido," *Prensa Libre,* 4 March 1988. Panics, by definition, don't reflect the reality of absolute numbers of kidnapped children. See Paula Fass, *Kidnapped: Child Abduction in America* (Oxford: Oxford University Press, 1997).

35. "Editorial: Tráfico de niños y adopción," *La Hora,* 23 November 1988.

36. Ricardo Gatica Trejo, "Localizan más niños de 'exportación,'" *El Gráfico,* 10 June 1988. As in Carlos Soto's 1987 account, newspaper articles often conflated the lump sum paid by foreign couples for adoption with the lawyer's earnings, or even with the amount allegedly paid to the birth mother for the child. In reality, birth mothers received a tiny fraction of the total sum, if anything.

37. "Editorial: Tráfico de niños y adopción," *La Hora,* 23 November 1988.

38. Ricardo Gatica Trejo interview, 29 January 2016.

39. Jorge Carpio Nicolle began his career as a journalist, founded the political party Unión del Centro Nacional (UCN) in 1983, and ran for president in 1985 and 1990. He was assassinated in 1993 in Chichicastenango, allegedly by a Civil Defense Patrol (PAC), local militias organized by the government. Larry Rohter, "Death Squads in Guatemala: Even the Elite Are Not Safe," *New York Times,* 23 August 1995.

40. National Security Archive (hereafter NSA), Erin Siegal McIntyre Donation, Guatemalan Adoption Box #1, folder 201000001-DOS-4. Siegal McIntyre submitted many requests under the Freedom of Information Act for her own book, *Finding Fernanda: Two Mothers, One Child, and a Cross-Border Search for Truth* (New York: Beacon Press, 2012). She continued to receive results after publishing the book, and later published a selection of these diplomatic cables in Erin Siegal McIntyre, *The U.S. Embassy Cables: Adoption Fraud in Guatemala 1987–2010* (Oakland, CA: Cathexis Press, 2010). Siegal McIntyre donated the rest of the unpublished results of her extensive FOIA requests to the National Security Archive. I cite them here with thanks for her generosity in making these materials freely available to other researchers.

41. NSA, Erin Siegal McIntyre Donation, Guatemalan Adoption Box #1, folder 201000001-DOS-4. September 1998 cable from the U.S. Embassy in Guatemala to the State Department.

42. Jorge R. Oliva, "Investiga tráfico de niños," *Prensa Libre,* 2 March 1988.

43. NSA, Erin Siegal McIntyre Donation, Guatemalan Adoption Box #1, folder 201000001-DOS-4. 1989 Cable.

44. NSA, Erin Siegal McIntyre Donation, Guatemalan Adoption Box #1, folder 201000001-DOS-4. August 1989 Cable.

45. Alvaro Gálvez Mis, "Acusación a notarios," *Prensa Libre,* 3 December 1988.

46. Cited in Centro de Estudios de Guatemala, *El negocio mas infame: Robo y tráfico de niños en Guatemala* (Guatemala City: Editorial Nuestra America, 1995), 8.

47. Alvaro Gálvez Mis, "Taracena: Se debe aprobar con urgencia la Ley de Adopción," *Prensa Libre,* 17 June 1989.

48. This was Abraham Rivera Sagastume, who preceded Taracena as head of the Commission for the Protection of Children. Gálvez Mis, "Taracena."

49. Fernando Linares Beltranena to Congressman Edmond Mulet, 22 October 1987, Archivo Privado de Fernando Linares Beltranena (AFLB).

50. "S.O.B." was in English in the original, while the rest of the note was in Spanish.

51. Congressman Edmond Mulet to Fernando Linares Beltranena, undated, AFLB. The UCN was a political party founded in 1983 by Jorge Carpio Nicolle and Mario Taracena Díaz-Sol, among others. See also "Mulet: Las luces y las sombras del candidato más formal," *Nómada*, 11 June 2019.

52. Hilda Morales Trujillo interview, 5 February 2016.

53. "Ley de adopciones engavetada," *El Gráfico*, 12 June 1989.

54. "Ley de adopciones engavetada," *El Gráfico*, 12 June 1989. Siegal McIntyre, *The U.S. Embassy Cables*, 29, 37. Laura Briggs, *Somebody's Children: The Politics of Transracial and Transnational Adoption* (Durham: Duke University Press, 2012), 204.

6. DISAPPEARED CHILDREN

1. Ministry of Social Welfare Archive, Archivo de la Secretaría de Bienestar Social (hereafter SBS) Adoption File 23-86. The file contains several contradictory accounts of this first encounter, including one version in which there were ten children. The version with five children is repeated most consistently.

2. SBS Adoption File 23-86.

3. SBS Adoption File 23-86. Daniel is a pseudonym. The adoption file includes his real assigned name, but it is likely that he retained this name after adoption. I use a pseudonym here to protect his privacy.

4. *Hasta Encontrarte: Niñez desaparecida por el conflicto armado*, Oficina de Derechos Humanos del Arzobispado de Guatemala (ODHAG), Guatemala City, 2000, 29. Erica Henderson, Catherine Nolin, and Fredy Peccerelli, "Dignifying Bare Life and Making Place through Exhumation: Cobán CREOMPAZ Former Military Garrison, Guatemala," *Journal of Latin American Geography* 13, no. 2 (2014): 97–116, and Sebastián Escalón, "Los dos entierros y el funeral de Martina Rojas," *Plaza Pública*, 1 October 2013. Guatemala's right-wing elite and former and current military officials continue to deny the plain evidence of what happened, claiming, "the guerrillas lost the military war but won the international publicity war." Roman Krznaric, *What the Rich Don't Tell the Poor: Conversations with Guatemalan Oligarchs* (Oxford: Blackbird Collective, 2022), 148.

5. Comisión para el Esclarecimiento Histórico (hereafter CEH), *Guatemala, Memory of Silence, Tzínil Natabál: Report of the Commission for Historical Clarification, Conclusions and Recommendations* (Guatemala City: United Nations Office of Project Services, 1999), 5.

6. CEH, *Guatemala, Memory of Silence,* 23; Comisión Nacional de Búsqueda de la Niñas y Niños Desaparecidos (National Commission for the Search for Disappeared Children), cited in Casa Alianza, Fundación Sobrevivientes, Secretaria de Bienestar Social, et al., *Adopciones en Guatemala: Protección o mercado?* (Guatemala City: Tipografía Nacional, 2007), 24.

7. CEH, *Guatemala, Memory of Silence,* 5, 23.

8. Marco Antonio (Maco) Garavito Fernández interview, 25 July 2017.

9. Marco Antonio (Maco) Garavito Fernández interview, 25 July 2017. See also *A Voz en grito: Testimonios de familiares de niñez desaparecida durante el conflicto armado interno en Guatemala* (Guatemala City: La Liga Guatemalteca de Higiene Mental, 2003). Marco Antonio Garavito Fernández, ed., *De barro y de hierro: Familiares de niñez desaparecida por el conflicto armado interno en Guatemala* (Guatemala City: La Liga Guatemalteca de Higiene Mental, 2002).

10. Irma Alicia Velásquez Nimatuj, "¿Dónde están los niños y niñas de la guerra?" *El Periódico*, 24 March 2018.

11. Secretaría de la Paz, *Niñez desaparecida en Guatemala como parte de la estrategia de la Guerra: Búsqueda, casos, y efectos* (Guatemala: Secretaria de la Paz, Dirección de los Archivos de la Paz, 2010), 139.

12. SBS Adoption Files 1-81 through 67-81, SBS Adoption Files 1-82 through 61-82, SBS Adoption Files 1-82 through 47-83, SBS Adoption Files 1-84 through 40-84, SBS Adoption Files 1-85 through 63-85, SBS Adoption Files 1-86 through 114-86, and SBS Adoption Files 1-87 through 53-87.

13. In addition to the published truth commission reports, the archive of the Catholic Church truth commission, AREMHI, contains a tabulation of forcibly disappeared children based on ongoing interviews with surviving family members. The Catholic Church has also helped reunite disappeared children with their families. See case 074-2002 AREMHI, Archivo del Proyecto Interdiocesano de Recuperación de la Memoria Histórica, Guatemala City.

14. CEH, *Guatemala, Memory of Silence*, 74.

15. CEH, *Guatemala, Memory of Silence*, 75, 5.

16. SBS Adoption File 23-86.

17. SBS Adoption File 39-84.

18. Supposed differences between *ladinos* and Maya are hotly debated and have changed over time. See J. T. Way, *The Mayan in the Mall: Globalization, Development, and the Making of Modern Guatemala* (Durham: Duke University Press, 2012), 3. For the social and racial policing of marginalized groups, see Jorge Ramón González Ponciano, "The *Shumo* Challenge: White Class Privilege and the Post-Race, Post-Genocide Alliances of Cosmopolitanism from Below," in *War by Other Means: Aftermath in Post-Genocide Guatemala,* ed. Carlota McAllister and Diane Nelson (Durham: Duke University Press, 2013). Racial divisions in Latin America have often erroneously been described as less rigid than in the United States, since there is no equivalent to the "one drop" rule. See Greg Grandin, *The Blood of Guatemala: A History of Race and Nation* (Durham: Duke University Press, 2000). The paradox of rigid racial lines that may nevertheless be crossed with a change in language or clothing is not unique to Guatemala. On race and hierarchy in Bolivia and Peru, see Laura Gotkowitz, ed., *Histories of Race and Racism: The Andes and Mesoamerica from Colonial Times to the Present* (Durham: Duke University Press, 2011).

19. Charles Hale, *Más que un indio: Racial Ambivalence and the Paradox of Neoliberal Multiculturalism in Guatemala* (Santa Fe: School of American Research Press, 2006); Irma Alicia Velásquez Nimatuj, *La pequeña burguesía indígena comercial de Guatemala: Desigualdades de clase, raza, y género* (Guatemala City: AVANSCO, 2011); Marta Elena Casaús Arzú, *Guatemala: Linaje y racismo,* 3rd ed. (Guatemala City: F&G Editores, 2007); Arturo Taracena

Arriola and Enrique Gordillo Castillo, eds., *Etnicidad, estado, y nación en Guatemala, 1944–1985,* vol. 2 (Antigua, Guatemala: CIRMA, 2004).

20. Arriola and Castillo, *Etnicidad, estado y nación,* 2:27.

21. The question of whether placing adoptees with families of different racial backgrounds itself constitutes a form of racial violence, even absent a context of political violence or genocidal massacres, has been raised in the United States and elsewhere. For example, in 1972 the U.S. National Association of Black Social Workers likened white families adopting Black children to "cultural genocide." This group only removed the reference to genocide from its public materials in 1994, and many adoption agencies now recommend same-race placements when possible. See Sarah Dorow, *Transnational Adoption: A Cultural Economy of Race, Gender, and Kinship* (New York: New York University Press, 2006), 52–53.

22. SBS Adoption File 23-86.

23. Accounts of the war in which women are protagonists tend to center on widows, though women from combatants to beauty queens also appear. See Victoria Sanford, *Buried Secrets: Truth and Human Rights in Guatemala* (New York: Palgrave Macmillan, 2003); Betsy Konefal, *For Every Indio Who Falls: A History of Maya Activism in Guatemala 1960–1990* (Albuquerque: University of New Mexico Press, 2010); Greg Grandin, *The Last Colonial Massacre: Latin America in the Cold War* (Chicago: University of Chicago Press, 2004); Beatriz Manz, *Paradise in Ashes: A Guatemalan Journey of Courage, Terror, and Hope* (Berkeley: University of California Press, 2005); Judith Zur, *Violent Memories: Mayan War Widows in Guatemala* (Boulder, CO: Westview Press, 1998); and Linda Green, *Fear as a Way of Life: Mayan Widows in Rural Guatemala* (New York: Columbia University Press, 1999). The most famous testimonial book about the Guatemalan armed internal conflict was spoken by a woman, as was the most interesting memoir by a former guerrilla fighter. Rigoberta Menchú, *I, Rigoberta Menchú* (London: Verso, 1984); and Yolanda Colóm, *Mujeres en la alborada: Testimonio* (Guatemala City: Artemis & Edinter, 1998).

24. Deborah Levenson-Estrada, *Trade Unionists against Terror: Guatemala City, 1954–1985* (Chapel Hill: University of North Carolina Press, 1994).

25. Grandin, *Last Colonial Massacre.*

26. Jennifer Schirmer, *The Guatemalan Military Project: A Violence Called Democracy* (Philadelphia: University of Pennsylvania Press, 1998), 88.

27. Outside the context of immediate genocidal attacks, Indigenous communities are constantly adapting to new conditions and creating new cultural configurations. What I want to suggest is that it was these transformations that were disrupted by the genocidal attacks, not the transmission of some sort of "timeless" Indigenous tradition. See Liliana Goldín, *Global Maya: Work and Ideology in Rural Guatemala* (Phoenix: University of Arizona Press, 2009). On essentialist notions about the continuity of past and present, see Edgar Esquit, "Nationalist Contradictions: Pan-Mayanism, Representations of the Past, and the Reproduction of Inequalities in Guatemala," in *Decolonizing Native Histories: Collaboration, Knowledge, and Language in the Americas,* ed. Florencia E. Mallon (Durham: Duke University Press, 2012).

28. SBS Adoption File 5-80.

29. There is a vast literature on genocide in a variety of different geographical and historical contexts, including comparative or critical global work, including Ben Kiernan, *Blood and*

Soil: A World History of Genocide and Extermination from Sparta to Darfur (New Haven: Yale University Press, 2009); and A. Dirk Moses, *The Problems of Genocide: Permanent Security and the Language of Transgression* (Cambridge: Cambridge University Press, 2021).

30. The Christian Solidarity Committee of the Dioceses of San Cristóbal, a religious organization in Mexico, arranged a letter-writing campaign to gather refugee testimony to distribute to the UN High Commissioner for Refugees, the Mexican Commission for Aid to Refugees, and the Bishop of Chiapas, Samuel Ruiz, including the letter from Pedro Ramírez. Archivo Histórico Diocesano de San Cristóbal de las Casas (AHDSC), Fondo Refugiados Guatemaltecos Mexico, box 191, folder 14.

31. United Nations, Convention on the Prevention and Punishment of the Crime of Genocide, General Assembly Resolution 260, 9 December 1948, Articles 2 and 3.

32. United Nations, Universal Declaration of Human Rights, General Assembly Resolution 217A, 10 December 1948, Article 13.

33. Guatemala ratified the Convention on the Prevention and Punishment of the Crime of Genocide before the CIA-led coup in 1954. Piero Gleijeses, *Shattered Hope: The Guatemalan Revolution and the United States 1944–1954* (Princeton: Princeton University Press, 1992).

34. Tara Zahra, *The Lost Children: Reconstructing Europe's Families after World War II* (Cambridge, MA: Harvard University Press, 2015). See also Tara Zahra, *Kidnapped Souls: National Indifference and the Battle for Children in the Bohemian Lands 1900–1948* (Ithaca, NY: Cornell University Press, 2008).

35. Emi MacLean, *Judging a Dictator: The Trial of Guatemala's Ríos Montt* (New York: Open Society Foundation, 2013), 7.

36. Marco Tulio Álvarez, *Las adopciones y los derechos humanos de la niñez guatemalteca 1977–1989* (Guatemala City: Secretaría de la Paz, Dirección de los Archivos de la Paz, 1999), 12.

37. Secretaría de la Paz, *Niñez desaparecida en Guatemala*, 31–32.

38. "Futuro incierto para miles de niños huérfanos, abandonados y de la calle," *La Hora*, 2 January 1992, cited a figure of 250,000 war orphans. The REMHI report estimated 200,000 war orphans. Proyecto Interdiocesano de Recuperación de la Memoria Histórica (REMHI), *Guatemala: Nunca más!* (Guatemala City: Oficina de Derechos Humanos del Arzobispado de Guatemala, 1998).

39. Green, *Fear as a Way of Life*, 29.

40. Archivo del Proyecto Interdiocesano de Recuperación de la Memoria Histórica (hereafter AREMHI), Caso 4017, Las Majadas, Aguacatán, Huehuetenango, 1982.

41. AREMHI, Caso Colectivo 17, Santa Cruz Verapaz, 1980.

42. AREMHI. Archival evidence of more than 3,300 forced disappearances at the Archivo del Grupo de Apoyo Mutuo in Guatemala City is currently being catalogued and digitized with the help of the Magill Library at Haverford College. See https://archivogam.haverford.edu. Testimonies by Maya survivors are collected at the University of Southern California Shoah Foundation's Visual History Archive in collaboration with the Fundación de Antropología Forense de Guatemala (Forensic Anthropology Foundation of Guatemala), which has gathered DNA samples and collaborated with groups seeking to reunite children with their families.

43. Sanford, *Buried Secrets*, 102.

44. Virginia Garrard-Burnett, *Terror in the Land of the Holy Spirit: Guatemala under Efraín Ríos Montt, 1982–1983* (Oxford: Oxford University Press, 2010), 111.

45. Archivo del Centro de Investigaciones Regionales de Mesoamérica (CIRMA), *Escuela de Comando y Estado Mayor: Manual de guerra contrasubversiva* (1980), 241. The manual is uncatalogued.

46. National Security Archive (NSA), U.S. defense attaché report on Plan Victoria 82, April 1982, https://nsarchive2.gwu.edu/NSAEBB/NSAEBB425/docs/1-820407%20DIA%20Views%20of%20a%20Coup%20Leader.pdf.

47. SBS, "Memoria de labores correspondiente al periodo 1982–1983 Secretaria de Bienestar Social de la Presidencia," 4. The Ministry of Social Welfare opened centers in the departments of Quiché (Joyabaj, Chimaltenango, Nebaj, Chajul, Cotzal, Uspantán), Chichicastenango (San Martín Jilotepeque, San Juan Comalapa), Cobán (Chisec), Huehuetenango (Nentón). The report noted the number of children "served" at each center but did not specify what this entailed. The numbers, in any case, are too round to be reliable. For example, 100 children were "served" at each center in Nebaj, Chajul, and Chisec.

48. SBS, "Memoria de labores correspondiente al periodo 1982–1983," 17.

49. In 1982, for example, the Guatemalan government reduced the Ministry of Social Welfare's budget by 246,405 *quetzales* even as it extended its geographical coverage. SBS, "Memoria de labores correspondiente al periodo 1982–1983," 34.

50. CIRMA, Colecciones Especiales, 10044618, *Revista Militar* 1, no. 7 (Sept-Dec 1982): 61.

51. CIRMA, *Revista Militar* 1, no. 7 (Sept.-Dec., 1982): 28. This was a military appropriation of a term, "ladinization," that had been used by anthropologists, including Richard Adams, who later disavowed the term. See Richard Adams, "Ladinización e historia: El caso de Guatemala," *Mesoamérica* 15, no. 28 (1994): 289–304.

52. Guatemalan model villages were designed according to counterinsurgency doctrine developed in Vietnam, and echoed colonial strategies of forcing Indigenous peoples to live in "*reducciones*," newly constructed Spanish-style towns, for the purposes of surveillance. Centro de Estudios Integrados de Desarrollo Comunal (CEIDIC), *Guatemala, polos de desarrollo: El caso de la desestructuración de las comunidades indígenas* (Mexico City: CEIDIC, 1988). See also Beatriz Manz, *Paradise in Ashes: A Guatemalan Journey of Courage, Terror and Hope* (Berkeley: University of California Press, 2004); and Sarah Foss, *On Our Own Terms: Development and Indigeneity in Cold War Guatemala* (Chapel Hill: University of North Carolina Press, 2022), chap. 7.

53. Sebastián Escalón, "Los niños que el ejército se llevó (II)," *Plaza Pública*, 28 August 2013.

54. CIRMA, "Apreciación de Asuntos Civiles (G-5) para el area Ixil," *Revista Militar* 1, no. 7 (Sept-Dec. 1982): 66.

55. CIRMA, *Escuela de Comando y Estado Mayor: Manual de Guerra Contrasubversiva*, 76. Emphasis in original. This is held uncatalogued at CIRMA.

56. CIRMA, *The Socio-economic Situation of Children in Guatemala* (La situación socio-económica de los niños en Guatemala) (Number 2903), Fondo Collección de Publicaciones

sobre Derechos Humanos. A reconstruction three years after the fact, this passage cites a 26 February 1986 interview with a member of the Guatemalan Church-in-Exile.

57. Schirmer, *The Guatemalan Military Project,* 58.

58. National Security Archive (NSA), Plan Operation Sofía, 316, https://nsarchive2.gwu .edu/NSAEBB/NSAEBB297/Operation_Sofia_lo.pdf.

59. Nara Milanich, "Degrees of Bondage: Children's Tutelary Servitude in Modern Latin America," in *Child Slaves in the Modern World,* ed. Gwyn Campbell, Suzanne Miers, and Joseph C. Miller (Athens: Ohio University Press, 2011), 116.

60. Secretaría de la Paz, *Niñez desaparecida en Guatemala,* 65. I use Maquín's real name because he has told his story and identified himself publicly.

61. Secretaría de la Paz, *Niñez desaparecida en Guatemala,* 102–110. Families in Guatemala, as in the United States and elsewhere, did not always consider it necessary to tell an adopted child that they were adopted until relatively late in the twentieth century. A Guatemalan column from 1937 argued *against* the prevailing assumption that adoptive children should not be told they were adopted. "Los hijos adoptivos deben conocer su verdadero origen," *El Liberal Progresista,* 1 September 1937.

62. *Discovering Dominga,* prod. Patricia Flynn and Mary Jo McConahay (Berkeley, CA: Berkeley Media, 2002), DVD.

63. Garavito Fernández, *De barro y de hierro,* 113.

64. Sebastian Rotella, "Finding Oscar: Massacre, Memory, and Justice in Guatemala," *ProPublica,* 25 May 2012. Steven Spielberg produced a documentary based on the article, *Finding Oscar,* dir. Ryan Suffern (Kennedy / Marshall, 2016). Oscar was three years old when he was disappeared, and Ramiro was five.

65. Mike Lanchin, "'I Helped Send My Adoptive Father to Jail for 5,000 Years,'" *BBC World Service,* 9 December 2018.

66. Oscar Ramírez Castañeda, talk given at Latin American Studies Association (LASA) after a screening of *Finding Oscar,* LASA, Boston, 26 May 2019.

67. Sebastian Rotella, "Guatemalan Massacre Survivor Wins Political Asylum in U.S.," *ProPublica,* 24 September 2012. Ramiro Cristales has also received political asylum, in Canada.

68. Sebastian Rotella, "Finding Oscar."

69. AHDSC, Fondo de Refugiados, box 177, folder 10.

70. According to the UN High Commissioner for Refugees (UNHCR), about 200,000 Guatemalans fled to Mexico; only 46,000 were officially registered and assisted by UNHCR. Elena Fiddian-Qasmiyeh, Gil Loescher, Katy Long, and Nando Sigona, eds., *Oxford Handbook of Refugee and Forced Migration Studies* (Oxford: Oxford University Press, 2014), 666. For parallels between the child refugees of the Guatemalan war and Central American child migrants in Mexico and the United States following the "unaccompanied minors crisis" beginning in 2014, see Rachel Nolan, "Guatemalan Child Refugees, Then and Now," *NACLA,* 13 November 2020.

71. Archivo Histórico Diocesano de San Cristóbal de las Casas (AHDSC), Fondo Refugiados Guatemaltecos Mexico, box 66, folder 12, 1 June 1985.

72. "Datos para la sistematización y evaluación 1989–1990," AHDSC, Fondo de Refugiados, Comité Cristiano de Solidaridad Chiapas (Mexico), 172.2. For example, the refugee

camp of Tierra Blanca had forty-three families making up a total population of 209 people, of whom seven were orphans.

73. "Programa de Educacion Primaria Bicultural para Niños Guatemaltecas Refugiados en México," AHDSC, Fondo de Refugiados, *Estudios Sociales 20,* box 7, folder 1, number 14.

74. Kathryn Sikkink, *Mixed Signals: U.S. Human Rights Policy and Latin America* (Ithaca, NY: Cornell University Press, 2004).

75. AHDSC, Fondo de Refugiados, box 1–11, folder 000000007, 414.

7. BEST INTERESTS OF THE CHILD

1. Greg Grandin, *The Last Colonial Massacre: Latin America in the Cold War* (Chicago: University of Chicago Press, 2004).

2. "Taking children" as a broad category to encompass this aspect of racist violence is used here in reference to Laura Briggs, *Taking Children: A History of American Terror* (Berkeley: University of California Press, 2020).

3. This approach to reading case files draws on Linda Gordon, *Heroes of Their Own Lives: The Politics and History of Family Violence* (Urbana: University of Illinois Press, 1998). For a debate over the merits and limits of using case files as sources for historical studies, see Linda Gordon, "Review of *Gender and the Politics of History* by Joan Wallach Scott," and Linda Gordon, "Response to Joan Wallach Scott," and Joan Wallach Scott, "Review of *Heroes of Their Own Lives*" by Linda Gordon, and Joan Wallach Scott, "Response to Linda Gordon," all in *Signs* 15, no. 4 (1990). See also Karen Tice, *Tales of Wayward Girls and Immoral Women: Case Records and the Professionalization of Social Work* (Urbana: University of Illinois Press, 1998).

4. SBS Adoption File 23-86.

5. SBS Adoption File 23-86.

6. Margarita López Raquec, *Acerca de los idiomas mayas de Guatemala* (Guatemala City: Ministerio de Cultura y Deportes, 1989). Many Indigenous people, especially those involved in seasonal agricultural labor or those who worked as market vendors, spoke some Spanish. But it is unlikely Daniel heard Spanish at home.

7. REMHI, *Guatemala: Nunca Más,* 504.

8. Licette Morales interviews, 14 April 2016 and 12 September 2016. Several women who worked as social workers during the war declined my requests to interview them. Licette Morales and several others not only agreed to be interviewed but gave permission to be quoted by name.

9. Licette Morales interviews, 14 April 2016 and 12 September 2016.

10. *Benedicto,* dir. Alejandra Gutiérrez Valdizán and Julio Serrano Echeverría (Plaza Pública, 2016).

11. A 1982 CIA report marked "top secret" and later declassified recorded that before a military sweep in an Ixil area, "Chief of Staff Lucas has cautioned his men not to harm innocent peasants, but he acknowledged that because most Indians in the area support the guerrillas it probably will be necessary to destroy a number of villages." *DCI Watch Committee Report,* CIA, top secret report, 5 February 1982, NSA Archive, https://nsarchive2.gwu.edu/NSAEBB /NSAEBB32/docs/doc19.pdf.

12. SBS Adoption File 23-86.

13. On families who were temporarily divided due to Indigenous migrant labor practices see Elizabeth Oglesby, "'We're No Longer Dealing with Fools': Violence, Labor, and Governance on the South Coast," in *War by Other Means: Aftermath in Post-Genocide Guatemala,* ed. Carlota McAllister and Diane Nelson (Durham: Duke University Press, 2013).

14. SBS Adoption File 23-85.

15. SBS Adoption File 23-85. Later papers suggest that they had seen photographs or read descriptions of Daniel before deciding to apply for adoption.

16. See, for example, SBS Adoption Files 4-80 and 14-84.

17. SBS Adoption Files 19-84, 6-84.

18. SBS Adoption File 23-85.

19. SBS Adoption File 23-85.

20. SBS Adoption File 23-85.

21. SBS Adoption File 74-86.

22. SBS Adoption File 31-85.

23. CEH, *Guatemala, Memory of Silence,* 15.

24. SBS Adoption File 23-85.

25. Margaret Atwood, "Margaret Atwood on What 'The Handmaid's Tale' Means in the Age of Trump," *New York Times Book Review,* 10 March 2017.

26. See Zahra, *Kidnapped Souls,* for the argument that state intervention into families was part of nationalist processes that predated totalitarianism.

27. Isabel Heinemann, "'Until the Last Drop of Good Blood': The Kidnapping of 'Racially Valuable' Children and Nazi Racial Policy in Occupied Eastern Europe," in *Genocide and Settler Society: Frontier Violence and Stolen Indigenous Children in Australian History,* ed. A. Dirk Moses (New York: Berghahn Books, 2004), 253. See also Isabel Heinemann, *Rasse, Siedlung, Deutsches Blut: das Rasse- und Siedlungshauptamt der SS und die rassenpolitische Neuordnung Europas* (Göttingen: Wallstein, 2003).

28. Some were fostered or held in SS boarding schools; not all were adopted. See Heinemann, "'Until the Last Drop of Good Blood,'" 260. See also Valentine Faure, "The Children of the Nazis' Genetic Project," *The Atlantic,* 22 February 2023, and Georg Lilienthal, *Der "Lebensborn e. V": Ein Instrument nationalsozialistischer Rassenpolitik* (Stuttgart: Gustav Fischer, 1985).

29. Antonio Vallejo Nájera, *Política racial del nuevo estado* (San Sebastián: Editorial Española, S.A, 1938). See also Enrique González Duro, *Los psiquiatras de Franco: Los rojos no estaban locos* (Barcelona: Ediciones Península, 2008).

30. Adrian Nathan West, "The Sleep of Reason," *New York Review of Books,* 23 May 2019.

31. On Spanish refugee children moved across national borders see Zahra, *Lost Children,* 16. See also Peter Anderson, "The Struggle over the Evacuation to the United Kingdom and Repatriation of Basque Refugee Children in the Spanish Civil War: Symbols and Souls," *Journal of Contemporary History* 52, no. 2 (April 2017): 297–318.

32. Ricardo Vinyes, *Irredentas: Las presas políticas y sus hijos en las cárceles Franquistas* (Madrid: Temas de Hoy, 2010); and Ricardo Vinyes, Montse Armengou, Ricard Belis, and Daniel Royo, *Los*

niños perdidos del franquismo (Barcelona: Plaza & Janés, 2002). Reports of stolen children have been the subject of ongoing struggle over historical memory in Spain. See Victoria Burnett, "Families Search for Truth of Spain's 'Lost Children,'" *New York Times*, 28 February 2009.

33. Neus Roig, *No llores que vas a ser feliz: el tráfico de bebés en España: de la represión al negocio* (Barcelona: Ático de los libros, 2018).

34. Hugh Thomas, *Spanish Civil War* (New York: Modern Library, 2001), 492. These charity organizations were run by the wives of elite Francoists.

35. Katya Adler, "Spain's Stolen Babies and the Families Who Lived a Lie," *BBC*, 18 October 2011; and Lucas Laursen, "The Missing Children," *BBC*, 24 June 2019.

36. As many as thirty thousand Argentines were disappeared, with an estimated five hundred children illegally appropriated. Marguerite Feitlowitz, *Lexicon of Terror: Argentina and the Legacies of Torture*, rev. ed. (New York: Oxford University Press), 289. As of 2023, the Grandmothers of the Plaza de Mayo had made over 130 matches reuniting families searching for the disappeared.

37. Rita Arditti, *Searching for Life: The Grandmothers of the Plaza de Mayo and the Disappeared Children of Argentina* (Berkeley: University of California Press, 1999).

38. Feitlowitz, *Lexicon of Terror*, 78, 68.

39. Similar crimes were recorded in Chile, though the numbers of affected families are still not known. Rafael Romo, "Chile's 'Children of Silence' Seek Truth," *CNN*, 31 October 2013. Birth parents formed an organization called Nos Buscamos, http://www.nosbuscamos.org.

40. On white families adopting Native American children see Dawn Peterson, *Indians in the Family: Adoption and the Politics of Antebellum Expansion* (Cambridge, MA: Harvard University Press, 2017).

41. The Carlisle School, infamous for its founder's slogan "kill the Indian in him, save the man," became the model for other federally funded institutions.

42. David Wallace Adams, *Education for Extinction: American Indians and the Boarding School Experience, 1875–1928* (Lawrence: University Press of Kansas, 1995).

43. See Margaret Jacobs, *White Mother to a Dark Race: Settler Colonialism, Maternalism, and the Removal of Indigenous Children in the American West and Australia, 1880–1940* (Lincoln: University of Nebraska Press, 2009), 406.

44. The 1978 Indian Child Welfare Act, which gave tribal governments more authority over child custody, was in part an extremely tardy response to this history and only passed after extensive Native activism and lobbying.

45. Jacobs, *White Mother to a Dark Race*. See also Margaret Jacobs, *A Generation Removed: The Fostering and Adoption of Indigenous Children in the Postwar World* (Lincoln: University of Nebraska Press, 2014); A. Dirk Moses, ed., *Genocide and Settler Society*.

46. Quoted in Margaret Jacobs, *White Mother to a Dark Race*, 427.

47. Truth and Reconciliation Commission of Canada, *Honouring the Truth, Reconciling for the Future* (Toronto: James Lorimer, 2015), 47.

48. Many studies of this issue are comparative. See Andrew Woolford, *The Benevolent Experiment: Indigenous Boarding Schools, Genocide, and Redress in Canada and the United States* (Lincoln: University of Nebraska Press, 2015).

49. Holly A. McKenzie, Colleen Varcoe, Annette J. Browne, and Linda Day, "Disrupting the Continuities among Residential Schools, the Sixties Scoop, and Child Welfare," *International Indigenous Policy Journal* 7, no. 2 (2016). Maria Bertsch and Bruce A. Bidgood, "Why Is Adoption Like a First Nations' Feast? Lax Kw'alaa, Indigenizing Adoptions in Child Welfare," *First Peoples Child & Family Review* 5, no. 1 (2010): 96–105.

50. Adoptees mounted a class action lawsuit against the Canadian government for loss of Indigenous identity through adoptions. "Ottawa Seeks Individual Settlements for Sixties Scoop Victims," *Globe and Mail*, 13 June 2017. The Canadian government settled in 2023 for US$2.09 billion.

51. Raven Sinclair, "Identity Lost and Found: Lessons from the Sixties Scoop," *First Peoples Child and Family Review* 3, no. 1 (2007): 66.

52. SBS Adoption Files 23-85, 83-84.

8. INSIDE PRIVATE ADOPTIONS

1. Fernando Linares Beltranena interview, 27 January 2016. All interviews with Linares Beltranena were conducted in English, which he said was his preference if quotations were to be published in English.

2. Centro de Investigaciones Regionales de Mesoamérica (hereafter CIRMA), Archivo de Inforpress Centroamericana, Report on intercountry adoption 1997, Caso: Guatemala, 5 folios (ICA, no. 1591). "American to Stand Trial over Guatemalan Adoptions," National Public Radio, 27 April 2017, and "Adoptions of Guatemalan Babies Prompt Closer Look," National Public Radio, 19 September 2007.

3. State adoptions slowed to a trickle by the 1990s. The Ministry of Social Welfare archives show that it finalized fifteen adoptions in 1990, twenty in 1991, eight in 1992, fourteen in 1993, and three in 1994.

4. The adoption files from the Archivo Privado de Fernando Linares Beltranena (hereafter AFLB) are cited with the first initial of the last name and date of finalization of the case.

5. Fernando Linares Beltranena interview, 27 January 2016.

6. The notarial files that are supposed to be held at the Archivo de Protocolos, Guatemala City, were also included in the full adoption files in Linares Beltranena's office.

7. Diane Nelson, *A Finger in the Wound: Body Politics in Quincentennial Guatemala* (Berkeley: University of California Press, 1999), 67, 66.

8. Cecilia Menjívar, *Enduring Violence: Ladina Women's Lives in Guatemala* (Berkeley: University of California Press, 2011).

9. Fernando Linares Beltranena interview, 27 January 2016.

10. AFLB. The originals of this form are in English.

11. Susan (pseudonym for an adoption agency worker who preferred I not use her name), telephone interview with author, 10 April 2017.

12. Hilda Morales Trujillo interview, 9 February 2016.

13. For example, Morales Trujillo performed twenty-nine notarial procedures relating to adoption out of 121 total notarial procedures in 1982 that she filed with the Archivo de Proto-

colos. The majority were connected to state orphanages. She mostly facilitated adoptions for non-U.S. families, including Scandinavian, Italian, Dutch, and French-Canadian couples.

14. Sarah Pointer, "PLAN Adoptions to close December 31," *News Register*, 26 December 2009; Soojin Chung, *Adopting for God: The Mission to Change America through Transnational Adoption* (New York: New York University Press, 2021). AFLB L 1990. Christian adoption agencies in the United States were the rule, not the exception. A report on intercountry adoption from 1997 noted that many North American adoption agencies brokering the adoptions of Guatemalan children had special requirements—for example, that couples be married at least a year or be under forty-five years old. A list of agencies noted "Christians preferred" (Covenant International, Inc.) or offered "priority for conventional Christian religion" (Dillon International, Inc.), or considered only "one divorce each acceptable" (Holt International Children's Services). CIRMA, Archivo de Inforpress Centroamericana, Report on Intercountry Adoption 1997, Caso: Guatemala, 5 folios (ICA, no. 1591), 2–3.

15. Some children who escaped from state orphanages ended up living in Concordia Park. See Sebastián Escalón, "Los niños que el ejército se llevó (II)," *Plaza Pública*, 28 August 2013.

16. Dina Castro interview, 18 February 2016.

17. This exchange is contained in AFLB P 1989.

18. Dina Castro interview, 18 February 2016.

19. AFLB K 1987.

20. Laura Briggs, *Somebody's Children: The Politics of Transracial and Transnational Adoption* (Durham: Duke University Press, 2012).

21. AFLB F 1989.

22. AFLB F 1989, AFLB G 1987, AFLB W 1990, AFLB M 1988, AFLB K 1987.

23. AFLB M 1988.

24. AFLB P 1989.

25. Underline in original. AFLB A 1987. The 1997 report on intercountry adoption notes of the children available for adoption: "Hispanic and Hispanic-Indian in appearance; more boys than girls." CIRMA, Archivo de Inforpress Centroamericana, Report on intercountry adoption 1997, Caso: Guatemala, 5 folios (ICA, no. 1591), 2–3.

26. AFLB F 1989.

27. AFLB H 1989.

28. For example, AFLB R 1989.

29. Capitalization in the original. AFLB K 1987.

30. AFLB H 1989.

31. AFLB K 1987.

32. AFLB L 1990, AFLB P 1989, AFLB K 1987.

33. AFLB H 1989.

34. This became more common in the 1990s. Linares Beltranena did not offer tourist packages along with adoptions. Hilda Morales Trujillo interview, 9 February 2016.

35. Jessica O'Dwyer, *Mamalita: An Adoption Memoir* (Berkeley, CA: Seal Press, 2010); Jennifer Grant, *Love You More* (Nashville, TN: Thomas Nelson, 2011); and Gil Michelini, *Daddy*

Come and Get Me: A Dad's Adventure through a Guatemalan Adoption (Fishers, IN: Emiliani Publishing, 2011).

36. AFLB K 1987.

37. These are direct quotations from the notarial documents in AFLB P 1989, but they are all very similar.

38. AFLB P 1989.

39. AFLB K 1987.

40. Margarita Pérez Soc, ed., *Voces rompiendo el silencio de Utatlán* (Comité de Víctimas Unidas de Santa Lucía Utatlán: Programa de Naciones Unidas para el Desarrollo, 2003), 44. This publication contains many testimonies recorded in 2003 in K'iche', transcribed, and translated into Spanish.

41. Pérez Soc, *Voces rompiendo el silencio de Utatlán,* 47.

42. Sarah Foss, "Community Development in Cold War Guatemala," in *Latin America and the Global Cold War,* ed. Thomas C. Field, Jr., Stella Krepp, and Vanni Pettinà (Chapel Hill: University of North Carolina Press, 2020).

43. Hilaria Feliza Vásquez interview, in Pérez Soc, *Voces rompiendo el silencio de Utatlán,* 186–187.

44. The *delantal,* the frilly apron, is a clear marker of social class in Guatemala. Attempting to read photographs to understand history, especially photographs of people who had less power than those photographing them, raises a number of issues. Susan Sontag wrote, "To photograph is to appropriate the thing photographed. It means putting oneself into a certain relation to the world that feels like knowledge—and, therefore, like power." Susan Sontag, *On Photography* (New York: Farrar Straus and Giroux, 1977), 4. I will not include copies of photographs here for obvious ethical and legal reasons. But I do find it worthwhile to discuss what they might reveal alongside the written text in files, which is more easily anonymized. See also Ariella Azoulay, *Civil Contract of Photography* (Cambridge, MA: MIT Press, 2006); and Nicholas Mirzoeff, *The Right to Look: A Counterhistory of Visuality* (Durham: Duke University Press, 2011).

45. Details from AFLB W 1990, AFLB G 1987, AFLB S 1987, AFLB L 1990, AFLB M 1988. AGT, Caso contra Edmond Lesieur Mulet, Juzgado 50 de Paz Penal, 25 November 1981.

46. AFLB S 1987.

47. AFLB L 1990.

48. AFLB J 1989.

49. Fernando Linares Beltranena interview, 27 January 2016. A "tip" is a *propina.*

50. Fernando Linares Beltranena interview, 27 January 2016.

51. AFLB S 1987.

52. AFLB S 1987.

53. Michelle Goldberg, *The Means of Reproduction: Sex, Power, and the Future of the World* (New York: Penguin, 2009). During oral arguments in 2022 in the case that overturned *Roe vs. Wade,* Justice Amy Coney Barrett asked about "safe haven" laws, which allow mothers who don't want to keep babies to drop them off anonymously in boxes at hospitals and fire stations. Barrett, a Catholic who belongs to a conservative faith group called People of Praise, asked whether these laws meant that a lack of access to abortion would no longer burden

women. A footnote to the final decision that received widespread media attention cited a report claiming that while nearly 1 million women wished to adopt in the United States in 2002, the "domestic supply of infants" had become nearly nonexistent. *Dobbs vs. Jackson Women's Health Organization,* 24 June 2022, 34.

54. Capitalization in the original. AFLB H 1987.

55. AFLB H 1987.

56. AFLB K 1987.

57. Ana María Moreno interview, 24 February 2016. I met Moreno in an apartment she shared with her longtime husband, the prominent sociologist Edelberto Torres-Rivas, who died in 2018. Moreno died in 2021.

58. Gifting children, especially to wealthier families, was not uncommon, so this story didn't sound as implausible in Guatemala as it might, say, in the United States. The mother effectively pretended the child was a *niño regalado.*

9. THE RECKONING

1. Daniel Rothenberg, "The Panic of the Robaniños: *Gringo* Organ Stealers, Narratives of Mistrust, and the Guatemalan Political Imagination" (Ph.D. diss., University of Chicago, 2017). *Robaniños* and *robachicos* were terms used interchangeably.

2. Abigail Adams, "Los cosechadores de órganos y Harbury: Relatos transnacionales de impunidad y responsibilidad en Guatemala después de la guerra," *Mesoamérica* 34 (1997): 595–632, 596.

3. "Aún sin saberse paradero de un recién nacido," *Prensa Libre,* 4 March, 1988. There was a similar panic in Mexico during an earlier period. See Susana Sosenski, *Robachicos: Historia del secuestro infantil en México 1900–1960* (Mexico City: Grano de Sal / UNAM, 2021).

4. Marc Lacey, "Guatemala System Is Scrutinized as Americans Rush In to Adopt," *New York Times,* 6 November 2006.

5. Deborah Levenson-Estrada, *Trade Unionists against Terror: Guatemala City, 1954–1985* (Chapel Hill: University of North Carolina Press, 1994), 66–67.

6. Michel-Rolph Trouillot wrote that silences were the result not of gaps left by chance in the archival record, but of certain events or people actively silenced by those with more power. Michel-Rolph Trouillot, *Silencing the Past: Power and the Production of History* (Boston: Beacon Press, 1995), 48.

7. Quoted in William Booth, "Witch Hunt," *Washington Post,* 17 May 1994; Laura Briggs, *Somebody's Children: The Politics of Transracial and Transnational Adoption* (Durham: Duke University Press, 2012), 191; and Diane Nelson, *A Finger in the Wound: Body Politics in Quincentennial Guatemala* (Berkeley: University of California Press, 1999), 66.

8. "Acusación en Europa," *Prensa Libre,* 10 November 1988; and "El Parlamento Europeo emite grave condena," *Prensa Libre,* 10 October 1988.

9. "Autoridades rescatan 14 infantes," *Prensa Libre,* 5 February 1987. The original story was published as "En el extrangero *[sic]*: Niños hondureños despedazados para traficar con sus órganos," *La Tribuna,* 2 January 1987.

10. Veronique Campion-Vincent, "The Baby-Parts Story: A Latin American Legend," *Western Folklore* 49, no. 1 (1990): 9–25, 10–11.

11. The classic reference on rumor as political speech from below is James C. Scott, *Domination and the Arts of Resistance: Hidden Transcripts* (New Haven, CT: Yale University Press, 1992). But rumors are just as often spread by the strong as by the weak, not only from below but from above. See Vanessa Freije and Rachel Nolan, "Interpretative Challenges in the Archive: An Introduction," *Journal of Social History* 55, no. 1 (Fall 2021): 1–6.

12. There have been lynchings of kidnappers in India and elsewhere. See for example "Rumors on WhatsApp Ignite Two Mob Attacks in India, Killing Seven," *New York Times,* 25 May 2017.

13. "Histeria por secuestro infantil en Guatemala," *La Prensa Gráfica,* 23 March 1994; "Psicosis por ola de secuestros de niños," *La República,* 28 March 1994; and "Psicosis por el robo de niños," *El Gráfico,* 28 March 1994. See also Edward Orlebar, "Child Kidnapping Rumors Fuel Attacks on Americans," *Los Angeles Times,* 2 April 1994.

14. Stanley Cohen, *Folk Devils and Moral Panics: The Creation of Mods and Rockers* (London: Routledge, 2007), 1.

15. Cohen, *Folk Devils,* vii.

16. See Stuart Hall, C. Critcher, Tony Jefferson, John Clarke, and Brian Roberts, *Policing the Crisis: Mugging, the State, and Law and Order* (London: Macmillan, 1978).

17. Victor Perera, "Behind the Kidnapping of Children for Their Organs," *Los Angeles Times,* 1 May 1994.

18. See Arlette Farge and Jacques Revel, *The Vanishing Children of Paris: Rumor and Politics before the French Revolution,* trans. Claudia Mieville (Cambridge, MA: Harvard University Press, 1993); Magda Teter, *Blood Libel: On the Trail of an Antisemitic Myth* (Cambridge, MA: Harvard University Press, 2008); Kimberly Theidon, *Intimate Enemies: Violence and Reconciliation in Peru* (Philadelphia: University of Pennsylvania Press, 2012); and Mary Weismantel, *Cholas and Pishtacos: Stories of Race and Sex in the Andes* (Chicago: University of Chicago Press, 2001).

19. Gema Kloppe-Santamaría, *In the Vortex of Violence: Lynching, Extralegal Justice, and the State in Post-Revolutionary Mexico* (Berkeley: University of California Press, 2020), 94.

20. Beth Conklin, *Consuming Grief: Compassionate Cannibalism in an Amazonian Society* (Austin: University of Texas Press, 2001), 10.

21. Barbara Katz-Rothman, *Weaving a Family: Untangling Race and Adoption* (Boston: Beacon, 2005), 136. See also Matthew Pratt Guterl, *Josephine Baker and the Rainbow Tribe* (Cambridge, MA: Belknap Press of Harvard University Press, 2014).

22. Rothenberg, "Panic of the Robaniños," 13.

23. Gary Alan Fine and Bill Ellis, *The Global Grapevine: Why Rumors of Terrorism, Immigration, and Trade Matter* (Oxford: Oxford University Press, 2010), 191, 189.

24. J. T. Way, *Agrotropolis: Youth, Street, and Nation in the New Urban Guatemala* (Berkeley: University of California Press, 2021), 68.

25. "Florece el mercado negro de organos humanos," *Prensa Libre,* 13 March 1994. Rumors also circulated on the radio and television, though these were not archived in a way that makes them accessible.

26. Nancy Scheper-Hughes, *Death without Weeping: The Violence of Everyday Life in Brazil* (Berkeley: University of California Press, 1992), 235.

27. Nancy Scheper-Hughes, "The Global Traffic in Human Organs," *Current Anthropology* 41, no. 2 (2000): 191–224, 202. Some of Scheper-Hughes's work on this topic has been controversial, since by her own account she sometimes posed as a patient seeking a transplant or as someone looking to buy a kidney.

28. "Desprestigio de Guatemala," *Prensa Libre,* 10 November 1988.

29. "Desprestigia a Guatemala," *Prensa Libre,* 11 November 1988.

30. "Pide investigar denuncia," *Prensa Libre,* 7 December 1988.

31. Claudio Porres interview, 22 March 2016.

32. Olga Valenzuela, "Adopción o tráfico?" *Prensa Libre,* 9 May 1988.

33. These were made available through extensive Freedom of Information Act requests by journalist Erin Siegal McIntyre, as noted in a previous chapter.

34. Siegal McIntyre, *U.S. Embassy Cables,* 9–10.

35. NSA, Erin Siegal McIntyre Donation, Guatemalan Adoption box #1, folder F-2010-00013-D05, September 1988 cable.

36. Historians argue over when the Cold War began and truly ended, especially in places outside Europe and the United States. Much of this work is either inspired by or arguing against Odd Arne Westad, *The Global Cold War: Third World Interventions and the Making of Our Times* (Cambridge: Cambridge University Press, 2005); and Westad, *The Cold War: A World History* (New York: Basic Books, 2017). Guatemala's recent history supports the longer view of the global Cold War. See also Carlota McAllister and Diane Nelson, eds., *War by Other Means: Aftermath in Post-Genocide Guatemala* (Durham: Duke University Press, 2013).

37. "Denuncia europea sin base," *Prensa Libre,* 12 November 1988.

38. NSA, Erin Siegal McIntyre Donation, Guatemalan Adoption box #1, folder 201000001-DOS-4, August 1989 cable.

39. Daniel Wilkinson, *Silence on the Mountain: Stories of Terror, Betrayal, and Forgetting in Guatemala* (Durham: Duke University Press, 2004), 30, 136.

40. "Legislarán para normar tráfico de órganos," *La Hora,* 12 March 1994.

41. NSA, Erin Siegal McIntyre Donation, Guatemalan Adoption box #1, folder 201000001-DOS-5 August 1994 cable.

42. "Foreigners Attacked in Guatemala," *New York Times,* 5 April 1994.

43. "Robaniños causan alarma en la zona 18," *La Hora,* 22 March 1994; and "Padres temen secuestro de niños en zona 18," *Prensa Libre,* 23 March 1994.

44. In North America, lynchings were—and are—collective violence in pursuit of social control. Lynchings are a form of public terror intended to shore up racist domination targeting Asians and Latin Americans as well as Black people in the largest numbers. See Monica Muñoz Martinez, *The Injustice Never Leaves You: Anti-Mexican Violence in Texas* (Cambridge, MA: Harvard University Press, 2018), Beth Lew-Williams, *The Chinese Must Go: Exclusion and the Making of the Alien in America* (Cambridge, MA: Harvard University Press, 2018), and Ashraf H. A. Rushdy, *American Lynching* (New Haven: Yale University Press, 2014).

45. Twentieth-century Brazil, Mexico, Ecuador, Peru, and Bolivia have also suffered high levels of "lynchings" *(linchamientos)* for similar structural reasons. Though both Indigenous

and non-Indigenous communities throughout Guatemala and Latin America have lynched suspected criminals, lynching is often described erroneously as only occurring in Indigenous communities. Christopher Krupa, "Histories in Red: Ways of Seeing Lynching in Ecuador," *American Ethnologist* 36, no. 1 (2009): 20–39; and Michael Pfeifer, ed., *Global Lynching and Collective Violence* (Champaign: University of Illinois Press, 2017).

46. Jim Handy, "Chicken Thieves, Witches, and Judges: Vigilante Justice and Customary Law in Guatemala," *Journal of Latin American Studies* 36, no. 3 (2004): 533–556; and Edelberto Torres-Rivas, ed., *Los linchamientos: ¿Barbarie o justicia popular?* (Guatemala City: FLACSO, 2003). See also MINUGUA, *Los linchamientos: Un flagelo contra la dignidad humana* (Guatemala City: Misión de Verificación de las Naciones Unidas en Guatemala, 2000); and Angelina Snodgrass Godoy, *Popular Injustice: Violence, Community and Law in Latin America* (Stanford: Stanford University Press, 2006).

47. Orlebar, "Child Kidnapping Rumors Fuel Attacks."

48. Rothenberg, "Panic of the Robaniños," 191.

49. Larson's name was redacted from the cable obtained through FOIA, but she was widely identified in the press. NSA, Erin Siegal McIntyre Donation, Guatemalan Adoption box #1, folder F-2010-00013-D05, August 1994 cable.

50. Rothenberg, "Panic of the Robaniños," 185, 192.

51. NSA, Erin Siegal McIntyre Donation, Guatemalan Adoption box #1, folder 201000001-DOS-5, March 1994 cable.

52. "Vecinos de Santa Lucía exigen libertad de detenidos," *Prensa Libre,* 12 March 1994.

53. Rothenberg, "Panic of the Robaniños," 238, 61.

54. Booth, "Witch Hunt."

55. Rothenberg, "Panic of the Robaniños," 246.

56. Abigail Adams, "Los cosechadores de órganos y Harbury," 598.

57. Booth, "Witch Hunt." Whatever criticisms I may have of the framing and language, this article contains useful on-the-ground reporting.

58. Elizabeth Kadetsky, "Guatemala Inflamed," *Village Voice,* 31 May 1994.

59. Jairo Alarcón, "Psicosis colectivo o resabios de la cultura del terror," *La República,* 14 April, 1994.

60. Ellen Sharp, "Vigilante: Violence and Security in Postwar Guatemala" (Ph.D. diss., University of California, Los Angeles, 2014). See also Jennifer L. Burrell, *Maya After War: Conflict, Power, and Politics in Guatemala* (Austin: University of Texas Press, 2013). Death squads remained active among the police during this period. Historian María de los Ángeles Aguilar connects the army and police's practices of "terminating the seed" with "social cleansing" campaigns to murder children living on the street in the 1990s. María de los Ángeles Aguilar, "'Destruyendo la semilla': Children and Adolescents as Internal Enemies of the Guatemalan State," presentation, Stanford University, 13 January 2023.

61. Snodgrass Godoy, *Popular Injustice,* 2, 15.

62. Gema Santamaría, "Legitimating Lynching: Public Opinion and Extralegal Violence in Mexico," in *Violence and Crime in Latin America,* ed. Gema Santamaría and David Carey (Norman: University of Oklahoma Press, 2017), 123.

63. The man was Ixil, from Nebaj. Rothenberg, "Panic of the Robaniños," 284.

64. I have corrected the spelling of the two tags, which appeared in an embassy cable spelled agrammatically as *"gringo roba niños"* and *"Yankis roban niños fuera."* See Erin Siegal McIntyre, *Finding Fernanda: Two Mothers, One Child, and a Cross-Border Search for Truth* (New York: Beacon Press, 2012), 68.

65. "Foreigners Attacked in Guatemala," *New York Times,* 5 April 1994.

66. "Las chispas de un estallido social," *Siglo Veintiuno,* 10 March 1994.

67. Nineth Montenegro, "Santa Lucia Cotz. ejemplo para toda la nación," *La República,* 10 March 1994.

68. Orlebar, "Child Kidnapping Rumors Fuel Attacks."

69. Orlebar, "Child Kidnapping Rumors Fuel Attacks."

70. "Foreigners Attacked in Guatemala," *New York Times,* 5 April 1994.

71. Linda Green, *Fear as a Way of Life: Mayan Widows in Rural Guatemala* (New York: Columbia University Press, 1999), 57.

72. Nelson, *A Finger in the Wound,* 69.

73. Adams, "Los cosechadores de órganos y Harbury," 631.

74. David Grann, "A Murder Foretold," *New Yorker,* 11 March 2011.

75. Francisco Goldman, *The Art of Political Murder: Who Killed the Bishop?* (New York: Grove Press, 2007). See also the documentary *The Art of Political Murder,* dir. Paul Taylor (HBO, Rise Films, Smoke House Pictures, 2020). In it, Guatemalan journalist Claudia Méndez Arriaza notes that despite definitive proof linking the army command to the murder, many Guatemalans still believe and repeat the false rumors.

76. Organ-trafficking rumors in other countries, including Brazil, also included stories about Japanese baby thieves. Scheper-Hughes, *Death without Weeping,* 233.

77. Guillermo Carranza, the Attorney General for Minors (Procurador de Menores), had helped spread this rumor. "Carranza: Los traficantes de niños fotografían a potenciales víctimas," *Siglo Veintiuno,* 15 January 1994.

78. Sharp, "Vigilante: Violence and Security in Postwar Guatemala," 63.

79. Daniel Valencia, "La comunidad que lincha," *El Faro,* 17 July 2011.

80. Peter Canby, "The Death Squad Dossier," *New York Review of Books,* 8 December 2022.

81. Lisa Cartwright, "Images of 'Waiting Children,'" in *Cultures of Transnational Adoption,* ed. Toby Alice Volkman (Durham: Duke University Press, 2005), 190. See Melissa Fay Greene, "30 Years Ago, Romania Deprived Thousands of Babies of Human Contact," *The Atlantic,* June / July 2020.

82. Cartwright, "Images of 'Waiting Children,'" 194.

83. Wendell Steavenson, "Ceausescu's Children," *The Guardian,* 10 December 2014.

84. Karen Rotabi and Nicole F. Bromfield, *From Intercountry Adoption to Global Surrogacy: A Human Rights History and New Fertility Frontiers* (London: Routledge, 2017), 38.

85. Kathleen Hunt, "The Romanian Baby Bazaar," *New York Times,* 24 March 1991.

86. Juan Carlos Llorca, "To Save Adopted Girl, California Couple Gives Her Up," Associated Press, 22 November 2008. Email 14 May 2008 quoted in Erin Siegal McIntyre, *The U.S. Embassy Cables,* 589.

87. Siegal McIntyre, *U.S. Embassy Cables,* 69, 71, 133.

88. Rothenberg, "Panic of the Robaniños," 118.

89. Susana Luarca interview, April 6, 2016.

90. Rothenberg, "Panic of the Robaniños," 115. Karen Avilés, "Se utilizó el hospital de Malacatán como expendio de menores," *La Jornada,* 24 September 1997, cited in Laura Briggs, "Making 'American' Families: Transnational Adoption and U.S. Latin America Policy" in ed. Anne Laura Stoler, *Haunted by Empire: Geographies of Intimacy in North American History* (Durham: Duke University Press, 2006), 356.

91. NSA, Erin Siegal McIntyre Donation, Guatemalan Adoption box #1, folder F-2010-00013-D05, November 1996 cable.

92. Convention of 29 May 1993 on Protection of Children and Co-operation in Respect of Intercountry Adoption (The Hague, Hague Conference on Private International Law, 1993), https://www.hcch.net/en/instruments/conventions/full-text/?cid=69.

93. Briggs, *Somebody's Children,* 204–205.

94. Fernando Linares Beltranena, "Cataplum! Destrucción de valores familiares: Nuevo código de menores," *Prensa Libre,* 12 September 1997, quoted in Briggs, *Somebody's Children,* 206.

95. Kay Warren, *Indigenous Movements and Their Critics: Pan Maya Activism in Guatemala* (Princeton: Princeton University Press, 1998), and Santiago Bastos and Manuela Camus, *Entre el mecapal y el cielo: Desarrollo del movimiento maya en Guatemala* (Guatemala City: FLACSO and Cholsamaj, 2006).

96. "Declara la legisladora Rosalina Tuyuc: Indígenas adoptan a niños desamparados," *El Gráfico,* 6 July 2008; and "En comunidades indígenas hay adopciones voluntarias," *El Gráfico,* 3 July 1998, quoted in Briggs, *Somebody's Children,* 209.

97. NSA, Erin Siegal McIntyre Donation, Guatemalan Adoption box #1, folder F-2010-00013-D05, August 2010 cable, providing background.

98. Susana Luarca interview, 6 April 2016.

99. Jacob Wheeler, *Between Light and Shadow: A Guatemalan Girl's Journey through Adoption* (Lincoln: University of Nebraska Press, 2011), 11.

100. Siegal McIntyre, *U.S. Embassy Cables,* 48. A similar attitude, that international adoptions were an affront to national pride, took hold in South Korea and other sender countries.

101. NSA, Erin Siegal McIntyre Donation, Guatemalan Adoption box #1, folder 2008-06662-D05, June 1997 cable.

102. "Report of the Special Rapporteur on the Sale of Children, Child Prostitution and Child Pornography, Ofelia Calcetas-Santos: Addendum, Report on the Mission to Guatemala," United Nations Commission on Human Rights, E / CN.4/2000/73 / Add.2, January 27, 2000, para. 91, p. 18. See also Jan McGirk, "Guatemala Starts Crackdown on Illegal Baby Trade," *The Independent,* 5 April 2000.

103. "Adoption and the Rights of the Child in Guatemala," Latin American Institute for Education and Communication (ILPEC) Guatemala, for UNICEF (2000), 49, 5, quoted in Briggs, *Somebody's Children,* 213. Full report at http://poundpuplegacy.org/files/Guatemala-UNICEFILPECENG.pdf.

104. "Adoption and the Rights of the Child in Guatemala," 7. The archive of the Ministry of Social Welfare holds adoption records from Elisa Martínez Orphanage dated as late as 1997.

105. Karen Dubinsky, *Babies without Borders: Adoption and Migration across the Americas* (New York: New York University Press, 2010), 116.

106. NSA, Erin Siegal McIntyre Donation, Guatemalan Adoption box #1, folder 201000001-DOS-5, February 2002 cable.

107. Koh Ewe, "These Adoptees Were Brought to the U.S. as Babies. Now Some Fear They Were Stolen," *Vice News,* 27 April 2022.

108. "A Place to Call Home," *Newsweek,* 14 July 2002.

109. Adoption Council of Canada, "Surveys of Countries Reveals Closures, Slowdown in International Adoption" (2004).

110. Norma Cruz interview, 1 December 2015.

111. The report gained credibility in Guatemala, at least on the left side of the political spectrum, because the Ministry of Social Welfare and the Catholic Church's truth commission workers participated. Casa Alianza, *Adopciones en Guatemala: Protección o mercado?* (Guatemala City: Casa Alianza, 1999).

112. Ignacio Goicoechea, "Report of a Fact-Finding Mission to Guatemala in Relation to Intercountry Adoption," Hague Conference on Private International Law, May 2007, https://assets.hcch.net/docs/18210249-187a-4607-b6b5-808e3f3fb7fa.pdf. See also Carmen Mónico, *Implicaciones del robo de niñas y niños en los sistemas de derechos humanos y bienestar de la niñez: Un estudio interpretativo de madres guatemaltecas que reportaron el robo de sus hijas y su posterior tráfico y adopción internacional* (Guatemala City: Instituto Universitario de la Mujer, Universidad de San Carlos de Guatemala, 2013).

113. Dayner Hernández and Loyda Rodriguez interview, 15 January 2016. The events described here are also recorded in the legal records, held at the archive of the Foundation for Survivors. Expediente Caso Primavera, Archivo Fundación Sobrevivientes.

114. Erin Siegal McIntyre, "The Limits of Jurisdiction," *Guernica,* 1 December 2014.

115. Jared Genser, "Fabrications, False Claims, and Material Omissions," 2015, http://perseus-strategies.com/wp-content/uploads/2015/01/Fabrications-False-Claims-and-Material-Omissions-A-Response-to-Guernica-Magazine's-Article-by-Erin-Siegal-McIntyre.pdf.

116. Mirah Riben, "September Solidarity for Guatemalan Kidnap Victims in the U.S.," 21 July 2009, http://familypreservation.blogspot.com/2009/07/september-solidarity-for-guatemalan.html.

117. Marc Lacey, "Guatemala System Is Scrutinized as Americans Rush in to Adopt," *New York Times,* 5 November 2006.

118. Wheeler, *Between Light and Shadow,* 2–3.

119. Elizabeth Larson, "Did I Steal My Daughter? The Tribulations of Global Adoption," *Mother Jones,* November / December 2007.

120. Siegal McIntyre, *Finding Fernanda,* 34.

121. NSA, Erin Siegal McIntyre Donation, Guatemalan Adoption Box #1, folder F 2008-06662-Do5.

122. Julio Prado interview, 27 November 2016. His novel is Julio Prado, *La noche viene sin ti* (Mexico City: Alfaguara, 2022).

123. NSA, Erin Siegal McIntyre Donation, Guatemalan Adoption Box #1, folder 201001905-Do5 / USCIS.

124. NSA, Erin Siegal McIntyre Donation, Guatemalan Adoption Box #1, folder F 2008-06662-D05. See also Laura Briggs, *Somebody's Children*.

125. "Adopciones: rechazan el 74% de las solicitudes," *Siglo Vientiuno*, 19 May 2007.

126. Miguel Ángel Albizures, "El abogado aguatero," *El Periódico*, 6 July 2007. Linares Beltranena brought Albizures before the Guatemalan Press Association (Asociación de Periodistas de Guatemala) and attempted—unsuccessfully—to force his expulsion after he wrote several columns criticizing the adoption market.

127. Miguel Ángel Albizures, "Adopción, el tema de siempre," *El Periódico*, 22 November 2007.

128. Andrino was head of the attorney general's Office for Children and Adolescents (Procuraduría de la Niñez y la Adolescencia). Marc Lacey, "Guatemala System Is Scrutinized as Americans Rush in to Adopt," *New York Times*, 5 November 2006.

129. NSA, Erin Siegal McIntyre Donation, Guatemalan Adoption Box #1, folder F 2008-06662-D05, May 2008 cable.

130. Rachel L. Swarns, "A Family, for a Few Days a Year" (video), *New York Times*, 8 December 2012.

131. "Report on Players Involved in the Illegal Adoption Process in Guatemala since the Entry into Force of the Adoption Law," Decree 77-2007, International Community against Impunity in Guatemala (CICIG), 1 December 2007, http://www.cicig.org/uploads/documents/informes/INFOR-TEMA_DOC05_20101201_EN.pdf.

132. Rudy Zepeda interview, 9 October 2015.

133. U.S. Department of State, Intercountry Adoption Information, Guatemala, https://travel.state.gov/content/travel/en/Intercountry-Adoption/Intercountry-Adoption-Country-Information/Guatemala.html, accessed 28 November 2022.

134. Marco Antonio (Maco) Garavito Fernández interviews, 23 November 2015, 28 January 2016, and 25 July 2017.

135. "Stolen Childhood," PBI Guatemala, September 2022, https://pbi-guatemala.org/en/news/2022-09/stolen-childhood-we-are-seeds-state-tried-kill-now-we-bloom-morning-light.

EPILOGUE

1. Jean-Sébastien (Alberto) Hertsens Zune interviews. I met with him several times: 11 November 2016 and 7 May 2016 and 24 July 2017 in Antigua, Guatemala, and 21 November 2016 and 31 July 2018 in Guatemala City. His story appears, in different form, in Rachel Nolan, "Destined for Export," *Harper's Magazine*, April 2019.

2. I had the opportunity to meet Tobar, but this account draws on detailed reporting by Luis Fernando Vargas for "Dime quién soy," *Radio Ambulante*, 30 October 2018.

3. *Case of Ramírez Escobar et al vs. Guatemala*, 9 March 2018, https://corteidh.or.cr/cf/jurisprudencia2/overview.cfm?lang=en&doc=1920.

4. Maggie Jones, "Why a Generation of Adoptees Is Returning to South Korea," *New York Times Magazine*, 14 January 2015.

5. Anne Brice, "Staffer's Search for Birth Mom Reveals Dark History of Guatemalan Adoption," *Berkeley News,* 9 July 2019. Cindy Espina, "Las cicatrices en sus manos, la historia de un reencuentro," *El Periódico,* 21 March 2021.

6. Religious and secular "solidarity" adoptions were not uncommon. See Maya Chinchilla, "Chapina 2.0: Reflections of a Central American Solidarity Baby," *Mujeres Talk,* 13 May 2013, https://mujerestalk.org/2013/05/13/chapina-2-0-reflections-of-a-central-american-solidarity -baby/.

7. "UNICEF Belgium Director Steps Down Amidst Adoption Fraud Allegations," *The Brussels Times,* 12 May 2019. Susanné Bergsten, "Sweden to Investigate Intercountry Adoptions," *Human Rights Watch,* 22 February 2021. Yves Denéchère and Fabio Macedo, "Étude historique sur les pratiques illicites dans l'adoption international en France" (Laboratoire Temps, Modes, Société [TEMOS], UMR CNRS 9016, Université d'Angers, Angers, France, January 2023). See also French Foreign Affairs Ministry, "International Adoptions Q & A," 24 November 2022, https://www.diplomatie.gouv.fr/en/the-ministry-and-its-network/news/2022/article /international-adoptions-q-a-24-nov-2022, and Morgan Le Cam, "Un rapport-choc sur les adoptions internationals," *Le Monde,* 10 February 2023.

8. The job of "searcher" also exists in Russia and South Korea, among other former and current sender countries. Maggie Jones, "Looking for Their Children's Birth Mothers," *New York Times Magazine,* 28 October 2007.

9. Teresa, name withheld, interview, 15 April 2016.

10. Sebastián Escalón, "Una niña de Guatemala," *Plaza Pública,* 17 September 2013.

11. Maggie Jones, "The Truth in Guatemala's Bones," *New York Times Magazine,* 30 June 2016.

12. Even among Indigenous children raised by their birth families, or by refugee families in Mexico, the pressures of the war had unexpected effects on Indigenous identity. Jakaltek Maya anthropologist Victor Montejo argued that after massive dislocations in the highlands in the early 1980s, different Maya groups that had not previously mingled due to geographic divides learned to speak to one another across linguistic subgroups, and became "Maya" in addition to Poqomam, Tz'utujil, or Q'anjob'al. Indigenous survivors created a pan-Maya movement involving new layers of identity, which some adoptees have elected to reclaim as their own after learning more about their birth families. Victor Montejo, *Voices from Exile: Violence and Survival in Modern Maya History* (Norman: University of Oklahoma Press, 1999). The documentary "Discovering Dominga" shows how complicated identity loss and reclamation issues can be for Indigenous adoptees. *Discovering Dominga,* prod. Patricia Flynn and Mary Jo McConahay (Berkeley, CA: Berkeley Media, 2002), DVD. It is worth noting that the politics of DNA testing are not at all straightforward in Guatemala or elsewhere, and have been controversial among Native American communities. Kim TallBear, *Native American DNA: Tribal Belonging and the False Promise of Genetic Science* (Minneapolis: University of Minnesota Press, 2013).

13. Comisión para el Esclarecimiento Histórico (CEH), *Guatemala, Memory of Silence, Tzínil Natabál: Report of the Commission for Historical Clarification, Conclusions and Recommendations* (Guatemala City: United Nations Office of Project Services, 1999), vol. 3, 48, 139.

14. Rudy Zepeda interview, 9 October 2015.

15. Marco Antonio (Maco) Garavito Fernández interview, 25 July 2017.

16. Elizabeth Jelin, *State Repression and the Labors of Memory,* trans. Judy Rein and Marcial Godoy-Anativia (Minneapolis: University of Minnesota Press, 2003).

17. "Laura Ingraham Says Migrant Children Separated from Parents Are Being Kept in What Are Basically 'Summer Camps,'" *Slate,* 19 June 2018. After she was criticized for comparing child detention centers to summer camps, Fox released a statement saying "Laura Ingraham's very personal, on-the-ground commitment to the plight of impoverished and abandoned children—specifically in Guatemala—speaks for itself." "Fox News's Laura Ingraham Says Immigrant Child Detention Centers Are 'Essentially Summer Camps,'" *Washington Post,* 19 June 2018.

18. Garance Burke and Martha Mendoza, "Deported Parents May Lose Kids to Adoption," Associated Press, 9 October 2018.

19. Ginger Thompson, "After Losing Freedom, Some Immigrants Face Loss of Custody of Their Children," *New York Times,* 22 April 2009.

20. See Laura Briggs, *Taking Children: A History of American Terror* (Berkeley: University of California Press, 2020); and Rachel Nolan, "As American as Child Separation," in *The Long Year: A 2020 Reader,* ed. Tom Sugrue and Caitlin Zaloom, 209–216 (New York: Columbia University Press, 2022).

21. Marco Antonio (Maco) Garavito Fernández interview, 25 July 2017.

Acknowledgments

This book has been a decade in the making, and I have incurred many debts of gratitude along the way. Thank you, first, to everyone in Guatemala, Mexico, El Salvador, and the United States who helped with this research and supported me in many ways as I built new lives in new (to me) places. My sincerest thanks to those I met and interviewed, for giving so generously of your time and sharing what were sometimes difficult stories. This book would have been impossible to write without the generosity and professionalism of a whole host of archivists and librarians, many of whom are facing unforgivable conditions of underfunding, low pay, and politically motivated threats—not to mention closure of the archives they have worked so hard to maintain and protect. To the archivists: thank you for all you do to preserve the historical record and help historians and journalists and students access it. None of this work exists without you.

My gratitude to everyone in Guatemala who helped with this research. Thank you to Silvia Mendéz, researcher extraordinaire. Her original research, support, and co-interviewing skills are not to be confined to the acknowledgments section. She also found many of the archival materials related to the earthquake discussed in Chapter 3. See the list of interviews for a partial indication of her work on this project. To Thelma Porres and Reyna Perez of CIRMA: you are the first stop and most crucial source of information for so many researchers both foreign and Guatemalan. My admiration and appreciation for all that you do. A special thanks to the very patient archivists at the Archivo General de Tribunales and at the Archivo Histórico de la Policía Nacional, which has been so unjustly attacked by the very government that should preserve it. My gratitude to Marco Antonio Garavito, with deep admiration for your commitment and La Liga's work on reunifications. My thanks to Fernando Linares Beltranena for allowing me to read his adoption archives.

Thank yous are not enough for Barbara Weinstein and Greg Grandin for the phone call telling me I had a spot at New York University, which changed my life. Thank you for all that came after, and for your unwavering support. To Sinclair Thomson for thoughtful, humane comments and advice throughout. To Ada Ferrer, for the space and guidance on how to write the first words of this book. To Kirsten Weld, for being the first to say that I could, and should, pursue this project and for much help and company along the way. The five of you are an inspiration both intellectually and personally. To Linda Gordon, for highly practical insight on how to think about social workers' case files. To Laura Briggs, for generously commenting on this project at both early and late stages. To Alejandro Velasco, for oral history wisdom at a crucial moment. To Stefanos Geroulanos, for a torrent of advice and encouragement. To all the other professors, lecturers, and teachers at New York University, Harvard College, University College Dublin, Brookline High School, and Pierce School who helped me think and grow.

My grateful thanks for material support go to the Mellon / ACLS Foundation, Woodrow Wilson Foundation, Fulbright, Boston University, Columbia University Society of Fellows and Heyman Center for the Humanities, and the Social Science Research Council. Thank you to the Graduate Student Union (GSOC), past and present (AWDU), for making it materially possible for me to go to graduate school, and for the education in organizing. Thank you to everyone who read, listened to, or commented on portions of this work at the Tepoztlán Institute, Universidad de San Carlos, Latin American Studies Association, Next Generation Guatemala, Columbia University, American Historical Association, and Rocky Mountain Council for Latin American Studies, Guatemala Scholars Network, Society for the History of Children and Youth, Yale University, New York City Latin American History Workshop, Bedford Correctional Facility, Centre for Ethics at the University of Toronto, and the Cold War Center at the Tamiment Library of New York University.

My warmest thanks to colleagues at Boston University, including the "goats" for keeping me going during the pandemic, and most especially to Susan Eckstein for being a terrific mentor, champion, and friend. Special thanks also to C. J. Ray, Shamim Butt-García, Marie Kimball, and Luz Fernández Toro for expert research assistance.

This book was in wonderful hands at Harvard University Press. My special thanks to Kathleen McDermott for her extremely useful edits—a rarity in times of editorial austerity—and commitment to the project. I was lucky to land two reviewers who made substantial critiques that improved the book manuscript. Thanks also to Kate Brick for unbeatable attention to detail and care taken over the production of the book. Thank you to Aaron Wistar, to the photographers and mapmakers whose beautiful work is featured in the book, and to the book's designers, Graciela Galup and Jason Alejandro. My deepest gratitude to those who read and commented on the entire manuscript: Sebastián Escalón, Joan Flores-Villalobos, Sarah Foss, Polly Lauer, and Sylvia Sellers-García. It is a convention to say that any remaining errors are mine alone, and that is very much the case. But many, many improvements were made thanks to their suggestions.

Thank you to Lydia Crafts and Sarah Foss for sharing sources and good company in Guatemala. To José Manuel Mayorga for friendship and insight, and to Cesár Hurtarte for being the first and very dear guide to all things Guatemalan. To the broader community of Guatemala scholars and journalists, for inviting me in and helping me out: Mario Castañeda, Kate Doyle, Julie Gibbings, Polly Lauer, Carlota McAllister, Claudia Méndez Arriaza, Kevin O'Neill, Louisa Reynolds, Victoria Sanford, Rachel Schwartz, Sylvia Sellers-García, Erin Siegal McIntyre, Dillon Vrana, and J. T. Way. Special thanks to Ashley Black for showing me the ropes at the Archivo General de Centroamérica that very first day, and for all the coffee breaks thereafter. Thank you to Casey Lutz and Catherine Nolan-Ferrell for making research in Chiapas both possible and enjoyable.

With thanks to my research group—Betty Banks, Joanna Curtis, and Matt Shutzer—and my writing group—Susanna Ferguson, Charles Peterson, Pedro Regalado, Matt Shutzer, and Yana Skorobogatov. For Mexico-based encouragement, thank you to Sara Hidalgo, Alfredo Núñez Lanz, Steven McCutcheon-Rubio, and Joanna Zuckerman Bernstein. With thanks to the NYU Latin America crowd, from whom I learned so much: Cayetana Adrianzen, Tony Andersson, Michelle Chase, Anne Eller, Josh Frens-String, Anasa Hicks, Sara Kozameh, Ernesto Semán, Marcio Siwi, Carmen Soliz, Christy Thornton, and Tony Wood. My thanks to my fellow fellows at Columbia for their company and thoughts on this project: Joelle M. Abi-Rached, JM Chris Chang, Chris Florio, Ardeta Gjikola, María González Pendás, Arden Hegele, and Whitney

Laemmli. Thanks to Emily Bloom, Eileen Gillooly, Reinhold Martin, and the others who made that place tick.

My most special thanks to Joan Flores-Villalobos, for all the fun and the serious reading together all these years—and for allowing me to steal all her best ideas and put them in this book. To Jeannette Estruth, for extreme feats of friendship and for talking me through this project daily, sometimes hourly.

Thanks to Chris Carroll, Willing Davidson, Deirdre Foley-Mendelssohn, Diego Fonseca, Emily Greenhouse, Betsy Morais, Rachel Poser, and Daniel Soar for the opportunities to get out more or read something else for a change.

With thanks to Eliza Griswold and Amy Waldman for showing me how to research and write a book and helping me believe I could do it, too. My thanks to the whole editorial staff at the *New York Times Magazine* for training me up, and for giving me the tape recorder I used for this project.

With thanks to the friends who talked through this project with me perhaps more times than they might care to remember: Molly Atlas, Jon Blitzer, Nick Casey, Maggie Doherty, Rachel Doyle, Deirdre Foley-Mendelssohn, Vanessa Freije, Maggie Jones, Laura Kolbe, Nicholas Kulish, Gideon Lewis-Kraus, Jessica Loudis, Casey Lurtz, Karan Mahajan, Francesca Mari, Katherine Marino, Andrew Martin, Sarah Esther Maslin, Seth Robinson, Hannah Rosefield, Louisa Thomas, and Anicia Timberlake. Thanks to everyone who fed and housed and bucked me up along the way. You know who you are.

With special thanks to my lifelong supports, Sophie Brickman and Leticia Landa. To Anna and Julia Siemon for loving me like an extra sister all these years. To Jim and Alexandra, my second set of parents. To Alba, Perla, Guayo, Lila, Guillermo, and Marie-Noelle for welcoming me into your family.

My thanks to Morgan Ostertag and the wonderful staff of the Children's Center of Brookline.

Finally, with thanks to my family for their love and support. Mom, you showed me what discipline and commitment looks like. Dad, you taught me to trust myself and follow my nose, even when it took me far away. Laura did it all first and showed me the way, as always. Dennis, Sam, and Anna made all of our lives sweeter and more fun. Sebastián, with thanks for the historical documents, and for so much more. To our little love, Gabriel.

A last, and special, thanks to all the adoptees who shared your stories with me and welcomed me into your communities—Gemma Givens, Alberto Zune, and the many others who have been in contact over the years. If you are reading this because you are looking for someone: I hope you find them.

Index